*Netaji: Collected Works*
*Volume 2*

# The Indian Struggle
# 1920—1942

*Netaji: Collected Works*
*Volume 2*

# The Indian Struggle
# 1920–1942

*Subhas Chandra Bose*

*edited by*
*Sisir Kumar Bose*
*and*
*Sugata Bose*

*NETAJI RESEARCH BUREAU, CALCUTTA*

**OXFORD**
UNIVERSITY PRESS

# OXFORD
UNIVERSITY PRESS

Oxford University Press is a department of the University of Oxford.
It furthers the University's objective of excellence in research, scholarship,
and education by publishing worldwide. Oxford is a registered trademark of
Oxford University Press in the UK and in certain other countries

Published in India by
Oxford University Press
YMCA Library Building, 1 Jai Singh Road, New Delhi 110001, India

© Netaji Research Bureau 1997

The moral rights of the authors have been asserted

First published 1997

All rights reserved. No part of this publication may be reproduced, stored in
a retrieval system, or transmitted, in any form or by any means, without the
prior permission in writing of Oxford University Press, or as expressly permitted
by law, by licence, or under terms agreed with the appropriate reprographics
rights organization. Enquiries concerning reproduction outside the scope of the
above should be sent to the Rights Department, Oxford University Press, at the
address above

You must not circulate this work in any other form
and you must impose this same condition on any acquirer

ISBN-13: 978-0-19-564149-3
ISBN-10: 0-19-564149-3

Printed in India by Repro Knowledgecast Limited, Thane

# Acknowledgements

We would like to thank Professor Krishna Bose and Professor Leonard A. Gordon for editorial advice, Mr Kartic Chakraborty for secretarial assistance, Mr Naga Sundaram for archival support and Manohar Mandal and Munshi for unstinted, practical help in running the Bureau's publication division. We wish also to record our gratitude to Oxford University Press for their speedy and efficient handling of the publication process.

We take this opportunity once again to express our deep appreciation to Netaji's wife Emilie Schenkl and their daughter Anita Pfaff for having generously assigned the copyright in Netaji's works to the Netaji Research Bureau.

Sisir K. Bose<br>
Sugata Bose

# CONTENTS

## THE INDIAN STRUGGLE 1920-1942

| | | |
|---|---|---|
| Editors' Introduction | | ix |
| Introduction | | 1- 38 |
| Chapter I | The Clouds Gather (1920) | .. 39- 52 |
| Chapter II | The Storm Breaks (1921) | .. 53- 79 |
| Chapter III | The Anti-Climax (1922) | .. 80- 92 |
| Chapter IV | The Swarajist Revolt (1923) | .. 93-103 |
| Chapter V | Deshabandhu C. R. Das in Power (1924-25) | .. 104-124 |
| Chapter VI | The Slump (1925-27) | .. 125-140 |
| Chapter VII | In Burmese Prisons (1925-27) | .. 141-156 |
| Chapter VIII | The Barometer Rises (1927-28) | .. 157-175 |
| Chapter IX | Signs of coming Upheaval (1929) | .. 176-194 |
| Chapter X | Stormy 1930 | .. 195-218 |
| Chapter XI | The Gandhi-Irwin Pact and After (1931) | .. 219-240 |
| Chapter XII | Mahatma Gandhi in Europe (1931) | .. 241-256 |
| Chapter XIII | The Fight Resumed (1932) | .. 257-287 |
| Chapter XIV | Defeat and Surrender (1933-34) | .. 288-307 |
| Chapter XV | The white Paper and the Communal Award | .. 308-326 |
| Chapter XVI | The Role of Mahatma Gandhi in Indian History | .. 327-333 |
| Chapter XVII | The Bengal Situation | .. 334-340 |
| Chapter XVIII | Epilogue 1934 | .. 341-345 |
| Chapter XIX | A Glimpse of the Future | .. 346-354 |

| Chapter XX | India Since 1857—A Bird's Eye view | .. 355-360 |
| Chapter XXI | From January, 1935 till September, 1939 | .. 361-378 |
| Chapter XXII | From September, 1939 till August, 1942 | .. 379-395 |
| | Appendix | .. 397-399 |
| | Index | .. 401 |

## PLATES

| | |
|---|---|
| Netaji Subhas Chandra in Vienna, 1934 | Frontispiece |
| Netaji Subhas Chandra in Berlin, 1942 | Facing page 385 |

# EDITORS' INTRODUCTION

Sisir K. Bose and Sugata Bose

*The Indian Struggle, 1920-1942* is Netaji Subhas Chandra Bose's major political study of the movement for independence in which he himself was a leading participant. The book provides a lucid, analytical narrative of the freedom struggle from the gathering clouds of the non-cooperation and Khilafat movements to the unleashing of the mighty storm of the Quit India and Azad Hind movements. The story of the political upheavals of the inter-war period is enriched by Netaji's reflections on the key themes in Indian history and a finely etched assessment of Mahatma Gandhi's role in it.

Bose wrote the first part of the narrative, 1920-1934, as an exile in Europe. He wrote it in about a year at a time when he was seriously ailing. Moreover, as he himself mentioned in his original preface, while writing what was essentially an historical narrative he had to draw largely from memory in the absence of adequate reference materials at his disposal in Vienna. The book was published by Lawrence and Wishart in London on 17 January 1935. It was particularly well-reviewed in the British press and warmly welcomed in European literary and political circles. The British Government in India, however, with the approval of the Secretary of State for India in London, lost no time in issuing a notification banning its entry into India. Samuel Hoare, the Secretary of State for India, alleged in the House of Commons that the action had been taken because the book tended generally to encourage methods of terrorism and direct action.

As the book did not reach the Indian reading public for well over a decade after its first publication, we can only guess the nature of reaction and response it might have evoked. It is interesting, however, to recall how it was received in Britain and the continent of Europe. Reviewing the book *The Manchester Guardian* gave the following assessment:

This is perhaps the most interesting book which has yet

been written by an Indian politician on Indian politics...His history of the last fourteen years, though written avowedly from the standpoint of the Left-Wing, is as nearly fair to all parties and everyone as can reasonably be expected of an active politician...He is interested in trade union movements, the peasants' revolt, and the growth of Socialism...Altogether the book leaves us with a wish to see Mr. Bose take a lead in Indian politics...

*The Sunday Times* found *The Indian Struggle* 'a valuable book for the enlightenment of opinion. It has a point of view difficult for the British mind to comprehend but it accurately describes a side of the Indian movement that cannot be ignored.' The diplomatic correspondent of *The Daily Herald* described it as 'calm, sane, dispassionate' and 'the ablest work I have read on current Indian politics. This is the book of no fanatic, but of a singularly able mind, the book of an acute, thoughtful, constructive mind, of a man who while still under forty, would be an asset and an ornament to the political life of any country.' *The Spectator* found the book 'valuable as a document of contemporary history'. The reviewer in *The News Chronicle* described Bose as 'unusually clear-headed for a revolutionary' and added:

> His picture of Gandhi is very interesting as an Indian view. It is firmly and convincingly drawn. He does full justice to the marvellous qualities of the saint without condoning in the least the 'Himalayan blunders' of the politician...

Bose had corresponded with Rabindra Nath Tagore while he was writing the book and had sought introductions from the poet to British intellectuals like Bertrand Russel and H.G. Wells. At one time he had evidently wished one such person to write a foreword to his book. Later, he either gave up the idea or the plan did not materialise. Nevertheless, from contemporary press reports it is clear that there was a stir among left-wing British politicians and intellectuals after the banning of the book in India. George Lansbury sent a message to Bose thanking him for the book from which he was 'learning a great deal'.

From Europe the most interesting commentary on the book

EDITOR'S INTRODUCTION  xi

came from the French savant Romain Rolland who, in the course of a letter to Netaji dated 22 February 1935, wrote:

...So interesting seemed the book to us that I ordered another copy so that my wife and sister should have one each. It is an indispensable work for the history of the Indian Movement. In it you show the best qualities of the historian: lucidity and high equity of mind. Rarely it happens that a man of action as you are is apt to judge without party spirit. Without sharing all your appreciations I find most of them well-founded and they all make us reconsider things with profit. What you say about the dualism in the part played by Gandhi and in his nature made a deep impression on me. Evidently this very dualism makes his personality so original...I am admiring your firm political sense. What a pity that all the ablest leaders of the Indian Social Movement are either imprisoned or exiled as you and Jawaharlal Nehru...

President de Valera of Ireland read the book with great interest and concluded his message by saying: 'I hope that in the near future freedom and happiness will come to the Indian people.' In Rome Bose personally presented a copy to Mussolini who in turn expressed sympathy for the Indian cause. There were reports that publishers there immediately became interested in an Italian edition. An Italian translation was eventually issued in 1942 under the auspices of the Italian Institute of Middle and Far Eastern Affairs. Japanese editions of the first part of the book were published on the eve of World War II and again during the war. It is known that a German edition was planned and was in preparation during Netaji's last sojourn in Europe but it never saw light of day.

The second part of the narrative, 1935-1942, was also written in Europe, eight years after the first part had been completed. Netaji left the manuscript with his wife Emilie Schenkl in Vienna who made it available after the end of the war. A reprint of the 1935 London publication was issued for the first time in India in 1948 and the latter part of the narrative, 1935-42, published separately in 1952. Netaji Research Bureau issued the first combined edition in 1964 and subsequently republished it as volume 2 of Netaji's *Collected Works* in 1981.

This is a carefully re-edited centenary edition. In presenting

Netaji's narrative in its entirety minor changes in chapter titles and arrangement have been made in the interest of the reader. The appendix in the original London edition appears in this volume as 'Epilogue 1934' and it precedes instead of following the chapter entitled 'A Glimpse of the Future'. In the appendix we have published the report of an interview with Bose in London in January 1938 which embodies his clarifications with regard to the references to Fascism and Communism in the chapter entitled 'A Glimpse of the Future'.

Netaji's letters, speeches and articles of the period covered in *The Indian Struggle, 1920-1942* can be found in volumes 3 to 11 of the *Collected Works*. This book's narrative ends in August 1942 with the comment: 'A new chapter in the history of India's struggle for freedom had begun.' What was left unstated was that in that final chapter of the Indian struggle Netaji was setting out to play a decisive role. Soon after he had completed revisions to the second part of his narrative, he embarked on a perilous submarine journey to Southeast Asia where he led the Azad Hind Fauj in the last war of Indian independence.

# INTRODUCTION

## I. The Background of Indian Polity

It is only during the last three decades that attempts have been made to give a true picture of the history of India since the earliest times. Prior to that it was customary for British historians to ignore the pre-British era of Indian history. Since they were the first to interpret political India to modern Europe, it was but natural that modern Europe should think of India as a land where independent ruling chiefs had been fighting perpetually among themselves until the British arrived and after conquering the land, proceeded to establish peace and order and bring the country under one political administration.

In order to understand India, however, it is essential to bear in mind at the outset two important facts. Firstly, the history of India has to be reckoned not in decades or in centuries, but in thousands of years. Secondly, it is only under British rule that India for the first time in her history has begun to feel that she has been conquered. Owing to her long history and to the vastness of her territory, India has passed through various vicissitudes of fortune. Neither for the individual nor for the nation is it possible to have an uninterrupted career of progress and prosperity. Consequently there have been in the course of India's history periods of progress and prosperity followed by intervals of decay and even chaos and the former have been always characterised by a very high level of culture and civilisation. Only through ignorance or through prejudice could one assert that under British rule India began to experience for the first time what political unity was. As a matter of fact, though for reasons of expediency India has been brought under one political administration by Great Britain and English has been enforced on the people everywhere as the state language, no pains have been spared to divide the people more and more. If there is nevertheless a powerful nationalist movement in the country today and a strong sense of unity, it is due entirely to the fact that the people have for the first time in their history begun to feel that they have been conquered and simultaneously they have begun to realise the deplorable effects —both cultural and material—which follow in the wake of political servitude.

Though geographically, ethnologically and historically India presents an endless diversity to any observer—there is none the less a fundamental unity underlying this diversity. But as Mr. Vincent A. Smith has said: 'European writers as a rule have been more conscious of the diversity than of the unity of India....India beyond all doubt possesses a deep underlying fundamental unity, far more profound than that produced either by geographical isolation or by political suzerainty. That unity transcends the innumerable diversities of blood, colour, language, dress, manners and sect.'[1] Geographically, India seems to be cut out from the rest of the world as a self-contained unit. Bounded on the north by the mighty Himalayas and surrounded on both sides by the endless ocean, India affords the best example of a geographical unit. The ethnic diversity of India has never been a problem—for throughout her history she has been able to absorb different races and impose on them one common culture and tradition. The most important cementing factor has been the Hindu religion. North or South, East or West, wherever you may travel, you will find the same religious ideas, the same culture and the same tradition. All Hindus look upon India as the Holy Land. The sacred rivers like the sacred cities are distributed all over the country.[2] If as a pious Hindu you have to complete your round of pilgrimage, you will have to travel to Setubandha-Rameswara in the extreme south and to Badrinath in the bosom of the snow-capped Himalayas in the north. The great teachers who wanted to convert the country to their faith had

[1] Vincent A. Smith, *The Oxford History of India*, Introduction p. 10.
[2] These and other facts and arguments will be found in Prof. Radha Kumud Mookherji's *The Fundamental Unity of India* (Longmans, 1914).

always to tour the whole of India and one of the greatest of them, Shankaracharya, who flourished in the eighth century A.D., built four 'Ashramas' (monasteries) in four corners of India, which flourish to this day. Everywhere the same scriptures are read and followed and the epics, the *Mahabharata* and the *Ramayana*, are equally popular wherever you may travel. With the advent of the Mohammedans, a new synthesis was gradually worked out. Though they did not accept the religion of the Hindus, they made India their home and shared in the common social life of the people—their joys and their sorrows. Through mutual co-operation, a new art and a new culture was evolved which was different from the old but which nevertheless was distinctly Indian. In architecture, painting, music— new creations were made which represented the happy blending of the two streams of culture. Moreover, the administration of the Mohammedan rulers left untouched the daily life of the people and did not interfere with local self-government based on the old system of village communities. With British rule, however, there came a new religion, a new culture and a new civilisation which did not want to blend with the old but desired to dominate the country completely. The British people, unlike the invaders of old, did not make India their home. They regarded themselves as birds of passage and looked upon India as the source of raw materials and as the market for finished goods. Moreover, they endeavoured to imitate the autocracy of the Mohammedan rulers without following their wise policy of complete non-interference in local affairs. The result of this was that the Indian people began to feel for the first time in their history that they were being dominated culturally, politically and economically by a people who were quite alien to them and with whom they had nothing whatsoever in common. Hence the magnitude of the revolt against the British domination of India.

In order to study the present political movement in India with the proper perspective, it is necessary to make a brief survey of the development of political thought and of political institutions in the past. The civilisation of India dates back to 3000 B.C., if not earlier, and since then, there has been on the whole a remarkable continuity of culture and civilisation. This undisturbed continuity is the most significant feature of Indian history and it incidentally explains the vitality of the people and of their culture and civilisation. The latest archæological excavations at Mohenjodaro and Harappa in North-Western India prove unmistakably that India had reached a high level of civilisation as early as 3000 B.C., if not earlier. This was probably before the Aryan conquest of India. It is too early to say what light these excavations throw on contemporary political history, but since the Aryan conquest of India, more facts and historical materials are available. In the earliest Vedic literature there is reference to non-monarchical forms of government. Where these existed, tribal democracy prevailed. In those days, 'Grama' (or village) was the smallest and 'Jana' (or tribe) was the highest social and political organisation among the Vedic communities.[1] In the later Epic literature, the *Mahabharata* for example, there is clear reference to republican forms of government.[2] There is also evidence that since the earliest times popular assemblies used to be held in connection with public administration. Throughout the Vedic literature one finds reference to two kinds of assembly—the Sabha and the Samiti (also called Samgati or Samgrama). The 'Sabha' has been interpreted to mean the advisory council of the selected few, while 'Samiti' has been interpreted as a gathering of the entire community. The 'Samiti' met on important occasions like royal coronations, times of war or national calamity, etc.[3]

In the next stage of political development one notices a distinct tendency towards the growth of monarchical power following the expansion of Aryan influence and

---

[1] *Development of Hindu Polity and Political Theories* by Narayan Chandra Bandyopadhyaya, p. 60. published by Chuckerverty Chatterjee & Co. Ltd., 15 College Square, Calcutta.

[2] K. P. Jayaswal, *Republics in the Mahabharata* (J. O. and B. Res. Soc., Vol. I, pp. 173-8).

[3] *Development of Hindu Polity and Political Theories* by Narayan Chandra Bandyopadhyaya, pp. 115-18.

domination in India. At this time there would be frequent wars between the independent states flourishing in Northern India, with a view to obtaining supremacy. The issue of these wars would be not political annexation but acceptance of the overlordship of the victor by the vanquished parties. The victorious king would be called 'Chakravartin' or 'Mandaleswara', and elaborate ceremonies—'Rajasuya' or 'Vajapeya' or 'Aswamedha'—would be held to celebrate such victories. This tendency towards the centralisation of authority grew stronger during the *Vedic* and *Epic* periods of Indian history till from the sixth century B.C. the movement for the political unification of India took definite shape. This movement reached its fulfilment during the next era—namely the Buddhistic or Maurya period—when the Maurya emperors were able to unify India politically for the first time and establish an empire.

After the retreat of Alexander the Great from India, Chandragupta Maurya founded his empire in 322 B.C. About this time and also later on, there were many republics in India. The Malavas, Kshudrakas, Lichchhavis and other tribes had republican constitutions. Mr. K. P. Jayaswal in his book *Hindu Polity* gives a long list of such republics. There is no doubt that when India was unified politically under one emperor, these republics continued to flourish as autonomous states recognising the suzerainty of one emperor. Besides, the popular assembly was a well-established institution during this period of Indian history. The greatest of the Maurya emperors was Asoka, the grandson of Chandragupta, who ascended the throne about 273 B.C. Asoka's empire embraced not only modern India but also Afghanistan, Baluchistan and a portion of Persia. Under the Maurya emperors, public administration reached a high level of efficiency. The military organisation was perfect for that age. The government was divided into separate departments under different ministers. The municipal administration of the capital, Pataliputra, near modern Patna, was also creditable. In short, the whole country was politically unified for the first time under one sound administration. And when Asoka accepted

Buddhism, the entire state machinery became the handmaid of the Buddhistic faith. Not being contented with political sovereignty or with propagating Buddhism within the limits of his empire, Asoka sent missionaries to all parts of Asia—from Japan on one side to Turkey on the other—to preach the lofty tenets of Buddhism. This period has been regarded by many people as the Golden Age of Indian history, when there was a uniform and all-round progress in every department of life.[1]

After some time decay set in and there was an interval of chaos—religious, cultural and political. Largely because of its exaggerated asceticism, Buddhism lost its hold on the Indian people and there was a revival of Brahmanical Hinduism. On the philosophical side, the Vedanta philosophy which was first propounded in the *Upanishads*, was restored to its pride of place. Socially, there was a revival of the *caste-system* and a new breath of realism took the place of the morbid asceticism of the later-day Buddhists. Political anarchy was ended through the rise of the *Gupta Empire* which flourished in the fourth and fifth centuries A.D. The greatest of the Gupta emperors was Samudragupta who ascended the throne in A.D. 330. During the Gupta period, the country was not only unified politically but art, literature and science flourished[2] and once again reached the high watermark of excellence. This renaissance took place under the influence of Brahmanical Hinduism and this period is therefore regarded by orthodox Hindus as a more glorious age than the preceding Buddhistic period. As under the Maurya emperors, India once again had active contact, both cultural and commercial, with Asia and also with some countries in Europe, like Rome. After the fifth century the political power of the Gupta emperors came to an end but the cultural renaissance continued unabated till once again it reached its peak in A.D. 640, when under King Harsha the country was once again unified politically.

[1] An impartial observer like the Greek Megasthenes bears testimony to the above facts.
[2] Impartial testimony is borne this time by the Chinese pilgrim and traveller Fa-hien.

This did not last very long and after some time, once again signs of decline appeared. Then there appeared a new element in Indian history—the Mohammedan invaders. Their raids into the heart of India began as early as the tenth century A.D. but it took them some time to conquer the country.[1] Mohammed Bin Tughlak succeeded for the first time in bringing a large portion of the country under one rule in the fourteenth century but it was reserved for the Moghul kings to unify the country and usher in a new era of all-round progress. During the sixteenth and seventeenth century under the rule of the Moghul emperors, India once again reached the pinnacle of progress and prosperity. The greatest of them was Akbar, who ruled in the latter half of the sixteenth century. The great merit of Akbar was not only the political unification of the country, but what was perhaps more important, the working out of a new cultural synthesis—in order to reconcile the new stream of culture with the old—and evolve a new culture.[2] The state machinery which he built up was also based on the whole-hearted co-operation of the Hindu and Mohammedan communities. The last great emperor among the Moghuls was Aurangzeb who died in 1707 and after his death the empire began slowly to break up.

From the above historical narrative it will be evident that democratic republican forms of government existed in India in the ancient times. They were usually based on a homogeneous tribe or caste. In the *Mahabharata* these tribal democracies are known as 'Ganas'.[3] Besides these full-fledged republics, in monarchical states also, the people enjoyed a large measure of liberty, as the king was virtually a constitutional monarch. This fact which has been consistently ignored by British historians has now been fully established through the researches of Indian histori-

---

[1] Sindh was conquered in the eighth century but this remained as an isolated phenomenon.
[2] Akbar even attempted to bring about a synthesis of religions. He evolved a new religion on an eclectic basis and called it 'Din Ilahi'. He had many supporters during his lifetime but after his death the new religion lost all following.
[3] As late as 1927 the writer has personally seen such institutions flourishing among the Khasi tribe in Assam in North-East India.

ans. Besides political matters, in other matters also, the people enjoyed a large measure of liberty.

Indian literature from the earliest times abounds in references to public bodies called 'Paura' and 'Janapada'. The former correspond to our modern municipalities—while the latter probably mean non-urban public bodies of some sort. Moreover, owing to the existence of caste, the people were self-governing in social matters, through a system of caste-democracy under the control of a 'Panchayat'.[1] There were popular 'Panchayats' in India since the oldest times, not only for carrying on the village administration—but also for administering the caste-regulations and maintaining discipline within the caste. Throughout the succeeding Buddhistic period the people enjoyed large self-governing powers. During this period, the 'assembly' and the '*vote*' were popular institutions. The advent of Maurya imperialism did not encroach on these powers nor did it destroy the republics which still continued to flourish. The Empire of the Guptas and of Harsha proceeded on the same lines. Under the Mohammedan rulers, though there was unbridled autocracy, the Central Government rarely interfered in provincial or local affairs. The governor of a 'Suba' or a province was of course appointed by the Emperor, but as long as revenue was regularly sent into the imperial coffers, the provincial administration was not interfered with in any way. Though occasionally a fanatical ruler would attempt proselytisation, on the whole the people enjoyed complete freedom in religious, cultural and social affairs, no matter who occupied the throne at Delhi. British historians are without exception guilty of overlooking this fact and when they loosely talk of despotism to which orientals are accustomed, they forget that behind this cloak of despotism, the people enjoyed a large measure of real liberty, which they have been denied under British rule. Both before and after the Aryan conquest of India, autonomous village institutions have been a consistent feature of the public life of India. This is true as much of

---

[1] Panchayat, which literally means a committee of five, is a very ancient institution.

the Aryan kingdoms of the north as of the Tamil kingdoms of the south.[1] But under British rule these institutions have been destroyed and the long arm of the bureaucracy stretches into the remotest villages. There is not one square foot of land where the people feel that they are free to manage their own affairs. With regard to political literature also, ancient India has much to boast of. The *Mahabharata* is a storehouse of knowledge and information for the student of political science. The *Dharma Shastras* also, with a mass of subsidiary literature, are of immense value. But most interesting of all is Arthashastra of Kautilya which probably belongs to the fourth century B.C.

To resume the thread of our narrative, with the gradual disruption of the Moghul Empire, the question arose as to which power would take its place. About this time, two indigenous powers made a bid for supremacy—the Mahratta power from Central India and the Sikh power from the north-west. The Mahratta power was consolidated by Sivaji (1627-80) who was great as a general and great also as a ruler. After his death the Mahratta power flourished till the end of the eighteenth century. Its expansion was checked in A.D. 1761 at the third battle of Panipat, where the Mahrattas were defeated, and it was finally overthrown in 1818 by the British. Though Mahratta rule was based on benevolent despotism it could boast of a highly efficient army and an excellent civil administration. The Sikh power was consolidated by Maharaja Ranjit Singh (1780-1839), who during his lifetime built up a fine army and an excellent civil administration. But after his death, no one with equal ability could take his place and when war broke out between the Sikhs and the British, the former were overthrown. Unfortunately for India, while she was going through a period of political anarchy and was attempting to evolve a new social and political order, she became the sport of the European powers. The Portuguese, the Dutch, the French and the British came in succession. Each of them, not content with carrying on trade or

---

[1] In this connection it is worthwhile studying the Chola Kingdom of South India of the tenth and twelfth century A.D.

preaching religion, tried to wrest political power from the warring chieftains. In the long run a lively struggle took place between the French and the British. Luck favoured the latter. Moreover, British diplomacy was more astute and their strategy more clever—while their Home Government gave them greater support than did France to her nationals. The French made South India the base of their operations and attempted to dominate India from the south. The British following historical precedent operated from the north, after seizing Bengal, and were more successful than the French.

After going through the pages of Indian history, chapter by chapter, we can draw the following general conclusions :

(1) A period of rise has been followed by a period of decline, to be followed again by a new upheaval.
(2) The decline is the result chiefly of physical and intellectual fatigue.
(3) Progress and fresh consolidation has been brought about by an influx of new ideas and sometimes an infusion of fresh blood.
(4) Every new epoch has been heralded by people possessing greater intellectual power and superior military skill.
(5) Throughout Indian history all foreign elements have always been slowly absorbed by Indian society. The British are the first and the only exception to this.
(6) In spite of changes in the Central Government, the people have all along been accustomed to a large measure of real liberty.

## II. Landmarks in British Rule in India

England first obtained her foothold in India through the East India Company. This company received a Royal Charter which conferred large powers in the matter of trade monopoly, acquisition of territory, etc. The East India Company succeeded in establishing itself in India towards the beginning of the seventeenth century as a trading concern. Gradually friction arose between the Company and the local Indian rulers of the day. And this led in some places, as Bengal, to armed conflict. During the course of one of these conflicts the then ruler of Bengal, Nawab Sirajudowla, was defeated by the combined forces of the Company and the Indian renegades who conspired against him. This was practically the beginning of the political conquest of India. A few years later, in 1765, the Emperor Shah Alam of Delhi, who was then the nominal ruler of India, granted the Dewani of Bengal, Bihar and Orissa to the East India Company. The grant of the Dewani meant that the entire revenue and financial administration of these areas passed into the hands of the Company. Thus the East India Company, while being a trading concern, became an administrative body as well. During the course of the next few years, there were complaints about the corruption and maladministration of the Company's officials. In 1773, therefore, an Act was passed, called Lord North's Regulation Act, which provided for governmental control over the policy and administration of the East India Company. The principal administrative change introduced with the passing of the Act was that the three Presidencies of Bengal, Bombay and Madras, which had been independent of one another, were brought under a Governor-General who with the help of four councillors was to rule over all the territories, his headquarters being in Bengal. There were manifold defects in the new system introduced and in addition to that, there were serious complaints of corruption against the administration of the Governor-General, Warren Hastings. After some time, therefore, another Act called Pitt's India Act was passed in 1784 which provided for a Board of Control. There were cabinet ministers on this board and the entire operations of the East India Company were brought under its control. The appointment of a Board of Control, composed partly of cabinet ministers, eventually led to the establishment of the supremacy of the British Parliament over India.

The East India Company had to renew its charter from time to time. The Charter Act of 1833 introduced a remarkable change in the status and function of the Company. With the passing of this Act, the East India Company ceased to exist as a trading concern and became a purely political and administrative body, governing India on behalf of the British Crown. According to the provisions of the Act, the direction of the entire civil and military administration and the sole power of legislation were vested in the Governor-General in Council. Twenty years later, that is in 1853, when the Charter Act was renewed, the Control of the Government over the Company was further strengthened. The Act required that one-third of the members of the Court of Directors of the Company should be nominated by the Crown. So far as India was concerned, further administrative changes were made. Bengal was made a separate province under a Lieutenant-Governor and the Government of India was thereby separated from the provincial governments. The Act also provided for a Legislative Council for India consisting of twelve members, all of whom were, however, to be officials. During the discussions in the House of Commons in connection with the renewal of the Charter in 1853, John Bright spoke strongly against the Company's administration, which he said had 'introduced an incredible amount of disorder and corruption into the state and poverty and wretchedness among the people'. He demanded that the Crown should assume direct responsibility for the administration in India. The advice was not heeded and a few years later the revolution (called by English historian the 'Sepoy Mutiny' and by Indian Nationalists the 'First War of Independence') broke out. After the suppression of the revolt, a new Act was passed called the Government of India Act, 1858. By this Act the Crown took over from the East India Company the entire administration of India. With the introduction of this Act, Queen Victoria issued a Royal Proclamation, which was read out by the Governor-General, Lord Canning, on November 1st, 1858, at Allahabad. In view of the responsibility of the British Cabinet to the British Parliament, the latter became the virtual arbiter of India's political destiny.

The next important step was taken in 1861 when the Indian Councils Act was passed. The Act provided for the Governor-General's Legislative Council which was to have not more than twelve and not less than six members, half of whom were to be non-officials. Besides the Central Legislative Council, Provincial Councils consisting partly of non-official members appointed by the Government were also introduced. Thus Bengal got a Provincial Legislative Council in 1862 and the North-West Provinces and Oudh (now called the United Provinces) in 1886.

The failure of the revolution of 1857 was followed by a period of reaction and during this period all anti-British movements in India were ruthlessly suppressed, while the people at large were completely disarmed. By the eighties of the last century the political depression was over and the public began to raise their head once again. This time the policy and the tactics of the liberty-loving and progressive Indians were quite different from those of 1857. An armed revolution being out of the question, constitutional agitation was substituted in its place. Thus in 1885, the Indian National Congress was founded for striving for self-government for India by constitutional means. The agitation conducted by the Indian National Congress made the Government of India feel that a further political advance was necessary. So in 1892 another Act was passed called the Indian Councils Act of 1892. Under this Act the Legislative Councils were given the right to put questions and to discuss the Budget, though voting on the Budget was not allowed. Further, provision was made in the Legislatures for a non-official element to be appointed by the Government. The Governor-General's Legislative Council was also increased by sixteen members.

With the dawn of the present century there was a national awakening in India on a large scale and Bengal, which had suffered longest from the British yoke, was the pioneer in the new movement. In 1905 the Viceroy, Lord Curzon, ordered the partition of that province. The official reason given for this action was one of administrative exigency —but the people felt that the object was to cripple the new renaissance in Bengal. A stormy agitation against the partition was set in motion in Bengal and this was accompanied by a powerful movement all over the country, in the course of which attempts were made to boycott British goods as a retaliatory measure against the Government. The pressure of these events forced the Government to make another meagre concession to popular clamour and so the Morley-Minto Reforms followed. Lord Morley was then the Secretary of State for India and Lord Minto the Viceroy of India. The Morley-Minto scheme of reforms was first announced in December 1906, and was finally passed into law as the Indian Councils Act of 1909. As a result of official inspiration, a few months before the announcement was made, a deputation of Mohammedan leaders led by the Aga Khan waited on the Viceroy on October 1st, 1906. In connection with the impending reforms they demanded that the Mohammedan community should have a certain number of seats reserved for them and that these seats should be voted for, not by the general body of Indian voters, but only by Mohammedan voters. This demand by the Mohammedan leaders of what is known in India as 'separate electorate' was granted in the Indian Councils Act of 1909. This Act provided for enlarged legislative councils both in the provinces as well as at the centre. Additional powers were given to the members in the matter of putting supplementary questions, moving resolutions, discussing the budget, etc. The method of election was however indirect and the Act was therefore regarded by many Indians as a retrograde measure in some respects as compared with the Indian Councils Act of 1892. The constituencies were very small, the largest of them having only 650 voters.[1]

After the introduction of the Morley-Minto Reforms, an Indian was for the first time appointed as member of the Viceroy's Executive Council and Sir (later Lord) S. P.

---

[1] This seems to be the view expressed by Sir Surendranath Bannerji in his book *A Nation in Making*, pp. 123-25.

Sinha was the first recipient of this honour. This was followed by the visit to India of King George V who was crowned at Delhi as Emperor—following the ancient Indian precedent. It was the Viceroy, Lord Hardinge, who was largely responsible for this arrangement, as also for the transfer of the capital of India from Calcutta to Delhi. Lord Hardinge had a wonderful historic sense and he thought that by these measures British rule would be more firmly installed in India. Others, like Lord Curzon, the former Viceroy, were opposed to these innovations and they felt on the contrary that Delhi had been the grave of many empires. However, the visit of the King Emperor in December 1911, and the annulment of the partition helped to assuage public feelings and anti-government agitation subsided to a large extent. Within the Indian National Congress a split had occurred in 1907 leading to the expulsion of the 'Nationalists' (or 'Extremists') from that body. Moreover, many of the leaders of the Congress Left Wing disappeared from the political arena for the time being—through imprisonment, as in the case of Lokamanya B. G. Tilak of Poona, or voluntary exile, as in the case of Sri Aurobindo Ghosh of Bengal. Things were therefore quiet till the Great War broke out, when the revolutionary party which had been born during the first decade of this century became very active. During the Great War public opinion in India demanded an announcement from the British Government regarding the policy of British rule in India. This demand was made all the more because Britain gave out that she was fighting for the freedom of small nations and of suppressed nationalities. To placate Indian opinion an announcement was made on August 20th, 1917, by Mr. E. S. Montagu, Secretary of State for India, that the policy of His Majesty's Government was that of 'the increasing association of Indians in every branch of the administration and the gradual development of self-governing institutions with a view to the progressive realisation of responsible government in India as an integral part of the British Empire'. In order to follow up this announcement, Mr. Montagu visited India and a joint report was made by the Secretary of State for India and the then Viceroy, Lord Chelmsford, on the question of the Indian constitutional reforms. The reforms proposed in the Montagu-Chelmsford report, were embodied in the Government of India Act, 1919. The most important innovation made in this Act was the system of government, called dyarchy. In the provinces the government was to be composed of two sections, called 'transferred' and 'reserved'. The transferred departments like Education, Agriculture, Excise and Local Self-Government were to be administered by ministers who must be elected members of the Legislative Council and who would be removable by a vote of that council. The reserved departments like Police, Justice and Finance were to be administered by members of the Governor's Executive Council, who would be appointed by His Majesty's Government and who would be independent of the vote of the Legislative Council. The Governor's Cabinet was thus to be composed of ministers administering 'transferred' departments and of members of the Executive Council administering 'reserved' departments. In the Central Government there was to be no dyarchy. All the departments would be administered by members of the Executive Council of the Governor-General, who would be appointed by His Majesty's Government and who would be independent of the vote of the Central Legislatures—the Lower House, called the Indian Legislative Assembly and the Upper House, called the Council of State. The Central Legislatures were to be composed only of representatives from British India and the Indian States ruled by Indian Princes were to be independent of the Central Government with regard to their internal administration, subject to the provisions of the treaties made between them and the British Government. The inadequacy of these reforms, the atrocities committed by the armed forces of the Crown in the Punjab in 1919 and the attempt of the Allied Powers to dismember Turkey—set in motion a powerful movement in India in 1920 under the leadership of Mahatma Gandhi. But in spite of the unprecedented awakening in the country no further political advance was made by the British

Government. The Government of India Act, 1919, contained a provision for the appointment of a Royal Commission, ten years later, that is in 1929, with the object of determining what further advance, if any, should be made in the direction of self-government. In accordance with this provision a Royal Commission was appointed in 1927 under the chairmanship of Sir John Simon.

The Commission reported in 1930. Thereafter a Round Table Conference of British and Indian representatives, nominated by the British Government, was convened for threshing out the details of the new Constitution. After three sessions of the Round Table Conference, the Government came forward with their own proposals regarding the new Constitution. These proposals were published in March 1933, in a White Paper. The White Paper was duly placed for consideration before a Joint Committee of both Houses of the British Parliament.[1]

### III. THE NEW AWAKENING IN INDIA

In considering the political conquest of India by such a small country as England the first point that strikes one is as to how such a feat could be at all possible. But if one knew the Indian temperament and Indian traditions, it would not be difficult to understand. The Indian people had never any feeling against the foreigner. This mentality had been developed partly through the philosophical outlook of the people as a whole and partly through the largeness of the country which made it possible to welcome as many people as could come into the country. In the past, India had been invaded by new tribes and peoples over and over again. But though they came as foreigners they soon settled down and made India their home. The feeling of strangeness disappeared and the foreigners became a part of the body-politic. On the whole, there was no intercommunal friction for any length of time after the

---

[1] The Report of the Joint Parliamentary Committee has been published on November 22nd, 1934. Even the meagre proposals of the White Paper have been further whittled down by the Joint Committee.

foreigners came in. An understanding would be soon effected and the foreigners would become members of the great Indian family.

Thus it was that when the European races—Portuguese, Dutch, French and English—first arrived in India they did not excite any suspicion or hostility or animosity. It was not a new phenomenon in the history of India—at least so the people thought. The fact that the majority of the foreigners were either peaceful missionaries or traders further served to disarm opposition. They were given facilities and even allowed to acquire territory for carrying on their peaceful avocation. Even when the foreigners took part in any political strife, they were always careful to side with a section of the people, so that they would never get the entire people against them. In this respect the diplomacy of the British was by far the best. The question crops up here as to why a section of the Indian people sought the help of the foreigners in their own internal disputes. The reply to that has been given already above. As contrasted with India, neighbouring countries like Afghanistan, Tibet and Nepal, have still remained comparatively independent, because people in these countries have been always suspicious of and hostile towards foreigners. Besides their diplomacy, there was one other factor which accounted for the success of the Europeans. That was their superior military skill. Unfortunately for India, though up to the sixteenth and seventeenth centuries she kept abreast of the modern world in her knowledge of the science and art of warfare, during the eighteenth and nineteenth centuries she was no longer up to date. Her geographical position had kept her isolated from modern Europe. The wars of the seventeenth, eighteenth and nineteenth centuries in Europe had effected a considerable improvement in the science and art of fighting and this knowledge was at the disposal of the European races, when they went over to the East. The first physical conflict between Indians and Europeans showed that the former were at a disadvantage in the matter of military skill. It is significant that before the British conquest of

India, the Indian rulers had Europeans in their service in the army as well as in the navy and many of them occupied high positions.

The first important success of the British in India happened in Bengal. The ruler was a young man, Sirajudowla, who was still in his twenties. Nevertheless, it must be said to his credit that he was the only man in the province who realised what a great menace the British were and he was determined to try his level best to throw them out of the country. If only he had had as much diplomacy as he had patriotism, he might have been able to alter the course of Indian history. In order to overthrow him, the English won over to their side the influential Mir Jaffar, by giving him a promise of the throne, and their combined forces were more than a match for Sirajudowla. It did not however take Mir Jaffar long to realise that he had been used as a tool by the British and that what they were really aiming at was political mastery for themselves. Sirajudowla was overthrown in 1757 but many decades were to pass before they could extend their supremacy to different parts of the country. In the meantime the rest of India, which was still independent, hardly realised the danger of British conquest. Being practically the first portion of India to come under British rule—the consolidation of British power naturally began first in Bengal. The overthrow of the old regime was naturally followed by a period of disorder and it took the British several years to put things in order. By the end of the eighteenth century, order had been established and the Government then had to face the question of building up their administration on a sound and permanent basis. In order to administer a big country the Government had naturally to educate on their own lines a new class of people who would be able to work as their agents. The British commercial houses also wanted Indians educated and trained on British lines. In the meantime British missionaries had been active in trying to impart their culture and their religion to the Indian people. Out of these different sources there arose a consciousness on the part of the Britishers of a cultural or civilising mission in India. It was this which produced the first revolt among the Indians. As long as the Britishers were merely trading, no one thought of them since they were petty traders. As long as they were merely ruling, people did not care, for Indians had in the past gone through many political vicissitudes and a change in government had never meant a change in their daily life—because no government in the past had interfered with local self-government. Out of the consciousness of a civilising mission there came the attempt on the part of Britain to 'anglicise' every sphere of the life of the Indian people. The missionaries became very active in propagating their religion, and educational institutions on the British model were founded by them, as well as by the state, in different parts of Bengal. The entire educational system was built up on the British model and English was made the medium of instruction, not only in the University but also in the secondary schools. In art and architecture also, British models were imposed on the country. In fact, in inaugurating the new educational system, the Government deliberately stated that their object was to train up a nation who would be English in everything, except in race. In the new schools, students began to think, to talk, to dress and to eat as Englishmen would. The new generation turned out by these schools was quite different from the old. They were no longer Indians in their equipment but English.

Faced with the menace of being swallowed up by a new religion and a new culture, the soul of the people revolted. The first visible embodiment of this revolt was Raja Ram Mohan Roy and the movement of which he was the father was the Brahmo Samaj movement. Ram Mohan Roy stood out as the apostle of a religious revival. He urged a return to the original principles of Vedantism and for a total rejection of all the religious and social impurities that had crept into Hinduism in later times. He also advocated an all-round regeneration of the social and national life and the acceptance of all that is useful and beneficial in the modern life of Europe. Raja Ram Mohan

Roy therefore stands out against the dawn of the new awakening in India as the prophet of the new age. The Raja was succeeded by Devendranath Tagore, father of the poet Rabindranath Tagore, as the head of the Brahmo Samaj. In appreciation of the pure life that he lived, which reminded one of the Rishis or saints of old, Devendranath Tagore was given the title of Maharshi (a great saint) by the people. His successor was Keshav Chandra Sen, one of the most prominent Indian personalities in the latter half of the nineteenth century. During the earlier portion of his life, Keshav Chandra Sen seemed to be inspired more by the sayings and teachings of Christ and in his public life he laid great emphasis on social reform. So vigorous was his personality and so enthusiastic was he in giving effect to his ideas that a split took place in the Brahmo Samaj. The older generation who were less radical called themselves the Adi or original Brahmo Samaj. Among the rest of the members a further split took place. The followers of Keshav Chandra Sen called themselves the Naba Bidhan, or the New Dispensation, while the rest called themselves the Sadharan (or general body) Brahmo Samaj. All branches of the Brahmo Samaj had however some principles in common. They all took their stand on the original doctrines of the Vedanta philosophy. They all condemned the use of images in religious worship and they all advocated the abolition of caste in society. The Brahmo Samaj movement spread all over India and in some places it was known by a different name —for instance, in Bombay Presidency it was known as the Prarthana Samaj.

The Brahmo Samaj had considerable influence on the new generation of English-educated Indians and even those who did not become converts to the Brahmo Samaj accepted the spirit of reform and progress for which it stood. But the ultra-modern ideas of the Samaj caused a revulsion of feeling among the old-fashioned Pandits, who attempted to justify all that there was in Hindu religion and in Hindu society. But this reactionary movement could not make any appeal to the new generation of youths. About this time, in the eighties of the last century, two prominent religious personalities appeared before the public who were destined to have a great influence on the future course of the new awakening. They were Ramakrishna Paramahansa, the saint, and his disciple Swami Vivekananda. Ramakrishna, the master, was brought up in the orthodox Hindu fashion, but his disciple was a young man educated at the university who was an agnostic before he met the former. Ramakrishna preached the gospel of the unity of all religions and urged the cessation of inter-religious strife. He emphasised the necessity of renunciation, celibacy and asceticism in order to live a truly spiritual life. As against the Brahmo Samaj, he advocated the necessity of symbolism in religious worship and condemned the ultra-modern imitative tendency of the Samaj. Before he died, he charged his disciple with the task of propagating his religious teachings in India and abroad and of bringing about an awakening among his countrymen. Swami Vivekananda therefore founded the Ramakrishna Mission, an order of monks, to live and preach the Hindu religion in its purest form in India and abroad, especially in America, and he took an active part in inspiring every form of healthy national activity. With him religion was the inspirer of nationalism. He tried to infuse into the new generation a sense of pride in India's past, of faith in India's future and a spirit of self-confidence and self-respect. Though the Swami never gave any political message, everyone who came into contact with him or his writings developed a spirit of patriotism and a political mentality. So far at least as Bengal is concerned, Swami Vivekananda may be regarded as the spiritual father of the modern nationalist movement. He died very young in 1902, but since his death his influence has been even greater. About the time that Ramakrishna Paramahansa flourished in Bengal, another prominent religious personality flourished in North-Western India. He was Swami Dayananda Saraswati, the founder of the Arya Samaj. The Arya Samaj movement had the largest following in the Punjab and the United Provinces. Like the Brahmo Samaj it advocated a return to the early Hindu scriptures and it condemned all later-day accretions and impurities. Like the Brahmo Samaj it also advocated the abolition of the caste-system which did not exist in the oldest times. In short, according to Swami Dayananda Saraswati, people were to go back to the pure Arya religion and live the life of the Aryas of old. His characteristic slogan was: 'Back to the Vedas'. Both the Brahmo Samaj and the Arya Samaj attempted proselytisation but the Ramakrishna Mission never made any such attempt, for Ramakrishna was against the creation of a new sect. But while the Brahmo Samaj was influenced to some extent by Western culture and Christianity, the Arya Samaj derived all its inspiration from indigenous sources. None of the three societies had any political mission, nevertheless whoever came under their influence rapidly developed a sense of self-respect and a spirit of patriotism.

The Brahmo Samaj was founded in 1828. By that time British rule in India had spread through a large porton of the country and people had begun to realise slowly that the new invaders were different from the old. They had come not merely to make money or to preach religion, but to conquer and to rule—and unlike the invaders of old they were not going to make India their home but were going to rule as foreigners. The realisation of this national menace quickly roused the masses to a sense of the danger that threatened them. Thus occurred the revolution of 1857. It was by no means merely a revolt of the troops—a sepoy mutiny—as English historians are wont to say—but a real national revolution. It was a revolution in which both Hindus and Mohammedans joined and they all fought under the flag of a Mohammedan. At that moment it looked as if the English would be thrown out of the country. But through sheer luck they won by the skin of their teeth. The failure of the revolution was due among other causes to lack of support from some quarters, viz., the Sikhs of the Punjab and to hostility on the part of the Gurkhas of Nepal. When the revolution was crushed, a reign of terror followed and the country was disarmed from end to end. The reaction lasted for a long time and no one dared to raise his head during that period. By the eighties of the last century a change set in. People began to recover their courage, and armed with the knowledge of the modern world, they began to devise new means of coping with the foreigners. Thus in 1885 was born the Indian National Congress, the object of which was not to organise another revolution but to fight for Home Rule along constitutional lines.

The renaissance in Western India, unlike that in Northern India, appeared more in the form of a movement for educational and social reform than as a religious movement. The father of this awakening was Justice M. G. Ranade who, later on, found a worthy disciple in Mr. G. K. Gokhale. In 1884, Mr. B. G. Tilak, Mr. G. G. Agarkar and Mr. V. S. Apte, founded the Deccan Education Society. Soon after, Mr. Gokhale joined the Society. Later on there arose differences between Lokamanya Tilak and Mr. Gokhale. The former was not interested in social reform like the latter and he belonged to the 'extremist' school of politics, while the latter was one of the outstanding 'moderate' leaders. In 1905, Mr. Gokhale founded the Servants of India Society, the object of which was to train 'national missionaries for the Service of India and to promote by all constitutional means the true interests of the Indian people'. Among the different measures adopted by Lokamanya Tilak to rouse the people was the revival of the Ganapati festival—which was a religious festival given a national interpretation by him—and the Shivaji festival held every year on the birthday anniversary of Shivaji, the great hero of Maharashtra.

In South India the Theosophical Society founded at Adyar near Madras in 1886 by Madame Blavatsky and Col. Olcott, played an important role in social and public life. Mrs. Besant joined the society in India in 1893 and became the President in 1907, which office she continued to hold till her death in 1933. Mrs. Besant became the great champion of Hinduism against all attacks. Even the errors and abuses of Hinduism she would explain away, rather than attack. Thereby she helped to bring back into the hearts of the people faith in their own culture and civilisation which had been badly shaken as a result of the impact of the West. The large following which she managed to gather round herself through her religious and educational work, was of great value and strength to her when in 1916-17 she took an active part in politics and carried on a raging and tearing campaign for demanding Home Rule for India.

By the beginning of the present century, the foreign government was able to strike its roots deeper into the soil of India. The political administration was no longer a centralised government with autonomy in the branches as in former times. It was a highly complicated system with its ramifications in every town and village of the country and with a bureaucracy ruling with a firm hand under orders from the centre. People began to feel for the first time in their history what foreign rule really meant. The beginning of the twentieth century found the Boers of South Africa fighting against the British for their freedom, the newly-awakened Japanese fighting the Russians for their existence and safety, and the Russian masses fighting the all-powerful Tsar for their bread and their liberty. About this time the pride and the haughtiness of the rulers reached its limit and signs of serious political unrest appeared in Bengal and in order to nip it in the bud, the then Viceroy, Lord Curzon, ordered the dismemberment of the province. This was the signal for a country-wide revolt and people everywhere began to feel that constitutional agitation was not enough. The partition of Bengal was taken as a challenge by the people and as a reply, for the first time in British Indian history, a movement was launched for the boycott of British goods. The political agitation gave a strong impetus to the growth of national art, national literature and national industry. Simultaneously, institutions were started where national education could be imparted and young men could be trained as scientists and engineers for organising new industries. The Government naturally did not like the new movement and steps were taken to put it down. As a reply to official repression, young men took to the bomb and revolver and the first explosion took place in 1907. This was the beginning of the revolutionary movement of the twentieth century and in order to suppress it the Government issued a notification in 1909, declaring as illegal many of the institutions for imparting physical training to the youths in Bengal. Simultaneously with the appearance of the revotutionary movement, there was a split within the ranks of the Indian National Congress. The Left Wing leaders, Lokamanya Tilak of Poona and Sri Aurobindo Ghosh and Mr. B. C. Pal of Bengal, wanted to adopt the boycott of British goods as a part of the Congress plan, and they were not content with the goal of self-government within the British Empire. The Right Wing leaders, Sir Pherozshah Mehta of Bombay, Mr. G. K. Gokhale of Poona and Mr. (later on Sir) Surendranath Bannerji of Bengal, stood for a more moderate policy. Lala Lajpat Rai of the Punjab occupied a middle position in this fight. An open rupture took place in the Surat Congress in 1907 when the Left Wing (also called 'Nationalists' or 'Extremists') were defeated and the Congress organisation passed into the hands of the Right Wing (also called 'Moderates' or 'Liberals'). Not long after this, Lokamanya Tilak was sentenced to six year's imprisonment for sedition, Sri Aurobindo Ghosh was forced into exile, while Mr. B. C. Pal gave up extremist politics. Driven out of the Congress, persecuted by the Government and deprived of their leaders, the Left Wingers (or the Extremists) had a bad time up to 1915 and the Moderates were the masters of the show. The Morley-Minto Reforms of 1909 which were welcomed by the Moderates and condemned by the Extremists, served as a temporary sop to the political agitators. With the outbreak of the Great War and the return of Lokamanya Tilak from imprisonment, there was a decided improvement in the political situation from the Indian point of view. In 1916 at the Lucknow session of the Indian National Congress, a compromise was effected between the two wings of the Congress and once again Extremists and Moderates appeared on the same platform. A further compromise was effected between the Congress and the All-India Moslem League at Lucknow. The upshot of this rapprochement was that the Congress and the Moslem League put forward the same demand for self-government and agreed about the representation to be given to Moslems in the legislatures under the reformed constitution, on the basis of 'separate electorate'. About this time a new factor appeared in Indian politics in the person of Mr. M. K. Gandhi who had returned to India from South Africa in December 1914, after winning laurels for himself in the passive-resistance movement against the South African Government. After the Lucknow Congress, an intensive campaign was started by Lokamanya Tilak, Mrs. Annie Besant and Mr. M. A. Jinnah for demanding Home Rule for India. Mrs. Besant was interned by the Government in this connection in 1917, but was released some months later, owing to the pressure of public agitation. The Extremists wanted to make Mrs. Besant the President of the next session of the Indian National Congress in Calcutta, but the Moderates were opposed to it. At the eleventh hour an agreement was reached and Mrs. Besant became President with the support of both parties. That was however the last Congress attended by the Moderates, for, the next year, they broke away and formed a separate organisation of their own, called the All-India Liberal Federation. In 1917, a statement was made by the Secretary of State for India, Mr. Montagu, on behalf of the British Government to the effect that the progressive realisation of responsible government was the goal of British rule in India. Soon after this Mr. Montagu came to India and together with the Viceroy, Lord Chelmsford, made a report on the coming reforms, called Montagu-Chelmsford report. This report was considered by a special session of the Congress held at Bombay, presided over by the late Mr. Hassan Imam, a distinguished advocate of Patna and ex-Judge of the High Court and was rejected by the Congress as unacceptable. On the basis of the Montagu-Chelmsford report, a new constitution was drawn up and passed by the British Government, called the Government of India Act, 1919. This constitution was regarded as inadequate and unsatisfactory by nationalist opinion in India. While attempts were made on the one hand to put India on the road to self-government, the Government of India forged fresh fetters for the people. A new Act was passed by the Government in the teeth of popular opposition, whereby people could be imprisoned without trial on political grounds for an indefinite period. A country-wide agitation was raised against this Act and it was led by Mahatma Gandhi. In the attempt to suppress the agitation in the Punjab, terrible massacres were committed by the troops in Amritsar under General Dyer. The Amritsar massacre caused an unparalleled indignation not only in India but also among all fair-minded people in England. After the Amritsar incident, two enquiry committees were appointed, one by the Congress and the other by the Government. Both the committees strongly condemned the action of the military, though the Congress Enquiry Committee went much further in its condemnation. But the steps taken by the Government to compensate the sufferers and to punish the wrong-doers were extremely inadequate. The Amritsar Congress, in December 1919, had decided to work the new constitution in spite of its unsatisfactory character, but when the attitude of the Government towards the Amritsar massacre was made known, there was a revulsion of popular feeling. Meanwhile the attempt of the Allied Powers to dismember Turkey produced discontent and resentment among the Indian Moslems who turned against the Government. In defence of the Sultan of Turkey who was also the 'Khalifa' or head of the Islamic Church, a movement was started by the Indian Moslems under the name of the Khilafat movement. At this stage an alliance was struck between the Khilafat leaders and Mr. Gandhi, the Congress leader. In September 1920, a special session of the Congress was held in Calcutta to determine the attitude of the Congress towards the reforms and particularly towards the elections to be held that year under the new Constitution. At the instance of Mr. Gandhi, the Congress decided to adopt a policy of non-co-operation towards the new Constitution. Three factors accounted for this decision—the atrocities in the Punjab, the attitude of Great Britain towards Turkey, and the inadequacy of the new constitutional reforms.

Lord Irwin, the ex-Viceroy of India, holds the view that every step in England and in the Dominions towards the development of responsible government has been accompanied at a greater or lesser interval by a corresponding advance in India. As examples he has mentioned that the Charter Act of 1833, the Indian Councils Act of 1861, the Indian Councils Act of 1892 and the Indian Councils Act of 1909, have followed popular movements in England or in other parts of the British Empire. There is considerable force in what Lord Irwin says. But one should go further and say that the Indian movement is organically connected with the world movement for liberty. In India, as elsewhere, the beginning of the nineteenth century was an important landmark. The revolution of 1857 followed in the wake of World revolution of 1848. The birth of the Indian National Congress took place at a time when there was a similar upheaval in other parts of the world. The movement of 1905 closely followed the Boer War in South Africa and was contemporaneous with the Russian Revolution of 1905. The attempted revolution during the Great War was a phenomenon visible all over the world, at about the same time. Last but not least, the movement of 1920-21 was contemporaneous with the Sinn Fein Revolution in Ireland, with the fight of the Turks for their independence, and it closely followed revolutions which brought freedom to countries like Poland and Czechoslovakia. There is no doubt, therefore, that the awakening in India is organically connected with the upheaval all over the world during the last and the present century.

### IV. Organisations, Parties and Personalities

To understand properly a narrative about the Indian struggle for freedom, it is necessary to have some idea of the different organisations, parties and personalities in India.

The most important party or organisation in India is the Indian National Congress, founded in 1885. It has its branches all over India. There is a central committee for the whole country called the All-India Congress Committee, which consists of about 350 members. This committee elects an executive committee for the year, called the Working Committee. Each province has a Provincial Congress Committee and under this committee there are district, sub-divisional (or tahsil or taluka), union and village Congress Committees. The different Congress Committees are all formed on the elective principle. The aim of the Congress is the 'attainment of complete independence by all peaceful and legitimate means'. The leader [1] of the Congress is Mahatma Gandhi—who is the virtual dictator. The Working Committee since 1929 has been elected according to his dictation and no one can find a place on that committee who is not thoroughly submissive to him and his policy.

Within the Congress there is a strong Left Wing who hold radical views on social and economic questions, i.e., questions relating to caste, to landlord versus peasant and to capital versus labour. This group also advocates a more vigorous and activist policy for the achievement of political freedom. On all such problems, Mahatma Gandhi holds a more compromising position. A few years ago the prominent members of the Left Wing were Mr. Srinivasa Iyengar, ex-Advocate-General of Madras and ex-President of the Congress, Pandit Jawaharlal Nehru of Allahabad, formerly an advocate by profession and son of the late Pandit Motilal Nehru, Dr. Mohammed Alam, an outstanding Moslem leader of Lahore and an Advocate, and Mr. K. F. Nariman of Bombay, a Parsi gentleman and an Advocate by profession, Dr. S. Kitchlew, a Moslem nationalist

---

[1] The President of the Congress is not the real leader. Whoever presides at a plenary session of the Congress continues as Congress President till the next session. The Congress President is elected as a result of nomination by the different Provincial Congress Committees.

leader of Lahore, also an Advocate, and the present writer. But since 1930, Mr. Srinivasa Iyengar has retired from the Congress and with the exception of Dr. Kitchlew and the writer,[1] the others have been won over by the Mahatma. Nevertheless, even without many prominent leaders the Left Wing is fairly strong. The position of Pandit Jawaharlal Nehru in this connection is an interesting one. His ideas and views are of a radical nature and he calls himself a full-blooded socialist—but in practice he is a loyal follower of the Mahatma. It would probably be correct to say that while his brain is with the Left Wingers, his heart is with Mahatma Gandhi.

Among the other leaders, Khan Abdul Gaffar Khan (popularly called the Frontier Gandhi), a Moslem leader of the Frontier Province, is at present exceedingly popular, but it is too early to describe his exact political complexion. Mr. P. D. Tandon, and other Congress leaders of the United Provinces, are followers of Pandit J. L. Nehru, though they are inclined towards the Left Wing. The Central Provinces leaders, Seth Govindh Das and Pandit Dwarka Prasad Misra, are also inclined towards the Left Wing. Among those who played a prominent part in the National Movement prior to 1920, Lokamanya Tilak of Poona, Mr. B. C. Pal of Calcutta, Sir S. N. Bannerjee of Calcutta, Mr. G. K. Gokhale of Poona and Sir Pherozshah Mehta of Bombay, are dead. The first two belonged to the Left Wing, while the rest belonged to the Right Wing. Of those who played an important part since 1920, the following leaders are now dead: Lala Lajpat Rai of Lahore, Deshabandhu C. R. Das of Calcutta, Pandit Motilal Nehru of Allahabad, Mr. J. M. Sengupta of Calcutta and Mr. Vithalbhai Patel of Bombay. Among the prominent leaders who retired from the Congress, but who are still alive, are Sri Aurobindo Ghosh of Calcutta who has been living a religious life in French Pondicherry since 1909, and Mr. Srinivasa Iyengar of Madras who retired from active politics in 1930.

Since May 1934, many of the Left Wingers have com-

---

[1] Swami Govindanand of Karachi has also consistently taken up a Left Wing position.

bined to form an All-India Congress Socialist Party. This party has so far found the largest support in the United Provinces and Bombay—but support is also forthcoming from all over the country. It is too early to say how this party will grow in future, because many of those who may play an important role are either in prison or out of India at the moment. At present a reshuffling of parties is going on and a realignment in politics will shortly take place.

Within the Indian National Congress there is an important and influential Moslem group and this group has its representatives in the Congress Cabinet—that is, the Working Committee. In this group are Moulana[1] Abul Kalam Azad of Calcutta, Dr. M. A. Ansari of Delhi, and Dr. Mohammed Alam of Lahore[2]. Among the Hindu leaders of the Congress there are some who are more inclined towards the Hindu Mahasabha—for instance Pandit Madan Mohan Malaviya of Benares and Mr. M. S. Aney of Berar.

Before 1918, the Congress had two groups—the Extremists (or Nationalists) and the Moderates (or Liberals). In 1907 the Extremists were driven out of the Congress, but in 1916 at the Lucknow Congress, a rapprochement was effected. In 1918, the Moderates being outnumbered by the Extremists, seceded from the Congress and started the All-India Liberal Federation. The present leaders of the Liberal Party are Sir Tej Bahadur Sapru of Allahabad, Sir Chimanlal Setalvad and Sir Pheroze Sethna of Bombay, the Right Hon. V. Srinivasa Sastri and Sir Sivaswami Iyer of Madras, Mr. Chintamani of Allahabad, and Mr. J. N. Basu of Calcutta. Among the present-day Congress leaders who are loyal supporters of the Mahatma, are Sardar Vallabhbhai Patel of Gujerat, Dr. M. A. Ansari of Delhi, Dr. Rajendra Prasad of Patna, Dr. Mohammed Alam and Sardar Sardul Singh of Lahore, Pandit Jawaharlal Nehru of Allahabad, Mr. Rajagopalachari of Madras, Mrs. Sarojini

---

[1] Moulana implies a learned Moslem divine, just as Pandit implies a learned Brahmin. But the word Pandit is used loosely in some parts of India, as Kashmir, in reference to all Brahmins, regardless of their learning.
[2] Mr. Sherwani of Allahabad, Mr. Asaf Ali of Delhi and Mr. Khaliquzzaman of Lucknow also belong to this group. The first two have been elected to the Assembly in the elections of November 1934.

Naidu, the celebrated poetess, Moulana Abul Kalam Azad of Calcutta, Mr. Abhayankar of Nagpur, Mr. Jairamdas Daulatram of Karachi and Dr. B. C. Roy of Calcutta. Among them Pandit Jawaharlal Nehru's popularity is, by general consent, the highest.

Besides the above political parties comprising members of all communities, there are communal organisations whose avowed object is to secure the loaves and fishes for members of their own community. Among the Moslems, the All-India Moslem League is the most important organisation, having been started as early as 1906. During 1920 and 1924, the Moslem League was eclipsed by the All-India Khilafat Committee. But after the abolition of the Khalifate in 1924, the Khilafat movement in India collapsed, and the Moslem League regained its former importance. Besides the Moslem League, there are other organisations of recent growth, like the All-India Moslem Conference. The prominent communal Moslem leaders are the Aga Khan, Mr. M. A. Jinnah (who was a Congress leader up to 1920), Sir Mohammed Iqbal of Lahore, Sir Mohammed Yakub of the United Provinces and Mr. Shafi Daudi of Patna. Moulana Shaukat Ali, once a prominent Congress and Khilafat leader, has, on several occasions, identified himself with the communal Mohammedans. Sir Abdur Rahim occupies a position between the communal leaders on the one side and the Nationalist Moslem leaders on the other.

As a counterblast to the All-India Moslem League, the Hindu Mahasabha has come into existence for the avowed object of protecting the rights of the Hindus. It has influential support in some parts of India. Among the prominent leaders are Mr. Ramananda Chatterji of Calcutta (Editor of the *Modern Review*), Dr. B. S. Moonje of Nagpur, Bhai Parmanand of Lahore, Mr. N. C. Kelkar of Poona. Pandit Madan Mohan Malaviya though intimately connected with the Congress also plays an important part in the Hindu Mahasabha. Besides the Moslem League and the Hindu Mahasabha there are other communal parties. For instance, the Anglo-Indians, the Indian Christians, the

Sikhs (of the Punjab) and the depressed classes among the Hindus have their own parties to safeguard their own interests, that is, to secure as much of the loaves and fishes as possible. Of these parties there is one which has played a comparatively important role—namely the Justice Party of Madras. The Justice Party of Madras has till recently been composed of non-Brahmins and its policy is pro-government, as compared with the Indian National Congress. Among the depressed classes, everywhere in India there is a strong nationalist bloc, working hand in hand with the Congress. The Sikhs of the Punjab are on the whole strongly nationalist.

While the political parties we first dealt with have a political programme and carry on some sort of agitation against, or opposition towards, the Government, the communal parties are more concerned with dividing amongst themselves such of the crumbs that are thrown at them from the official tables. In accordance with the time-worn policy of *divide et impera*, the Government greatly encourage these parties—just to spite the Indian National Congress and try to weaken its influence. This was clearly exhibited in 1930 and later, when the Indian representatives to the Round Table Conference were not selected by a vote of the Indian people—but were nominated by the British Government and in making these nominations, the communal parties, who have no concern with the fight for political freedom, were given exaggerated importance. As a matter of fact, whenever the occasion demands, leaders are created overnight by the British Government and, thanks to the British Press, their names are made known to the whole world. When the Government of India Act, 1919, was under consideration, the late Dr. T. M. Nair of Madras, was made a leader in London, in opposition to the Congress leaders at the time. In 1930 and after, Dr. Ambedkar has had leadership thrust upon him by a benign British Government, because his services were necessary to embarrass the nationalist leaders.

Next in importance to the Indian National Congress are the labour and peasant parties. Labour organisation has, however, made more headway than the peasants' organisation. The All-India Trade Union Congress was first started in 1920 and Mr. N. M. Joshi was one of the founders of that organisation. Since then the Trade Union Congress has had a stormy career. In 1929 at the Nagpur session, presided over by Pandit Jawaharlal Nehru, a split took place, the Right Wing represented by Mr. N. M. Joshi, Mr. V. V. Giri, Mr. Shiva Rao, Mr. R. R. Bakhale, and others, breaking away from the Congress and starting another body called the Trade Union Federation. The Trade Union Federation now works hand in hand with the British Trades Union Congress and is affiliated to the International Federation of Trade Unions of Amsterdam. The politics of this body is closely allied to the politics of the Liberal Party. In 1931, at the Calcutta session of the Trade Union Congress, presided over by the writer, a further split took place, as a result of which the extreme section broke away and started the Red Trade Union Congress. This section is alleged to work under the inspiration of the Communist International, but their organisation has not exhibited much activity ever since its birth. The present Trade Union Congress, to which the writer belongs, holds a middle position between the Trade Union Federation and the Red Trade Union Congress. In other words, it is definitely socialist but is opposed to the policy and tactics of the Third International. But neither is it affiliated to the Second International at Zurich or to the International Federation of Trade Unions at Amsterdam. Unlike the Trade Union Federation, the Trade Union Congress has no faith whatsoever in the British Trades Union Congress and in Indian politics, the Trade Union Congress has more in common with the Indian National Congress than with the Liberal Federation. The President of the Congress now is Pandit Harihar Nath Sastri of Cawnpore and the Secretary is Mr. Shib Nath Banerji of Calcutta. It is interesting to speculate what part Mr. M. N. Roy, formerly of the Communist International, will play in future in the workers' movement in India and also in the political movement. Though he is still regarded as a communist by many, in view of his past activities, associations and writings—the Communists themselves call him a counter-revolutionary. He is now serving a term of six years' imprisonment in India for his former activities, but meanwhile his followers in the workers' organisations in Bombay are working in the Trade Union Congress and in opposition to the Red Trade Union Congress, which is alleged by many to be a Communist body. Since Mr. M. N. Roy severed his connection with the Communist International, a split has taken place among those workers' leaders who were formerly alleged to be Communists. The group headed by Mr. Dange of Bombay, have declared for Mr. M. N. Roy, while the other group denounce him as a counter-revolutionary.

Since 1920, a peasants' awakening has taken place all over India and the Indian National Congress has been indirectly responsible for its birth. But up till now no All-India organisation has been formed. The peasants' movement is very strong in the United Provinces and has been organised there in the name of the Kisan (Peasant) League. The Left Wing Congressmen of the province are intimately connected with the peasants' movement and their general outlook is radical. In Gujerat, too, where Mahatma Gandhi's influence is greatest, there is a strong peasants' movement—but this movement is entirely under Congress influence and the right-hand man of the Mahatma, Sardar Patel, is the leader of the peasants. The peasants' movement in Gujerat has not so far been developed on a class-conscious basis, but a radical turn in the movement is bound to come before long. In the Punjab the Kirti (Workers) Kisan (Peasant) Party is influential and some elements in the party seem to be under the influence of communistic ideas. The party would have made more rapid progress if it had a prominent personality at its head. In Bengal, the peasants' movement has made much progress and has been organised under the name of Krishak (Peasant) Samities (Societies)—but it has been handicapped by want of sufficient honest and able leaders. So far, the political movement in Bengal has drawn the best and ablest workers, but in view of the new alignment that is going to take place in Indian politics before long, it is not likely that there will be a dearth of workers in the peasants' movement in future. In Central India, too, the peasants' movement is fairly strong but in South India—in the Madras Presidency—it is rather backward. Only in some parts of the northern portion of Madras Presidency, called Andhra, is the movement strong.

There is an independent movement among the students and also among the youths in India. From time to time,* All-India Congresses of students and of youths are held—but there is no permanent All-India Committee to co-ordinate these activities. These two movements are generally conducted on a provincial basis. In Bengal, of all the provinces, the students' movement is the strongest. The last All-India Congress of students was held at Lahore in December 1929. The youth movement is organised in different provinces under different names. In Bengal the name 'Yuba Samity' or 'Tarun Sangha' is popular. In the Punjab and the United Provinces, the name 'Naujawan Bharat Sabha' is more in vogue. The first Congress of Youths was held in Calcutta in December 1928, and was presided over by Mr. Nariman, the Congress leader of Bombay. The second and the last Congress was held in Karachi in March 1931, and was presided over by the writer. The students' and youth organisations work in close co-operation with the Indian National Congress, though they have a more radical outlook and programme.

Last but not least, the women's movement is an important factor in the public life of India today. This movement has advanced by rapid strides during the last fourteen years. One of the miracles for which the Mahatma is responsible to a very large extent, is this awakening. This movement has been intimately connected with the Indian National Congress, nevertheless, independent women's committees have come into existence all over the country. The movement is, generally speaking, organised on a provincial basis and in many provinces—as in Bengal—provincial Congresses are held from time to time. In all the Congress Committees in India, women now have an honoured place and in the Supreme Executive of the Congress—the Working Committee—there is at least one woman representative. Two of the recent annual sessions of the Indian National Congress have been presided over by women—by Mrs. Besant in 1917 and Mrs. Sarojini Naidu, the poetess, in 1925.

Besides the political organisations of women referred to above, there are other organisations working solely with social and educational aims. These organisations are conducted on an All-India basis and All-India Conferences are held from time to time. Among these organisations is the All-India Women's Conference which held its last session in Calcutta towards the end of 1933.

To sum up, the most important organisation in India today is the Indian National Congress. It stands for the whole country and for all communities. It strives for political freedom for India—but it also aims for an all-round development of national life and for the amelioration of all social evils. With the exception of the communal parties all the other organisations or parties in the country are on the whole friendly towards the Congress, and work in close co-operation with it. The undisputed leader of the Congress today is Mahatma Gandhi—but within the Congress there is a powerful radical Left Wing.[1] The Mahatma has so far maintained a middle position on all such questions as capital and labour, landlord and peasant, as well as the social question of caste. The Left Wing, however, is working for a more radical and uncompromising policy on social and economic issues and it is not unlikely that before long the Congress will adopt its views.

---

[1] The present writer belongs to this wing.

CHAPTER I

THE CLOUDS GATHER (1920)

The annual session of the Indian National Congress met at Amritsar in the Punjab in December 1919, under the shadow of the atrocities perpetrated there earlier in the year. In spite of the opposition of Mr. C. R. Das, Mr. B. C. Pal and Mr. B. Chakravarti, the Bengal leaders, a resolution was passed in favour of working the New Constitution (called the Government of India Act, 1919) and thanking the Secretary of State for India, Mr. Montagu, who had played so important a part in launching it. Mr. Gandhi, who had been largely responsible for the decision arrived at by the Amritsar Congress, welcomed the Royal proclamation announcing the assent to the Government of India Act, 1919, and in his weekly paper, *Young India*, he wrote on December 31st, 1919: 'The reforms Act coupled with the proclamation is an earnest of the intention of the British people to do justice to India and it ought to remove suspicion on that score.... Our duty therefore is not to subject the Reforms to carping criticism but to settle down quietly to work so as to make them a success.'

But during the next nine months events moved with dramatic suddenness. What actually happened can best be described in the words of Mr. Gandhi himself. When he was tried by a British Judge, Mr. Broomfield, in March 1922, for writing seditious articles in his paper, Mr. Gandhi made a remarkable statement in the course of which he explained why after having co-operated with the British Government all his life, he was ultimately forced to turn against it. Therein he said: 'The first shock came in the shape of Rowlatt Act, a law designed to rob the people of all real freedom. I felt called upon to lead an intensive agitation against it. Then followed the Punjab horrors beginning with the massacre at Jallianwalla Bagh (in Amritsar) and culminating in crawling orders, public floggings and other indescribable humiliations. I discovered, too, that the plighted word of the Prime Minister to the Mussalmans of India regarding the integrity of Turkey and the holy places of Islam was not likely to be fulfilled. But in spite of the foreboding and the grave warnings of friends, at the Amritsar Congress in 1919, I fought for co-operation and working the Montagu-Chelmsford Reforms, hoping the Prime Minister would redeem his promise to the Indian Mussalmans, that the Punjab wound would be healed and that the Reforms, inadequate and unsatisfactory though they were, marked a new era of hope in the life of India. But all that hope was shattered. The Khilafat promise was not to be redeemed. The Punjab crime was whitewashed and most culprits were not only unpunished but remained in service and some continued to draw pensions from the Indian revenue, and in some cases were even rewarded. I saw, too, that not only did the reforms not mark a change of heart, but they were only a method of further draining India of her wealth and of prolonging her servitude.'

As already indicated in Section III of the Introduction on 'The New Awakening in India', the new legislation, popularly known as the Rowlatt Act,[1] was enacted on March 18th, 1919, for conferring permanently on the Government of India extraordinary powers for the arrest of individuals and their imprisonment without trial, when the war-time emergency ordinances lapsed. In February, 1919, Mr. Gandhi started an agitation against the Rowlatt (or 'Black') Bill when it was introduced in the Imperial Legislative Council.[2] In trying to suppress this agitation in the Punjab, indescribable atrocities were perpetrated by the forces of the Crown. At Jallianwalla Bagh in Amritsar on April 13th, there was a massacre of unarmed men, women and children who had gathered on the occasion of a public meeting. This was followed by a reign of terror under Martial Law, in the course of which many people were publicly flogged, while others were forced to crawl on their

---

[1] According to Sir Surendranath Bannerji, 'the Rowlatt Act was the parent of the Non-co-operation movement'. (*A Nation in Making*, London, 1927, p. 300.).

[2] Now called the Indian Legislative Assembly.

bellies when passing along certain streets. Two committees were appointed to inquire into these incidents and submit a report—a non-official committee appointed by the Indian National Congress and an official committee appointed by the Government of India, called the Hunter Committee. The Congress Enquiry Committee published unimpeachable evidence of the most brutal atrocities committed by the forces of the Crown, including outrages on helpless women. The findings of the Hunter Committee did not go as far as those of the Congress Enquiry Committee, nevertheless, they were sufficiently damaging for any government. After the publication of these two reports the public naturally expected that in view of the new era to be ushered in by the Constitutional Reforms, the Government of India would take courage in both hands and punish the wrong-doers, while granting adequate compensation for all those who had been killed or injured or had been otherwise made to suffer.

By the middle of 1920 it was clear, however, that the Government of India did not propose to take any such action.[1] The attitude and conduct of the Government appeared to the public eye as tantamount to condoning all the inhuman atrocities that had been perpetrated. This created a revulsion of feeling all over the country, even in circles favourably disposed towards the Government and the New Constitution. There can be little doubt that if the Government of Lord Chelmsford, the then Viceroy and Governor-General of India, had in 1920 taken drastic action against the authors of the Punjab atrocities, the confirmed 'Co-operator', Mr. Gandhi, would not have been forced to the path of non-co-operation, nor would the Indian National Congress have set aside the resolution adopted at the Amritsar Session in December 1919. Thus, on the rock of

---

[1] In the Imperial Legislative Council an Indemnity Act was passed in order to protect all the officers who had taken part in the Punjab atrocities. Besides the Lieutenant-Governor of the Punjab, Sir Michael O'Dwyer, was untouched, and General Dyer, who was responsible for the Jallianwalla Bagh massacre and for the administration of Martial Law, was merely declared unfit for future service in India. Even the meagre action taken by th Government was disapproved by the House of Lords and unprecedented public subscriptions were raised in England for the authors of the Punjab tragedy.

Jallianwalla Bagh was wrecked the ship of co-operation built by the Secretary of State for India, Mr. Montagu, through his sympathetic gestures and his elaborate intrigues during his visit to India in 1917-18.

It is an open secret that while Mr. Montagu and Lord Chelmsford were touring India with a view to preparing their joint memorandum on the new constitutional reforms, the former was engaged in rallying public support in favour of working the New Constitution. Before he left India in 1918, Mr. Montagu succeeded in definitely winning over the Moderate section in the Indian National Congress. When the National Congress met at a special session in Bombay in 1918 to consider the Montagu-Chelmsford Report, the Moderate Congressmen who were then being led by Sir Surendranath Bannerji and Mr. Srinivasa Sastri, absented themselves and soon after they seceded from the Congress and formed a separate political party under the name of All-India Liberal Federation, pledged to work the New Reforms. The Special Congress at Bombay in 1918 pronounced the Montagu-Chelmsford Report as unacceptable. Nevertheless, in December 1919, the Amritsar Congress resolved to work the constitution drafted on the basis of that report and also thanked Mr. Montagu. Thus, in spite of all the unfortunate events of 1919, Mr. Montagu, was able through his personal influence, to keep the Congress back from the path of opposition. It was only the Government of India's attitude towards the Punjab atrocities that proved to be the proverbial last straw.

A British politician in 1934 will naturally inquire why attempts were not made in 1920 to win over the Moslem Community when it was apparent that the Indian National Congress was heading towards an oppositionist policy. On this point, Mr. Montagu was not inactive and he did his level best to influence the British Cabinet, but the odds were against him. During the Great War, Indian Mohammedans had expressed their uneasiness as to what the policy of Britain towards Turkey would be when the time came for discussing peace-terms. To placate them the British Prime Minister, Mr. Lloyd George, had made a conciliatory statement on January 5th, 1918, in which he said, among other things, that Great Britain would not pursue a vindictive policy and had no intention of depriving the Turks of the rich lands of Asia Minor and Thrace which were predominantly Turkish. At the end of the war, however, when it was clear that the allies were aiming at nothing less than the complete dismemberment of Turkey, a deputation of Indian Moslems was sent to Europe in March 1920, to plead the cause of the Turks. This deputation which was led by Moulana Mohammad Ali, the younger of the Ali brothers, failed to achieve anything in spite of the best efforts of Mr. Montagu, the Secretary of State for India. By the middle of 1920, Indian Moslems began to feel that in all probability Turkey would cease to exist as an independent state—that the head of the Islamic Church, the Khalifa, who was also the Sultan of Turkey, would be deprived of his territories in Europe and in Asia and that the Holy Places of Islam would pass into non-Moslem hands. The realisation of this unavoidable calamity produced a blaze of resentment among every section of the Moslem Community in India. But however deep their resentment might be, they were not in a position to take up arms against the victorious British Government. Therefore all that they could think of doing was to oppose the working of the New Constitution.

About the middle of 1920, anti-British feeling was stronger among the Moslems than among the rest of the Indian population. Mr. Montagu had been able to divide the nationalist forces but he had failed to win over any section of the Moslems, though he had left no stone unturned in his efforts to placate them and had ultimately to resign from the Cabinet for ventilating their grievances.[1]
An organisation was set up by the Moslems under the

---

[1] In 1922 the Government of India urged on the British Cabinet that the Indian demand for the revision of the Treaty of Sevres should be made public. The chief items of that demand were—restoration of Asia Minor and Thrace to the Turks; suzerainty of the Sultan over the Holy Places and the evacuation of Constantinople by the Allied troops. Mr. Montagu thought that he had been authorised by the Cabinet to give publicity to the demand—but as the Cabinet disowned him, he had to resign.

name of the All-India Khilafat Committee with the object of restoring to the 'Khalifa', the head of the Islamic Church, the temporal power which he had enjoyed as Sultan of Turkey before the Great War. The leadership of this Khilafat movement was assumed by the Ali Brothers, Moulana Mohammed Ali, the younger but more influential, and Moulana Shaukat Ali, the elder. Both of them were Oxford graduates. Moulana Mohammad Ali had been a journalist and Moulana Shaukat Ali a highly-paid officer in the Excise Department of the Government of India. During the war both of them had been interned for carrying on propaganda against the British Government and in favour of the Turks. The agitation following in the wake of their incarceration had made them prominent in the public eye and when the Khilafat movement began, it was natural that they should be invested with the crown of leadership. Moreover, their dress and mode of life, shaped according to orthodox Moslem ideas, made a strong appeal to the Moslem masses and served to make them tremendously popular.

The Punjab atrocities and their sequel made a rebel of the once loyal Mr. Gandhi. He who had pleaded for co-operation at Amritsar in December 1919, and had succeeded in carrying the Congress with him, was in 1920 collecting his forces for leading a revolt against the British Government. Before he returned to India in 1914, he had tried the method of passive resistance in South Africa, in his fight for the rights of Indians against the South African Government and had found it extremely helpful. In February, 1919, before the Rowlatt Bills became law, he had started an agitation on the same lines, called the 'Satyagraha'[1] movement, against the Bills—but the agitation had proved to be abortive for the time being, because of

---

[1] 'Satyagraha' means literally 'persistence in truth'. It has been translated variously as non-co-operation, passive resistance, civil-disobedience, civil-resistance. The Satyagraha pledge was first taken at a public meeting in Johannesburg in South Africa, on September 11th, 1906, against the Asiatic Law Amendment Ordinance. According to Mr. Gandhi, Satyagraha eschews the use of violence in every form and has not the remotest idea of injuring the opponent. Mr. Gandhi states in his preface to Satyagraha in South Africa that before 1919 he had occasion to experiment with Satyagraha five times in India.

the outbreak of violence. He was, however, fully prepared to use the same method once again in organising a non-violent revolt against the British Government. He had disciplined his body and mind for a life of suffering. He had, moreover, brought with him a group of loyal followers from South Africa and during his six years' stay in India, had won many supporters for his cause. He only wanted more allies in order to be able to capture the leadership of the Indian National Congress. About this time the Ali Brothers and other Moslem leaders were preparing to launch Khilafat movement and they, too, were looking out for allies. Nothing could please them more than to find that the premier nationalist organisation of the country would take up the cause of Turkey. So an alliance was at once struck between Mr. Gandhi and the Ali Brothers on the basis of two issues, viz. the Punjab atrocities and the Khilafat grievances. The Ali brothers and their followers while keeping up a separate organisation—the All-India Khilafat Committee—would join the Indian National Congress and agitate for the redress of the Punjab and Khilafat wrongs and for the attainment of political freedom, which was the only guarantee against such wrongs in future. On the other hand, the Indian National Congress would lend its full support to the Khilafat organisations in the country and agitate for the redress of the Khilafat or Turkish grievances.[1]

The elections to the legislatures under the new Constitution—called the Government of India Act, 1919—were due in November 1920. The Amritsar Congress had resolved in December 1919, to work this Constitution but in the meantime public opinion had changed considerably. A special session of the Congress was therefore summoned in Calcutta in September 1920, under the Presidency of

---

[1] In November 1919, a Khilafat Conference was held in Delhi composed of both Hindus and Moslems under the guidance of Mr. Gandhi, to consider what steps should be taken to help the cause of the Khalifa (who was also the Sultan of Turkey). At this conference, Moulana Hasrat Mohani, an influential Moslem, suggested the boycott of British goods while Mr. Gandhi proposed non-co-operation with the Government. It was not till 1920, however, that the Khilafat Movement was actually launched.

Lala Lajpat Rai, the well-known Punjab leader. Mr. Gandhi was fully aware that his new policy of opposition to the reformed constitution would not be accepted by an influential section in the Congress. He had, therefore, strengthened himself by an alliance with the Moslem leaders and the All-India Khilafat Committee. In fact, he was sure of his position in the country that if the Congress had rejected his plan of non-violent non-co-operation, he could have launched his campaign with the support of the Khilafat organisations. Matters did not however, come to such a pass. Besides the Moslem leaders, Mr. Gandhi had a powerful ally in Pandit Motilal Nehru, the leading advocate of Allahabad and the leader of the United Provinces. The opposition to Mr. Gandhi's plan was sponsored by Mr. C. R. Das, the leading advocate of Calcutta and the leader of Bengal and Pandit Malaviya and Mrs. Besant, both ex-Presidents of the Congress, who had influential support from many provinces. Shortly before the Calcutta Congress, Lokamanya Tilak died. He was the only possible rival of Mr. Gandhi and at the time of his death, one could not say definitely what attitude he would take up if he were to attend the Calcutta Congress. At the Amritsar Congress he had taken up a middle position between Mr. Gandhi's proposal of co-operation and Mr. B. C. Pal, Mr. B. Chakravarti, and Mr. C. R. Das's proposal of opposition. Lokamanya Tilak held that the proper attitude should be one of responsive co-operation. In other words, the Congress should accept and work what was useful and beneficial in the New Constitution and reject what was useless or harmful. The closest followers of Lokamanya Tilak have declared since his death that he adhered to this view till the time of his death. Throughout his public career Lokamanya Tilak had been the leader of the Left Wing of the Indian National Congress, called the Extremists or Nationalists—as opposed to the Right Wing, called the Moderates or Liberals. He was a man of profound erudition and unbounded courage and sacrifice. His six years' incarceration in a far-off Burma prison had brought him additional lustre and popularity and if he had pitted himself against Mr. Gandhi at the Calcutta Congress, the position of the latter would have been a difficult one. With Lokamanya Tilak's death, however, it was smooth sailing for Mr. Gandhi. He moved the adoption of a policy of progressive non-violent non-co-operation which would begin with the renunciation of titles bestowed by the Government and with the triple boycott (namely, boycott of legislatures, law-courts, and educational institutions) and would end in non-payment of taxes. This resolution was carried by a large majority, 1,855 votes out of 2,728 being in his favour.

The resolution of the Special Congress in Calcutta came up for consideration at the regular annual session held at Nagpur in December, 1920, under the presidency of the veteran Congress leader from Madras, Mr. Vijayraghavachariar. Mr. Das and his followers mustered strong at Nagpur hoping to cross swords with Mr. Gandhi once again. But through the latter's tactful handling of the situation an understanding was arrived at between him and Mr. Das. The boycott of the legislatures, to which Mr. Das was chiefly opposed, was no longer a live issue, as the elections had already taken place. It was, therefore, possible to persuade Mr. Das to come to an agreement. When this was done, the non-co-operation resolution was ratified with practical unanimity, though Pandit Malaviya, Mrs. Besant, Mr. Jinnah and Mr. B. C. Pal remained irreconcilable.

Besides ratifying the resolution on progressive non-co-operation, including the boycott of legislatures, law-courts and educational institutions, the Nagpur Congress took a very important step in altering the Constitution of the Indian National Congress. Hitherto, the goal of the Congress, as defined in the Constitution, had been 'Self-Government within the British Empire'. This had antagonised all those Congressmen who believed in the severance of the British connection or who refused to be tied down to the Empire. To enable the Left-Wingers to return to the Congress fold, the goal of the Congress was declared to be 'Swaraj' (which means literally self-rule) and it was left to individual Congressmen, to define 'Swaraj' in their own way. Mr. Gandhi, however, defined 'Swaraj' to mean 'Self-Government within the Empire, if possible—and outside, if necessary'.

Before the Nagpur Congress the machinery of the Congress had been a loose one. There were branches only in the big cities and throughout the year, no work was done according to a systematic plan. At Nagpur, it was decided to re-organise the Congress on a country-wide basis. The smallest unit would be the Village Congress Committee. Several such Committees would combine to form a Union Congress Committee. Then there would be formed in succession—subdivisional (also called Taluka or Tahsil), district, provincial and All-India Congress Committees. The All-India Congress Committee would be a body of about 350 members consisting of representatives from the different provinces. This Committee would elect a Working Committee of 15 members which would be the Supreme Executive of the Congress for the whole country. Further, the provinces were re-organised on a linguistic basis. For instance, the Madras Presidency was divided into Andhra, which is Telegu-speaking and Tamil-Nadu, which is Tamil-speaking. The basis of the new Congress Constitution was of a democratic and parliamentary character. Besides setting up a new Constitution, the Nagpur Congress laid down a definite plan of work for the coming year.

Regarding the means to be followed by the Congress for attaining Swaraj, a change was made in the Constitution. Hitherto the Congress had been tied down to 'constitutional' means, but in future the Congress could adopt 'all peaceful and legitimate' means. This change had to be made in order to enable the Congress to resort to non-co-operation, which could be regarded as unconstitutional. Regarding both the goal and the means, the decision of the Nagpur Congress represented the golden mean between the views of the Right-Wingers, like Pandit Malaviya and Mr. Jinnah and the youthful Left-Wingers who swamped the Congress for the first time in 1920. The latter desired the goal of the Congress to be complete independence to

THE CLOUDS GATHER (1920) 49

be attained by all possible means. It was Mr. Gandhi, however, who by virtue of his tremendous influence and popularity was able to keep the Left-Wingers at bay. The Constitution that was adopted at Nagpur and which holds good even today, was practically his own draft. A year before, at Amritsar, he had been authorised by the Congress to revise the existing Constitution of that body.

Among the other resolutions adopted were those relating to the revival of hand-spinning and hand-weaving, removing of untouchability [1] among the Hindus and the collection of a fund of ten million rupees in memory of the late Lokamanya Tilak. (The idea of bringing back into use the ancient spinning-wheel in order to produce cloth as a cottage industry had struck Mr. Gandhi a year before.) While the above resolutions were all of a useful or beneficial character, there was one resolution which must be regarded as a great blunder. That was the decision to wind up the British Branch of the Indian National Congress and stop publication of its organ, the paper *India*. With the carrying into effect of this resolution, the only centre of propaganda which the Congress had outside India was shut down.

The Nagpur Congress, like the Calcutta Congress, was a great triumph for Mr. Gandhi. It was his Constitution and his plan of work that was adopted there. The gathering was an unprecedented one, twenty thousand people attending the Congress. Public enthusiasm was at a very high pitch and among the distinguished visitors were two Labour members of the British Parliament, Mr. Ben Spoor and Col. Wedgwood. The Nagpur Congress was an important landmark in the history of the Indian Nationalist Movement. It stood for a complete break with the Moderates, but it did not represent a complete victory for the Extremists. The latter, as we shall see subsequently, would have to work for many years before they could bring the Congress round to their point of view.

Considered objectively, the plan which Mr. Gandhi placed before the Congress and the country was not some-

[1] This is explained later on.

thing altogether new in the recent history of India. The fight which the people of Bengal had waged against the Government as a protest against the partition of their province in 1905 by the then Viceroy, Lord Curzon, had many features in common with the war of non-violent non-cooperation started in 1920 under the leadership of Mr. Gandhi. In 1905, Bengal had resorted to the boycott of British goods and of state-owned educational institutions and there had simultaneously been a revival of national industries and a growth of national schools and colleges, free from state interference of every kind. Moreover, leaders like Mr. B. C. Pal had refused to give evidence before British law-courts on the ground that they refused to recognise their jurisdiction. Sri Aurobindo Ghosh, the leader of the Extremist section of the Nationalist Movement in Bengal in those days, had compared this policy with the policy of the Irish Sinn Fein Party. Several decades earlier, the country had witnessed another movement which could also be regarded as a precursor of Mr. Gandhi's non-cooperation. Before scientists in Europe learnt to produce synthetic indigo, Bengal was an important supplier of indigo. The indigo plantations in those days were owned by Britishers and these foreign landlords were oppressive and brutal in their behaviour towards the tenants. When their brutality became unbearable, the tenants in Jessore and Nadia took the law into their own hands. They refused to pay rent, stopped cultivating indigo and made it impossible for the British landlords to live there and terrorise them. (A graphic description of these incidents can be found in the book *Nil-Darpan* of the well-known Bengali writer, Dinabandhu Mitra.) Thus the people had already learnt to rid themselves of oppression through their own exertions, where they found that the Government neglected its duty.

It is a well-known fact that Mr. Gandhi had in his earlier life been considerably influenced by the teachings of Jesus Christ and the ideas of Leo Tolstoy. It canont therefore be claimed that he was altogether original in his ideas or novel in his practice. But his real merit was a twofold one. He translated the teachings of Christ and the ideas of Tolstoy and Thoreau into actual practice and demonstrated that it was possible to fight for liberty without resorting to violence. Firstly, he used 'non-co-operation' not for remedying local grievances, but for winning national freedom and he well-nigh demonstrated that it was possible to paralyse the civil administration of a foreign Government thereby and bring the Government to its knees. A happy combination of factors helped to bring Mr. Gandhi to the forefront in 1920. The attempted revolution during the Great War had failed and the Revolutionary Party had been crushed. There was consequently no possibility of another revolution in 1920. Nevertheless, the country wanted a bold and vigorous policy on the part of the Congress and the only alternative was a movement like the one which Mr. Gandhi started. Secondly, the death of Lokmanya Tilak on the eve of the Calcutta Congress removed from the field the only possible rival of Mr. Gandhi. Thirdly, as a result of his long and careful preparation, Mr. Gandhi was fully prepared to assume the undisputed leadership of the Indian National Congress in 1920. Through ascetic discipline he had equipped himself for a life of suffering and during the period of his apprenticeship in Indian politics, from 1914 to 1920, he had been able to gather round him a band of loyal and trusted followers. Fourthly, he had acquired experience in the use of the weapon of 'Satyagraha'. Though his movement against the Rowlatt Bills in 1919 had proved to be abortive, he had won considerable success in South Africa. Before 1919 he had occasion, moreover, to make use of Satyagraha five times in India with very good results. Last but not least, he had gathered round his head a halo of saintliness which was of inestimable value to him in a country where the people revere the saint more than the millionaire or the Governor.

In spite of the democratic constitution of the Indian National Congress, at Nagpur, Mr. Gandhi emerged as the virtual Dictator of the Congress. He was, moreover, spontaneously acclaimed by the people as Mahatma (meaning literally a high-souled man or saint). That was the highest tribute that the Indian people could give him.

Throughout the year 1919, lightning and thunder had raged in the political sky of India—but towards the end of the year the clouds lifted and the Amritsar Congress seemed to herald an era of peace and quiet. But the promise of Amritsar was not fulfilled. Once again the clouds began to gather and towards the end of 1920 the sky was dark and threatening. With the new year came whirlwind and storm. And the man who was destined to ride the whirlwind and direct the storm was Mahatma Gandhi.

CHAPTER II

THE STORM BREAKS (1921)

The defection of the Moderates from the Congress was responsible for lowering to some extent the intellectual level of that body. But this loss was more than compensated by the rallying of the masses round the Congress banner. Moreover, Mahatma Gandhi did get as his trusted colleagues some veteran Congressmen whose reputation stood high in the country and who now renounced their professional work in order to give their whole time to the Congress. Mr. C. R. Das,[1] the leader of Calcutta Bar, who had already made a name in Indian politics as also in Bengali literature, gave up his princely income and plunged into the Non-co-operation Campaign. From Allahabad came Pandit Motilal Nehru, the leader of the Allahabad Bar, who also gave up his professional work. He was joined by his son—Pandit Jawaharlal Nehru—also an advocate by profession, who was destined to make a name for himself in the days to come. From the Punjab, Lala Lajpat Rai, the uncrowned king of that province who had been a lawyer in his earlier life, came forward to join the Mahatma. From the Bombay Presidency, the Mahatma got the support of the Patel Brothers, Mr. Vithalbhai and Mr. Vallabhbhai, both advocates by profession—and also Mr. N. C. Kelkar of Poona, who was the successor of late Lokamanya Tilak in Maharashtra (the southern and eastern portion of Bombay Presidency). The leaders of the Central Provinces who joined the Mahatma were Dr. Moonje, an eye-physician and Mr. Abhayankar, an advocate. The leader of Bihar was Mr. Rajendra Prasad, who renounced a fat income and a most promising career at the Patna Bar in order to work for the Congress. From the Tamil-speaking portion of Madras Presidency came Mr. Rajagopalachari,

[1] So great was the popularity of Mr. C. R. Das at the time that he was spontaneously given the title of 'Deshabandhu' by the people. 'Deshabandhu' means literally 'friend of the country'.

Mr. A. Rangaswami Iyengar and Mr. Satyamurti, and from the Telegu-speaking portion Mr. Prakasam, all lawyers by profession. On the supreme executive of the Congress there also sat the Ali brothers—Moulana Mohammed and Moulana Shaukat Ali, Moulana Abul Kalam Azad, one of the most learned of the Moslem divines and Dr. Ansari of Delhi—all of whom represented the new awakening among the Indian Moslems. Thus it will be seen that it was a very good team that Mahatma Gandhi was able to collect at the outset of his campaign.

Among those who gave up their professional work in response to the appeal of the Congress, the lawyers played a most important part. The example of lawyer-princes like Deshabandhu Das and Pandit Motilal Nehru was followed by lesser lights among the lawyer-fraternity throughout India and as a result, the Congress ranks were replenished by a large number of the whole-time workers of standing and influence. The appeal of the Congress for boycott of law-courts met with a fair measure of success. While a large number of lawyers gave up their practice for good, there was, on the other hand, an intensive campaign to dissuade litigants from approaching British law-courts and persuade them to settle their disputes by arbitration. As a matter of fact, arbitration-boards under the control of the Congress came into existence all over the country and owing to their efforts the Government revenue from litigation was considerably reduced. Along with the boycott of law-courts, a campaign was started for promoting temperance and stopping the use of intoxicants of all kinds. The success of this campaign was remarkable throughout India and in many provinces the excise revenue (that is, the revenue from the trade in liquor and other intoxicants) was reduced to one-third of what it formerly was. In some provinces, as in Bihar, the Government felt obliged to conduct a campaign for popularising the use of liquor and other intoxicants in order to increase their revenue.

The temperance movement was exceedingly popular among the masses and it fulfilled a moral as well as an economic purpose, while it caused considerable embarrassment to the Government. This movement was accompanied by a campaign for the removal of untouchability. In certain parts of India, especially in the south, some castes like sweepers, scavengers, etc. had been treated as untouchables. That is to say, the other castes would not dine with them, would not take food or drink served by them and, in some places, would not allow them to enter the temples. This custom was a factor working against the solidarily of the Indian people and from the moral and human standpoint was quite unjustifiable. It was therefore but natural that when the Congress resolved to launch a campaign for winning political freedom for India, it should also seek to emancipate the masses from the shackles of social bondage of every kind.

In order to afford some measure of economic relief to the masses, the Congress advocated the boycott of foreign cloth and the revival of hand-spinning and hand-weaving on a large scale. The idea of boycotting foreign cloth was not a new one—since the cry of boycott of British cloth had been first raised in Bengal as early as 1905. The revival of hand-weaving was also not a new proposal, since the Indian handloom industry had held its own against the competition of foreign and Indian mills. But the idea of reviving hand-spinning, which had practically gone out of use, was a novel and a daring one. It was difficult at first to find the men or women who could teach others to spin. The Mahatma, who was himself a good spinner, arranged to turn out batches of men and women who themselves could spin and teach spinning. Within a short time thousands of men and women were sent out all over the country, including the remotest villages, to teach the villagers how to spin. It was also difficult at first to get or buy spinning-wheels. They had to be manufactured in the cities and sent out to the villages, till the village carpenters learned to make them once again. The cloth woven in handlooms out of hand-spun yarn was called 'Khadi' or 'Khaddar' and was more coarse than mill-made cloth. As the production of this cloth began to increase, it automatically became the uniform of all Congressmen in India. They were required to set an example to the people by voluntarily wearing coarse 'Khadi' and discarding fine mill-made cloth.

To undertake the above work, both men and money were required. The Mahatma therefore appealed to the nation for ten million members for the Congress and a fund of ten million rupees (13½ rupees=one pound approximately). The response to this appeal proved to be most encouraging but in order to go round collecting money and enlisting members, an initial band of workers was necessary. This band of workers had to be supplied by the student community and the year 1921 therefore opened with an extensive campaign for the boycott of schools and colleges. Students responded to the appeal in large numbers and the response was the greatest in Bengal where the imagination of the youths had been stirred by the colossal sacrifice made by Deshabandhu C. R. Das. It was these student-workers who carried the message of the Congress to all corners of the country, who collected funds, enlisted members, held meetings and demonstrations, preached temperance, established arbitration-boards, taught spinning and weaving and encouraged the revival of home industries. Without them, all the influence of Mahatma Gandhi would not have carried the country very far.

There has been much criticism of the policy of withdrawing students from educational institutions in 1921. Nevertheless, if one dispassionately reviews the situation in the country in 1920-21 the conclusion will be irresistible that the Congress had no option in the matter, if it desired its resolutions to be translated into action. It should also be stated that though originally the Congress did not take in hand the task of establishing 'national' institutions, later on such institutions were started all over the country. Those students who had withdrawn from state-owned or state-controlled institutions in a spirit of non-co-operation but who desired to continue their studies under more salutary conditions, could join the newly-started national institutions and continue their studies. Such institutions were started in Bombay, Ahmedabad (in Bombay Presidency), Poona (in Bombay Presidency), Nagpur (in Central Provinces), Benares (in the United Provinces), Patna (in Bihar), Calcutta and Dacca (in Bengal). Some of these were for literary education, while others were for technical or medical education—but spinning was compulsory in all of them. In many places there were separate institutions for girls. Many of these institutions still exist and some of them are in a flourishing condition. Besides these educational institutions, another set of institutions spontaneously grew up all over India. These were called 'Ashramas'. Built on the model of the hermitage of old, they were homes for the whole-time political workers. New recruits were also trained there and the local office of the Congress would often be housed in the same premises. The Ashramas also served sometimes as centres for spinning and weaving. From these centres raw cotton and yarn would be distributed among the spinners and weavers and would be received back as yarn and cloth respectively. In many Ashramas there would also be a reading-room and a library for the use of the Congress workers and of the local public.

In the programme of progressive non-co-operation adopted at Nagpur in December 1920, there was, besides the triple boycott, an item regarding the renunciation of titles conferred by—and resignation of all posts held under —the Government. A comparatively large number of men gave up their titles but an insignificant number resigned their jobs and among the latter was myself. I had passed the Indian Civil Service in England in 1920, but finding that it would be impossible to serve both masters at the same time—namely the British Government and my country—I resigned my post in May 1921, and hurried back to India with a view to taking my place in the national struggle that was then in full swing. I reached Bombay on July 16th and the same afternoon I obtained an interview with Mahatma Gandhi. My object in seeking an interview with Mahatma Gandhi was to get from the leader of the campaign I was about to join, a clear conception of his plan of action. During the last few years I had made some study of the methods and tactics employed by revolutionary leaders in other parts of the world and in the light of that knowledge I wanted to understand the Mahatma's mind and purpose.

I remember vividly the scene of that afternoon. On arriving at Mani Bhawan, the usual residence of the Mahatma in Bombay, I was ushered into a room covered with Indian carpets. Almost in the centre, facing the door, sat the Mahatma surrounded by some of his closest followers. All were clad in home-made Khadi. As I entered the room, I felt somewhat out of place in my foreign costume and could not help apologising for it. The Mahatma received me with his characteristic hearty smile and soon put me at ease and the conversation started at once. I desired to obtain a clear understanding of the details—the successive stages —of his plan, leading on step by step to the ultimate seizure of power from the foreign bureaucracy. To that end I began to heap question upon question and the Mahatma replied with his habitual patience. There were three points which needed elucidation. Firstly, how were the different activities conducted by the Congress going to culminate in the last stage of the campaign, namely, the non-payment of taxes? Secondly, how could mere non-payment of taxes or civil disobedience force the Government to retire from the field and leave us with our freedom? Thirdly, how could the Mahatma promise 'Swaraj' (that is, Home Rule) within one year—as he had been doing ever since the Nagpur Congress? His reply to the first question satisfied me. The response to his appeal for ten million members and ten million rupees having been found to be satisfactory, he had proceeded to the next item in his plan—namely, the boycott of foreign cloth and the propagation of home-made Khadi During the next few months, his efforts would be concentrated on the Khadi campaign. And he expected that the Government would take the initiative in attacking the Congress, the moment it realised that the peaceful constructive activities of the Congress were proving to be successful. When the Government did so, the time would come for disobeying governmental decrees and marching to prison. The prisons would before long be filled to overflowing and then would come the last stage of the campaign—namely, the non-payment of taxes.

The Mahatma's replies to the other two questions were not convincing. I asked him if he expected that the boycott movement would create so much distress in Lancashire that pressure would be brought to bear on Parliament and the Cabinet to make peace with India. But the Mahatma gave me to understand that he did not consider that to be the means whereby the Government would be forced to come to terms with the Congress. What his real expectation was, I was unable to understand. Either he did not want to give out all his secrets prematurely or he did not have a clear conception of the tactics whereby the hands of the Government could be forced.[1] Altogether, his reply to the second question was disappointing and his reply to the third was no better. What was to him a question of faith—namely, that Swaraj would be won within one year —was by no means clear to me and personally speaking, I was prepared to work for a much longer period. However, I had no other course but to feel thankful for what I had been able to learn after an hour's conversation. But though I tried to persuade myself at the time that there must have been a lack of understanding on my part, my reason told me clearly, again and again, that there was a deplorable lack of clarity in the plan which the Mahatma had formulated and that he himself did not have a clear idea of the successive stages of the campaign which would bring India to her cherished goal of freedom.

Depressed and disappointed as I was, what was I to do? The Mahatma advised me to report myself to Deshabandhu C. R. Das on reaching Calcutta. I had already written to the latter from Cambridge that I had resigned the Indian Civil Service and had decided to join the political movement. Stories had reached us in England that he had given up his princely career at the Bar and was going to devote his whole time to political work, while making a gift of his entire property to the nation. In my eagerness

[1] Looking back on the incident today, it strikes me that possibly the Mahatma expected a 'change of heart' on the part of the British Government, leading to an acceptance of India's national demands.

to meet this great man, I overcame the somewhat depressing effect of my interview with Mahatma Gandhi and I left Bombay with the same excitement and the same enthusiasm with which I had landed there. On reaching Calcutta, I went straight to the house of Deshabandhu Das. Once again I was disappointed. He was out on a long tour in the interior of the province and I had no option but to wait for his return. When I heard that he was back, I called again. He was out at the time but I was received with great kindness and cordiality by his wife, Srijukta Basanti Devi. Before long he arrived on the scene. I can still picture before my mind's eye his massive figure as he approached me. He was not the same Mr. Das whom I had once approached for advice when he was one of the leaders of the Calcutta Bar and I a student, expelled from the University for political reasons. He was not the same Mr. Das who was earning thousands in a day and spending thousands in an hour. Though his house was no longer a palace, he was however the same Mr. Das, who had always been a friend of youth, could understand their aspirations and sympathise with their sorrows. During the course of our conversation I began to feel that here was a man who knew what he was about—who could give all that he had and who could demand from others all they could give—a man to whom youthfulness was not a shortcoming but a virtue. By the time our conversation came to an end my mind was made up. I felt that I had found a leader and I meant to follow him.

On settling down in Calcutta I proceeded to take stock of the situation in the country and particularly in the province of Bengal. Throughout the country there was unparalleled enthusiasm. The 'triple boycott' had been fairly successful. Though the legislatures were not empty, no Congressmen had gone there. The lawyers had on the whole made a good response and the student community had come out of the ordeal with flying colours.[1] The ap-

---

[1] The people had taken up enthusiastically the propaganda for the removal of untouchability and for the stoppage of the drink and drug traffic.

peal for Congress members and for funds had borne good fruit, and feeling highly encouraged at the state of affairs the Mahatma had launched in July a campaign for the boycott of foreign cloth and the revival of spinning and weaving. On the anniversary of the death of Lokamanya Tilak, August 1st, 1921, there were huge bonfires of foreign cloth all over the country. A symbolic meaning was also given by the Congress leaders to these bonfires which were to burn to ashes all the dross, all the dirt and all the weakness that was in the country. The whole-hearted support of the Moslem community and the novelty of the method of non-co-operation brought more strength to the movement, while the slogan of 'Swaraj within one year' drew into the field many people who would have been appalled by the prospect of a long period of suffering.

In Bengal two important events took place—the Assam-Bengal Railway Strike and the no-tax campaign in Midnapore District. The railway strike paralysed completely all rail and steamer traffic in East Bengal and Assam. The strike was conducted under the leadership of Bengal Congress Committee and in the earlier stages it was so successful that it made the people conscious of the power that they could wield if only they could combine against the authorities. As a timely settlement was not made, the strike dragged on for a long period and it ultimately collapsed, bringing disaster in its train. It was in connection with this strike that Mr. J. M. Sen Gupta first came into prominence before the public eye. The other event of importance was the no-tax campaign in Midnapore District. In 1919 at the instance of Sir S. P. Sinha (afterwards Lord Sinha), a member of the Executive Council of the Governor of Bengal, an Act had been passed purporting to introduce a measure of Self-Government for the villages—whereby union-boards would be established for every group of villages in the province. There had been considerable criticism of this measure mainly on two grounds—firstly, the power that should be transferred to the villagers was still retained in the hands of the district officials (for instance, the power to appoint and dismiss village policemen) and secondly, the establishment of union-boards entailed additional taxation in return for which no advantages would accrue. The Act provided that it was open to the Provincial Government to introduce it in any district or to withdraw it therefrom. Under the leadership of Mr. B. N. Sasmal, an advocate, the people of Midnapore started an agitation for the withdrawal of the Act from their district, and to strengthen their demand they refused to pay the taxes imposed by the newly-established union-boards. The usual repressive measures were taken to force the new Act on the district. Forcible seizure of property, harassment and prosecution of the villagers, intimidation by military police and by soldiers—all were tried but without success. The orgy of repression continued throughout the year 1921, but the Act had ultimately to be withdrawn in 1922. The success of this no-tax campaign gave considerable strength and self-confidence to the people of Midnapore and popularity to their leader, Mr. B. N. Sasmal.

It is necessary to interrupt our narrative here and to refer to the attitude adopted by the authorities in 1921. At first, the Viceroy, Lord Chelmsford, did not take Mahatma Gandhi seriously. In January, the Duke of Connaught, uncle of the present King, visited India with the object of inaugurating the new legislatures. His visit was boycotted by the Indian National Congress and there were boycott demonstrations wherever the Duke went. These demonstrations annoyed the Government of India and their attitude of indifferent neutrality began to change slowly. In April, Lord Chelmsford was succeeded by Lord Reading, the brilliant ex-Lord Chief Justice of England. Soon after his arrival, in the month of May, an interview was arranged between him and Mahatma Gandhi. At this interview, Lord Reading gave an assurance to the Mahatma that he would not interfere with the work of the Congress as long as there was no resort to violence. He further stated that in a speech of his, Moulana Mohammed Ali, the right-hand man of the Mahatma, had made an appeal for resorting to violence and that the Government were thinking of prosecuting him. The Mahatma promised to see to it that the

## THE STORM BREAKS (1921)

Moulana gave a public assurance that he would eschew violence in every way and this promise was duly carried out. Though there was nothing wrong or humiliating in the whole affair, to the public eye it appeared as if both the Mahatma and the Moulana had been outmanoeuvred by the astute Viceroy. Though the contemplated prosecution of Moulana Mohammed Ali was dropped after this interview, he and other Moslem leaders were arrested in September for their participation in the Khilafat Conference at Karachi in August and were sentenced to two years' 'rigorous imprisonment'. At this Conference, a resolution was passed calling upon all Moslems to give up service under the Government, whether in a civil or in a military capacity and this constituted a breach of the law. After the conviction of the Ali brothers and their associates, Mahatma Gandhi came forward to take up the challenge. The same resolution was signed and published by forty-six Congress leaders, and it was repeated from a thousand platforms all over India. But the Government did not make a single arrest and took no notice of this defiance on the part of the Congress. In September, the Indian Legislative Assembly—the Central Parliament set up under the New Constitution—passed a resolution urging an examination and revision of the constitution earlier than 1929. No immediate reply to this came from the side of the Government but the following year, the Secretary of State for India, Lord Peel, in a despatch on the subject dated November 3rd, 1922, stated that it was too early to contemplate a revision of the constitution.

From the above narrative it might appear as if throughout 1921 Mahatma Gandhi was riding on the crest of a wave and had no obstacles to encounter. This impression is not altogether correct. No doubt there was a tremendous volume of mass opinion on his side—but so far as the intelligentsia were concerned, there were certain elements opposed to him. In the first place, the Indian Liberals were everywhere arrayed against him and in most provinces they had accepted office as Ministers. This cooperation on the part of the Liberals was the direct result of the efforts of Mr. Montagu, the Secretary of State for India, and as long as he remained in office—that is, till March 1922—they were enthusiastically in support of the Constitution. After his resignation from the British Cabinet, reaction set in and Liberal leaders began to feel that it was becoming increasingly difficult for them to continue their co-operation. In April 1922, Sir Tej Bahadur Sapru resigned from the Executive Council of the Viceroy and in May 1923, Mr. Chintamani, Liberal Leader of the United Provinces, resigned the office of Minister of Education in that province. Gradually the Liberals all turned against the Government and by 1927 the change was so great that when the Simon Commission was appointed, Congressmen and Liberals could preach boycott from the same platform.

Closely allied with the Indian Liberals in mentality and outlook were the University authorities who had been hard hit by the Congress policy of boycott of educational institutions. Though their influence had been drowned for the time being by the rising tide of non-co-operation, they continued to exert what influence they still possessed against the Congress. In this effort they had the support of no less a personality than India's illustrious poet, Dr. Rabindranath Tagore. The poet arrived in Bombay from Europe about the middle of July. As a matter of fact, I travelled in the same boat with him. During our voyage, I had occasion to discuss with him the new policy of non-co-operation adopted by the Conress. He was by no means hostile to the idea. He was only anxious that there should be more of constructive activity, so that ultimately a state within the state could be built up, entirely on the co-operation and support of the people. What he suggested was analogous to the constructive side of the Irish Sinn Fein movement and was completely in accord with my views. But immediately after his arrival in India, he was surrounded by a group of people who were opposed to the Non-co-operation Movement and who began to point out to him only the shortcomings of that movement—as well as the personal views of the Mahatma on modern science and modern medicine, which had no connection with the political programme of the Congress. Under the impression that the Non-co-operation Movement was aiming at a break with Western science, culture and civilisation, the poet delivered a forceful address in Calcutta under the caption 'Unity of Culture' and roundly condemned any attempt to isolate India from the culture and civilisation of the rest of the world and deprecated the boycott of educational institutions. Congress circles could not take this assault lying down but it was impossible to find a literary man of the same standing as the poet to reply to his attack. However, the premier novelist of Bengal, Sarat Chandra Chatterji, ventured to give a reply in an address on 'The Conflict of Cultures'. The burden of his address was that though culture had a universal basis, each country had its own specific culture which was the creation of its national genius. India had to preserve and develop her own culture and if in doing so, she had to boycott the educational institutions which were under British influence, there was nothing objectionable in it. An attack from the poet was exceedingly unwelcome to the Mahatma, particularly because they had been great friends ever since the latter's return to India from South Africa. The Mahatma had therefore to pay several visits to the poet in order to pacify him. With the lapse of time the poet's opposition was completely disarmed and he became one of the staunchest supporters of the Mahatma in his subsequent campaigns.

While opposition to the Mahatma's policy of non-co-operation came from the intellectuals, opposition to his cult of non-violence came from another quarter—namely, the Revolutionary Party. During the Great War, thousands of revolutionaries had been imprisoned and most of them were subsequently released as a result of the amnesty declared in 1919. Many of them did not approve of the doctrine of non-retaliation which they apprehended would demoralise the people and weaken their power of resistance. There was a possibility that the ex-revolutionaries as a class would go against the Congress owing to ideological differences. As a matter of fact, a section of them had already started propaganda in Bengal against the Non-co-operation Movement. Strangely enough, funds had been provided by the British Mercantile Community under the name of the Citizens' Protection League. The money was distributed through the medium of an Indian advocate who did not disclose the source of the funds. Deshabandhu C. R. Das was anxious to disarm the hostility of the ex-revolutionaries and, if possible, to win their active support for the Congress campaign. He, therefore, arranged a conference in September between them and the Mahatma, at which he also was present. The ex-revolutionaries had a heart-to-heart talk with the Mahatma and he and the Deshabandhu tried to convince them that non-violent non-co-operation, instead of weakening or demoralising the people, would strengthen their power of effective resistance. The upshot of the conference was that all those present promised to give a full chance to the Congress to strive for Swaraj and promised to do nothing to hamper its work, while many of them agreed to join the Congress organisation as loyal and active members.

The conference between the Mahatma and the ex-revolutionaries took place behind closed doors in September 1921, when he and other members of the Congress Working Committee were staying as guests of Deshabandhu C. R. Das. This was the first occasion when I had an opportunity of coming into personal contact with the prominent leaders of the Congress. Besides the Deshabandhu, the outstanding personalities then were Pandit Motilal Nehru, Lala Lajpat Rai and Moulana Mohammed Ali. It is difficult to say how far the Mahatma would have succeeded in 1921 without their active support. To realise the importance of Lalaji and Deshabandhu one has only to visualise the political situation in the Punjab and in Bengal in their absence. And in 1921, Nehru Junior (Pandit Jawaharlal Nehru) was not so well known or experienced that he could have replaced his father. Besides the influence which the first three leaders had in their own provinces, their importance was also due to the fact that they were the three outstanding intellectual stalwarts of the Congress. Many of the blunders committed by the Mahatma as a political leader could have been avoided if they had been in a position to advise him. Since the death of these three giants, the leadership of the Congress has fallen to a low intellectual level. The Congress Working Committee today is undoubtedly composed of some of the finest men of India—men who have character and courage, patriotism and sacrifice. But most of them have been chosen primarily because of their 'blind' loyalty to the Mahatma— and there are few among them who have the capacity to think for themselves or the desire to speak out against the Mahatma when he is likely to take a wrong step. In the circumstances the Congress Cabinet of today is a one-man show.

In 1921, besides the above three leaders, the Ali brothers (Moulana Mohammed and Moulana Shaukat Ali) had a unique position among the public. This was due partly to their own activities and their suffering during the Great War—partly to the new awakening among the Moslems— but largely to the propaganda conducted in their favour by the Mahatma. The Mahatma associated himself so closely with them that they came to be looked upon as the right and the left hand of the Mahatma. In their company the Mahatma toured the country and one clearly remembers that in those days whenever there was a popular shout of 'Victory to Mahatma Gandhi' (Mahatma Gandhi ki Jai), it would be accompanied by a shout of 'Victory to the Ali Brothers' (Ali Bhajo-ki Jai). Though after some years the Ali brothers parted company with the Mahatma, I do not think one could find fault with the latter for his intimate association with them. The real mistake in my opinion did not lie in connecting the Khilafat issue with the other national issues, but in allowing the Khilafat Committee to be set up as an independent organisation throughout the country, quite apart from the Indian National Congress. The result of this was that when later on Ghazi Mustafa Kemal Pasha, as the leader of the New Turkey, forced the Sultan to abdicate and abolished the office of Khalifa altogether, the Khilafat question lost all meaning and significance and the majority of the members of the Khilafat organisations were absorbed by sectarian, reactionary and pro-British Moslem organisations. If no separate Khilafat Committees had been organised and all Khilafatist Moslems had been persuaded to join the ranks of the Indian National Congress, they would probably have been absorbed by the latter when the Khilafat issue became a dead one.

After the middle of the year, the political situation began to grow tense. Neither the Government nor the Congress knew at the time when the storm would break, but signs of the coming clash began to appear in different parts of the country. Throughout all these episodes the public took the offensive and the Government played a defensive role. Reference has already been made to the no-tax campaign in Midnapore district in Bengal and to the defiant conduct of the Congress leaders after the incarceration of the Ali brothers in September, following the Khilafat Conference at Karachi. Two other incidents are worth mentioning—the 'Akali' movement in the Punjab and the Moplah rebellion in Malabar in the south. The Akalis were a section among the Sikhs analogous to the Puritans among the Christians. They wanted primarily to reform the administration of the Sikh shrines or Gurudwaras. These shrines were mostly very rich and were administered by a set of 'Mohants', who though required to act merely as trustees living an ascetic and abstemious life, generally lived a thoroughly disreputable life at public expense. The Akalis wanted to dispossess these Mohants and bring the shrines under the administration of popular committees. As always happens in an enslaved country, the Government rallied to the support of the vested interests—the Mohants. Thus a movement directed against the Mohants soon developed into a movement against the Government. The tactics of the Akalis were in keeping with the Congress policy of non-violent non-co-operation and consisted in sending 'Jathas' or groups of men and women to take possession of the shrines. They were arrested and put into prison or mercilessly beaten and forcibly dispersed. This movement went on for a year till, in November 1922, the Government came to its senses and introduced legislation in the Punjab Legislative Council to concede what the Akalis had demanded from the beginning. The Moplahs of Malabar were a section of the Moslem community. Their rising was directed against the local Hindus; nevertheless it was also an attack on the Government and as such, caused them considerable anxiety and embarrassment. It has significance also because it was the first incident to loosen Hindu-Moslem unity.

In spite of these isolated phenomena of revolt, till November 1921, there was no sign of a country-wide conflict, far less of the Swaraj promised 'within one year'. Congress circles were therefore getting uneasy and depressed, when the Government came to the rescue. An announcement was made that the Prince of Wales would visit India and that he would land in Bombay on November 17th. The motive behind the visit was, of course, to assuage public feeling and rally public support for the Government. The Congress Working Committee promptly issued instructions for a boycott of the Prince's visit. It was stated that, though the people had nothing against the Prince personally, since he was coming to strengthen the bureaucracy which they were engaged in fighting, they had no option but to boycott his visit. As a first step towards this boycott, a 'hartal' or boycott demonstration was called for November 17th, when there should be a complete suspension of business all over the country. On that day, the boycott demonstration in Bombay was not a success. There was a clash between supporters of the Government and those of the Congress which resulted in prolonged rioting. But in Northern India, especially in Calcutta, the demonstration was a unique success, due largely to the wholehearted co-operation of the Khilafat organisations. So great was the success in Calcutta that the Anglo-Indian Papers, the *Statesman* and *Englishman,* wrote the next day that Congress volunteers had taken possession of the city and the Government had abdicated and they demanded immediate and drastic action against the Congress volunteers. Within twenty-four hours, the Government of Bengal issued a notification declaring them to be illegal. This was followed by similar notifications in other parts of the country.

We had been spoiling for a fight in Calcutta and the official notification therefore was thrice welcome to us. The general opinion was in favour of an immediate reply to the official challenge. But our leader, Deshabandhu Das, was cautious. He wanted time to take stock of his following in the province and to consult Mahatma Gandhi and the Working Committee. Secret circulars were sent out at once to different parts of the province for a report as to the measure of public support that would be forthcoming if the Congress started open defiance of the official ban. In less than a week encouraging reports began to pour in from the districts. A meeting of the Provincial Congress Committee of Bengal was thereupon summoned behind closed doors towards the end of November to decide our course of action. This committee was a body of about 300 members representing the Congress organisations of Bengal. By that time I had become a member of that body and I was able to participate in the deliberations. It was unanimously decided to start civil disobedience and in view of the state of emergency, all the powers of the committee were vested in its President, Deshabandhu Das, —and he was further authorised to nominate his successors. Thus he was appointed the Congress Dictator for the province—a procedure which was to be followed subsequently all over the country.

Contrary to the advice given by the younger hot-heads of the party who wanted to commence with a big demonstration, the leader decided to make a modest beginning. He wanted, he said, to work up the movement slowly and restrict the fight to a single clear issue. That issue was: would the Government take action if batches of five volunteers went out peacefully to hawk Khadi cloth—not in uniform as we had suggested, but in mufti? If they did so, then the public would regard the action of the Government as wholly arbitrary and unjustified and all sections would then rally to the support of the Congress. On this issue the fight began and I was put in charge of the campaign. My work as the Principal of the National College could not be continued and more so, because the students and some members of the staff were anxious to join the campaign. We issued an appeal for volunteers who would go out to defy the official ban and accept all the consequences. The response was discouraging. Apparently the public were still lukewarm and some stimulus was required to stir them up. The leader suggested that his son and his wife should go out as volunteers in order to set an example to others. We opposed the idea especially on the ground that no lady should be permitted to go out as long as there was a single man left. But the leader was adamant in his decision. So the next day young Das, who was about the same age as myself—went out at the head of the volunteers and was at once taken to prison.[1] There was an immediate change in the atmosphere and more volunteers began to enlist—but even that was not enough. So the turn came for Mrs. Das. Accompanied by her sister-in-law, Mrs. Urmila Devi and another associate, Miss Suniti Devi, she went out at the head of volunteers. When the news spread in the city that Mrs. Das and other ladies had been taken to prison, there was wild excitement. In utter indignation young and old, rich and poor began to pour in as volunteers. The authorities were alarmed and they converted the city into an armed camp. But our battle was half-won.

Indignation was not confined to the public but spread within the ranks of the hitherto loyal police. At the police-station, as Mrs. Das stepped into the prison-van, to be conveyed to prison, numbers of police constables came up to her and vowed that they were going to resign their jobs the same day. There was consternation in Government circles. No one knew at the time how far the con-

---

[1] According to the rules of non-co-operation, a Congressman was required not to put up a defence when brought up for trial before a British law-court. The prosecution therefore had an esay time and it would not generally take more than a few minutes to dispose of the cases.

tagion would spread. Orders were issued at once by Government that the pay of police constables would be substantially increased. The same evening at a dinner party in the Government House there was a sensation. Mr. S. N. Mullick, a leading Liberal politician (who was afterwards a member of the Council of the Secretary of State for India)—when he heard of Mrs. Das's arrest—left Government House immediately as a protest. So tense was the excitement that before midnight the Government had to order the release of Mrs. Das and her associates, and the public were given to understand that the arrests had been made through a mistake. From the next day thousands of students and factory-workers began to enlist as volunteers. Within a few days the two big prisons in the city were filled with political prisoners. Camp-prisons were then opened but they too were filled in no time. The Government then resorted to drastic action. Orders were issued for the arrest of Deshabandhu Das and his close associates, and by the evening of December 10th, 1921 we were all in prison.

But these arrests acted as a further stimulus and as more people were arrested the prison-administration became more unmanageable. Orders were given for the release of a large number of political prisoners but no one would leave the prison, and moreover, it was impossible to identify them. Sometimes they would be taken to the prison office on the pretext of being transferred to some other prison or of being interviewed by their relatives and there they would be set free. When this trick was discovered, no prisoner would leave his cell when called by a prison-official. Prisoners were thereupon taken forcibly to the prison-gate and set at liberty. Outside prison, tactics were changed. Arrests were stopped and orders were given that sticks and batons should be used freely by the police in dealing with crowds and demonstrators. In some cases demonstrators were removed in police-vans to out-of-the-way places thirty miles from the city and there asked to walk back home. A liberal use was also made of the hose in order to give the demonstrators free cold baths in

# THE STORM BREAKS (1921)

winter.

But it was clear to everybody that these makeshift arrangements and tactics would not do. The situation was going out of hand from the official point of view. The novelty of the tactics employed by the Congress had nonplussed the Government. They could of course have made a reckless and ruthless use of force on a large scale to put down the movement as they did subsequently, but they were embarrassed by the presence of the Prince of Wales in India. The Prince of Wales was due to arrive in Calcutta—the storm centre of the 1921 movement—on December 24th, and about a week before that, the Viceroy, Lord Reading, arrived there. The members of the Calcutta Bar had previously agreed to invite him to a banquet, as he was ex-Lord Chief Justice of England. But in view of the arrest of Deshabandhu Das, they cancelled the engagement. The Government of India thus found themselves in an exceedingly difficult position as they met with opposition everywhere. In the first place, though the civil disobedience movement was strongest in Bengal, it was fairly strong throughout Upper India and no province was free from it. In addition to this the Akali movement in the Punjab, the no-tax campaign in the Midnapore district in Bengal, and the Moplah Rebellion in Malabar in South India intensified the crisis. Outside India, the Sinn Fein Movement in Ireland had been largely successful, a treaty with Great Britain having been signed on December 6th, 1921. Some months earlier, Afghanistan had entered into a treaty with Mustafa Kemal Pasha and this was followed by a treaty between Persia and Soviet Russia. In Egypt, the Nationalist Wafd Party of Syed Zaghlul Pasha was strong and active. Thus it was apparent that the entire Moslem world was combining against Great Britain and this had an inevitable reaction on the Moslems of India. In these circumstances it was no surprise that the Government of Lord Reading should be anxious for a settlement with the Congress. A peace-maker was found in Pandit Madan Mohan Malaviya, the veteran nationalist leader, who for reasons of his own, had kept away from the 1921 movement. He came to interview Deshabandhu Das in the Presidency Jail with a message from the Viceroy. The offer that he brought was that if the Congress agreed to call off the civil disobedience movement immediately, so that the Prince's visit would not be boycotted by the public, the Government would simultaneously withdraw the notification declaring Congress volunteers illegal and release all those who had been incarcerated thereunder. They would further summon a Round Table Conference of the representatives of the Government and the Congress to settle the future constitution of India.

The leader had a long discussion with Moulana Abul Kalam Azad, the outstanding Moslem leader of Calcutta and with Pandit Malaviya. Some other points had to be decided, including the question of the release of the Ali brothers and their associates, who had been sentenced to two years' hard labour at Karachi in September. On this point the official reply was that since they had not been sentenced in connection with the civil disobedience movement, the Congress should not press for their release as a part of the terms of settlement. But the Viceroy was prepared to give an assurance that they would actually be released in due course. When Deshabandhu Das broached the subject to us and asked for our opinion, the younger section, including myself, vehemently opposed the idea of an armistice on those terms. Thereupon he entered into an elaborate discussion with us and advanced the following arguments in support of his contention that a compromise should be made at once. Rightly or wrongly, he said, the Mahatma had promised Swaraj within one year. That year was drawing to a close. Barely a fortnight was left and within this short period something had to be achieved in order to save the face of the Congress and fulfil the Mahatma's promise regarding Swaraj. The offer of the Viceroy had come to him as a godsend. If a settlement was made before December 31st and all the political prisoners were released, it would appear to the popular imagination as a great triumph for the Congress. The Round Table Conference might or might not be a success, but if it failed and the Government refused to concede the popular demands—the Congress could resume the fight at any time and when it did so, it would command greater prestige and public confidence.

The above logic was irrefutable and I felt convinced. Under the joint signatures of Deshabandhu Das and Moulana A. K. Azad, a telegram was sent to Mahatma Gandhi recommending for acceptance the proposed terms of settlement. A reply came to the effect that he insisted on the release of the Ali brothers and their associates as a part of the terms of settlement and also on an announcement regarding the date and composition of the Round Table Conference. Unfortunately, the Viceroy was not in a mood for any further parleying and wanted an immediate decision. All that the Deshabandhu could do in the circumstances was to send for his friends who were then outside prison and urge upon them that they should use all possible means to get the Mahatma to agree. These friends did so and many telegrams passed between Calcutta and Sabarmati, the usual residence of the Mahatma near Ahmedabad. Ultimately the Mahatma did come round, but by then it was too late. The Government of India, tired of waiting, had changed their mind. The Deshabandhu was beside himself with anger and disgust. The chance of a lifetime, he said, had been lost.

The feeling among the political prisoners, as also among the Congress rank and file, was that the Mahatma had committed a serious blunder. Only a minority, who had blind faith in him, refused to pass any judgment. However, since the opportunity had been lost, there was no option but to make the best of a bad situation. The Deshabandhu had been elected President of the ensuing Congress which was to meet at Ahmedabad in the last week of December. His half-written speech, which was a vindication of the principles and methods of the non-co-operation movement, was sent to the Congress and the presidential chair was filled, in his absence, by Hakim Ajmal Khan, the outstanding leader of Delhi. There was great enthusiasm at the Ahmedabad Congress and the main resolution was one which called upon the whole country to adopt a policy of individual and mass civil disobedience. Every man and woman was exhorted to join the National Volunteer Corps, defy the emergency ordinances and court imprisonment. The Congress further appointed the Mahatma as the Dictator for the whole country, following the precedent of the Bengal Congress Committee, who had appointed the Deshabandhu as the Dictator for the province.

There was an interesting episode at the Ahmedabad Congress. Moulana Hasrat Mohani, an influential Moslem leader of the United Provinces, moved a resolution to the effect that the goal of the Indian National Congress should be defined in the constitution as the establishment of a republic (the United States of India). So impassioned was his eloquence and so responsive was the audience, that one felt as if the resolution would be carried by a large majority. But the Mahatma rose to oppose the resolution and with great sobriety argued against the proposition, with the result that it was thrown out by the house. The proposition was, however, to be brought up over and over again at subsequent Congresses till it was accepted at the Lahore Congress in 1929, the mover on that occasion being none other than the Mahatma himself.

With the dissolution of the Congress, the year 1921 came to an end. Nothing of a startling character happened on or before December 31st. The promised Swaraj did not come. A few months earlier, at the conference with the ex-revolutionaries of Bengal, the Mahatma had said that he was so sure of getting Swaraj before the end of the year that he could not conceive of himself as living beyond December 31st, without having won Swaraj. He had further said that provincial autonomy and diarchy in the Central Government he could have for the mere asking, but he wanted full Dominion status and if he had that, he would be prepared to unfurl the Union Jack over his Ashrama. As the curtain was rung down on December 31st, 1921, these words floated like dreams before my mind's eye.

## THE STORM BREAKS (1921)

Before the end of the year, with the exception of Mahatma Gandhi, all the other important leaders were in prison. As a matter of fact, at the time of the negotiations between the Deshabandhu and the Viceroy, none of the outstanding intellectual stalwarts was in a position to advise the Mahatma as to the proper course for him to adopt. If they had done so, then, in all probability, events would have taken a different course. There can of course be no doubt that within twelve months the country had made tremendous progress and much of the credit for that belonged to the Mahatma. But what has to be regretted is that he did not show sufficient diplomacy and prudence when the crucial hour arrived. In this connection I am reminded of what the Deshabandhu used frequently to say about the virtues and failings of Mahatma Gandhi's leadership. According to him, the Mahatma opens a campaign in a brilliant fashion; he works it up with unerring skill; he moves from success to success till he reaches the zenith of his campaign—but after that he loses his nerve and begins to falter.

Before we close this chapter it would be desirable to take stock of the year's achievements and failures. The year 1921 undoubtedly gave the country a highly-organised party-organisation. Before that, the Congress was a constitutional party and mainly a talking body. The Mahatma not only gave it a new Constitution and a nation-wide basis —but what is more important, converted it into a revolutionary organisation. The tricolour national flag—red,[1] green and white—was adopted all over the country and assumed great importance. Uniform slogans were repeated everywhere and a uniform policy and ideology gained currency from one end of India to the other. The English language lost its importance and the Congress adopted Hindi (or Hindustani) as the *lingua franca* for the whole country. Spontaneously, Khadi became the official uniform for all Congressmen. In short, all the features of a modern political party became visible in India. The credit for such achievements naturally belongs to the leader of the move-

---

[1] The colour red in the national flag has now been altered to saffron.

ment—Mahatma Gandhi. He has unfortunately been guilty of many serious blunders—'Himalayan blunders' to use his own language. And the fact that even today he is enthroned in the hearts of his countrymen does not mean that he has been free from errors of judgment but that his positive achievements have been really so great that his countrymen are prepared to forgive his mistakes.

It is necessary, in this connection, to refer to some of the shortcomings inherent in the movement from the very beginning and which were to reveal themselves more and more with the lapse of time. In the first place, too much power and responsibility was handed over to one man. The disadvantages of such a state of things were not so great, while Deshabandhu C. R. Das, Lala Rajpat Rai and Pandit Motilal Nehru were alive, since they could control the Mahatma to some extent. But since their death the entire intellect of the Congress has been mortgaged to one man and those who dare to think freely and speak out openly are regarded by the Mahatma and his disciples as heretics and treated as such. Secondly, the promise of 'Swaraj' within one year was not only unwise but childish. It made the Congress appear so foolish before all reasonable men. No doubt the Mahatma's disciples have tried subsequently to explain away the point by saying that the country did not fulfil the conditions and so Swaraj could not be won within one year. The explanation is as unsatisfactory as the original promise was unwise—because arguing in the same way, any leader can say that if you fulfil certain conditions you can be free in one hour. In making political forecasts, no leader worth the name should impose impossible conditions. He should estimate what conditions are likely to be fulfilled and what results are likely to be achieved in a given set of circumstances. Thirdly, the introduction of the Khilafat question into Indian politics was unfortunate. As has already been pointed out, if the Khilafatist Moslems had not started a separate organisation but had joined the Indian National Congress, the consequences would not have been so undesirable. In that case, when the action of the Turks themselves made the Khilafat issue a dead one, the Khilafatist Moslems would have been completely absorbed into the ranks of the nationalists.

The storm that was brewing in 1920 actually broke in November 1921. During November and December it raged with great intensity and when the new year dawned, such was the prospect that it was impossible to predict how long it would last. The year 1922 was, however, destined to provide an anti-climax, as we shall presently see.

CHAPTER III

## THE ANTI-CLIMAX (1922)

It is not possible at this distant date to understand how profoundly the people of India believed in 1921 that Swaraj would be won before the end of that year. Even the most sophisticated people shared this optimism. I remember listening once to the speech of an able Bengalee advocate at a public meeting in 1921, in the course of which he asserted in all seriousness: 'We are surely going to get Swaraj before the year is out. If you ask me how we are going to win it, I cannot answer. But we are going to win it all the same.' On another occasion in 1921, I was discussing with an exceptionally able Calcutta politician some instructions issued by the Mahatma. He had declared that all funds at the disposal of the Congress should be spent before the end of the year and that nothing should be left over for the next. To a normal rational mind this seemed improper, but defending the Mahatma, this friend said, 'We have deliberately chosen not to look beyond December 31st'. All this may appear now as madness; nevertheless, it gives some idea of the exuberance of naive enthusiasm and optimism that had taken possession of the country that year.

With the dawn of the new year, 1922, a special effort was made by the Mahatma to whip up public enthusiasm. It was therefore decided to proceed to the last item in his plan—namely, the non-payment of taxes. On February 1st, 1922, he sent an ultimatum to the Viceroy, Lord Reading, saying that if within seven days the Government did not demonstrate a change of heart, he would commence general non-payment of taxes in Bardoli subdivision in Gujerat (northern part of Bombay Presidency). It was reported that in Bardoli subdivision there were many people who had worked with Mahatma Gandhi in the passive-resistance movement in South Africa and had acquired experience in work of that kind. The beginning of the no-tax campaign in Bardoli would be the signal for starting a similar campaign all over the country. Elaborate arrangements were also made to start a no-tax campaign [1] in Bengal simultaneously, and the United Provinces and Andhra (northern portion of Madras Presidency) were also well-prepared for a campaign of that sort. The ultimatum of the Mahatma threw the whole country into a fever of excitement. With bated breath everybody began to count the hours as they sped by. Suddenly there came a bolt from the blue which left the people speechlees and dumbfounded. That was the incident at Chauri-Chaura.

On February 4th, at a place called Chauri-Chaura in the United Provinces, the villagers in a fit of exasperation set fire to the police-station and killed some policemen. When this news reached the Mahatma, he was horrified at the turn of events and immdiately summoned a meeting of the Congress Working Committee at Bardoli. At his instance, the Committee decided to suspend the civil-disobedience movement (that is, the defiance of laws and governmental decrees, including non-payment of taxes) entirely throughout India for an indefinite period and all Congressmen were enjoined to confine themselves to peaceful constructive work. The 'constructive programme' included hand-spinning and hand-weaving, removal of untouchability, promotion of intercommunal unity, suppression of the drug traffic, extension of 'national' education, suppression of litigation and establishment of arbitration-boards —without voluntarily violating any law or governmental ordinance existing at the time.

The Dictator's decree was obeyed at the time but there was a regular revolt in the Congress Camp. No one could understand why the Mahatma should have used the isolated incident at Chauri-Chaura for strangling the movement all over the country. Popular resentment was all the greater because the Mahatma had not cared to consult representatives from the different provinces and because the situation in the country as a whole was exceedingly favourable for the success of the civil-disobedience campaign. To

---

[1] Non-payment of the Chowkidari tax, which all villagers then had to pay for the upkeep of the village police, etc.

sound the order of retreat just when public enthusiasm was reaching the boiling-point was nothing short of a national calamity. The principal lieutenants of the Mahatma, Deshabandhu Das, Panidt Motilal Nehru and Lala Lajpat Rai, who were all in prison, shared the popular resentment. I was with the Deshabandhu at the time and I could see that he was beside himself with anger and sorrow at the way Mahatma Gandhi was repeatedly bungling. He was just beginning to forget the December blunder when the Bardoli retreat came as a staggering blow. Lala Lajpat Rai was experiencing the same feelings and it is reported that in sheer disgust he addressed a seventy-page letter to the Mahatma from prison.

In semi-official circles another explanation has been given of the sudden *volte-face* of the Mahatma. It is alleged that elaborate arrangements had been made by the Government in secret to render his no-tax campaign at Bardoli a debacle and that a large portion of the next instalment of taxes had been already collected. Official circles, sympathetic to the Mahatma, conveyed secret information to him regarding the counter-measures adopted by the Government and warned him of the possibility of a failure, in case he launched the campaign. When Mahatma Gandhi was brought face to face with these facts, he realised the hopelessness of the situation and thinking that without a successful campaign at Bardoli, he could not work up the movement in the country, he decided to use the Chauri-Chaura incident as a pretext for calling off the civil-disobedience movement. Those who know the Mahatma more intimately will not, however, accept this explanation.

While the followers were fretting and funing against the Dictator, the astute ex-Lord Chief Justice of England was not idle. Throughout 1921 he had given the Mahatma a long rope, but since the Ahmedabad Congress he began to look for an opportunity for putting a stop to his activities. In his weekly paper *Young India*, the Mahatma had written some articles—the finest he has ever written and which will rank for all time among his inspired writings—which the Government held to be seditious. They could therefore arrest him and get him sentenced to a long term of imprisonment. But the point they had to consider was what the effect of such an action would be on the masses who idolised the Mahatma. Lord Reading, it was reported, was genuinely afraid that in spite of all the non-violence which the Dictator preached, his arrest would be followed by widespread disorder, rioting and bloodshed. And coming after Lord Chelmsford, under whose regime the Amritsar massacres had taken place, he had no desire to repeat the terrible events of 1919. He was therefore anxiously and nervously looking for an opportunity to strike at the Mahatma when the latter himself took a step which had a depressing effect all over the country and produced a revolt within the Congress itself. That was the proper psychological moment for Lord Reading to act—if only the Secretary of State for India, Mr. Montagu, would not stand in his way. Fortunately for the Government of India, early in March, owing to differences with the Cabinet in England, Mr. Montagu was forced to resign. The last obstacle was therefore removed and on March 10th, 1922, Mahatma Gandhi was made a prisoner.

The trial of Mahatma Gandhi was a historic event. In describing the trial proceedings, Deshabandhu C. R. Das in his presidential speech at the Gaya Congress in December 1922, drew an analogy with the trial of Christ before Pontius Pilate. A similar comparison was also drawn by the well-known Y.M.C.A. leader, the late Mr. K. T. Paul.[1] In the trial, the Mahatma who described himself as a farmer and a weaver, made a lengthy statement describing how 'from a staunch loyalist and co-operator I have become an uncompromising disaffectionist and non-co-operator'. And he ended his statement with these words: 'The only course open to you, the Judge and the Assessors, is either to resign your posts and thus dissociate yourselves from evil if you feel that the law you are called upon to administer is an evil and that in reality I am innocent, or to inflict on me the severest penalty if you be-

[1] *The British connection with India*, by K. T. Paul, London, 1927, p. 50.

lieve that the system and the law you are assisting to administer are good for the people of this country and that my activity is therefore injurious to the public weal.'

The English Judge, Mr. Broomfield, sentenced him to six years' imprisonment.

The resignation of Mr. Montagu was an indication of the growing power of the Conservatives in the Coalition Cabinet of Mr. Lloyd George, the Premier. Under pressure from the Tory members, Mr. Lloyd George delivered in August his famous 'steel-frame' speech in which he described the Civil Service as the steel-frame of the Indian administration which must remain British, no matter what other changes may overtake India. This speech caused widespread resentment in India, because people were looking forward to the day when the power and the emoluments of the Civil Service would be curtailed and the people given thereby a due place in the administration of their country. About this time, Lord Winterton, the new Under-Secretary of State for India, visited India. One of the purposes of his visit was to herald a new policy with regard to the Indian Princes and Ruling Chiefs. The year before, when the Prince of Wales visited India, he had noticed a great difference between his reception in British India and in the Indian States. In British India, his visit had been boycotted by the public, whereas in the States he had no such unpleasant experience. Since that moment, the British Government were led to adopt a new attitude towards the Princes—an attitude of greater friendship and cordiality. The Princes, on their part, utilised the occasion for persuading the Government of India to introduce legislation with a view to suppressing hostile agitation and propaganda conducted against the Princes from British India. Accordingly in September 1922, a Bill was introduced in the Assembly called the Indian States (Protection against Disaffection) Bill. The Bill was thrown out by the Assembly but the Viceroy 'certified' it as urgent and necessary and it became law. It is noteworthy in this connection that the new Under-Secretary of State for India, Lord Winterton, in his conferences with the Viceroy and the Governors of

Bombay, Madras and Bengal, advocated this new attitude towards the Princes and after his visit representatives of the Government of India began to sing praises of the Princes whenever a suitable opportunity presented itself.

In October there was a General Election in England. The Coalition Government broke up and the Conservatives came into power with Mr. Bonar Law at their head and with Viscount Peel and Lord Winterton as Secretary and Under-Secretary of State for India respectively. The next month, Sir Basil Blackett was sent out to India as the Finance Member to the Government of India. The current of reaction began to grow stronger and stronger in India. The Indian Liberal leaders, who under the influence of Mr. Montagu had been led to work the Constitution and to accept office as Ministers, found their position increasingly difficult. Sir Tej Bahadur Sapru had already resigned from the Viceroy's Executive Council in April, following the resignation of Montagu in March. And in March 1923, when the situation became unbearable for him, Mr. Chintamani, the Minister for Education in the United Provinces, resigned. During the whole of 1922 the only decent acts which the Government did was to concede the demands of the people in Midnapore district in Bengal and of the Akali Sikhs in Punjab. In Midnapore, the new Village Self-Government Act, as a protest against which the no-tax campaign had been started, was withdrawn, and in Punjab a new law was passed under which all the Sikh shrines were taken out of the control of the Mohants and handed over to popular committees.

We must now interrupt our narrative and enquire as to what the leaders had been doing in the meantime. In the first week of December 1921, Lala Lajpat Rai and most of his principal colleagues had been rounded up by the police at a meeting of the Punjab Congress Committee. A few days later, Deshabandhu Das and most of his colleagues, including the Secretary of the Bengal Congress Committee, Mr. B. N. Sasmal, and myself had been placed under arrest. Following this, Pandit Motilal Nehru and most of the important Congressmen in the United Provinces had been clapped into prison. According to the rules of non-co-operation, no Congressman could put up a defence before a British Court of Law. Consequently, everywhere the prosecution had an easy task. Most of the trials would not last more than a few minutes and the same magistrate would dispose of hundreds of cases in one afternoon. In the case of Deshabandhu Das, however, the trial dragged on for two months and since Mr. Sasmal and I had been made his co-accused in the same case, we had to suffer the agony of a uselessly long trial. It was freely talked about at the time that in view of the prestige and influence commanded by the Deshabandhu, the magistrate was unwilling to convict him without some show of legality. Time was therefore given again and again to the prosecution to collect evidence to prepare their case against him. The prosecution case rested on certain notices, alleged to have been signed by him, which were in violation of the Government proclamation, banning as illegal all volunteer organisations. Those who worked in the office of the Bengal Congress Committee knew, as a matter of fact, that these notices had not been signed by him. Nevertheless, the official expert in handwriting gave evidence on oath that the signatures were genuinely of the Deshabandhu and on the strength of this so-called expert evidence, he was convicted and sentenced to six months' imprisonment. These as well as other illegalities relating to his arrest were pointed out in a statement made by him before the court towards the end of his trial, in the course of which he sought to prove that the Government never hesitate to break the law when it suits their own purpose. Before sentence was passed, a message was sent on behalf of the prosecution saying that if he accepted the Bardoli resolution, regarding the suspension of civil disobedience, the Government would set him free at once, but he refused to entertain any such proposal.

Soon after our conviction we were transferred to another prison in Calcutta, the Alipore Central Jail, where we had an opportunity of meeting representatives from all the districts in Bengal. Except among the orthodox followers of the Mahatma who were in a minority, the general feeling was one of resentment at the Bardoli decision. This feeling was directed more against the Mahatma, since he was the Dictator of the All-India Congress Committee and the Bardoli resolution had been passed at his instance. Accepting the Bardoli retreat as an accomplished fact, the Deshabandhu tried to devise means for rousing public enthusiasm once again by a change in tactics. He thus conceived of his plan of non-co-operation within the legislatures. According to this plan, Congressmen, instead of boycotting the elections, would stand as candidates at the polls and after capturing the elected seats, would carry on a policy of uniform, continuous and consistent opposition to the Government. The boycott of the legislatures, as conceived by the Calcutta Congress in 1920, had proved to be a failure. While the nationalists had kept away from the legislatures, undesirables had captured those bodies. These people, instead of assisting the popular movement in the country, had lent their support to the Government. Through their help the Government was able to demonstrate to the world that in their policy of repression they had the support of the elected members of the legislatures. According to the Deshabandhu, in a revolutionary fight, the points of vantage should not be left in the hands of the enemy. Therefore all elected seats in the legislatures, as also in all public bodies (namely, municipalities, district boards, etc.), should be captured by Congressmen. Where there was room for doing any solid constructive work, they could do so. But failing that, they could at least keep up a systematic opposition to the members and agents of the Government, and thereby prevent them from doing mischief. Further, the election campaign would give the Congress an occasion and an opportunity for doing its own propaganda simultaneously all over the country. The adoption of this new policy did not imply that they were to abandon any of the other activities of the Congress, but simply meant an extension of those activities to include capture of the elected seats in the legislatures and all public bodies.

Discussion regarding this new plan were carried on vigorously from day to day in the Alipore Central Jail. It soon appeared that in all these discussions the main contention of the opponents was that the Government of India Act, 1919, hardly left any room for useful opposition within the legislatures. Owing to the presence of Britishers and of other members nominated by the Government, it was difficult, if not impossible, for the elected members to secure a majority either in the Indian Legislative Assembly (the Central Legislature) or in the Provincial Legislatures. Further, the Viceroy, in the case of the former and the Governors, in the case of the latter, had powers of veto and certification, whereby they could always override the decision of the legislatures. The reply to this was that even if the elected members did not have a majority, they could still keep up a continuous opposition against the Government and thereby strengthen the agitation outside the legislatures. Secondly, it would be possible for the elected members to secure a majority in at least some of the legislatures and if the Viceroy or the Governor set aside the decision of any legislature, the Government would stand condemned before the bar of public opinion, both inside India and outside. Lastly, under the existing constitution, a vote against the Ministers or their departments could not be overriden by the Governor of any province, and if the provincial legislature voted down the salaries of Ministers, they would automatically be thrown out of office and the working of the diarchical constitution would have to be suspended. As these discussions went on for some weeks, two parties crystallized among the political prisoners in the Alipore Jail and they proved to be the nuclei of the future 'Swaraj' and 'No-Change' parties. In May 1922, the annual conference of Congressmen in Bengal, called the 'Provincial Conference', was held in Chittagong. Mrs. C. R. Das was elected President of the Conference because of the gallant part she had played in last year's movement. In her presidential speech, she stated that the Congress might have to consider a change in tactics and suggested, among other things, that the policy of non-co-operation within the legislatures was worth considering. It was not difficult to guess who had inspired her speech and taking it as a feeler sent out by her husband, a storm of controversy was at once let loose all over the country. It was clear therefrom that the orthodox followers of the Mahatma would not think of any deviation from the plan that he had laid down before his arrest and that a stiff fight would take place before the new plan could be adopted by the Congress. This prospect, far from discouraging us, helped to whip up our enthusiasm. The Deshabandhu had frequent discussions with his supporters in prison and he chalked out his future line of action in great detail. Among the measures that he contemplated was the starting of daily papers in English and in the vernacular—and out of this speculation came the birth of his paper *Forward*, which was started in 1923 and soon attained distinction as one of the leading nationalist papers in India.

During 1922 conflicts between political prisoners and the prison authorities took place in many prisons in India. Matters came to a head in two prisons in Bengal—at Barisal and Faridpur. Political prisoners in these prisons demanded decent treatment at the hands of the authorities and refused to submit to the humiliating treatment generally meted out to prisoners in Indian Jails. The authorities were stubborn and resorted to flogging, but even that could not break the backbone of the political prisoners. Meanwhile, intense public indignation was roused by the news of the flogging. Even the tame Bengal Legislative Council was stirred to action and within the Government itself, differences of opinion broke out. The Member in charge of Jails, Sir Abdur Rahim, disapproved flogging of political prisoners, but he could not carry the Government with him. As a protest he resigned the portfolio of Prisons which was taken up by the then Home Member of the Bengal Government, Sir Hugh Stephenson.

After the arrest of Mahatma Gandhi, in March, the Congress Working Committee was at a loss to decide what to do. Thereupon, a Committee was appointed, called the 'Civil Disobedience Enquiry Committee', for the purpose of touring the country and reporting on the possibility of starting civil disobedience again. The general feeling among the members of this committee was that it was not possible to start civil disobedience so soon. But the point that was difficult to settle was what the Congress should do in the meantime. Should the Congress be content with carrying on its peaceful constructive work or should it adopt the new plan suggested by the Deshabandhu? The committee made an extensive tour of the country and submitted a report after some months. The members of the Committee were equally divided in their conclusions. Hakim Ajmal Khan (Delhi), Pandit Motilal Nehru (Allahabad) and Mr. Vithalbhai J. Patel (Bombay) were in favour of adopting the Deshabandhu's plan of entering the legislatures and Dr. M. A. Ansari[1] (Delhi), Mr. K. R. Iyengar (Madras) and Mr. C. Rajagopalachari (Madras) were against it. As the report was published shortly before the Gaya session of the Congress to be presided over by Deshabandhu Das, his hands were strengthened by the report.

Towards the end of September 1922, there were unexpected floods in the northern districts of Bengal. Though floods and famines are of frequent occurrence in the India of today, the floods of 1922 were of an unprecedented magnitude. Four large districts of Bengal were affected, crops were destroyed, houses washed away and cattle killed. As a result of the floods, there were several cases of death also. The whole countryside was one vast expanse of water. The Congress organisations throughout the province promptly responded to the appeal for relief and I was among the first batch to arrive at the flooded area for the purpose of organising relief. Thanks to the efforts of Sir P. C. Roy, the famous chemist and the President of the Relief Committee and to the generosity of the public, a fund of more than 400,000 rupees was raised, besides large contributions in cloth, foodstuffs and fodder (for the cattle). On this occasion the Government of Bengal contributed a sum of 20,000 rupees and in justifying the niggardliness of the Government, the Maharaja of Burdwan, a member of the Governor's Executive Council, stated that

---

[1] In the light of this fact it is surprising that Dr. Ansari should be one of the sponsors of the Council-entry proposal in 1934.

the Government was not a charitable institution. The relief operations conducted by the public, without any aid from the Government were so successful that they added greatly to the prestige of the Congress, whose members were largely responsible for them. In fact, we had the good fortune to be complimented on our work by the Governor of Bengal, Lord Lytton, personally when he inspected the flooded areas. Since then, the Congress has always taken a leading part in organising relief operations on the occasion of floods and famines.

Between August and December two other noteworthy events took place. The first was the meeting of the All-India Trade Union Congress at Lahore, which was presided over by Deshabandhu Das. In his presidential speech he made a striking declaration to the effect that the Swaraj he was striving to win was not for a section of the people —but for the masses who comprised 98 per cent of the population. Before and after this meeting, he always took a keen interest in the trade union movement and was for some time the President of the Labour Association of the Tata Iron & Steel Company at Jamshedpur. The other event was the meeting of the Young Men's Conference in Calcutta which was the precursor of the youth movement in the province. This Conference revealed the desire on the part of the youths to have a movement and an organisation of their own, quite apart from the Indian National Congress.

Towards the end of November, a meeting of the All-India Congress Committee was held in Calcutta at which there was a trial of strength between the supporters of Deshabandhu and of the Mahatma. This was a prelude to the annual session of the Congress. In the last week of December in an atmosphere tense with excitement the plenary session of the Indian National Congress assembled at Gaya. According to preliminary forecasts, Mr. Das's plan was likely to be defeated. But no one could tell at the time how the voting would go. It was clear, however, that Mr. Das would have influential support from all the provinces, especially from Bengal, the United Provinces, the Punjab, Central Provinces and Maharashtra (part of Bombay Presidency) After stormy debates in the Subjects Committee, the matter came up for voting before the open session of the Congress. Mr. Srinivasa Iyengar, a prominent leader from Madras, who was the leader of the Madras Bar and had resigned the post of Advocate-General of Madras, moved an amendment to the effect that representatives of the Congress should contest the elections but should not participate in the work inside the legislatures. On this amendment the principal voting took place and resulted in a big majority for the supporters of the Mahatma. Great was their enthusiasm and the hero of the day was the Madras leader, Mr. Rajagopalachari, who stood up before the Congress as the apostle of Gandhism.

The position of Mr. Das became rather anomalous. He was the President of the Congress, but the plan he advocated had been rejected. To settle his future course of action, he summoned a meeting of his supporters. It was decided that he should resign the membership of the Congress and organise his party under the name of 'Swaraj Party'. The next day when the All-India Congress Committee met for the purpose of laying down the programme of work for the next year, that is 1923, Pandit Motilal Nehru stood up to make an announcement about the formation of the Swaraj Party. The announcement came as an unexpected blow and cast a shadow on the jubilant faces of the Mahatma's supporters. Most of the outstanding intellectuals were on the side of the Deshabandhu and there was no doubt that without them, the Congress would lose much of its strength and importance. The announcement first made by Pandit Motilal Nehru was confirmed when Mr. Das in winding up the deliberations, submitted his resignation of the office of president, since he desired to work in opposition to the official resolutions with the object of persuading the country to accept his plan of work.

The supporters of Gandhiji left Gaya satisfied at their victory but not happy, because of the split that had taken place. The Swarajists parted with a sense of defeat, but with the determination to fight and win.

CHAPTER IV

## THE SWARAJIST REVOLT (1923)

The Swarajist leaders returned from Gaya to their own provinces with a stiff programme of work before them. The general understanding was that Deshabandhu Das should conduct the propaganda in Bengal, Central Provinces and South India; Pandit Motilal Nehru in Upper India and Mr. Vithalbhai Patel in Bombay Presidency. The Nationalist Press as a whole was anti-Swarajist. Therefore the Swarajists had to depend mainly on lecturing as a means of propaganda. In Calcutta we published a daily paper of four pages, called *Banglar Katha*, to supplement our propaganda and I had to become editor overnight under the orders of the leader. In Madras, Mr. A. Rangaswami Iyengar, afterwards editor of *Hindu*, was very helpful. His paper, *Swadesmitram*, a Tamil daily, became an exponent of the Swarajist policy and he also started an English weekly under the same name, to help our propaganda. In Poona the extremely influential Marathi paper, *Kesari*, became a champion of our cause. After Lokamanya Tilak's death, Mr. Kelkar had been the editor of *Kesari* and as he became a staunch supporter of the Swaraj Party, the resources of his paper *Kesari* were placed at the disposal of the party.

When the Deshabandhu returned to Bengal after the Gaya Congress, he found his position considerably weakened. The Congress machinery had passed into the hands of our political opponents, who now came to be known as 'No-Changers', because they were against any change in the existing plan and programme of the Congress. When we first took stock of our following, we found that we were in a minority. It was difficult for us at first to raise funds because we had rebelled against the official programme of the Congress. Nevertheless, we were a disciplined and determined band of workers and with unbounded enthusiasm we addressed ourselves to our task. One of the tactics we followed at the time, consisted in summoning frequent meetings of Congress organisations throughout the country and asking for a reversal of the resolutions passed at the Gaya Congress. At first our party used to be defeated at such meetings but we gradually made headway and when our party was able to secure a majority in one place, the news would encourage our fellow-workers in other places.

After preliminary propaganda had been done all over India, the first Swarajist Conference was held in March at Allahabad at the house of Pandit Motilal Nehru. The constitution and plan of campaign of the Swaraj Party was drawn up at the Conference. When the constitution was being discussed, a controversy arose with regard to the ultimate aim of the Swaraj Party. Was Dominion Status to be the goal of the Party or Complete Independence? On this point the constitution of the Congress was not clear. It merely stated that Swaraj was our goal but did not define what was meant by Swaraj. As the Swaraj Party was more practical, it wanted to define clearly what Swaraj meant, but a complete agreement was not possible on the question, because there were two groups among the Swarajists. It was therefore decided, as a compromise, to declare in the constitution that the 'immediate' objective of the party was the attainment of Dominion Status. Thus was the conflict between the young and the old settled for the time being.

The Swarajist Conference over, Mr. Das set out on a long tour in South India. It was a tremendously uphill work. The Madras Presidency was at the time one of the strongholds of Gandhism and Mr. Das deliberately undertook to storm that citadel first. In spite of the grilling heat of a South Indian summer he had a very successful tour. His success there had repercussions in other parts of the country. On his return to Calcutta he undertook the direction of the propaganda in Bengal with very good results. About this time the party decided to requisition frequent meetings of the All-India Congress Committee. At each successive meeting it was found that the votes of the Swarajists were increasing. By the middle of the year 1923, such progress was made that the Working Committee (the Cabinet of the Congress) composed entirely of 'no-changers', could no longer command a majority in the All-India Congress Committee and had therefore to resign. But though the 'no-changers' were not strong enough to hold office, neither was the Swaraj Party. So a third party, which in the absence of a better name may be called the 'Centre Party', came into office. This party did not accept the Swarajist plan but they were not die-hard Gandhists either. They advocated some sort of understanding between the two rival groups in the Congress. About the same time the 'no-changers' were also defeated in Bengal and in the Bengal Congress Committee, a Centre Party, which was under the influence of the Swarajists, came into office. Under this arrangement, Moulana Akram Khan became the President of the Bengal Congress Committee. But the former Secretary, Dr. P. C. Ghosh, refused to hand over office. Therefore, two rival Congress Committees began to function simultaneously, each claiming to be the representative body. Some months elapsed before the constitutional question was settled by the Working Committee, when a decision was given in favour of the Committee of which Moulana Akram Khan was the president.

In most provinces, especially in Bengal, feelings between the two parties were exceedingly bitter, though their aim was a common one, namely to win Swaraj for India. The prevailing bitterness made responsible Congressmen think seriously as to how they could bring about some sort of compromise between the warring groups. Then came the suggestion to hold a special session of the Congress in Delhi in September, 1923. This decision was a blow for the supporters of Gandhiji, because the Swarajists were sure to press their plan at the Delhi Congress once again and with better chances of winning than they had at Gaya. Moulana Abul Kalam Azad, one of the most intelligent and distinguished Mohammedan leaders, was elected President of the Delhi Congress and in his presidential speech he advocated the Swarajist policy of contesting the elections and carrying on fight within the legislatures.

Shortly before the Delhi Congress, Moulana Mohammed Ali, the younger and more influential of the Ali brothers and Dr. Kitchlew, the well-known Punjab leader, were released from prison. Their arrival was welcomed by the 'No-Change' Party whose policy and action they supported. Nevertheless, the Swarajists had made so much progress that nothing could hamper them any more. Deshabandhu Das attended the Congress at the head of a large contingent of delegates and the Bengal votes served to turn the scales. As soon as it was clear that the Swarajists would win the day, the 'No-Change' Party agreed to compromise. Moreover, Moulana Mohammed Ali claimed to have received some secret message (which he called 'wireless message') from the Mahatma, asking him to bring about a compromise between the rival Congress groups. Therefore, without much wrangling, a compromise resolution was passed at the special Congress in Delhi in September 1923, to the effect that Congressmen were permitted to take part in the forthcoming elections and carry on a uniform, continuous and consistent opposition against the Government within the legislatures, but the Congress as an organisation would have no responsibility in the matter.

The Swarajists left Delhi overjoyed. After nine months of hard and untiring work in the teeth of opposition and in the face of considerable unpopularity, they had won the day. But they could not rest on their oars. They had barely two months' time to prepare for the forthcoming elections. And they had a tough fight in front of them.

Luck, however, favours the brave. So it did the Swarajists. In spite of gloomy forecasts they had remarkable success. In the Central Provinces, the election returns were excellent and it was clear that by their obstructive tactics the Swarajists would be able to paralyse the work of the Local Legislative Council. The election returns for Bengal were also encouraging and for the Indian Legislative Assembly a strong contingent of Swarajists was returned. By mutual agreement it was arranged that Pandit Motilal Nehru would lead the Swaraj Party in the Assembly, while the Deshabandhu would lead the party in the Bengal Legislative Council, where he was hopeful of bringing about a constitutional deadlock. The success of the Swarajists in capturing the elected seats in the Central and Provincial legislatures was followed by similar success in other directions. The elections to the local bodies (municipalities and district boards) in the United Provinces were held in 1923 and under the direction of Pandit Motilal Nehru the Swaraj Party in that province had considerable success and as a result many of the municipalites and district boards came under Swarajist control. In the field of journalism, too, the Swarajists made much progress. In Calcutta, the Deshabandhu launched his daily paper *Forward* in October, soon after his victory at Delhi. As some of the organisers of the paper were suddenly put into prison without trial, I was entrusted with the organisation of the paper. Though the launching of the paper entailed very hard work on our part, success followed rapidly and in its career the paper was able to keep pace with the growing popularity and strength of the Party. Within a short time *Forward* came to hold a leading position among the nationalist journals in the country. Its articles were forceful, its news service varied and up-to-date and the paper developed a special skill in the art of discovering and exposing official secrets.

During 1923 the movement was on the whole of a constitutional nature with the exception of a civil-disobedience (or Satyagraha) campaign in Nagpur. The authorities in Nagpur prohibited the carrying of national flags along certain streets in Nagpur. As a protest against this order, processions were sent into the prohibited area with flags, etc. The campaign went on for some months and a large number of people were sent to prison. The issue soon became an All-India one, because the order in question was regarded as an insult to the National Flag and people began to pour in from all parts of the country in order to defy the order and court imprisonment. Ultimately, better counsels prevailed in Government House and a compromise was arrived at, whereby the demand of the people in this connection was substantially conceded. It should be observed in this connection that the above campaign—generally known as the Nagpur Flag Satyagraha Campaign—was run by the orthodox Gandhists who were anxious to demonstrate that the Gandhi method had not become sterile and was still capable of stirring up the country.

While the Swarajists represented the main body of rebels against orthodox Gandhism in 1923, the same year saw the birth of another revolt against Gandhism which was to acquire greater importance in the years to come. Being dissatisfied with the Gandhian ideology, a small group in Bombay under the leadership of Mr. Dange,[1] took to studying Socialist literature. They had a club of their own and published a weekly journal for preaching socialism. Among the Congress leaders the only patron they had at the time was the late Mr. Vithalbhai Patel. They soon took up labour organisation in Bombay and before many years elapsed, they became the first group of Communists in India. Following Bombay, a similar group was started some time later in Bengal under the name of the "Workers' and Peasants' Party"—but it was never able to acquire as much importance or make as much headway as the Bombay Group. The reason is not far to seek. Bengal, of which Calcutta is both the heart and the brain, has for a very long time been one of the strongholds of the nationalist movement. There the movement is based on an influential and patriotic petit-bourgeois class. Moreover, Bengal does not possess an indigenous and influential capitalist class, as does Bombay. Consequently, class-differentiation has never appeared in Bengal in that sharp and acute form in which it has appeared in Bombay. The petit-bourgeois element is not so strong or influential in Bombay as it is in Bengal and the national movement there is of more recent growth than in Bengal. In these circumstances it is not to be wondered at that the intellectual revolt against Gandhism in Bombay should take a Socialist or Communist turn. In Bengal, on the other hand, the revolt against Gandhism

---

[1] Mr. Dange was convicted in 1925 in connection with the Cawnpore Bolshevik Conspiracy Case and again in connection with the Meerut Communist Conspiracy Case in 1933, after a trial lasting nearly four years.

took a revolutionary more than a Communist turn. This phenomenon we shall consider in a later chapter on the 'Bengal Situation'.
We have already seen in the previous chapter that when in March 1922, Mr. Montagu resigned from the Cabinet, the forces of reaction got the upper hand both in England and in India. The Coalition Cabinet of Mr. Lloyd George soon came to an end and a General Election took place in October 1922, which brought the conservatives into power. In November 1922, Sir Basil Blackett was appointed Finance Member to the Government of India. One of his first deeds was to double the Salt Tax in February 1923, when he produced his first budget. Now the Salt Tax is traditionally unpopular in India—partly because the people are prevented by law from making salt out of the soil or the water given them by nature and partly because the Salt Tax hits the poor hardest. The doubling of the Salt Tax, therefore, was the worst move which the Government could have taken. The Indian Legislative Assembly promptly threw out this provision of the Finance Member but the Viceroy, Lord Reading, as promptly restored it by virtue of his power of certification. In June, the Government gave further offence by appointing a Commission— called the Lee Commission—to inquire into the status, position and grievances of the All-India services which are manned mainly by Britishers. Everyone felt at the time that the only result of the appointment of this commission would be to enhance the pay and emoluments of Britishers in India.[1] Thus, while the Government showed a readiness to incur more expenditure in order to please Britishers—they showed reluctance in curtailing unnecessary expenditure, though the Inchcape Committee had made several useful recommendations in this behalf.[2] In addition to this measure, the Government of India took another step which was

---

[1] This apprehension was fully justified when the Lee Commission submitted its report and the Government of India gave effect to the recommendations in a lavish manner.

[2] A Retrenchment Committee presided over by Lord Inchcape had been appointed by the Government for suggesting possible lines of economy. This Committee submitted its report in March 1923.

severely criticised at the time and which roused resentment in certain parts of the country. This was the deposition of the Maharaja of Nabha from his throne (or Guddee). Though the Government made certain allegations against the Maharaja as a justification for their action—the popular feeling in the country was that the Maharaja was neither better nor worse than the general run of Maharajas in India, that he was deposed solely because of his avowedly nationalistic views. Since the Maharaja was a Sikh and he was reported to have cherished sympathy for the Akali movement, his deposition roused a great deal of indignation among the Sikh community.

While the fores of reaction were gaining in strength in official circles and the Swarajists were preparing their great onslaught on the bureaucratic citadel, the Indian Legislative Assembly, even without the nationalists, was neither tame nor inactive. During the year, resolutions demanding a speedy constitutional advance were passed twice. Moreover, towards the end of its term, the Assembly passed a Reciprocity Bill which was introduced by Dr. (now Sir) H. S. Gour. This Bill was aimed at the Dominions and Colonies of the British Empire where Indians were not given equal rights and it provided for retaliation against all those countries, which placed disabilities on Indians, inflicting on their nationals in India the same disabilities which Indians had to suffer there. This Bill was the result of the injustice meted out to Indians in the Crown Colony of Kenya in Africa. In Kenya where the Indian settlers outnumbered the white settlers by three to one, the latter wanted to usurp all political power and exclude the former altogether. In the Kenya legislature they had a law passed giving the vote to all white settlers above twenty-one. They refused at first to extend the vote to Indian settlers, but ultimately offered them a separate electorate with a more limited franchise. This offer was declined by the Indians because it would put the stamp of second-class citizenship on them. The Kenya Indians appealed to India for help and in April 1923, the Rt. Hon. V. S. Sastri[1] led a deputa-

---

[1] Mr. V. S. Sastri who became the head of the Servants of India

tion to England to plead their cause before the authorities at Whitehall. A fairly satisfactory agreement was drawn up between the India Office and the Colonial Office—called the Wood-Winterton [1] Agreement but the Tory Cabinet did not give effect to it. Mr. Sastri therefore had to return disappointed. After his return to India, the Reciprocity Bill was introduced in the Assembly by Dr. H. S. Gour.

The above picture of India in 1923 would not be complete without reference to some of the communal dissensions which appeared in 1923 and which were to assume a more ugly shape in the years to come. Punjab was the scene of most of the troubles in 1923. Early in the year there was a Hindu-Moslem riot in Multan and this was followed by a similar riot in Amritsar, near the scene of the Jallianwala Bagh massacre in 1919. About this time, Mr. (now Sir) Mian Fazli Hussain became a minister in the Punjab and his extreme partiality for Moslems in the matter of appointments to public services caused considerable heart-burning among Sikhs and Hindus. Later in the year, a movement was started among Indian Moslems in opposition to the Indian National Congress—called 'Tanzeem' and 'Tabligh'—which aimed at organising the Moslems as a strong and virile community. This movement gained adherents for some time but before long it fell into disfavour and was replaced by communal or sectarian organisations of a different kind. While the above movement was going on among the Moslems, the Hindus were not altogether idle. Their communal organisation—called the Hindu Mahasabha—sought to strengthen itself by deciding at its annual meeting in August to admit the depressed classes to all the rights and privileges enjoyed by high-caste Hindus. Corresponding to the 'Tanzeem' and 'Tabligh' movement among the Moslems, a 'Sangathan' movement was started among the Hindus. Further, in order

---

Society after Mr. Gokhale's death had been made a Privy Councillor, while Mr. Montagu was Secretary of State for India.

[1] The Hon. Edward Wood, better known as Lord Irwin and now as Lord Halifax, was the Under-Secretary of State for the Colonies, while Lord Winterton was the Under-Secretary of State for India.

to reclaim those Hindus who for some reason or other had left the Hindu fold in the past, the 'Shuddhi' (or purification) movement was started. By performing the Shuddhi ceremony, it was made possible for a non-Hindu to become a Hindu. The apostle of this movement was Swami Shraddhananda,[1] A highly respected leader of the Hindu Mahasabha, through whose influence thousands of non-Hindus, including Moslems and Christians, were converted to Hinduism. About this time, the Swami was endeavouring to reconvert the Malkana Rajputs who had originally been Hindus but had subsequently embraced the Islamic faith and this attempt caused annoyance to many of the Moslem leaders.

While the communal storm was brewing in India, the Ali brothers remained true to their nationalist creed. Moulana Mohammed Ali, the younger brother, was elected to preside over the annual session of the Congress at Coconada in Madras Presidency. There was no heated controversy as at Gaya and the deliberations took place in an atmosphere of extreme cordiality. There was, however, a breeze over the Hindu-Moslem question which fortunately did not develop into a storm. Deshabandhu Das had drawn up a Hindu-Moslem Pact for settlement of the communal question in Bengal and he desired the Congress to put the seal of approval on it. The Coconada Congress, however, did not do so and the pact was rejected on the alleged ground that it showed partiality for the Moslems and violated the principles of Nationalism. Another pact which had been drawn up by Lala Lajpat Rai and Dr. M. A. Ansari for the settlement of the communal question was referred by the Coconada Congress to the All-India Congress Committee for consideration. These pacts indicated that the better minds among the Congress leaders had begun to realise the possibility of a communal rift and the necessity for making some sort of settlement before the breach widened. But sufficiently speedy or sufficiently drastic action was not taken, with the result that the differences did become

---

[1] Swami Shraddhananda was subsequently murdered by a Moslem fanatic probably out of his resentment at the Shuddhi movement.

more acute and grave and the country had to face a communal storm as soon as the political tension created by the Swaraj Party subsided after the death of Deshabandhu Das in June 1925.

From the nationalist point of view, the year 1923 had begun badly but it ended well. In January, there was division and depression. In December, there was hope and confidence. Despite signs of communal disturbance here and there, the political barometer had once again begun to rise. In England too, the forces of reaction had received a temporary setback. In May 1923, Mr. Baldwin replaced Mr. Bonar Law as Premier and in November of the same year he appealed to the country on the issue of Protection versus Free Trade. The Conservatives were thrown out of office as a consequence and the beginning of 1924 saw a Labour Government installed in office for the first time in British history. The Near East policy of the previous Cabinets had failed. Before the end of 1922, Mustapha Kemal Pasha had succeeded in driving the Greeks out of Anatolia. Before the end of 1923 he succeeded in driving the allied troops out of Constantinople. And by March 1924, he felt sufficiently strong to abolish the Khalifate altogether and bring into existence a new and powerful Turkey.

CHAPTER V

## DESHABANDHU C. R. DAS IN POWER
### (1924-25)

The year 1924 opened with an outlook hopeful in every direction, but the Swarajists had no time to rest. The elections to the Calcutta Municipal Corporation, the largest municipality in India, were to be held in March. Thanks to the Minister for Local Self-Government, Sir Surendranath Bannerji, the Calcutta Municipal Act had been amended in 1923. Therein, larger powers had been conferred on the municipality, the franchise had been considerably enlarged and the elective element strengthened. Under the constitution, it was possible for the Swaraj Party to capture the municipal administration if they were successful at the polls. An intensive campaign was therefore started early in 1924 with the object of capturing the elected seats. So great was the enthusiasm of the people who attended in their thousands the meetings addressed by the Swarajist leaders that the election forecast was a very favourable one. As a matter of fact the Swaraj Party was returned with a very safe majority, a large number of the successful Swarajist candidates being Moslems. This result was all the more creditable because the elections were held on the basis of separate electorate, whereby Hindu voters alone could vote for Hindu candidates and Moslem voters for Moslem candidates. At the first meeting of the newly-elected municipal councillors, Deshabandhu Das was elected Mayor and Mr. Saheed Suhrawardy, a Moslem gentleman, Deputy Mayor. The Corporation soon after appointed me as the Chief Executive Officer, that is, the head of the municipal administration.[1] Though my appointment to this important post at the age of twenty-seven was generally

---

[1] Under the new constitution of the Calcutta Municipal Corporation there was a division of function—the Chief Executive Officer being the head of the administration and the Mayor being the head of the Corporation as a whole. Under the old constitution both these functions were combined in the 'Chairman'.

approved in Swarajist circles, it did not fail to cause a certain amount of heart-burning in some circles within the party. To the Government it gave great annoyance and it was not without a great deal of hesitation that they decided to give their approval, as they were required to do under statute.

The election of the Deshabandhu as the Mayor under the new constitution symbolised our capture of the Calcutta Municipality and was attended by popular demonstartions. Under the new regime, new measures calculated to benefit the citizens were set in motion in quick succession. The newly-elected Swarajist Councillors and Aldermen, including the Mayor, all came dressed in home-made Khadi. Among the employees of the Municipality, Khadi became the official uniform. Many of the streets and parks were renamed after India's greatest men. For the first time an Education Department was started and a distinguished Indian graduate of Cambridge [1] was put in charge. Free primary schools for boys and girls sprang up all over the city, Health Associations, financed by the Municipality, were started in every ward of the city by public-spirited citizens for carrying on health propaganda among the people. Dispensaries were opened by the Municipality in the different districts for giving free medical treatment to the poor. In purchasing stores, preference was given to Swadeshi (i.e. home-made) goods. In making new appointments, the claims of Moslems and other minorities were recognised for the first time. Infant clinics were established in different parts of the city and to each clinic was added a milk-kitchen for supplying milk free to the children of the poor. Last but not least, the Municipality arranged to give civic receptions to Nationalist leaders like Mahatma Gandhi, Pandit Motilal Nehru and Mr. V. J. Patel, when they visited the city and the previous custom of giving civic receptions to Viceroys, Governors and officials was discontinued once for all.

The above measures adopted for promoting the wel-

[1] K. P. Chattopadhyaya who has continued to hold office till the present day. At present there are about 40,000 boys and girls in the Municipal Schools.

fare of the citizens brought a new civic consciousness.[1] People for the first time began to look upon the Municipality as their own institution and upon Municipal officers and employees as Public Servants and not bureaucrats. But the British vested interests in the city felt that they were losing their importance and that they could no longer dominate the Municipality. At that time nearly all the departmental heads were Britishers, but with one or two exceptions, I had no difficulty whatsoever in dealing with them. The majority of them were quite loyal to the new Swarajist administration and some of them were even enthusiastic in praising it. Though within a few months the efficiency of the administration was considerably raised and citizens' complaints were attended to more promptly than before, the official bloc in the Corporation, as also the Government, continued their policy of opposition, with the result that constant friction used to take place. In the matter of appointments, they were opposed to the Swarajist policy of doing justice to the minorities. With regard to the drainage problem of the city, they were also in conflict with the Swarajists. The scheme sponsored by the Government for the new drainage works was rejected by the Swarajists as being unscientific and useless. In this they had the support of the Drainage Engineer of the Municipality, the late Mr. O. J. Wilkinson and of the Director of Public Health, Dr. C. A. Bentley, while the Chief Engineer, Mr. J. R. Coats, was on the side of the Government. The drainage controversy between the Municipality and the Government continued for a long time and it took the Government ten years to give in to the Municipality on the drainage question.[2]

The doings of the Swaraj Party in the Calcutta Corporation would not have embarrassed the Government so much but for the fact that there was a simultaneous pressure on the latter from many quarters. In the Indian

---

[1] To give expression to this new consciousness, a weekly journal called the *Calcutta Municipal Gazette* was started by the Municipality.

[2] The drainage scheme which has been adopted now was drawn up by the Indian Chief Engineer, Dr. B. N. Dey, who is still holding that office.

Legislative Assembly the Swaraj Party was fairly strong, and on behalf of the party notice of a resolution was given demanding the release of Mahatma Gandhi. Mahatma Gandhi had fallen seriously ill on January 12th and had been operated upon. This news had caused anxiety and alarm from one end of the country to the other and there was a very strong public demand for his release. On the morning of February 5th, the day on which the above resolution was to be moved, the Mahatma was quietly released. A few days later, on February 8th, Pandit Motilal Nehru, the leader of the Swaraj Party in the Assembly, moved a resolution demanding that a Round Table Conference be convened for drawing up a Constitution for India, establishing full responsible Government and that the new Constitution be placed before a newly-elected Indian Legislature and be submitted before the British Parliament for being embodied in a statute. Replying to this resolution on behalf of the Government of India, Sir Malcolm Hailey promised an investigation into the complaints against and criticism of the Constitution. If after the investigation it was found that there was possibility of constitutional advance within the four corners of the Act, the Government would have no objection in making recommendations to the British Cabinet to that effect. But if, on the other hand, further constitutional advance involved an amendment of the Government of India Act, 1919, then the Government could not promise any action at that stage. This reply was extremely disappointing and as a retort, the Assembly threw out some of the demands for grants and refused leave to introduce the entire Finance Bill. The Finance Bill had therefore to be restored with the help of the special powers of certification vested in the Viceroy.

The debate over the demand for a Round Table Conference was followed by the appointment of a Committee with the following terms of reference—to inquire into the difficulties arising from or the defects inherent in the working of the Government of India Act, 1919; to investigate the feasibility and desirability of securing remedies for such difficulties and defects, consistent with the structure, policy and purpose of the Act, either by action taken under the Act and the rules or by such amendments of the Act as appear necessary to rectify any administrative imperfections. This Committee was presided over by the Home Member, Sir Alexander Muddiman and among the members were Sir Tej Bahadur Sapru (Allahabad), Sir Sivaswami Aiyer (Madras), Mr. M. A. Jinnah (Bombay) and Dr. Paranjpye (Poona)—all of them being Liberal (Moderate) politicians—who submitted a minority report. The Committee as a whole reported that there were serious defects in the Constitution and in the manner in which it had been worked. The majority of the members, consisting mostly of officials, recommended a number of minor modifications which would help the working of the Constitution. The minority reported that such modification of the Constitution would be of little avail and that a satisfactory operation of the Constitution would be possible only when it was revised with a view to introducing responsible government in the provinces and at least a measure of responsibility in the Central Government. It would be noted in this connection that the Swaraj Party in the Assembly did not cooperate with the Muddiman Committee in any way and the report of the Committee was altogether disappointing from the Swarajist point of view.

While the major issues were being tackled by its members in the Assembly, the Swaraj Party was following obstructive tactics in all the provincial legislatures. In the Assembly there was hardly any room for obstruction or deadlock because the Viceroy could easily override the legislature by his special powers of 'veto' and 'certification'. Moreover, all the departments of the Central Government were administered by members who were under the full control of the Viceroy and were neither elected members of the Assembly nor removable by a vote of that body. In the provinces, on the other hand, the departments called 'transferred' departments were administered by 'ministers' who were elected members of the provincial legislature and were subject to the vote of that body—while the other departments, called 'reserved' departments, were administered by members who were quite independent of the vote of the legislature.[1] The Swarajist tactics in the provincial legislatures therefore consisted in attacking the ministers and their 'transferred' departments. The salaries of the ministers would be either rejected altogether, in which case no ministers could be appointed at all—or votes of no-confidence in the ministers would be moved repeatedly so that no set of ministers could continue in office long. At the same time attempts would be made to throw out the Budget of the transferred departments which could not be restored by certification. By such tactics, the Governor of the province would be forced to suspend the working of the transferred departments, take over the administration into his own hands and go on ruling as he would in the pre-reform days. In the Central Provinces Legislative Council where the Swarajists had an absolute majority—the entire Budget was thrown out without any difficulty and no ministers could therefore be appointed. In Bengal the situation was somewhat similar to that in the Central Provinces. The salaries of the ministers were rejected and repeated attempts to restore them proved unavailing. The ministers had therefore to lay down their office. Thus, in the Central Provinces and in Bengal, the working of the constitution was rendered impossible. It is not possible to describe the enthusiasm of the public when diarchy was overthrown in those two provinces. It was regarded as a great triumph for the Swarajists and this victory brought a sense of elation all over the country. In 1920, the Congress had tried to paralyse the new constitution, by boycotting the polls but this attempt had failed, because not a single seat had remained vacant and undesirable men had flooded the legislatures. In 1924, on the other hand, the Swarajists, by carrying the fight inside the legislatures, were able to wreck the constitution, in at least some of the provinces.

People belonging to the Liberal Party and even 'No-Changer' Congressmen have not sometimes been able to

---

[1] Because of this dual system, the constitution was called 'diarchy'.

understand the utility of the Swarajist policy of constitutional obstruction. They argue that if ministers are allowed to continue in office they could do more good than if those departments are taken over by the Governor and his officials. As against that, the Swarajists argue that three years' experience (1920-1923) has shown that there is hardly any scope for useful work for a minister under the constitution of 1919. All the more important departments, like public security, justice, prisons, finance, etc. are in the hands of officials and the budget allotments for these departments are made first. What is left is handed over to the ministers and this amount is so inadequate that it barely suffices for their minimum establishment, rendering it quite impossible to undertake nation-building work on a decent scale. Moreover, the principal officials working under the ministers, including their secretaries, cannot be subjected to disciplinary action by them and being quite independent of the legislature in the matter of their pay and emoluments, they are not responsive to popular sentiment. In these circumstances, the unhampered working of the constitution cannot benefit the country in any way—whereas successful obstruction not only brings pressure to bear on the Government by putting obstacles in its path, but also develops a spirit of resistance in the country as a whole. As a matter of fact, when the constitution of the Swaraj Party was first drawn up in March 1923, it was explicitly stated in the preamble that the object of the Swarajist policy was to create an atmosphere of resistance to the bureaucracy, without which the Government could never be made to respond to popular demands.

While the Swarajists were enjoying the first flush of victory, the Labour Secretary of State for India, Lord Olivier, in a striking speech delivered in the House of Lords, analysed the causes which led to the birth of Swarajism in India. Among the causes he mentioned were—firstly, the resolution passed by the House of Lords supporting General Dyer, the author of the Jallianwalla Bagh massacre; secondly, the 'steel-frame speech' of the Premier, Mr. Lloyd George, in 1922, eulogising the Indian Civil Service; thirdly, the doubling of the Salt Tax by the Government of India, in 1923, in the teeth of tense popular opposition and despite the adverse vote of the Indian Legislative Assembly; and fourthly, the injustice meted out to Indians in the Crown Colony of Kenya in Africa. This clever and sympathetic analysis of the causes of the Indian unrest leading to the birth of the Swaraj Party, showed that for once at least the India Office in London was able to appreciate public sentiment and public opinion in India. It is to be regretted, therefore, that this understanding was not followed up by appropriate action.

Not content with his activities in the legislature, the Municipality and in other directions, the Deshabandhu launched another important movement at this time—the Tarakeswar Satyagraha movement. Not far from Calcutta, at a place called Tarakeswar, there is an old temple of 'Baba Taraknath' or 'Shiva'. As in the case of other holy shrines, there was considerable property attached to the temple, which had been endowed in order to provide for its upkeep. Following the Hindu custom, there was a trustee, called the Mohunt, in charge of the temple and the attached property. Though the Mohunts are expected to live a chaste and abstemious life, there were allegations against the Mohunt of Tarakeswar with regard to his personal character and to his administration of the endowed property. As Tarakeswar happens to be one of the most holy places of pilgrimage in Bengal and is visited every year by people from all parts of the province, the allegations made against the Mohunt were widely known. After the success of the Akali movement in the Punjab, pressure was brought to bear on the Bengal Congress Committee for starting a similar movement at Tarakeswar. Notices were served on the Mohunt calling upon him to mend his ways but as these attempts were of no avail, in April 1924, the Deshabandhu launched a movement for taking peaceful possession of the temple and the attached property, with a view to placing them under the administration of a public committee. The Mohunt appealed to the Government for help and as soon as volunteers began to move towards the temple and the palace of the Mohunt—the police appeared on the scene. The usual Satyagraha scenes were re-enacted at Tarakeswar—peaceful volunteers moving up from one side and the police attacking them mercilessly on the other and occasionally making arrests. Owing to the intervention of the Government, the issue became a political one. Once again, in order to set an example to the people, the Deshabandhu sent his son to prison at the head of the volunteers. Within a short time, the movement became extremely popular and there was a warm response from every corner of the province.[1]

In May 1924, the annual conference of Bengal Congressmen, called the Provincial Conference, was held at a place called Sirajganj. Prior to this the Deshabandhu had drawn up an agreement between Hindus and Moslems, covering religious as well as political questions, but it had been rejected by the Coconada Congress in December 1923, on the ground that it conceded too much to the Moslems. This agreement, known as the Bengal Pact—was placed before the Sirajganj Conference for ratification. There was a stormy debate and the political opponents of the Deshabandhu, joined by some reactionary Hindus, put up a formidable opposition. Nevertheless, the passionate eloquence of the leader carried the day and the Bengal Pact was adopted by a large majority. After this, another resolution was discussed and passed which was to stir up a hornet's nest in the days to come. This was the Gopinath Saha resolution. Some months earlier, a young student, named Gopinath Saha, had attempted to assassinate the Commissioner of Police of Calcutta, Sir Charles Tegart. Through mistaken identity, he shot at and killed another Englishman, Mr. Day. At the trial before the High Court of Cal-

---

[1] The Satyagraha campaign went on for several months. The Mohunt ultimately was forced to come to a compromise with Deshabandhu C. R. Das and an agreement was drawn up whereby the temple and the major portion of the property was to be handed over to a public committee. This agreement had to be placed before a court of law but at this stage a third party, under the name of the Brahman Sabha, raised objections. While the whole matter was under consideration, the Deshabandhu died. After his unfortunate death, the agreement was set at nought and the result of the Satyagraha campaign was nullified.

cutta, Saha made a statement which created a sensation at the time. He stated in effect that he really had intended to murder the Police Commissioner and expressed his sincere sorrow for having killed the wrong person. He was glad to pay with his life and hoped that every drop of his blood would sow the seeds of freedom in every Indian home. Saha was sentenced to death by High Court and duly hanged. But, after his death, resolutions were passed in several meetings in Bengal appreciating his courage and spirit of sacrifice, while condemning his action. A similar resolution was unanimously passed at the Sirajganj Conference and it caused considerable annoyance to the Government.

While these stirring events were happening in Bengal, interesting developments were taking place elsewhere. Mahatma Gandhi, as we have already seen, was released on February 5th. He went to a seaside resort near Bombay for rest and change of climate. After some weeks he was able to take interest once again in public affairs and gradually to assume his normal activities. Speculation at once arose as to what attitude Gandhiji would take up with regard to the Swaraj Party. On principle he was of course bitterly opposed to the Swarajist policy of 'Council-entry', nevertheless, he did not adopt a hostile attitude. It may be that he found the position of the Swarajists to be too strong in the country to be able to overthrow them and so he bowed to the inevitable. Or it may be that he felt that the changed circumstances in the country warranted a change in tactics. Be that as it may, he met the Swarajist leaders, Deshabandhu Das and Pandit Motilal Nehru and arrived at an understanding with them. This agreement, known as the Gandhi-Das Pact, was to the effect that the Mahatma was to devote himself to the Khadi campaign, while the Swarajists were to be in charge of the political campaign. In order to carry on his work without any interference on the part of the Congress or the Swaraj Party, the Mahatma was empowered to organise an autonomous body to be called the All-India Spinners' Association. This body was to have its own funds and its own Secretariat.

The Swaraj Party, on the other hand, was to carry on its work as an autonomous body independently of the Congress and to have its own Secretariat[1] The alliance thus struck between the Mahatma and the Swaraj Party soon ripened into friendship as a result of conciliatory statements made by the former from time to time. On one occasion, for instance, he said in his characteristic style, 'My political conscience is in the keeping of the Swarajists'. On another occasion he is reported to have remarked: 'I shall cling to the Swaraj Party as a child clings to its mother.'

After establishing peace within the Congress camp through his understanding with the Swaraj Party, the Mahatma turned to another acute problem. Since 1923, Hindu-Moslem dissensions had appeared in different parts of India and Mahatma Gandhi was farsighted enough to realise that if the evil was not nipped in the bud, it would soon grow into a national calamity. The communal storm might not break while the Swarajist campaign, supported by both Hindus and Moslems, was in full swing—but the moment there was a lull in the campaign, the evil was sure to rear its head. So in September 1924, at his instance a Unity Conference was convened at Delhi. The Conference was largely attended, even the Anglican Metropolitan of India and representatives of the Britishers in India, participating in it. At the time of the Conference the Mahatma embarked on a three weeks' fast as a self-imposed penance for the wrongs committed by members of different communities who by their action disturbed inter-communal peace in India. The Conference was a successful one. A formula was devised for promoting unity between the different communities in India and a Conciliation Board of fifteen members was set up which was to intervene whenever and wherever any communal trouble arose. In spite of the success of the Unity Conference, practical results did not follow. In March 1924, Mustapha Kemal Pasha took the extraordinary step of abolishing the Khalifate altogether. Those Moslems who had been drawn towards

---

[1] This agreement was ratified at the annual session of the Congress held at Belgaum in December, over which Mahatma Gandhi presided.

the Indian National Congress owing to the desire to secure support for the Khilafat campaign, no longer felt any urge to remain friendly towards the Congress. The Khilafat Committees themselves went out of existence in most parts of India and many of the erstwhile members of those organisations were absorbed into reactionary mushroom organisations. About this time the All-India Moslem League came back to life again. This body had been the premier organisation for Moslems in India till 1920. Since that year it had been practically replaced by the All-India Khilafat Committee which had succeeded in drawing most of the active elements among the Indian Moslems. The abolition of the Khalifate by the Turks themselves, struck at the root of the Khilafat Committees in India and indirectly helped the revival of the All-India Moslem League. In December 1924, when the All-India Moslem League met once again, the Khilafatists were defeated for the first time since 1920. The newly-revived All-India Moslem League, as we shall see later, became more sectarian and reactionary than it had been prior to 1920.

About the middle of 1924, matters began to approach a crisis once again. This crisis was of course different in character from that of 1921-22. The Government felt hardpressed from all sides. Not only in Bengal, but throughout the country, the local bodies (municipalities, district boards, etc.) were coming under the control of the Nationalists, and to that extent official power and influence were being eliminated. In all the legislatures, a stiff fight was being waged and in two provinces, Central Provinces and Bengal, the working of the new constitution was paralysed. In Bengal, the Tarakeswar Satyagraha, though it began as a movement for the reform of the temple administration, soon, developed into a political movement and gradually assumed serious proportions. Over and above this, according to the Government, there was a strong undercurrent of revolutionary activity and the Government were particularly annoyed by public resolutions, praising the revolutionary Gopinath Saha, though the appreciation was of a qualified and conditional character. In August, when the influence of the Swaraj Party was at its height, the annual conference of the Party was held in Calcutta. Leaders from the different provinces were present on the occasion. The attendance was large and the enthusiasm very great. That was the signal for the Government to strike. During the last twelve months they had not been altogether inactive and had been closely following events. Soon after the Delhi Congress in September 1923, a number of Congress workers belonging to the Swaraj Party of Bengal had been suddenly arrested and put in prison without any trial under an old regulation called 'Regulation III of 1818'. The explanation given by the Government at the time was that the revolutionary movement was raising its head again and it was therefore necessary to resort to speedy suppression. Though the arrests created considerable resentment at the time, it was not followed by any further developments and the excitement gradually subsided. After a year, the Government decided to repeat those tactics again. They did not know how to suppress the Swaraj Party otherwise. The activities of the Party, except in the case of the Tarakeswar Satyagraha and similar campaigns, were carried on within the bounds of the law, but they caused considerable embarrassment to the Government; nevertheless the Government could not take any legal proceedings against the Swarajists. All attempts to suppress the Tarakeswar Satyagraha campaign had not only failed but had served to evoke greater enthusiasm on the part of the people. In sheer desperation the Government therefore decided to strike at the root of the organisation and since that was not possible through a trial in a court of law, they resolved to imprison some of the principal organisers of the Swaraj Party without trial.

On October 25th, 1924, in the early hours of the morning, they made a clean sweep of a large number of Congressmen in Calcutta and other places in Bengal. These arrests were made partly under Regulation III of 1818, and partly under an emergency ordinance (called the Bengal Ordinance) promulgated by the Viceroy at midnight on October 24th. This ordinance conferred on the Government of Bengal powers of arrest and imprisonment similar to those conferred on the Government of India by Regulation III of 1818, and the ordinance was issued in order to help the Government of Bengal to order arrest and imprisonment without trial of persons in Bengal, without any reference to the Government of India. Among those arrested were two prominent Swarajist members of the Bengal Legislative Council, Mr. Anil Baran Roy and Mr. S. C. Mitra,[1] and myself. Some of the warrants, as in the case of three of us, had been issued under the Regulation, whereas in the case of the others, they had been issued under the newly-promulgated Bengal Ordinance. The warrants under the Regulation had been signed as early as July last, the day after the Government were finally defeated in their attempt to retain the ministers in office and work the diarchical constitution. It has not been explained yet as to why the warrants had not been executed for nearly three months. The conjecture generally made is that the Bengal Government waited for sanction to a larger number of arrests and also for the promulgation of the Bengal Ordinance. Moreover, the whole matter had to be placed before the then Labour Secretary of State for India, Lord Olivier, and so the delay was unavoidable. With regard to the *raison d'etre* of these arrests, the public notion at the time was that the pressure of the Swarajists in the local bodies (especially the Calcutta Municipality), in the legislatures and at Tarakeswar had unnerved the Government. And the reason why they struck only in Bengal, was that the anti-Government forces were strongest in that province.

The large number of arrests made so suddenly and unexpectedly on October 25th, created tremendous excitement in the country. Official circles came out with the excuse that a revolutionary conspiracy was on foot and the arrests had to be made before anything serious happened.

---

[1] Mr. Anil Baran Roy has since retired from politics and joined the Ashrama of Sri Aurobindo Ghosh at Pondicherry. Mr. S. C. Mitra has since joined the Assembly and been a prominent member of the opposition between 1928 and 1934.

But it was hard to persuade the public that those who had been arrested were engaged in a revolutionary conspiracy. Public clamour against the arrests continued to be very strong and one month after my arrest, Government began to think seriously of releasing me. But the prestige of the police, at whose instance the arrests had been made, stood in the way and the proposal had to be dropped. The agitation over my arrest was the strongest at the time because the public thought that the object of the Government was to strike at the Swarajist administration of the new Corporation. Everyone knew, including the extreme loyalists, that I was engaged day and night in my municipal duties and had been forced to give up politics altogether, since I was appointed Chief Executive Officer of the Calcutta Corporation. Official and semi-official circles were therefore at pains to put forward an excuse for the arrests which would find some credence among the public. The Anglo-Indian papers of Calcutta, *The Statesman* and *The Englishman* (now defunct), came out with statements to the effect that I was the brain of the revolutionary conspiracy. My solicitors at once filed legal proceedings against both the papers for defamation. The proceedings dragged on for months and in the meantime attempts were made to secure the help of the Government in the suit in the matter of obtaining proofs to substantiate the charges made against me in the Press in support of the Government. As the Government did not agree to help in the matter, an attempt was made to secure the assistance of the India Office in London. By that time there had been a change in the Cabinet in England. A General Election had taken place in October and as a result of the scare created by the Zinovieff letter, there had been a landslide in favour of the Conservative Party. Following the defeat of the Labour Party at the polls, the Labour Secretary of State for India, Lord Olivier, had made room for the Conservative Secretary of State, Lord Birkenhead. Though the India Office was inclined to help the Anglo-Indian papers in the suit brought against them for defamation, they were unable to find any documentary evidence to prove my complicity in a revolutionary conspiracy. *Forward*, the Swarajist paper of Calcutta, happened to get hold of and publish a letter, written to Calcutta from London on the subject, in which an agent of the India Office was reported to have said that I had been arrested on the verbal testimony borne against me by certain people, but that there was no documentary evidence against me. The publication of this letter further embarrassed the Government.

No one in India felt these persecutions more than Deshabandhu Das did. In a magnificent speech delivered from the Mayoral chair of the Calcutta Corporation, he gave vent to the deep indignation which stirred the public at the time. He accepted full responsibility for what the Chief Executive Officer had done and challenged the Government to arrest him. The Government did not accept the challenge but replied in a different way. They opened negotiations with him for a settlement of the entire Indian question. At that time, Mahatma Gandhi was politically a back-number. He had confined himself to the Khadi campaign, having retired from the political movement which was under the control of the Swarajist leaders. The memory of the negotiations in December 1921, had left an impression on the official mind that it was possible to come to an understanding with the Deshabandhu if the major issues were tackled in an earnest and sincere manner. Lord Lytton personally had a very high appreciation of him as a man. And at the time no official felt the pressure of the popular movement more than the Governor of Bengal did. In those days, to settle with the Congress meant to settle with Deshabandhu C. R. Das. Therefore, unknown to the outside world, negotiations between the Deshabandhu and the Governor of Bengal, Lord Lytton, went on for some months.

With his shrewd political instinct, the Deshabandhu thought of making use of the public feeling roused by the arrests of October 1924. He appealed at once for a fund to be used for national reconstruction. The economic situation in the country was not favourable and many people thought that the response to the appeal would be disappointing. But the leader knew better. In spite of unfavourable forecasts, he had a very good response and that was a further proof of public confidence in him. At the end of the year, the annual session of the Congress was held at Belgaum in Bombay Presidency. This Congress was presided over by Mahatma Gandhi and it was the last Congress attended by Deshabandhu. The proceedings were marked by extreme cordiality between the Mahatma and the Swarajist. The principal programme of work adopted for the coming year was the extension of home-spinning and home-weaving and it was enjoined on every member of the Congress to produce a certain quantity of yarn as his membership subscription. The only other significant fact about the Belgaum Congress was the attempt of Mrs. Annie Besant to get her Commonwealth of India Bill ratified by the Congress. This Bill, which was to confer Home Rule on India, had been drafted by her and her intention was to have it introduced in the British Parliament as a private Bill. She felt that her hands would be considerably strengthened if the Congress gave the stamp of approval to her pet constitution, but none of the Congress leaders would be drawn into her net. She therefore had to leave the Belgaum Congress disappointed.

The political situation remained unchanged when the year 1925 was ushered in. Deshabandhu Das continued in power. In the early part of 1925, there was a further trial of strength between the Government and the Swarajists in Bengal. The Ordinance which the Governor-General had promulgated in October 1924, conferring on the Bengal Governor powers of summary arrest and imprisonment without trial, was to expire in April 1925. Thereafter, if the Bengal Government desired to have those powers, they would have to introduce legislation to that effect in the Bengal Legislative Council. A Bill was therefore duly introduced and the Government strained every nerve to have it passed into law. As the Swarajists were really in a minority in the Legislative Council, the Government felt hopeful that they would be able to carry the legislation through. The Deshabandhu was then taking rest at Patna as he had been suffering from a nervous breakdown. But in spite of his ill-health, he resolved to inflict a crushing defeat on the Government in person. On the appointed day he arrived at the Council Hall in time and had actually to be carried in an invalid-chair. Once again the laurels of the day were his. The Bill was thrown out, but by virtue of the extraordinary powers given to the Governor under the Constitution, he was able to certify the Bill as law.

Soon after this incident the annual conference of Bengal Congressmen was summoned at Faridpur and in view of the critical situation in the country, Deshabandhu Das was elected President. Against all medical advice, he resolved to go there and preside over the deliberations. People did not understand at the time why he was so insistent on attending this conference. Anything that he said would have drawn the same amount of attention even if it happened to be a Press statement. The real reason, however, as to why he wanted to go there was that he had to give a public indication of his demands, for the benefit of the Government. Moreover, he wanted to demonstrate to the Government that his views were acceptable to the bulk of Congressmen so that the Government would feel that in the event of a settlement being arrived at, the Deshabandhu was in a position to deliver the goods. At that time the Government attached a great value to the Bengal Provincial Conference, because Bengal was then the storm centre and contained some of the most radical elements in the Indian National Congress. Therefore a proposal which was carried in Bengal, would in all probability be acceptable to Congressmen elsewhere. Deshabandhu Das made a speech which was regarded as rather tame for a Bengal audience. He discussed the question of Dominion Status versus Independence as the goal of Congress, and declared that he stood for the former. Moreover, he spoke in condemnation of terrorism. The speech as a whole appeared to be an appeal to the Government and to the more extreme elements among Indians to adopt a compromising attitude so that the ground could be prepared for a settlement. It was, however, not welcomed by the youthful section of the audience and there was a possibility that he would be defeated when the matter was put to the vote. Nevertheless, so great was his personal influence at the time and so transparent his sincerity of purpose that he carried the day. The deliberations of the Faridpur Conference were on the whole satisfactory to the authorities with whom the Deshabandhu was engaged in negotiating.

Soon after this, Lord Reading left India for London, as the Conservative Cabinet and the Secretary of State for India, Lord Birkenhead, wanted to consult him. By that time it was in the air that negotiations had been going on between Deshabandhu Das and the Government, though hardly anyone knew any details. It was announced that after consulting Lord Reading, Lord Birkenhead would make an important pronouncement about India. Everyone in India awaited his speech with the greatest interest and eagerness.

Then came a sudden bolt from the blue. In June 1925, when Deshabandhu Das was having a rest in the hill-station of Darjeeling, the summer capital of the Bengal Government, he fell seriously ill. After a brief attack he suddenly died. The whole country was at once plunged in grief. He was at the height of his glory and was expected to achieve great things for his country. While *in memoriam* meetings and processions were going on in the country, the British Cabinet in London made up their mind as to what they should do. Their arch-enemy was dead; therefore, things would settle down now for a while. They would accordingly not decide anything in a hurry but would watch developments. But it had already been announced that Lord Birkenhead would make an important pronouncement about India on July 7th, 1925, Therefore, the announcement carefully prepared on behalf of the Cabinet had to be entirely suppressed and in its place Lord Birkenhead, on the previously announced date, made an uninteresting speech. Besides talking about platitudes, he merely endorsed Lord Reading's panacea for India's ills in the form of development of industry and the stabilisation of finance.

The death of Deshabandhu on June 16th, 1925, was for India a national calamity of the first magnitude. Though his active political career consisted of barely five years, his rise had been phenomenal. With the reckless abandon of a Vaishnava devotee, he had plunged into the political movement with heart and soul and he had given not only himself but his all in the fight for Swaraj. When he died, whatever worldly possessions he still had, were left to the nation. By the Government he was both feared and admired. They feared his strength, but admired his character. They knew that he was a man of his word. They also knew that though he was a hard fighter, he was none the less a clean fighter, and further, he was also the man with whom they could bargain for a settlement. He was clear-headed, his political instinct was sound and unerring and unlike the Mahatma he was fully conscious of the role he was to play in Indian politics. He knew, more than anyone else, that situations favourable for wresting political power from the enemy do not come often and when they do come, they do not last long. While the crisis lasts, a bargain has to be struck. He knew also that to sponsor a settlement, when public euthusiasm is at its height, needs much courage and may involve a certain amount of unpopularity. But he was nothing if not fearless. He was conscious of his exact role, namely that of a practical politician, and he was therefore never afraid of courting unpopularity.

In contrast with the Deshabandhu, the role of the Mahatma has not been a clear one. In many ways he is altogether an idealist and a visionary. In other respects, he is an astute politician. At times he is as obstinate as a fanatic; on other occasions he is liable to surrender like a child. The instinct, or the judgment, so necessary for political bargaining is lacking in him. When there is a real opportunity for a bargain, as in 1921, he is liable to stick out for small things and thereby upset all chances of a settlement. Whenever he does go in for a bargain, as we shall see in 1931, he gives more than he takes. On the whole, he is no match in diplomacy for an astute British politician.

After the death of Deshabandhu Das the Mahatma spent several months in Bengal trying to raise a memorial fund in honour of the departed great and helping to reorganise the Congress machinery in the absence of the leader. His public activities, nevertheless, continued on the whole to be non-political in character and the political mantle of the Deshabandhu therefore fell on Pandit Motilal Nehru, the Swarajist leader in the Assembly. While Lord Reading was still in England and Lord Lytton, the Governor of Bengal, was acting as the Governor-General of India, the Pandit attempted to resume the threads of the negotiations which the Deshabandhu had been carrying on with the Government. But the Government in London had already decided to drop the negotiations for the time being and watch developments. Nothing therefore came out of this attempt of Pandit Motilal Nehru.

June 1925 proved to be a turning point in the recent history of India. The disappearance of the towering personality of the Deshabandhu from the political arena was for India a colossal misfortune. The Swaraj Party, which owed so much to him, was paralysed after his death and dissensions gradually arose within the Party. Nevertheless, the Party at the time of his death was an institution of which anyone would be proud. The *Capital* of Calcutta, the organ of British commercial interests, writing after his death, compared the Swaraj Party with the Sinn Fein Party of Ireland and remarked that during forty years of its existence, it had seen nothing like it before. This discipline of the Party, according to the paper, was German in character. The weakening of the Swaraj Party served to strengthen the forces of reaction in India and in England, while it let loose a flood of communal strife in India which had, up till then, been held back by the superior forces of Nationalism. Today, as we look back on the year 1925, we cannot help feeling that if Providence had spared the Deshabandhu for a few years more, the history of India would probably have taken a different turn. In the affairs of nations, it often happens that the appearance or disappearance of a single personality means a new chapter in history. Thus has been the influence of Lenin in Russia, of Mussolini in Italy and of Hitler in Germany in recent world-history.

CHAPTER VI

## THE SLUMP (1925-27)

Considering the influence of Mahatma Gandhi in 1921 and 1922, the rise of the Swaraj Party must be regarded as something unaccountably remarkable. Though the leaders and the rank and file of the party had the highest respect for the personality of the Mahatma, the Party was frankly an anti-Gandhi Party and it was strong enough to force the Mahatma to voluntary retirement from politics. This retirement continued virtually till the Calcutta Congress in December 1928. Now what was the secret of the Swaraj Party's success? To understand that one must know more about the practical shape which Gandhism took, and as to how the mass mind reacted to the personality of the Mahatma, during the period 1920-22.

Though Hindu society has never had an established church like Europe, the mass of the people have been profoundly susceptible to the influence of Avatars,[1] priests and 'gurus'.[2] The spiritual man has always wielded the largest influence in India and he is called a 'Saint' or 'Mahatma' or 'Sadhu'. For various reasons, Gandhiji came to be looked upon by the mass of the people as a Mahatma before he became the undisputed political leader of India. At the Nagpur Congress in December 1920, Mr. M. A. Jinnah, who was till then a Nationalist leader, addressed him as 'Mr. Gandhi', and he was shouted down by thousands of people who insisted that he should address him as 'Mahatma Gandhi'. The asceticism of Gandhiji, his simple life, his

---

[1] According to many Hindus, God incarnates Himself from age to age in order to save the good and destroy the wicked and in order to establish the reign of Truth on earth. These incarnations are called Avatars. According to other Hindus, these Avatars are not divine incarnations but human souls in the highest stage of development—that is, when they have realised their oneness with Godhead. According to popular belief there have been nine Avatars up till now—and the tenth is to come at the end of the present wicked age.

[2] 'Guru' is a religious preceptor. In India only a truly spiritual man can be a religious preceptor.

vegetarian diet, his adherence to truth and his consequent fearlessness—all combined to give him a halo of saintliness. His loin-cloth was reminiscent of Christ, while his sitting posture at the time of lecturing was reminiscent of Buddha. Now all this was a tremendous asset to the Mahatma in compelling the attention and obedience of his countrymen. As we have already seen, a large and influential section of the intelligentsia was against him, but this opposition was gradually worn down through the enthusiastic support given by the masses. Consciously or unconsciously, the Mahatma fully exploited the mass psychology of the people, just as Lenin did the same thing in Russia, Mussolini in Italy and Hitler in Germany. But in doing so, the Mahatma was using a weapon which was sure to recoil on his head. He was exploiting many of the weak traits in the character of his countrymen which had accounted for India's downfall to a large extent. After all, what has brought about India's downfall in the material and political sphere? It is her inordinate belief in fate and in the supernatural—her indifference to modern scientific development—her backwardness in the science of modern warfare, the peaceful contentment engendered by her latter-day philosophy and adherence to Ahimsa (non-violence) carried to the most absurd length. In 1920, when the Congress began to preach the political doctrine of non-co-operation, a large number of Congressmen who had accepted the Mahatma not merely as a political leader but also as a religious preceptor—began to preach the cult of the new Messiah. As a consequence, many people gave up eating fish and meat, took the same dress as the Mahatma, adopted his daily habits like morning and evening prayer and began to talk more of spiritual freedom than of political Swaraj. In some parts of the country the Mahatma began to be worshipped as an Avatar. Such was the madness that seized the country at the time that in April 1923 in a politically-minded province like Bengal, a resolution moved at the Jessore Provincial Conference to the effect that the goal of the Congress was not spiritual Swaraj but political Swaraj was defeated at the end of a heated debate. In 1922, when the writer was in prison, Indian warders in the service of the Prisons' Department would refuse to believe that the Mahatma had been cast in prison by the British Government. They would say in all seriousness that since Gandhiji was a Mahatma, he could assume the shape of a bird and escape from prison any moment he liked. To make matters worse, political issues would no longer be considered in the cold light of reason, but would be unnecessarily mixed up with ethical issues. The Mahatma and his followers, for instance, would not countenance the boycott of British goods because that would engender hatred towards the British. Even so intellectual a personality as the celebrated poetess, Mrs. Sarojini Naidu, in her speech at the Gaya Congress in December 1922, condemned the Swarajist policy on the ground that councils were places of 'Maya',[1] where Congressmen would be tempted by bureaucratic overtures. And worst of all was the tendency on the part of the orthodox followers of the Mahatma to regard everything that he said as gospel truth without reasoning or arguing and to accept his paper *Young India* as their Bible.

For a people so prone to mysticism and supernaturalism, the only hope of political salvation lies in the growth of a sane rationalism and in the modernisation of the material aspect of life. It was therefore distressing to many sober Nationalists to find that through the conscious influence of the Mahatma, some of the above weak traits in the Indian character were again becoming prominent. Thus there arose a rationalist revolt against the Mahatma and his philosophy. As the Swaraj Party headed this revolt, elements from the Right and from the Left that were tired of the irrationalism of the Mahatma—were drawn towards it. Among the Right elements were those who preferred constitutional action to civil disobedience and the Deshabandhu by virtue of his social position and his vocation as an advocate, was able to command their confidence. Among the Left elements was the younger generation of Congressmen who did not find the ideology and method of the Ma-

---

[1] 'Maya' means an illusion or something false that charms and tempts.

hatma to be sufficiently radical for the modern world and who looked upon the Deshabandhu as a more radical (or revolutionary) force in Indian politics. It was the unique personality of Deshabandhu Das that was able to combine into one party such dissimilar elements, to wrest the Congress machinery from the hands of the orthodox 'No-Changers' and to carry on a fight against the bureaucracy on many fronts. But in his absence, there was no one competent enough to continue his many-sided activities or to keep together the diverse elements that composed the Swaraj Party. The result was that the Swaraj Party remained in power only so long as the Mahatma did not emerge from his voluntary retirement. When he did emerge in 1929, the Swarajist leader, Pandit Motilal Nehru, surrendered without even the show of a fight.

The death of Deshabandhu C. R. Das may be regarded as the beginning of a period of all-round depression in the country. If Mahatma Gandhi had come out of his retirement exactly at this juncture, things might have taken a different course, but unfortunately for India, he did not do so. The Deshabandhu's personality was, among other things, a powerful cementing factor within the Swaraj Party and also in the domain of Hindu-Moslem relations. It served, moreover, to tone up the attitude of the Party to an extremist pitch. In his absence, dissensions began to appear within the Party. The most important of these was the revolt of the Maharashtrian Swarajists led by Mr. M. R. Jayakar of Bombay and Mr. N. C. Kelkar of Poona. The Maharashtrian Swarajists had never fully believed in the 'uniform, continuous and consistent' opposition of the Swaraj Party, but they had nevertheless followed the Deshabandhu and his policy with unquestionable loyalty. They believed in the theory of 'responsive co-operation' propounded by Lokamanya Tilak at the time of the Amritsar Congress in December 1919. This theory implied that there should be co-operation with the Government in so far as they adopted measures calculated to benefit the country, but non-co-operation or opposition in so far as their policy was harmful to the public interest. The Maharashtrian

Swarajists looked upon the Deshabandhu as their leader since the time of Lokamanya's death and had therefore given their support and allegiance to his policy, regardless of their personal views. When Pandit Motilal Nehru assumed the leadership of the Swaraj Party, differences broke out between him and his Maharashtrian followers. The breach gradually widened until in an unlucky moment the Pandit lost his patience with them and in a fit of temper, characteristic of him, declared that 'the diseased limb (viz. the Maharashtrian group) of the Swaraj Party should be amputated'. This statement so offended the Maharashtrians that they resolved to sever all connection with the Pandit and the Swaraj Party and to start the Responsivist Party. Other dissensions also appeared within the Swaraj Party, later on. These developments indicated that while Pandit Motilal Nehru had superior intellectual qualities and a personality that could draw admiration and respect, he lacked that emotional appeal which alone can keep a party together through fair weather and foul.

In the domain of Hindu-Moslem relations, too, the Deshabandhu was a unifying force. His 'Bengal Pact' which had been rejected by the Coconada Congress in December 1923, but had been ratified by the Provincial Conference in May 1924, had served to convince all Moslems that he was their real friend. That such a man was at the head of the Swaraj Party helped to rally Moslem support for that Party and as a matter of fact, the Swaraj Party in the Bengal Legislative Council had a large number of Moslem members who had been elected on a basis of separate electorate. With the death of the Deshabandhu, the Moslem community no longer retained their former confidence in the Swaraj Party. Moreover, the political tension created by the Swaraj Party which had served to hold back the rising tide of communalism, subsided after his death and the country was then plunged in intercommunal strife which usurped the field for about two years. There was another unfortunate development following the death of the Deshabandhu—namely the weakening of the extremist attitude of the Party. When the Swaraj Party first came into existence, it had drawn elements both from the Right and from the Left. During the lifetime of the leader the Left elements had the upperhand because he himself belonged to the Left. But in his absence the Right elements were able to raise their head. Th emergency of intercommunal strife also helped to bring to the fore people who generally fought shy of politics and who were averse to doing anything which involved suffering and sacrifice. In Bengal the Left Wing was at a disadvantage for some time, because a large number of Congressmen belonging to that group were in prison either under Regulation III of 1818 or under the Bengal Ordinance.

From the middle of 1925 onwards there was a gradual watering down of the original Swarajist Policy of undiluted opposition. In June, Pandit Motilal Nehru accepted a seat on the Skeen Committee appointed by the Government to report on the Indianisation of the Army. Not long after this, Mr. S. B. Tambe,[1] a prominent member of the Swaraj Party of the Central Provinces, accepted an appointment as a member of the Governor's Executive Council and this step was approved of by Mr. N. C. Kelkar and other prominent Maharashtrian Swarajist leaders. About this time the Indian Legislative Assembly was given the right of electing its own President and Mr. Vithalbhai J. Patel, one of the most thorough-going obstructionists in the Swaraj Party, stood as a candidate and was duly elected to this office. Though the acceptance of that office involved a certain amount of co-operation with the Government, Mr. Patel performed his functions with remarkable ability and conspicuous success—so much so that though he always acted within the limits of the Constitution and with scrupulous fairness, he came to be dreaded by the Treasury Benches for his independent and impartial rulings. The popularity which the Swaraj Party gained during the period of its existence, was due in no small measure to his work as President. Working with a wretched Constitution and without any parliamentary precedents to back him, Mr. Patel

---

[1] Mr. Tambe later on became the acting Governor of the Central Provinces when the Governor went home on leave for some months.

was, nevertheless, able to maintain the rights and privileges of the members of the House of which he became the custodian and gave to the Opposition Party and its leader the status they would be entitled to in a free country enjoying a democratic Constitution.

In September 1925, the report of the Reforms, Enquiry Committee, better known as the Muddiman Committee, was placed before the Assembly. The Home Member, Sir Alexander Muddiman, moved the acceptance of the Majority Report of the committee and as an amendment to that, the Swarajist leader, Pandit Motilal Nehru, put forward what has been called the 'National Demand'. The National Demand, as formulated by the Pandit, was the result of a compromise with non-Swarajist members of the Assembly and represented the Greatest Common Measure of agreement among the non-official members. The National Demand was to the effect that constitutional reforms practically amounting to the immediate grant of Dominion Status should be conceded by the British Parliament and that a Round Table Conference between the British and Indian representatives should meet in order to discuss the ways and means for implementing those reforms. The reply given to the demand by the official spokesman in the Assembly at the time and later on by the Viceroy, amounted to a refusal.

Before the end of the year, Lala Lajpat Rai, joined the Assembly as a Swarajist and was elected Deputy Leader of the Party. About this time the Responsivist Party, headed by Mr. M. R. Jayakar and Mr. N. C. Kelkar, the erstwhile Swarajist leaders, was launched. It differed from the Swaraj Party on two main points. It advocated discriminate opposition, as opposed to the Swarajist policy of indiscriminate opposition to the Government in the Legislatures. Further, it did not approve of the pro-Moslem attitude of the Swaraj Party or of the Indian National Congress and on the contrary, it allied itself more with the Hindu Mahasabha. The accentuation of Hindu-Moslem differences in 1925 and after, threw more Hindu Congressmen into the arms of the Hindu Mahasabha and the politics of the Hindu Mahasabha, was, generally speaking, identical with that of the Responsivist Party. Both the Hindu Mahasabha and the Responsivist Party thought that the Moslem community by co-operating with the Government was able to strengthen its position and further its interests, to the detriment of Hindu interests—while the Indian National Congress through its policy of indiscriminate opposition was unable to do anything for the Hindus. This feeling was strengthened as a result of the conduct of Mr. (Now Sir) Mian Fazil Hussain, who by accepting the office of Minister in the Punjab, was able to promote Moslem interests in that province to the exclusion of Hindu and Sikh interests. The position of the Hindu Mahasabha and of the Responsivist Party received further support from the Hindu community through the reactionary and communal attitude adopted by the Moslem League at its sitting at Aligarh in December 1925, in which prominent leaders like Moulana Mohammed Ali, Mr. M. A. Jinnah, Sir Abdul Rahim and Sir Ali Imam participated.

The next elections to the Legislatures being due in 1926, the 1925 session of the Congress held at Cawnpore had to decide the attitude to be adopted by the Congress on the occasion. It was considered desirable that the Indian National Congress should itself take up the task of running the elections, instead of leaving it to the Swaraj Party. The Cawnpore Congress, presided over by Mrs. Sarojini Naidu,[1] arrived at this decision without much controversy, because by then the opposition of the Mahatma and his orthodox followers had been disarmed, but the question that raised a storm was as to the policy to be followed in the Legislatures. Should it be a policy of unmitigated opposition, or non-co-operation, as originally advocated by the Swaraj Party, or should it be a policy of discriminate opposition—or responsive co-operation—as urged by the newly-formed

[1] Mrs. Naidu was the second woman to be elected President of the Congress, the first being Mrs. Besant who presided over the Calcutta Congress, in 1917. A distinguished poetess, she had been closely associated with the Mahatma in the non-co-operation movement since 1920. She continues till today as one of his closest adherents and has been a member of the Congress Working Committee with hardly any break.

Responsivist Party? In support of the Swarajist policy, there stood Pandit Motilal Nehru and Lala Lajpat Rai, whereas opposed to them were Pandit M. M. Malaviya, Mr. Jayakar and Mr. Kelkar. The former won the day but before a year passed, Lala Lajpat Rai left the Swarajist fold and together with Pandit Malaviya [1] formed the Independent Party which played the same role in Northern India as the Responsivist Party in Central and Western India. By the time Lala Lajpat Rai left the Swaraj Party another prominent personality joined the Party. He was Mr. Srinivasa Iyengar, former Advocate-General[2] of Madras and the leader of the Madras Bar. Mr. Iyengar on being returned to the Assembly in 1926 was at once elected Deputy Leader of the Party and soon after, was elected President of the 1926 session of the Congress held at Gauhati in Assam.

The general attitude of the Government after the death of Deshabandhu Das was on the whole reactionary. The only exception was in the matter of the abolition of the Excise Duty, which welcome event took place in December 1925. The Excise Duty was first imposed as a tax on Indian mill-made cloth in 1894. The ostensible object of this duty was to obtain revenue for the Government but the real object was to help the British textile industry, which did not view with equanimity the growth of an indigenous textile industry in India. Though since 1916 the duty on textile imports had been kept at a higher level than the Excise Duty on Indian mill products, the latter was keenly resented by Indian Nationalists and especially by the Indian business community. The abolition of the duty was therefore meant as a sop to the Indian textile interests. Beyond this Act, no other friendly gesture was

---

[1] Pandit Malaviya, though a veteran Congressman and an ex-President of the Congress, did not accept the Swarajist policy. During the period 1923-26, he was a member of the Assembly but did not belong to the Swaraj Party. After the general election of 1926 he continued as an Independent. The change in the politics of Lala Lajpat Rai was due to the Hindu-Moslem tension in the Punjab and the influence of the Hindu Mahasabha.
[2] The position of the Advocate-General of Madras would correspond to the position of the Solicitor-General in England.

made by the Government of India or in England. The Labour Party, however, made a friendly move by adopting the Commonwealth of India Bill drafted by Mrs. Besant for conferring Home Rule on India and authorised Mr. George Lansbury to introduce it as a Private Bill in the House of Commons. The Bill received its first reading in December 1925, but it proved to be still-born. Nevertheless, it had some value as a gesture.

The history of 1926 is largely a history of Hindu-Moslem strife. As happens everywhere, the slackening of the Nationalist movement diverted the energies of the people to internal questions and disputes. The abolition of the Khalifate by the Turks in 1924 led many of the Nationalist Moslems in India to give up the Khilafat movement and to divert their whole attention to the Nationalist cause. But some of the Nationalists as well as the more reactionary Moslems continued to keep up the Khilafat Committees, as Moulana Shaukat Ali did in Bombay, and where that was not possible, they started other organisations of a sectarian reactionary character, under different names. This reactionary movement among the Moslems called forth a similar reactionary movement among the Hindus and branches of the Hindu Mahasabha began to grow up all over the country. The Hindu Mahasabha, like its Moslem counterpart, consisted not only of erstwhile Nationalists, but also of a large number of men who were afraid of participating in a political movement and wanted a safer platform for themselves. The growth of sectarian movements among both Hindus and Moslems accentuated intercommunal tension. The opportunity was availed of by interested third Parties who wanted to see the two communities fight, so that the Nationalist forces could be weakened. The causes which generally led to intercommunal rioting were the slaughter of cows which outraged Hindu feelings and the playing of music before mosques at prayer time, which gave offence to Moslem feelings. Friction would also be caused if a Moslem mosque or a Hindu temple was defiled in any way. Once there was a mental tension between the two communities in a particular locality, such incidents could easily throw the spark to light the flame of communal passion and it was not difficult for third parties to employ agents to do this dirty work.

The worst episode in the events of 1926 was the Hindu-Moslem riots in Calcutta which broke out in May and again in July. The trouble arose through an Arya Samajist [1] procession playing music while passing before a mosque. The Arya Samajists claimed that they had been having the procession for many years without any trouble. The Moslems declared on the contrary that the music was interfering with their worship inside the mosque. Fighting went on for many days and many were killed on both sides. Ultimately when both parties were exhausted, they made peace. Though matters did not reach a crisis elsewhere as it did in Calcutta, there was considerable tension all over the country. For the Congress Party the hour was dark. The elections to the Legislatures were due in November and they were going to be held under the shadow of Hindu-Moslem riots. The field would not be as open to Congressmen as it had been in 1923. New organisations representing reactionary Hindus and reactionary Moslems had come into existence and they would put up their own candidates. During the elections of 1926 a strong propaganda was carried on by a section of the Moslems to the effect that if the Hindus were going to carry on their non-co-operation with the Government, the Moslems should have nothing to do with them, but should endeavour to work the Constitution. On the other side the Hindu Mahasabha raised the cry that if the Hindus non-co-operated while the Moslems secured the help of the Government, they would be placing themselves at a serious disadvantage as compared with the Moslems. The Hindu Mahasabha therefore urged the modification of the Swarajist policy of non-co-operation. Nevertheless, among the Hindu electorate the influence of the Congress was much greater than that of the Hindu Mahasabha, though among the Moslem electorate, the influence of reactionary and sectarian organi-

---

[1] As explained in Section III of the Introduction, the Arya Samaj is a reformist sect of the Hindus with a large following in Upper India.

sations proved to be stronger than that of the Congress at the General Election of 1926.

The General Election of November 1926 being contested by Nationalists in the name of the Congress, there was a great improvement in their strength in many of the Provincial Legislatures, e.g. in Madras, and Bihar. The wholehearted co-operation of all sections of Congressmen, which was not forthcoming in 1923 when the Swaraj Party ran the elections, was responsible for the improvement. But in one respect the election results were worse than in 1923. In 1923 a large number of Nationalist Moslems had been elected as Swarajists but in 1926 their places were generally taken by their reactionary co-religionists. In provinces like Bengal and Punjab with a large Moslem population, the situation inside the Legislatures was not favourable for the Congress Party. In the Central Provinces which had been the stronghold of Swarajism and in portion of the Bombay Presidency, the Nationalist strength was divided, because of the formation of the Responsivist Party. With the formation of a Responsivist Party in the Central Provinces Legislative Council and of a Moslem bloc in the Bengal Legislative Council, it became possible for the Government to appoint Ministers in these two provinces, where none had existed for three years. In the Indian Legislative Assembly also, the Nationalist strength being somewhat weakened by the formation of a Responsivist bloc on the one side and by a Moslem bloc on the other, the Government had a comparatively easier time than they had in the previous Assembly. Apart from the Legislatures, a certain amount of disintegration was also visible in the rank and file of the Congress. In provinces like Punjab, Bombay Presidency and the Central Provinces, this was due to the activities of the Responsivist Party. In provinces like Bengal where the Responsivists had little influence, the disintegration was caused by warring factions within the Congress Party. In Bengal after the death of Deshabandhu Das, through the influence and support of the Mahatma, the late Mr. J. M. Sengupta had succeeded to the leadership. He had not been in office for a year before opposition to his leadership appeared. The opposition ultimately crystallised under the leadership of Mr. B. N. Sasmal, at one time a most popular figure in Bengal Congress circles. The fight went on till 1927. For some time there were two rival Provincial Congress Committees in Bengal and in the elections to the Calcutta Municipal Corporation, held in March 1927, two sets of Congress candidates were set up. Mr. Sasmal's party was defeated in this fight and that led to his temporary retirement.

In the face of dissensions outside and inside the Congress, the leaders had a trying time in 1926. For a time it looked as if nothing could stem the rot that had set in. The brunt of the responsibility had to be borne by Pandit Motilal Nehru who was deprived of the leadership of Mahatma Gandhi, who had retired from active politics, and of Deshabandhu Das who had died the year before. The National Demand put forward by him in the Assembly in September 1925, had been turned down by the Government In the circumstances what could he do? He was not in a position to start a campaign of civil disobedience in the country. Therefore he decided to withdraw from the Assembly as a protest against the attitude of the Government. Much adverse criticism was made of this decision at the time—nevertheless, there is hardly any doubt that there was no alternative to this step except one of abject acquiescence in the policy of the Government. In March 1926, after a speech exceedingly dignified but somewhat defeatist in its tone, Pandit Motilal Nehru walked out of the Assembly followed by all the Swarajist members. Following this move in the Assembly, the Swaraj Party also withdrew from the Provincial Legislatures.

But the dark clouds of 1926 had a silver lining. In spite of intercommunal dissensions and disturbances, the production of Khadi was going up by leaps and bounds. Freed from other distractions, the Mahatma was able to concentrate on this work. Under his leadership the All-India Spinners' Association was extending its branches all over the country. Through this organisation, the Mahatma was once again building up his own party which was to be of invaluable service to him when he desired to recapture the Congress machinery once again. To make up partly for the many defections in the Congress Party, Mr. Srinivasa Iyengar joined the party wholeheartedly about this time. He had great reputation and prestige in the Madras Presidency and this he placed at the disposal of the Congress. Through his help the movement in the Madras Presidency was greatly strengthened and a strong Congress Party was set up in the Madras Legislative Council. In the Assembly he performed with great ability the duties of the Deputy Leader of the Congress Party. After presiding over the Gauhati Congress in December 1926, he spent a very busy time in going round the country for restoring intercommunal unity. In this task he was assisted by the Ali brothers who were actively associated with the Congress till 1928, though their estrangement with the Mahatma began in 1926.[1]

The most encouraging sign of the year was the awakening among the youths all over the country. They were disgusted with the narrow sectarianism of the older generation and wanted to chasten public life with the pure breath of nationalism. The youth movement appeared under different names in different provinces, but the impulse behind it was the same everywhere. There was a feeling of impatience and revolt at the rotten state of affairs—a sense of self-confidence and a consciousness of the responsibility which they had towards their country. In the Punjab the movement appeared under the name of Naujawan Bharat Sabha and was to play an important role in the years to come. In Nagpur, the capital of the Central Provinces, the youths started, on their own responsibility, a movement called the Arms Act Satyagraha. The object of this campaign was to defy the Arms Act which prohibited Indians from possessing or bearing arms, and it was started by a popular local Congress leader, Mr. Awari, who was given the title of 'General'

---

[1] It is generally believed that the estrangement between the Ali brothers and the Mahatma took place over the Hindu-Moslem riots at Kohat in North West Frontier Province. In this dispute the Ali brothers took the side of the Moslems and complained that the Mahatma had taken the side of the Hindus.

by his followers. It was announced at the commencement of the campaign, that the Satyagraha movement was being started as a protest against the conduct of the Government who had imprisoned without trial a large number of public workers in Bengal.

Taking advantage of the weakness of the Congress in 1926, the Government continued its reactionary policy in 1927, though since April 1926, India had a new Viceroy in Lord Irwin, who was a totally different stamp from his predecessor Lord Reading. The report of the Skeen Committee was published in April 1927 and it provided that one-half of the cadre of the Indian Army would be completely Indianised in twenty-five years. The report of the Committee was disappointing and it was not signed by Pandit Motilal Nehru who had resigned his membership of the Committee before the report was drafted. But even the meagre recommendations of the Committee, which by the way was presided over by the Chief of Staff of the Indian Army, were not given effect to, at the instance of the Secretary of State for India, Lord Birkenhead. The *mala fides* of the Government will be all the more evident from the fact that during Sir Tej Bahadur Sapru's tenure of office as a member of the Viceroy's Executive Council, the Army Staff had prepared a plan whereby the whole army could be Indianised within thirty years.

Another unwelcome move of the Government in 1927 was the stabilisation of the rupee at 1s. 6d. The traditional exchange ratio was 1s. 4d. and this was favourable to India. In the teeth of popular opposition, the Government fixed the value of the rupee by 12½ per cent, the Finance Member, Sir Basil Blackett, automatically put a premium on imports into India. But that was not the only disadvantage which India was subjected to. As a result of the new ratio, the Indian peasant producing raw material for the world market received so much less money than before and his purchasing power in relation to Indian goods was thereby considerably reduced. There is no doubt that the new ratio was responsible to a large extent in accentuating the economic crisis in India. Along with the new ratio, Sir Basil Blackett wanted to have an Indian Reserve Bank as a part of his plan for controlling the currency—but this Bill [1] was fortunately thrown out by the Assembly and the Viceroy did not make it law through 'certification'.

The only event of a somewhat satisfactory nature during the earlier half of 1927 was the Capetown Pact between India and South Africa. The Government of South Africa headed by General Hertzog, an ardent nationalist, wanted to adopt a dual policy of segregation and repatriation with regard to the Indian settlers. A delegation was sent from India, composed of Sir Mohammed Habibullah, the Right Hon. V. S. Sastri and Sir George Paddison to plead the cause of the Indians. As a result of their persuasion, the following agreement was arrived at. The Areas Reservation Bill for segregating Indians was altogether abandoned by the South African Government. Emigration of Indians was, however, to be encouraged, though a higher bonus would be given than before. Indians born in South Africa who wanted to make that country their home, were to be assisted by the Government to attain the 'White' standard of life. Though the Pact was only partially satisfactory, it was better than nothing and the Viceroy, Lord Irwin, fully supported the Indian case in this matter. The Pact provided for an 'Agent' of the Indian Government who would reside in South Africa and Mr. Sastri was sent out from India as the first 'Agent'.

In the international sphere the step taken by England in breaking off relations with Russia in 1927, was to have repercussions in India. Since then the activities of the Communist Party in India increased considerably. This was helped by the weakening of the Nationalist forces in the country and the growth of labour unrest in 1927 and 1928.

---

[1] The Bill was first ruled out of order by the Assembly President, Mr. V. J. Patel, whereafter it was introduced again in an altered form. The Congress Party succeeded in throwing out the section relating to the management of the Bank, whereupon the Bill was withdrawn by Sir Basil Blackett.

CHAPTER VII

## IN BURMESE PRISONS[1] (1925-27)

In the early hours of the morning of October 25th, 1924, I was roused from my sleep as I was wanted by some police officers. The Deputy-Commissioner of Police, Calcutta, on meeting me, said : 'Mr. Bose, I have a very unpleasant duty to perform. I have a warrant for your arrest under Regulation III of 1818.' He then produced another warrant authorising him to search my house for arms, explosives, ammunition, etc. Since no arms, etc. were forthcoming, he had to content himself with taking a pile of papers and correspondence. To avoid public attention, he drove me to prison in his own car but so utterly unexpected was my arrest that known faces, whom I met on my way, never thought that my destination was His Majesty's Prison at Alipore. At the Alipore New Central Jail I was surprised to find that there were others in the same boat with me. The prison authorities did not seem to be happy to receive us. Special arrangements had to be made for segregating us from the rest of the prison population and they had hardly any surplus accommodation. As the day advanced, our numbers began to swell and to our great delight (there is nothing so welcome in prison as companionship) when the time for evening lock-up came, we found that we were eighteen in number.

As I was the Chief Executive Officer of the Calcutta Municipal Corporation at the time, my sudden arrest dislocated the work of the Municipality. The Government therefore gave special orders that till the beginning of December I could attend to my office work in prison and that my Secretary could see me from time to time with office files and documents. In all these interviews a police-

---

[1] The writer has been in custody eight times but he has tried to chronicle the events of only one such experience, since it is more intersting than the others.

officer would be present besides a jail-officer and usually some of the worst police-officers would be detailed to conduct these interviews. I had frequent trouble with them and had to put up with a great deal of unpleasantness and on some occasions I had to rebuke some of them for their impertinence. As a punishment I was given orders of transfer to another prison (Berhampore Jail) in the interior of the province where it would be difficult for people to interview me. Neither at Alipore nor at Berhampore did I have much trouble with the prison-staff. Some of the Government orders were of course humiliating, but for that we did not blame the prison-staff. My trouble with the police-officers, however, continued at Berhampore. Most of my time was spent in study and many were the plans we discussed about the work that we would do when we left prison once again. As the arrests continued from day to day, the prison population began to increase to our great delight. My stay at Berhampore did not last more than two months. On January 25th, 1925, I suddenly received orders of transfer to Calcutta. On my way I learnt to my great surprise that my real destination was Mandalay Prison in Upper Burma. At midnight I reached Calcutta and was taken into the Lalbazar Police-station to spend the night there. The room in the police-station was a dirty hole and thanks to mosquitoes and bugs, it was impossible to have a wink of sleep. The sanitary arrangements were horribly bad and there was no privacy at all. I then realised the truth of what others had said before, namely, that if there is a hell on earth, it is the Lalbazar Police-station. As I lay down, counting the number of beams in the ceiling to while away the time, I heard familiar voices in an adjoining room. So the good Government had sent me companions even there ! In the early hours of the morning when it was still dark, a police-officer appeared on the scene. This was Mr. Lowman, Assistant-Inspector General of Police, who, we learned later, was to escort us to Mandalay. The doors of the cells were opened and out came seven familiar faces, all bound for the same destination. A surprise indeed !

Under cover of darkness, surrounded by armed guards, we came out of the police-station. Two prison vans were standing in front with their doors invitingly open. In one, our worldly belongings were placed; in the other the living luggage was deposited. With terrific speed, the prison vans moved out of the yard, and merged in the darkness that still hung over the landscape. After a while both the vans drew up and as we alighted, we realised that we were on the river bank. There was a ship standing near the bank, but we were all put into a small motor-boat. For three hours we cruised about on the river and when it was time for the ship to sail, we were quietly taken up into the ship from the farther side. By nine o'clock in the morning, we were sailing down the river towards the sea. In front of our cabins heavily-armed guards were stationed, and great was the curiosity of the other passengers to know who we were and why these elaborate arrangements had been made. When we reached the high seas, the armed guards in front of our cabins were withdrawn and only plain-clothes officers were left to look after us. Our four days' voyage was rather interesting. Mr. Lowman was jovial and communicative and we discussed all possible subjects, including our estimate of Governors, Executive Councillors, public leaders, etc. I even raised the question of the torture of political prisoners by the police. Mr. Lowman at first denied the charge but at the end he admitted that on some occasions such misdeeds had been committed. On the whole, though I began with a strong prejudice against him, I came to hold a favourable opinion of him and this opinion was confirmed as a result of my subsequent meetings and talks with him. The night before we reached Rangoon, Mr. Lowman had almost a nightmare. He complained in the morning that he could not sleep well as he dreamt that some of the state prisoners had escaped through the port-hole in the evening. From Rangoon to Mandalay it was a long journey of twenty hours. We had a very large police escort and at every stop on our way, they would line up on both sides of the train. From the fuss they made, one would think that we were either high state-officials or wild animals.

Till then Mandalay was but a name to us. I had a hazy idea that it was the capital of the last independent kingdom of Burma and the scene of the second Burmese war. But I remembered distinctly that it was the place where Lokamanya Tilak had been imprisoned for nearly six years and later on Lala Lajpat Rai for about a year. It gave us therefore some consolation and pride to feel that we were following in their footsteps. From the station we drove inside the fort to the prison and we passed on our way the houses in which Lalaji and Sardar Ajit Singh had lived during their internment. Outlined against the morning sky we saw beautiful structures which, we were told, were the palace and state-buildings of the old kingdom. The memory of the good old days that were no more, produced a pang in our hearts and we began to wonder when Burma would once more be able to fly her flag of independence. As our carriages drew up in front of the grey walls of Mandalay prison, our day-dreaming came to an end. The massive gates of the prison-house yawned and we were soon swallowed up. The interior of a Burmese prison is somewhat different from that of an Indian prison and the first few minutes were spent in examining our new surroundings. The first thing we realised was that the jail-buildings were built not of stone nor of brick, but of wooden palisading. The buildings looked exactly like cages in a zoo or in a circus. From the outside and especially at night, the inmates of these buildings appeared almost like animals prowling about behind the bars. Within these structures we were at the mercy of the elements. There was nothing to protect us from the biting cold of winter or the intense heat of summer or the tropical rains in Mandalay. We all began to wonder how we were going to live our life there. But there was no help and we had to make the best of a bad situation. In the yard adjoining ours, so we were told, Lokamanya Tilak had spent about six years of his life. Among the prison-staff we found many men who had been there when Lokamanya Tilak was a prisoner. From them and later on from the Inspector-General of Prisons himself, we heard interesting anecdotes of him and how he spent his days in prison. Not less interesting for us than the anecdotes were the lemon-trees which he had planted with his own hands. From one of the state prisoners, Mr. Jibon Lal Chatterji, who had preceded us, we took our first lessons in the Burmese language. I was not there long before I developed a strong liking for the Burmese people. There is something in them which one cannot help liking. They are exceedingly warm-hearted, frank and jovial in their temperament. They are of course quick-tempered and are sometimes liable to lose their self-control when under the influence of temper. But that did not appear to me as a very serious shortcoming. What struck me greatly was the innate artistic sense which every Burman has. If they have any faults, it is their extreme *naivete* and absence of all feeling against foreigners. In fact, I was told later that for a Burmese woman, a foreigner has greater attraction than a member of her own community.

Our Superintendent, Captain (later on, Major) Smith, was exceedingly nice in his dealings with us and there was never any misunderstanding between us. Even when we had to fight the Government or go on hunger-strike, our friendly relations were not disturbed. With the Chief Jailor we had frequent trouble and we would receive constant pin-pricks from him. He would justify himself by saying that he had to act under orders, but till the end I was not able to find out who was really responsible for these pin-pricks. However, after some time, when the subordinate staff realised that if we were given trouble we could also make trouble, they settled down to a friendly alliance with us. The head of the Prison Department was Lieut.-Col. Tarapore, a Parsi gentleman, a very tactful, intelligent and well-meaning official. Though state-prisoners in Mandalay or in other prisons of Burma had occasional misunderstandings with him, I must admit and that with great pleasure, that on the whole he endeavoured to treat us well. His difficulty was that in the first place, the Bengal Government who were ultimately responsible for us, were exceedingly vindictive. Secondly, the Government of India, the highest authority in the land, were too far away and too indifferent. Thirdly, the Burma Government, though not vindictive towards us, did not want to do anything on their own responsibility. Lieut.-Col. Tarapore was a great enthusiast of prison-reform and at his instance the Burma Government invited Mr. Patterson, one of His Majesty's Prison Commissioners in England, to visit Burma and advise them on prison-reform there. But with all his enthusiasm Lieut.-Col. Tarapore could not achieve much because of his reactionary environment. I remember that a very important piece of reform which he had once attempted had to be given up because of opposition in other quarters. To the ordinary Burman, accustomed to smoking tobacco from a very early age, tobacco is more important than food. As tobacco was banned in Burmese prisons, the prisoners would commit innumerable jail-offences in trying to smuggle it from outside. The Inspector-General of Prisons rightly thought that if tobacco were given to the prisoners in a legal way, there would be a drop in the number of prison-offences and the illegal traffic would also be stopped to a large extent. He, therefore, introduced a rule that as a reward for good behaviour prisoners would be given a certain quantity of tobacco every day. Though the reform was not sufficiently far-reaching, it was an improvement on the existing state of things. The experiment was tried for a year but at the end of that period, most of the Prison Superintendents reported against the experiment and the Finance Department also raised difficulty about funds. The reform had consequently to be dropped. Towards the end of our stay in Burma, another important reform was attempted by him. Prisoners were taken out of prison and employed for roadmaking. They were accommodated in camps, were allowed more freedom than in prison and were also given a certain allowance in addition to their food. I do not know what the ultimate result of the experiment was, but about the time that I left Burma, difficulty was being experienced in finding suitable officers for running these camps. In our talks with him, the Inspector-General used to complain that he did not have officials possessing the necessary education and character who could forget their prison-environment and treat the prisoners as human beings.

During my stay in Burma I was able to make a study of criminal psychology and of the problems of prison-reform. In supplying us with necessary literature, the Inspector-General was of great assistance. The prison population in the different jails in Burma also afforded a valuable subject-matter for study. It is neither possible nor necessary to give here some of the results of my study and observation, but I shall content myself with making one observation. It is generally thought that those who are convicted for murder, are the worst specimens of humanity and are past redemption. On the contrary, my experience is that among the prisoners, murderers are generally a better type. This is so at least in those cases in which murder has been committed in a fit of temper or temporary insanity. Professional thieves and pick-pockets, on the other hand, represent the worst type. In the condemned cells (where prisoners are locked before they are hanged) I would see from time to time fine specimens of humanity, sometimes boys in their 'teens who were going to be hanged simply because they had lost their self-control for a moment and killed someone in a fit of temper. The ease with which the High Court in Burma would confirm death sentences appeared amazing to me. The conduct of the High Court was all the more monstrous in view of the fact that in Burma people had for centuries been accustomed to take the law into their own hands and Upper Burma and Mandalay had come under British rule as late as 1885.

From time to time we would receive visits from many interesting people including officials. From the Home Member down to the petty magistrate no one would ignore us, since Indian state prisoners were to them interesting specimens of humanity. Among the visitors was Mr. Patterson, a Prison Commissioner from England, who greeted us as 'eight of the most dangerous men in India'. A regular visitor was Mr. Brown, the Deputy Commissioner (i.e. District Officer) of Mandalay. Whatever may have been his attitude towards the people of Mandalay, with the state prisoners his dealings were those of a straightforward gentleman. He was a cultured man and we enjoyed our discussions with him. He was, moreover, helpful to us in supplying literature and in mediating, whenever we fell out with the prison officials. Our relations with the prison officials suddenly became strained, when Captain Smith went on leave. He was succeeded by Major Findlay. While Captain Smith had a genial temperament, Major Findlay had a rough exterior and a rather saturnine temperament. We soon fell out with Major Findlay over trifling matters and this led to hunger-strike. Through Mr. Brown's mediation, the misunderstanding was however cleared up. Thereafter, when we came to know one another more intimately, I discovered that he was an exceedingly nice and straightforward man. Another official who acted as Superintendent for a time was Major Sheppard, with whom there was constant friction, but since he did not stay long, matters did not reach a crisis.

Ours was not the first batch of state prisoners to be deported to Burma. About a year before we arrived, another batch had been sent across there. When the first batch came they were not confined in the same prison, but were transferred in twos to different prisons in Burma. They had a very hard time and as they were separated, they could not put up a joint fight for improving their conditions. During this period two of the state prisoners, Mr. Jibon Lal Chatterji and Mr. Bhupendra Kumar Dutt, sent a representation to the then Secretary of State for India, Lord Olivier, severely criticising the conduct of the Political Branch of the Bengal Police, called in India the Intelligence Branch. The main thesis was that agent-provocateurs were employed by the police for entrapping innocent but over-enthusiastic young men and that the bogey of a revolutionary conspiracy was deliberately raised by the Intelligence Branch because they could thereby draw extra allowances, like 'danger allowance', and could also have at their disposal large sums of money for employing informers. Certain facts and figures were given by way of substantiating this charge. This letter somehow found its way to the Indian Press and after its publication it was quoted by the Swarajist leader, Pandit Motilal Nehru, in a speech in the Assembly, attacking the policy of imprisoning people without trial. The publication of the letter so annoyed the Government that severe restrictions were imposed on the state prisoners in Burma. After some time the temper of the Government cooled down and the state prisoners were allowed then to come together in one prison. An exception was however made in the case of Mr. Bhupendra Kumar Dutt, whom the Government wanted to punish for the publication of the letter.

In prison we were able to meet from time to time Burman political prisoners from whom we learned a lot about the intricacies of Burma politics. Among those whom we met there were some priests (called in Burma 'hpongyis'). These priests, or hpongyis, whom I met in prisons of Burma, are some of the finest specimens of humanity I have ever met. Burma is a land where there is no caste and no class. It is probably the most classless country outside Russia. Buddhism there is a living religion and the priests who live that religion are held in high esteem. For centuries, they have been imparting free elementary education to men and women, with the result that in the matter of literacy, Burma today is far ahead of India. Since the British annexation, the hpongyis alone have kept up the flame of dying nationalism, since they were never reconciled to British domination or to British culture. Under their leadership for many a year, guerrilla warfare was carried on. Owing to their consistent opposition to the foreign Government, they are intensely hated by all Britishers, official and non-official. Strangely enough, though they are anti-British, they are nevertheless pro-Indian and they are strongly opposed to separation from India. Apart from the cultural affinity they have with India, they feel that when they are separated from India, it will be more difficult for them to fight Great Britain for their political freedom. Among the mass of the Burmese people the influence of the priests is very strong. The English-educated Burmans are politically a divided community. The majority are politically opposed to the priests and are anti-Indian and pro-British.[1] A minority among them is however allied politically with the priests. The English-educated Burmans generally think that separation from India will improve their lot, though the fact remains that it is the Britishers who have the best of everything in the country and not the Indians. The 'anglicised' Burmans generally have no idea or intention of fighting for their freedom and they think that once the Indians are eliminated from Burma, everything will be all right for them. The hpongyis or priests, on the contrary, are politically-minded and they follow the policy and tactics of Indian National Congress. When I was in Burma, the uncrowned king of the Burmans was Rev. U. Ottama, a priest.[2] The impression that I had during my stay there was that the priests had the largest following in the country. They had boycotted the Burma Legislature since 1920 and they did not have their representative there. That led the Government to think that the Burmans really wanted separation from India, as the English-educated Burmans generally were saying. The recent elections have shown, however, that the people are against separation. The significance of the last elections will be understood better when it is remembered that they were fought on the basis of the old electoral roll and that the request of the anti-separationist party for a revision of the electoral roll prior to the elections, was turned down. Among the separationists (the English-edu-

---

[1] The New Constitution, outlined by the Joint Parliamentary Committee on the basis of separation from India, is likely to prove disappointing to English-educated Burmans and may bring about a change in their general attitude.

[2] Rev. U. Ottama is now an exile living in Calcutta and is not allowed to return to Burma. His health is completely shattered as a result of repeated incarceration. When I was in Burma an interesting incident took place. Rev. U. Ottama was in prison and a rumour got afloat that he had been secretly transported to a prison in India. In the Burma Legislative Council, questions were put on this point. The Home Member, himself a Burman, felt annoyed at the questions and replied that U. Ottama was one of ten thousand criminals in his jails and he could not be expected to know where he was confined at the time. At this insulting reference to U. Ottama, all the non-official members of the Legislative Council walked out as a protest. They resolved to dissolve their separate parties and started a united party—called the People's Party.

cated Burmans) as also among the anti-separationists, it is very difficult to have a united party, because personal considerations play an important role in Burma. The priests who are anti-separationists are, on the whole, a compact party. Among the English-educated Burmans, when I was in Burma, there were several parties, the most important of them being the Twenty-One Party [1] —so called because twenty-one persons joined together and formed the party. The Nationalist Party in Burma is called the G.C.B.A.— that is, the General Council of Burmese Association and there are as many G.C.B.A.'s as there are parties. Many people wonder today, why Britain is so keen on separating Burma from India—but if one knew Burma, there would be no reason to wonder. Many Britishers think that even if India be a lost Dominion, it is still desirable to try and keep Burma. Burma is so thinly populated, is so rich in minerals and in certain parts has such a pleasing climate that it would be fit for colonisation by Britishers. Besides, Burma is the gateway of the Far East and has an important strategic position.

Interesting as Burmese politics was to me, the country and the people were even more so. I spent a great deal of my time in studying the ancient history of Burma and in discovering the old cultural contacts between the two countries. There is no doubt that many Kshatriya tribes migrated to Burma from India. They, as well as the people from Ceylon and South India, brought to Burma, Buddhism and the Pali literature. The culture and philosophy of Burma have been largely influenced by India. The alphabets have been taken from Sanskrit and even the script is much like some of the Indian scripts. The pagodas (temples) of Burma which have a unique charm of their own, are not devoid of Indian influence. In Pagan and in other old centres of Burmese culture, one can still see structures which form the transition between the typical Hindu temple and the typical Burmese pagoda. I have already said that the artistic sense of the ordinary Burman

---

[2] The policy of the Twenty-One Party was to work the Constitution, while that of the G.C.B.A. was to boycott it.

is of a very high order. One had only to see the exquisite handiwork of the prisoners in Mandalay and other prisons to believe this. In Mandalay, on two or three jail holidays in the year, the Superintendent would give the prisoners permission to sing and dance. On these days they would organise a variety performance. They would play dramas and sing songs specially composed for the occasion, would dance their exquisite national dance and would even improvise a jail orchestra to supply the necessary music. All this was possible only among a people with a highly-developed artistic sense.

In October 1925, our national religious festival—the Durga Pujah—falling due, we applied to the Superintendent for permission and for funds to perform the ceremony. Since similar facilities were given to Christian prisoners in Indian prisons, the Superintendent gave us the necessary facilities, in anticipation of Government sanction. The Government, however, not only refrained from giving sanction but censured the Superintendent, Major Findlay, for acting on his own responsibility. Thereupon we informed the Government that they should reconsider their decision, otherwise we would be forced to go on hunger strike. The reply being in the negative, we commenced hunger strike in February 1926. All our correspondence with the outside world was at once stopped. Nevertheless, three days after the hunger strike began, the Calcutta paper, *Forward*, published the news of our hunger strike and also the ultimatum we had sent to Government. About the same time *Forward* published extracts from the report of the Indian Jail Committee of 1919-21. Before this Committee a high official of the Prison Department, Lieut-Col. Mulvany, had given evidence to say that he had been forced by his superior officer, the Inspector-General of Prisons of Bengal, to withdraw the health reports he had sent of some state-prisoners in his jail and to send in false reports instead. These disclosures raised a storm of indignation among the public. In the Indian Legislative Assembly which was then sitting in Delhi, Mr. T. C. Goswami, a Swarajist member, moved the adjournment of the House over the hunger strike in Mandalay Jail and referred to the evidence of Lieut.-Col. Mulvany to the effect that false reports about the state prisoners are manufactured by the Prison Department. The Home Member found himself in an uncomfortable position and promised to redress the grievances of the state prisoners on hunger strike. No sooner was the debate over than a searching inquiry was instituted with a view to finding out how *Forward* got the necessary material for publication. However, the Government issued orders without delay that they would sanction the money that had been spent by us and that in future they would provide facilities and funds for our religious requirements. So after fifteen days' starvation, having won our point, we ended the strike.

In the latter half of 1926 an interesting development took place. The Legislatures were dissolved and fresh elections were due in November. My fellow-prisoner, Mr. S. C. Mitra, was offered a constituency for the Indian Legislative Assembly by the Bengal Congress Party, and I was offered a Calcutta constituency for the Bengal Legislative Council. Both of us accepted the offer and decided to stand. While Mr. Mitra was returned unopposed, I had a formidable opponent in Mr. J. N. Basu, the leader of the Liberal Party in Bengal. At the last election Mr. Basu had retained his seat by defeating the Swarajist candidate and the Congress Party thought that it was necessary to put me up against him in order to dislodge him. He was exceedingly popular in his constituency and was a fine type of gentleman and we had nothing against him except his Liberal Politics. This was the key-election of the year in Bengal and so the Party had to put forward its best efforts in order to win. The election was reminiscent of the early Sinn Fein elections in which political prisoners were candidates and the slogan was—'Put him in to get him out'. Modern electioneering methods were used by the Party, including the use of rockets for distributing leaflets and posters showing the candidate behind prison bars. The voters felt that my success would be a public vote of confidence in me and force the Government either to release me or send me up for trial. So I got a thumping majority. But the Government of India was less responsive to public opinion than the Government in Ireland and my incarceration continued.

Meanwhile, as a result of the unfavourable climatic conditions and of the hunger strike earlier in the year, my health had begun to give way. Matters grew serious when during the winter of 1926 I had an attack of bronchopneumonia. After the attack, I could not shake off the temperature and simultaneously I began to lose weight. I was therefore transferred to Rangoon for examination by a medical board. The medical board composed of Lieut.-Col. Kelsall and my brother, Dr. Sunil C. Bose, made a recommendation to the effect that I should not be detained in prison. While I was awaiting the orders of Government in Rangoon Jail, I had a quarrel with the Superintendent, Major Flowerdew (now the Inspector-General of Prisons, Bengal), whereupon I was transferred to Insein Jail. My transfer to Insein proved to be a godsend. On arrival I found as Superintendent, Major Findlay, who had been the Superintendent of Mandalay Jail for some time. He was painfully surprised to see the condition of my health. After keeping me under observation for three weeks, he wrote a very strong note to Government about my health. On receiving this note the Government were forced to act. But they were still opposed to the idea of releasing me. In the meantime they had made an offer in the Bengal Legislative Council saying that if I wanted to go to Switzerland at my own expense, they would release me and put me on board a ship at Rangoon sailing for Europe. This offer I had rejected, partly because I could not accept the conditions attached to the offer and partly because I did not like the idea of going to Europe direct from Burma for an indefinite period. After the rejection of this offer, the next order that I received from Government was for my transfer to Almora Jail in the United Provinces. Once again arrangements for my transfer were made with the utmost secrecy and early one morning in May 1927, I was removed from Insein Jail to a boat sailing from Rangoon.

On the fourth day I reached Diamond Harbour at the mouth of the river Hooghly. Before our boat reached Calcutta, she was stopped and I was met by Mr. Lowman (who was then the head of the Intelligence Branch of the Police) who wanted me to alight. Thinking that he wanted to smuggle me out of Calcutta, I refused. But I was assured that His Excellency the Governor had placed his launch at our disposal and that I had to appear before a Medical Board who were waiting for me there and I then agreed. The board composed of Sir Nilratan Sirkar, Dr. B. C. Roy, Lieut.-Col. Sands and Major Hingston, the Governor's physician, examined me and sent their report by wire to the Governor at Darjeeling. I spent the day in the Governor's launch, and next morning Mr. Lowman, with a telegram in his hand, came to inform me that the Governor had ordered my release. Saying this, he handed over the official order of release. It was May 16th, 1927, but the order was signed on May 11th. It looked like intriguing. I asked Mr. Lowman why they had made a show of a medical examination on May 15th, when the release order had actually been signed on the 11th. He would not reply at first, but on being pressed he said that on May 11th, other orders had also been signed and kept in readiness, including my transfer to Almora and it had been decided that the final decision would come from Darjeeling after the Governor received the report of the Medical Board. Later on, I was to discover that when the Medical Board were considering what report they would make, the police-officers tried their best to make them submit a report in favour of my transfer to Almora, or of my departure to Switzerland, with a view to preventing my release, but fortunately for me, the board refused to do so. Thus, it was clear that till the last moment the Police Department tried to prevent my release. They would undoubtedly have succeeded, if anyone else had been the Governor. Fortunately for me, the new Governor, Sir Stanley Jackson, had come with an open mind and he was a strong man. With the unerring instinct of a trained politician he had sensed the grievance of the people. He had realised within a few days of his arrival that what the people demanded was some protection from the tyrannical Police Department. Under Lord Lytton's regime, the Police Department had ruled and the Commissioner of Police of Calcutta had been the virtual Governor of Bengal. All that was now changed. Within a few weeks of his taking over reins of office, Sir Stanley Jackson gave everyone to understand that henceforth he was to rule Bengal and not the Commissioner of Police. When any conflict arose between the public and the police he endeavoured to do justice even at the risk of offending the latter. For nearly four years he was able to avoid trouble through his firmness and tact. Only when the whole of India was plunged again into the throes of another gigantic upheaval, did Bengal become once again the political storm-centre of India.

CHAPTER VIII

THE BAROMETER RISES (1927-28)

By the middle of 1927 the darkest hour had ended and the horizon began to light up. Disgusted with the narrow sectarianism, selfishness and fanaticism, which had seized the country after the death of the Deshabandhu, the soul of the people began to stir itself again. In the new awakening the contribution of the youth was the largest. The leadership of the Congress was, on the whole, found wanting. Mahatma Gandhi was suffering from acute mental depression and was living in retirement from active politics. Pandit Motilal Nehru had left for Europe, partly owing to professional reasons and partly because of the serious illness of his daughter-in-law. In the circumstances, the responsibility of leadership was vested in Mr. Srinivasa Iyengar and he endeavoured to rise to the occasion. He spent much of his time in 1927 in touring the country for restoring intercommunal amity and friendship. His crowning achievement during the year was a successful session of the Unity Conference in Calcutta in November, convened and presided over by him, which was to pave the way for the coming upheaval in which all communities and parties were to join once again. In Bengal, where the worst demonstration of communal passion had taken place during 1926, there were signs of the dawn of a new era. In August, as a result of a vote of no-confidence in the Bengal Legislative Council, the Ministers were once again thrown out. About this time a strike broke out in the biggest railway workshop of the Bengal Nagpur Railway at Kharagpur, seventy miles from Calcutta. The workers' organisation was so strong that the Company had to climb down and meet the demand of the workers. In November, the Unity Conference in Calcutta helped to clear the atmosphere and restore the friendly feelings hitherto existing between the Hindu and Moslem communities. Later in the month, when the annual meeting of the Bengal Congress Committee [1] was held, there were signs of enthusiasm among the Congress workers of Bengal. The most potent impetus to the new awakening came, however, from the side of the Government.

It was an auspicious moment for the Indian Nationalists when in November 1927 the Viceroy, Lord Irwin, made an announcement, regarding the appointment of the Indian Statutory Commission. The appointment was made under Section 84a of the Government of India Act, 1919, which provided for decennial reviews of the political situation in India, somewhat reminiscent of the political surveys made by the British Parliament into the affairs of the East India Company at the time of the renewal of the Company's Charter. Since the Statutory Commission was due in 1929, it was rather surprising to find a Tory Government accelerating the date of the Commission. The Indian National Congress had been pressing since 1920 for a Round Table Conference for revising the Constitution, with a view to the early introduction of Dominion Home Rule, but this demand had been consistently turned down by the British Government. The Conservative Party had never taken kindly to the Reforms of 1919, for which the Liberal, Mr. Montagu, had been largely responsible, though Indian opinion considered them inadequate and unsatisfactory. They, therefore, wanted to dispose of the Indian question themselves while they were in power, so that the Labour Party, if they happened to succeed them, would not be able to make any further concessions to the Indian demand for Home Rule. Since the next General Election in England was due in 1929, the Conservative Cabinet found it necessary to appoint the Statutory Commission in 1927.

The Commission was composed of Sir John Simon (Chairman), Viscount Burnham, Lord Strathcona, Hon. Edward Cadogan, Mr. Stephen Walsh, Major Attlee and Col. Lane Fox. (Mr. Walsh resigned and was succeeded by Mr. Vernon Hartshorn.) There were seven members,

---

[1] At this meeting of the Bengal Congress Committee the writer was elected President and Mr. Kiron Sankar Roy, Secretary.

of whom two were Labourites, one (viz. the Chairman) was a Liberal, and the rest were Conservatives. Thus the cooperation of all the political parties in Britain was secured for the work of the Commission. The Commission was charged with inquiring into 'the working of the system of government, the growth of education and the development of representative institutions in British India and matters connected therewith and to what extent it is desirable to establish the principle of responsible government or to extend, modify or restrict the degree of responsible government then existing therein, including the question whether the establishment of second chambers of the local legislatures is or is not desirable'. It was stated on behalf of the Government that Indians had perforce to be excluded from the Commission because it was an exclusively Parliamentary Commission and the necessity of having a Parliamentary Commission was explained by the Viceroy in the following words : 'It would be generally agreed that what is required is a Commission which would be unbiased and competent to present an accurate picture of facts to Parliament; but it must also be a body on whose recommendations Parliament should be found willing to take whatever action a study of these facts may indicate to be appropriate.' Simultaneously with the announcement of the Commission, the Viceroy and the Governors of Provinces invited a number of public men in order to explain to them the motive and intention of the Government. The Commission was appointed by Royal Warrant of November 26th, 1927, and Lord Birkenhead, the Secretary of State for India, while speaking in the House of Lords the same month on the appointment of the Commission, challenged Indian politicians to produce an agreed constitution for India.

The announcement regarding the Statutory Commission evoked a chorus of condemnation from the Congress leaders of all parts of India as also from the public at large. The public had become so much accustomed to the idea of self-determination for India, that they no longer regarded the British Parliament as the arbiter of India's destiny. It was therefore but natural that the Congress should, without hesitation or delay, decide to boycott the Commission (popularly known as Simon Commission). That was, of course, no surprise for the Government. But what did surprise them was the decision of the Indian Liberals to boycott the Commission. It was not the violation of the principle of self-determination which offended them but the exclusion of Indians from the All-White Commission. In the face of this non-co-operation on the part of the British Government, how could the Liberals maintain their pet theory of Indo-British collaboration? The attitude of the Liberals was explained by a resolution passed at a public meeting held at Allahabad in December, which was presided over by Sir Tej Bahadur Sapru and which considered 'the exclusion of Indians a deliberate insult to the people of India, as not only does it definitely assign to them a position of inferiority, but what is worse, it denies them the right to participate in the determination of the constitution of their own country'. The tenth session of the Liberal Federation held at Bombay the same year and presided over by the same gentleman, decided to reject the Simon Commission.

Following the Unity Conference in November, the All-India Moslem League met in Calcutta in December. The League passed a resolution recommending Hindu-Moslem unity on the lines laid down by the Unity Conference. It also urged the boycott of the Simon Commission and accepted the principle of joint electorates with reservation of seats for Moslems. This decision was a triumph for the Nationalist Moslems and it was possible only because such prominent Moslems as Mr. M. A. Jinnah and the Ali brothers participated in the Conference and advocated the Nationalist point of view. The same month the All-India Trade Union Congress met at Cawnpore and it witnessed for the first time a compact body of Communists who stood for an independent Socialist Republic and for a definite break with the British Trade Unions in Amsterdam. Towards the end of December the annual session of the Indian National Congress was held at Madras and was presided over by Dr. M. A. Ansari, the Nationalist Moslem leader of Delhi.

The Madras Congress is memorable for two reasons. A resolution was of course passed boycotting the Simon Commission 'at every stage and every form'. But along with that another resolution was passed directing the Executive to convene an All-India All Parties Conference with a view to drawing up a constitution for India acceptable to all parties. A somewhat contradictory resolution was also passed declaring the goal of the Indian people to be 'complete independence'.

The proceedings of the Madras Congress clearly indicated that the appointment of the Simon Commission had been made at an auspicious moment and it had wonderful effect in whipping up the enthusiasm of the people. From one end to the other, the country exhibited a solidarity which it had seldom shown before in recent times. It was this feeling of solidarity, as also the resolve to give an effective reply to Lord Birkenhead's challenge in the House of Lords, which was responsible for the decision to convene an All-Parties Conference. Apart from the effect produced by the appointment of an All-White Commission, there was another factor which at this time put an indelible stamp on the Congress. That was the awakening among the youths. The youthful element in the Congress had been demanding a more extremist ideology for some time past and under their influence, resolutions had been passed from time to time by Provincial Conferences recommending to the Indian National Congress that the goal of the Indian people should be defined as complete national independence. The resolution of the Madras Congress regarding independence[1] was therefore but the logical fulfilment of a process going on within the Congress for a long time. Along with this resolution the Madras Congress took a significant step in appointing to the Working Committee, representatives of the Left Wing. And as General Secre-

[1] This resolution was passed unanimously at the Madras Congress but after the Congress was over, Mahatma Gandhi declared that it had been 'hastily conceived and thoughtlessly passed'. Lala Lajpat Rai declared that it was passed because 'many people believed that Dominion Status also meant national independence'. At the Lahore Congress in December 1929, a similar resolution was moved by the Mahatma and unanimously adopted.

taries for the coming year were appointed Pandit Jawaharlal Nehru (i.e. Nehru Junior), Mr. Shuaib Qureshi and the writer. Thus the Madras Congress may be regarded as standing for a definite orientation towards the Left.

Another factor which lent significance to the proceedings of the Madras Congress was the return of Pandit Jawaharlal Nehru from Europe and his participation in the Congress deliberations. Pandit J. L. Nehru had had a most interesting career. After completing his studies at Cambridge he had been called to the Bar. But when in 1920 the non-co-operation movement was launched, he threw up his professional work and joined the Mahatma. According to popular gossip, he was largely responsible for persuading his father, Pandit Motilal Nehru, to do the same. He did not agree with the Swarajists on the question of working inside the Legislatures and since they came into power, he had voluntarily occupied a back seat in the councils of the Congress. Latterly he had been to Europe with his sick wife and during his stay there he studied some of the latest developments in Europe and especially in Soviet Russia. Since his return to India he gave expression to a new ideology and declared himself to be a Sociolist, which was extremely welcome to the Left Wing in the Congress and to the youth organisation in the country. The new phase in his public career was first given expression to at the Madras Congress.

The solid wall of opposition put up against the Simon Commission came as an eye-opener to the Government. Something had to be done to soften the opposition. Therefore, soon after his arrival in India, in February 1928, Sir John Simon wrote to the Viceroy suggesting that the sittings of the Commission should be in the nature of a 'Joint Free Conference' consisting of the seven British members and a body of representatives chosen by the Indian Legislatures. In response to an inquiry from Sir Sankaran Nair, Sir John Simon further stated that the reports submitted by the Committees appointed by the Legislatures would be attached to the main report to be submitted to Parliament by the Commission. In spite of the above modification proposed by Sir John Simon, leaders of all parties soon after declared in a manifesto issued from Delhi that their opposition to the Simon Commission still held good. In the Indian Legislative Assembly, Lala Lajpat Rai moved a resolution repudiating the Simon Commission and this was duly carried. No committee could accordingly be appointed by the Assembly to co-operate with the Simon Commission. Of the Provincial Legislatures, the Central Provinces Legislative Council alone was able to resist the appointment of a committee. In spite of the opposition of the Congress and Liberal Parties, all the other Provincial Legislatures, however, appointed committees to co-operate with the Commission.

The arrival of the Simon Seven in India in February 1928, was greeted with an All-India 'hartal' or boycott-demonstration, organised under the direction of the Congress Working Committee. Enthusiasm all over the country and particularly in Bengal was very great. The public expected a positive lead from the Congress leaders, which could bring the boycott home to those against whom it was directed. But no such directions came from the Congress headquarters. Only in Bengal, the Provincial Congress Committee on its own responsibility launched an intensive campaign for the boycott of British goods, the day the Commission landed in Bombay. There is absolutely no doubt that if the Congress Working Committee had taken courage in both hands, they could have anticipated the movement of 1930 by two years and the appointment of the Simon Commission could have been made the starting point of such a movement. When the writer visited the Mahatma in May 1928, at his Ashram, at Sabarmati, he reported to him the public enthusiasm which he had met with in many provinces and begged him to come out of his retirement and give a lead to the country. At that time the reply of the Mahatma was that he did not see any light, though before his very eyes the peasantry of Bardoli were demonstrating through a no-tax campaign that they were ready for a struggle. During the whole of 1928 and 1929, there was so much unrest in the labour world that if a political campaign had been started at that time, it would have been well-timed. Moreover, in 1928 and 1929, there was more enthusiasm and excitement in provinces like Punjab and Bengal than in 1930. In 1930, when the movement was launched by the Mahatma, the labour unrest had subsided to a large extent and the situation in some provinces was much quieter than before. After starting the movement in 1930, the Mahatma observed in his paper, *Young India,* that he could have launched the campaign two years earlier. The responsibility for not utilising the situation in 1928 devolves not only on the Mahatma but also on the Swarajist leaders who had the Congress machinery in their hands at the time, but who had unfortunately lost their dynamic impulse. If a leader like Deshabandhu Das had been available then, the events following the boycott of the Prince of Wales' visit to India in 1921 would have been repeated in 1928.

Undeterred by the opposition which faced them, the Simon Seven travelled from place to place. Wherever they went, they met black flags, hostile demonstrations and shouts of 'Simon go back'. The Government tried to organise counter-demonstrations with the help of a section of the Moslems and a section of the depressed classes but such attempts did not meet with success. Though the boycott campaign was kept strictly within the limits of non-violence, elaborate arrangements were made wherever the Commission went and in some places unnecessarily harsh repression was resorted to. In the clashes that took place between the unarmed public and the armed police in different parts of the country, generally there were no serious consequences except in one place—Lahore. There the black procession which was being led by Lala Lajpat Rai was charged by the police with sticks and batons. Lala Lajpat Rai, who was in the front rank of the procession, was seriously injured in the attack and was laid up in bed for some time. He recovered to some extent at first but there was some permanent injury to his heart which caused a relapse leading to his death. Great sorrow and indignation followed the death of Lalaji and since the Simon Commission was indirectly responsible for his death, the Commission became more unpopular with the people who used to idolise the great Punjab leader.

The activities of the leaders were not confined to a negative boycott of the Commission. The great task ahead of them was to give a fitting reply to the challenge of Lord Birkenhead by producing an agreed constitution. To that end, the All-Parties Conference met at Delhi in February and March 1928. The most thorny problem which the Conference had to tackle was the question of Hindu-Moslem-Sikh representation in the Legislatures under the new Constitution. When the Conference re-assembled in May at Bombay, the outlook appeared gloomy, because no progress whatsoever had been made. Thanks to the prudence of Mahatma Gandhi, the Conference instead of publicly recording its failure, appointed a small committee with Pandit Motilal Nehru as Chairman, to determine the principles of the new Constitution for India and draft a report thereon. The Committee met frequently at Allahabad and ultimately issued its report[1] in August which was unanimous, subject to certain reservations made in the preamble, and was signed by Pandit Motilal Nehru, Sir Ali Imam, Sir Tej Bahadur Sapru, Mr. M. S. Aney, Sardar Mangal Singh, Mr. Shuaib Qureshi, Mr. G. R. Pradhan and the writer. The Report of the Committee, popularly known as the Nehru Committee, was cordially welcomed by all Nationalists in the country as it rendered the work of the Simon Commission superfluous. Mahatma Gandhi sent his warmest congratulations to Pandit Motilal Nehru who had worked so much over the report and for whom it was a great achievement. The report was placed before the plenary session of the All-Parties Conference in Lucknow in August and was unanimously adopted. It was again placed before the All-Parties Convention in December 1928, in Calcutta, and objections were raised at that meeting by the representatives of the Moslem League, Sikh League and Hindu

---

[1] Report of the Committee appointed by the All-Parties Conference to determine the principles of the Constitution for India. Published by the Indian National Congress, Allahabad, 1928.

Mahasabha. The opposition of the Moslem League was the most serious and served to rouse the opposition of the other two bodies.

It was stated in the preamble to the Nehru Report that the Committee could not be unanimous on the question of the fundamental basis of the Constitution, since a minority[1] would not accept Dominion Status and pressed for complete national independence, as the basis of the Constitution. The majority of the members of the Nehru Committee, however, adopted Dominion Status as the basis of the Constitution without restricting the liberty of action of those political parties whose goal was complete independence. The Constitution outlined in the Report was only for British India. With regard to the Indian States, the Report stated that the Central Government should exercise the same rights in relation to, and discharge the same obligation towards, the Indian States, arising out of the treaties or otherwise, as the present Government of India had exercised and discharged. A future federal linking up of the Indian States with the rest of India was, however, looked forward to, whenever the States were ready for the surrender of rights which federation necessitated. The Report recommended autonomy for the provinces and suggested the creation of Sind and Karnataka as separate provinces. The Executive, both in the provinces and at the centre, was to be responsible to the Legislature. The Central Legislature was to be composed of a Senate and House of Representatives—the Senate to be elected by the Provincial Legislatures. Every adult of either sex was to be entitled to vote and there would be joint electorates for Hindu, Moslem and other communities. For a minority community, there would be reservation of seats for a period of ten years only. In Bengal and Punjab there would be no reservation of seats at all. There would be a Supreme Court for India and a radical restriction of appeals to the Privy Council. The Civil Services would be under the control of the Central Government. The Report further enumerated nineteen fundamental rights which were to be embodied

---

[1] The present writer was among them.

in the Statute. The residuary powers were to be vested in the Central Government.

The greatest achievement of the Nehru Committee was the settlement of the question of Hindu-Moslem-Sikh representation in the Legislatures under the proposed Constitution. Such an achievement would not have been possible so soon after the recent intercommunal disturbances, but for the new situation created by the appointment of the Simon Commission. The Report provided for a common electorate for all communities. Minority communities would be entitled to a reservation of seats in the Legislature in proportion to their population and they would, in addition, have the right to contest the elections for the other seats. The reservation would, however, be only for a period of ten years. For Bengal and Punjab, the Committee decided to have no reservation at all. The Hindus, who are in a minority in these two provinces, did not demand any reservation, as being against the principle of nationalism— and the Committee considered it unfair and unreasonable that there should be a reservation of seats for the majority community—namely, the Moslems. As for the Sikhs, they were prepared to forego reservation of seats for their community if the other two communities did so—and if they did not, then the Sikhs demanded representation in excess of their numbers. Besides the question of principle which appealed to the Nehru Committee, practical considerations also showed that the best solution of the Bengal and Punjab problem would be not to have any reservation there. In Bengal, under the existing Constitution, the Moslems have 40 per cent of the elected seats and the Hindus 60 per cent—while the Moslem population is about 54 per cent and the Hindu population about 46 per cent. In Punjab under the existing Constitution, the Moslems have 50 per cent of the elected seats, the Hindus 31 per cent and the Sikhs 19 per cent, while in population the Moslems are 55 per cent, the Hindus 34 per cent and the Sikhs 11 per cent. The Hindu-Moslem-Sikh representation now in vogue is based on the 'Congress-League Scheme' which was adopted as a compromise between the Indian National Congress and the All-India Moslem League at Lucknow in 1926. In proportion to their population, the Moslem representation in Bengal and Punjab was reduced under the 'Congress-League Scheme', because in the other provinces the Moslems got representation far in excess of their numbers and the adjustment of Hindu-Moslem interests was made on an All-India basis. Moslem representation as provided under the Congress-League Scheme was no longer acceptable to the Moslems of Bengal and Punjab. At the same time the Nehru Committee found it well-nigh impossible to fix another proportion which would be acceptable to the parties concerned. Therefore, from the practical point of view also, the Committee found it advisable to decide on non-reservation of seats in Bengal and Punjab.

While the Nehru Committee was engaged in threshing out the principles of the New Constitution, interesting events were taking place elsewhere. In May 1928, I was called upon to preside over the Maharashtra Provincial Conference at Poona. The enthusiasm I met with there was striking. In my speech I advocated some new lines of activity for Congressmen which I had decided on during my prolonged incarceration in Burma. For instance, I urged that the Congress should directly take up the task of organising labour and that youths and students should start organisations of their own for looking after their own interests and also for serving their country. I also urged separate political organisations for women, in addition to their participation in the Congress organisations. From Poona I went to Bombay and found that the youths there had already founded the Bombay Presidency Youth League and were preparing to take the initiative in national service at a time when the Congress Committee was not giving the lead expected of it. The month of June found a no-tax campaign in full swing in the Bardoli sub-division in Gujerat where in 1922 the Mahatma had sounded the order of retreat. A 20 per cent increase in land revenue assessment had been ordered by the Government and the peasants under the leadership of Mr. Vallabhbhai Patel (the younger of the Patel brothers) refused to pay and resorted to

Satyagraha. The usual police repression followed, including the confiscation of property and land. A heroic non-violent battle was waged by the peasantry of Bardoli for several months and ultimately the Government had to yield. The whole of Bombay Presidency—and particularly Bombay city—rallied to the support of the Bardoli peasants and women took an active part in the movement. The Bardoli campaign was the precursor of the larger fight that Bombay was to wage in 1930. Out of this campaign Mr. Vallabhbhai Patel emerged with a great reputation. Prior to this he was of course known as one of the sincerest and staunchest lieutenants of the Mahatma but the Bardoli victory brought him into the front rank of India's leaders. In appreciation of his heroic service, the Mahatma gave him the title of 'Sardar' (meaning leader) by which he is now generally called.

At the time of the All-Parties Conference in Lucknow in August, a new development took place. While the settlement of the communal question made by the Nehru Committee was welcome to the younger Nationalists, the recommendation regarding a dominion form of government, coming as it did after the Madras Congress resolution on independence, was quite unacceptable to them. Their intention, therefore, was to oppose the adoption of the Report at the All-Parties Conference at Lucknow. Such a step would have given great satisfaction and delight to the enemies of the Congress, would have weakened the forces working for national unity and would have increased the prestige of the Simon Commission instead of destroying it. A private meeting of members of the Congress Left Wing was therefore held at Lucknow to decide our course of action and Pandit Jawaharlal Nehru and I suggested that instead of dividing the House and thereby wrecking the All-Parties Conference, we should content ourselves by voicing our protest at the Conference and then proceed to organise an Independence League in order to carry on an active propaganda in the country in favour of independence. This suggestion was accepted by the meeting of Left-Wingers and following it, Pandit J. L. Nehru and I made our position clear at the All-Parties Conference on the question of independence, but refrained from dividing the House. After the Conference, we started organising branches of the Independence League all over the country and in November, at a meeting held at Delhi, the Independence League was formally inaugurated.

The 'Independence Movement' started at Lucknow was contemporaneous with another movement—viz. the Students' Movement. When the boycott of the Simon Commission was launched in February, students all over Bengal and particularly in Calcutta, took an active part in it. Disciplinary action was taken against many of them by the College authorities and the students then began to feel the want of an organisation of their own for fighting for their interests. Out of this experience the Students' Movement in Bengal was born.[1] The first All-Bengal Conference of students was held in August in Calcutta and was presided over by Pandit Jawaharlal Nehru. After the Conference, students' organisations were started all over Bengal and somewhat later, similar organisations were started in other provinces as well. The unrest in the student world was accompanied by unrest in the labour world as well. The year before, there had been a strike at Kharagpore not far from Calcutta, among the railway workers. In 1928 a strike broke out in the Tata Iron & Steel Works[2] at Jamshedpur, about 160 miles south-west of Calcutta, in which 18,000 workers were involved. The strike dragged on for some months. Ultimately a settlement was arrived at between the workers and the management, which was extremely favourable to the former. Even more important than the Tata Strike was the Textile Strike in Bombay in which at least 60,000 workers were involved. This strike was in the first stage

---

[1] Pandit Jawaharlal Nehru and the writer were among the few public men who encouraged the students at the time to organise themselves.

[2] Owing to pressure from the workers the writer took up the leadership of the strike when it was about to collapse. The strike was then revived and strengthened and it led to an honourable settlement. Unfortunately differences broke out among the workers after the settlement and this had disastrous consequences. The Tata strike served for the writer as an initiation into the workers' movement, with which he has been intimately connected ever since.

a phenomenal success and caused serious embarrassment not only to the mill-owners but to the Government as well. Following this, there was a strike in the workshop of the East India Railway at Lillooah near Calcutta in which 10,000 workers were involved, in the Tinplate Company at Jamshedpur in which 4,000 workers were involved, in the Oil and Petrol Works at Budge-Budge about twenty miles from Calcutta, in which 6,000 workers were involved, and last but not least, in the Jute Mills in and near Calcutta, in which about 200,000 workers were involved. The Bombay textile strike deserves special mention because it was under the leadership of a compact disciplined party who were alleged to hold communistic ideas and some of whom at least declared themselves later at the Meerut Conspiracy Case Trial to be avowed Communists. Most of the above strikes were conducted by the more militant section in the Trade Union Congress and they were therefore gaining in importance from day to day. Towards the end of the year, when the Trade Union Congress met at Jharia in the mining area, it was found that the Left Wing had considerably increased their numbers and among them, the Communists were a compact and well disciplined group. A new move was taken at this Congress in as much as the Trade Union Congress was affiliated to the League against Imperialism.[1]

December was as usual a month of Congresses and conferences. The most important among them were the All-India Youth Congress (which was going to hold its first session), the All-Parties Convention and the Indian National Congress. The Youth Congress was presided over by Mr. K. F. Nariman, the Parsi leader from Bombay, who had grown extremely popular with the Congress Left Wing. A lawyer by profession, he was at first a Swarajist member of the Bombay Legislative Council where he distinguished himself as an able fighter. He, however, came into prominence through his attempt to expose publicly the colossal waste

---

[1] The League against Imperialism was at first declared to be a non-Communist body and the Indian National Congrss as well as the All-India Trade Union Congress were affiliated to it. Later on when the League became virtually a Communist body, the National Congress and the Trade Union Congress ceased to affiliate themselves any longer.

of money which had resulted from the Back Bay Reclamation Scheme of the Bombay Government. He had to face a defamation suit in the Court of law because of the allegations he made, but he came out of it with flying colours. Mr. Nariman, since he came into prominence, continued to uphold and give expression to extremist views until he was made a member of the Congress Working Committee at the instance of the Mahatma. The Youth Congress was important in as much as it indicated the emergence of a new factor in the public life of the country and gave expression to a mentality somewhat different from that which prevailed within the precincts of the National Congress.[1]

The All-Parties Convention held in Calcutta during the Congress week had unfortunate consequences. All those who did not have a hand in drafting the Nehru Report now made a dead set against it. Mr. M. A. Jinnah, who a year earlier had advocated a progressive nationalist point of view at the Moslem League Conference in Calcutta, now came forward with his famous 'fourteen points' in order to amend the communal settlement embodied in the Nehru Report. He demanded, among other things, one-third of the elected seats in both Houses of the Indian Legislature for Moslems, reservation of seats for Moslems in Bengal and Punjab on a population basis, vesting of residuary powers in the provinces, etc. This attitude served to make Mr. Jinnah popular with his reactionary co-religionists but undermined the value and importance of the Nehru Report. Following the Moslems, the Sikhs also made extreme demands, while the representatives of the Hindu Mahasabha refused to make any further concessions beyond what had been already embodied in the Nehru Report, and they even criticised adversely the concessions made by the Nehru Committee to the Moslem demands. It was difficult to get the support

---

[1] In his speech as the Chairman of the Reception Committee the writer advocated activism, as opposed to the passivism which was being preached from Sabarmati Ashrama of the Mahatma and Pondicherry Ashrama of Sri Aurobindo Ghosh. He also pleaded for modernisation of the material side of life. The speech caused resentment among the followers of the Mahatma and Sri Aurobindo Ghosh.

of the Moslem League for the Nehru Report, because of the parties within that body, based largely on personal considerations. For instance, the group led by the late Sir Mohmmed Shafi took up a *non-possums* attitude on the communal question, and on the political question advocated co-operation with the Simon Commission. The Nationalist bloc stood for wholehearted acceptance of the Nehru Report and for complete boycott of the Simon Commission. The group led by Mr. Jinnah had a reactionary attitude on the communal question but advocated the boycott of the Simon Commission. A meeting of the Moslem League was summoned at Delhi in March 1929, to consider the question and there was a clash between the warring sections, so that the meeting ended in pandemonium.

In December 1927, when the Madras Congress decided in favour of convening an All-Parties Conference, it appeared as if the decision was a right one. This feeling was confirmed when the Nehru Committee was able to produce a unanimous report and the All-Parties Conference at Lucknow in August 1928 adopted it. But subsequent experience has shown that it was a mistake for the Congress to take this step, as it was a mistake for the Congress to participate in a Round Table Conference in which other people were present who had no right to be there. The responsibility for producing a constitution belongs solely and exclusively to the party that fights for freedom. A report drafted by an All-Parties Committee can have value only if it is ratified by all parties in the country. But such ratification is never possible in a country which has been under foreign rule for some time. In such a country, there are bound to be parties which are under the thumb of the Government and these parties can always hold up the ratification of a document like the Nehru Report. Moreover, what is the value of such ratification when the other parties are not going to fight for freedom? The party that fights, should not, therefore, look up to any other party to produce the constitution for which it alone is fighting.

The most important conference of the year was the annual session of the Indian National Congress held in Calcutta and presided over by Pandit Motilal Nehru. The attendance at the Calcutta session was the largest since the inception of the Congress and all arrangements were made on a colossal scale. Within the Congress there were two groups—the older group who would be content if they had a Dominion form of Government and who were therefore in favour of accepting the Nehru Report *in toto*, and the Left Wing who adhered to the resolution of independence passed at the Madras Congress and wanted to accept the Nehru Report only on the basis of complete national independence. At a meeting of the All-India Congress Committee held in Delhi in November, a compromise had been arrived at between the two groups, at the instance of Pandit Motilal Nehru. At the Calcutta session of the Congress, however, the Mahatma refused to accept the Delhi formula on the ground that it was self-contradictory and the breach between the two groups was thus opened once again. Attempts for a compromise were made by the Mahatma and Pandit Motilal Nehru, but the maximum concession which they could make fell short of the minimum demand of the Left Wingers. Though the Left Wing leaders were inclined to avoid an open split, the rank and file of the Left Wing would not think of a compromise. Thus the main resolution of the Congress moved by Mahatma Gandhi was opposed by the entire Left Wing, who supported the amendment moved by the writer. The Mahatma's resolution stated that 'subject to the exigencies of the political situation, the Congress will adopt the Nehru constitution in its entirety, if it is accepted by the British Parliament on or before December 31st, 1929; but in the event of its non-acceptance by that date, or its earlier rejection, the Congress will organise non-violent non-co-operation by advising the country to refuse taxation and in such other manner as may be decided upon'. An amendment to the effect that the Congress would be content with nothing short of independence, which implied severance of the British connection, was moved by the writer and was supported, among others, by Pandit Jawaharlal Nehru. The amendment was lost by 973 votes to 1350—but the vote could hardly be called a free one, as the followers of the Mahatma made it a question of confidence and gave out that if the Mahatma was defeated, he would retire from the Congress. Many people therefore voted for his resolution not out of conviction, but because they did not want to be a party to forcing the Mahatma out of the Congress. Nevertheless, the voting showed that the Left Wing was strong and influential.

The Calcutta Congress, coming after the Madras Congress, was in the nature of an anti-climax. The President-elect on the day of his arrival was given an ovation which would excite the envy of kings and dictators, but when he left, there was disappointment writ large on every face. There was tremendous enthusiasm all over the country at the time and every one had expected the Congress to act boldly. But while the country was ready, the leaders were not. The Mahatma, unfortunately for his countrymen, did not see light. Hence the temporising resolution of the Calcutta Congress which only served to kill precious time. Only madness or folly could have led one to hope that the mighty British Government would concede even Dominion Home Rule without a struggle. During the sittings of the Congress a procession of 10,000 workers visited the Congress pandal to demonstrate their solidarity with struggle for national freedom and to appeal to the Congress to take up the cause of the starving workers. But all these signs of upheaval made no impression on the leaders. The decision that should have been made soon after the appointment of the Simon Commission—and certainly not later than the Calcutta Congress—was not made till the Lahore Congress in December 1929. But by then the situation was to deteriorate.

CHAPTER IX

## SIGNS OF COMING UPHEAVAL (1929)

The net result of the Calcutta Congress, as we have seen, was to put the clock back. But a far-sighted politician like the Mahatma could read the signs of the times. The Left Wing opposition at the Calcutta Congress had indeed been formidable and if his leadership was to be retained, he would have to deal with the opposition in a diplomatic manner. The tactics employed by the Mahatma during the next twelve months were indeed superb. As we shall presently see, he took the wind out of the sails of the Extremists,[1] by himself advocating independence at the next Congress and divided the ranks of the opposition by winning over some of the Left Wing leaders. The Left Wing opposition had become a menace to all sections among the older leaders, to the Swarajists as much as to the 'No-changers', and the Calcutta Congress had found the Swarajist Pandit Motilal Nehru standing side by side with the 'No-Changer' Mahatma Gandhi, in order to fight the common danger. This temporary alliance was further strengthened during the ensuing months and with the help of a section of the Left Wing leaders, it became possible for the Mahatma to regain his hold on the Congress machinery and his prestige in the country, which had been badly shaken by the proceedings of the Calcutta Congress.

No one can seriously maintain that a shrewd politician like the Mahatma really expected the Government to climb down and to concede Dominion Home Rule without a fight, merely as a result of a written ultimatum delivered by the Congress. Therefore, one would be entitled to hold that at the Calcutta Congress the Mahatma was merely playing

---

[1] He began this propaganda soon after the Calcutta Congress by stating publicly that if by December 31st, 1929, the Government did not concede Dominion Status to India, he would become an 'Independence-wallah' on January 1st, 1930. This time-limit of one year was reminiscent of his promise of Swaraj within one year in 1921.

for time, because he was personally unprepared to launch a fight in the immediate future. As a matter of fact, even at the Lahore Congress in December 1929, the Mahatma had no plans for launching an anti-Government campaign of any sort—though he moved the resolution on independence, which was unanimously adopted by the Congress. Not till February 1930, after much searching of heart, did he make up his mind to start a civil-disobedience movement in the country, beginning with the campaign for the manufacture of salt. But though the Congress did not give a bold and intelligent lead to the country during the whole of 1929, the unrest did not abate in any way. On the contrary, the forces making for revolution began to grow stronger and stronger, while owing to lack of co-ordination much dissipation of energy resulted. Besides the main current of the Congress movement, three other lines of activity were clearly visible at this time. There was an undercurrent of revolutionary activity with a certain amount of following in northern India, an unrest in the labour world which extended to every part of the country, and an awakening among the middle-class youths which was manifest everywhere.

The visible expression of the revolutionary movement was afforded by two incidents which occurred at Lahore and at Delhi. At Lahore an Inspector of Police, Mr. Saunders, a Britisher, was assassinated. It was reported that the revolutionaries believed that Mr. Saunders was responsible for the attack on Lala Lajpat Rai at the time of the anti-Simon demonstration in Lahore in 1928, which ultimately resulted in his death and that his assassination was an act of reprisal. The other incident was the throwing of a bomb in the Assembly at Delhi during a sitting and two young men, Sardar Bhagat Singh and Mr. Batukeshwar Dutt, were arrested in connection therewith. After these overt acts, there was a round-up of a large number of young men from all over the country and an All-India conspiracy case was started at Lahore about the middle of 1929. For some reason or other, the Lahore conspiracy case excited not only public interest but public sympathy as well. The reasons probably were that prior to his arrest, Sardar Bhagat Singh was known to be the leader of the youth movement (called the Naujawan Bharat Sabha) in the Punjab, and the fearless and defiant attitude adopted by him and his comrades, after their arrest and during their trial, made a deep impression on the public. Moreover, Sardar Bhagat Singh came from a wellknown patriotic family—being a nephew of Sardar Ajit Singh, who had been deported to Burma in 1909 along with Lala Lajpat Rai. The Naujawan Bharat Sabha was first started as a thorough-going nationalist movement, in order to fight communalism and religious fanaticism in the Punjab. If the official allegations are to believed, the Sabha developed into a revolutionary organisation and some members of the Sabha also went in for terrorist activities. Whatever the truth or otherwise of the allegations may be, there is no doubt that the Sabha developed a frankly Socialistic tendency. And incidentally it may be remarked that all youth organisations in the Punjab have a strong Socialist bent. In March 1931, when a session of the All-India Naujawan Bharat Sabha was held at Karachi, members of the Punjab Naujawan Bharat Sabha openly declared that they were against terrorism and that they believed in mass action on Socialist lines.

Soon after their arrest, the Lahore Conspiracy Case prisoners, headed by Sardar Bhagat Singh, made a demand that they should be accorded better treatment than ordinary criminals on the ground that they were political prisoners and under trial, who should be deemed to be innocent until they were actually convicted. After trying usual constitutional methods, when they found that no remedy was forthcoming, they resorted to hunger-strike. Among the prisoners was a young man from Calcutta, Mr. Jatindra Nath Das, who was at first rather averse to hunger-strike because he regarded it as a dangerous game to play. The enthusiasm of the rest forced him to join the strike but before doing so, he warned them that come what may, he would not turn back until their demands were fully conceded. There was an intense agitation throughout the country over the hunger-strike and there was a public demand that the

Government should remedy their just grievances and thereby save their lives. When the condition of the prisoners grew serious, the Government made half-hearted attempts at compromise. For instance, they offered better treatment to the hunger-strikers on medical grounds. But their demand was not merely for better treatment for themselves, but for all prisoners similarly circumstanced and on the ground that they were political prisoners. To this demand the Government would not yield and so the strike went on. Besides an intensive Press agitation, meetings and demonstrations were held all over the country demanding humane treatment for political prisoners. In connection with a demonstration of this kind in Calcutta, a number of prominent Congressmen, including the writer, were arrested in September and sent up for trial for sedition.

As the days rolled by, one by one the hunger-strikers dropped off but young Jatin was invincible. He never hesitated, never faltered for one small second—but marched straight on towards death and freedom. Every heart in the country melted but the heart of the bureaucracy did not. So Jatin died on September 13th. But he died the death of a martyr. After his death the whole country gave him an ovation which few men in the recent history of India have received. As his dead body was removed from Lahore to Calcutta for cremation, people assembled in their thousands and tens of thousands at every station to pay their homage. His martyrdom acted as a profound inspiration to the youths of India and everywhere youth and student organisations began to grow up. Among the many messages that were received on the occasion was one which touched the heart of every Indian. It was a message from the family of Terence McSwiney, the Lord Mayor of Cork, who had died a martyr under similar conditions in Ireland. The message ran thus : 'Family of Terence McSwiney have heard with grief and pride of the death of Jatin Das. Freedom will come.'

Jatin Das was twenty-five at the time of his death. While a student he had joined the non-co-operation movement in 1921 and had spent several years in prison. After a break of many years he had resumed his studies again at a Calcutta College. At the time of the Calcutta Congress in 1928 and after, he had taken a leading part in organising and training volunteers and in the Bengal Volunteer Corps, of which the writer was the Chief Officer or G.O.C., he held the rank of Major. The Bengal Volunteer Corps came into existence at the time of the Calcutta Congress. For the Congress and the National Exhibition connected with it, a large body of volunteers had been necessary and the writer had been entrusted by the Congress authorities with the organisation and training of the Corps. Though the Corps was a peaceful and unarmed body, military discipline and training in military drill was imparted to the volunteers and they were also given a semi-military uniform. After the Congress was over, the Volunteer Corps was maintained and branches were opened all over the province. In this arduous work, Jatin had played an important role. The officers and rank and file of the Volunteer Corps therefore took a leading part in the funeral demonstrations.

In this connection the attitude of the Mahatma was inexplicable. Evidently the martyrdom of Jatin Das which had stirred the heart of the country did not make any impression on him. The pages of *Young India* ordinarily filled with observations on all political events and also on topics like health, diet, etc. had nothing to say about the incident. A follower of the Mahatma who was also a close friend of the deceased, wrote to him inquiring as to why he had said nothing about the event. The Mahatma replied to the effect that he had purposely refrained from commenting, because if he had done so, he would have been forced to write something unfavourable.

The news of the self-immolation of Jatin Das was received in Delhi when the Assembly was in session. For a moment it looked as if the heart of the Government throbbed. But the throbbing was a momentary phenomenon. What emotion was roused at the time was soon drowned in official diplomacy and duplicity. The Government promised to take up the question of the treatment of political prisoners but after a great deal of deliberation and delay, when the public excitement had somewhat abated, they finally produced their proposals. It was then found that the remedy suggested was worse than the disease. At the outset the Government refused to class anyone as a political prisoner—so that the principal demand of the Lahore hunger-strikers was turned down. The Government proposed instead that prisoners would in future be put into either of three classes—A, B, and C or Divisions, I, II and III respectively. C class prisoners would be treated exactly like ordinary criminals; B class prisoners would be treated slightly better than C class in the matter of food, letters, interviews and other facilities—while A class prisoners would be treated somewhat better than B class. The distinction at the time of classification would be made according to the social status of the prisoner. When these rules were applied in practice, it was found that at least 95 per cent of the political prisoners were classed as C; about 3 or 4 per cent were classed as B and less than 1 per cent as A. The effect of the new rules therefore was to give somewhat better treatment to a microscopic minority in order to break the solidarity of the political prisoners. The principle of 'divide and rule' was thus extended to the domain of prison administration. The only welcome feature in the new rule was that it abolished in theory the classification of certain prisoners as 'European', who used to get better food, clothing and accommodation than Indians of the highest rank. In practice, however, the writer has personally seen that in many provinces, e.g. Bengal, Central Provinces and Madras, the facilities previously enjoyed by 'European' prisoners are still being continued. And in the Madras Penitentiary, where the writer was confined for two months in 1932, he even found the placard 'European Ward' in front of the ward occupied by 'European' prisoners and on his objecting to it, the placard was removed. In this connection it should be admitted that when the new rules were drafted, the Assembly members, including the Swarajists, did not put up the opposition expected of them. And some members like Mr. Jinnah, who had no experience of prison life, even thought that the rules would prove to be a blessing.

As has been already remarked, the years 1928 and 1929 witnessed an unprecedented awakening among the youths.[1] The halting attitude of the Congress at Calcutta and the stale tactics of the Swarajists in the Legislatures roused the youths to a sense of their duty. The success of the first session of the Youth Congress in Calcutta served as an inspiration and a further impetus came from the undying example set by Jatindra Nath Das through his martyrdom. Throughout 1929, youth and student organisations grew up all over Bengal, as branches of the Provincial Youth Association and Provincial Students' Association. Besides the political conferences held in different districts of Bengal from time to time, separate conferences for youths and for students began to be held from now onwards. In other provinces too, the same phenomena were visible. In Poona, the Maharashtra Youth Conference was held and Pandit Jawaharlal Nehru presided over it. In Ahmedabad, the Bombay Presidency Youth Conference met in October 1929, and was presided over by Mrs. Kamaladevi Chattopadhyaya, sister-in-law of Mrs. Sarojini Naidu, who within a short time had become a popular figure among the youths. In september, the first session of the Punjab Students' Conference was held in Lahore and was presided over by the writer. Following this, the Central Provinces Youth Conference was held in November at Nagpur and the Berar Students' Conference at Amraoti in December, both being presided over by the writer. In the Madras Presidency, too, similar conferences were held. At the end of the year, at Lahore, during the Congress week, an All-India Congress of Students was held and was presided over by Pandit Madan Mohan Malaviya, the Vice-Chancellor of the Benares Hindu University.

The awakening among the youths was contemporane-

---

[1] This was followed immediately by a similar awakening among women. In Bengal the Deshabandhu had started in 1921 the 'Nari Karma Mandir' for training women for national service. After his death this institution ceased to exist. In 1928 when the writer resumed his public activities, a political organisation for women was started under the name of the 'Mahila Rashtriya Sangha' in Calcutta, which was followed by many other organisations all over the country.

ous with a widespread unrest in the labour world and there were strikes all over the country. But the strike which unnerved the Government most was the textile strike which commenced in 1928 in Bombay, because it was conducted by a compact party of well-educated men and women following communistic ideas. The employers and the Government made common cause in their efforts to break the strike and a large number of rowdy blacklegs were imported from outside for the purpose. When the strike showed signs of weakening, the Government struck hard. A round-up of trade union leaders holding advanced ideas was made simultaneously all over India in March 1929, and thirty-one of them were brought to Meerut, near Delhi, for trial in connection with an All-India Communist Conspiracy Case. They were brought to Meerut from all places for trial, probably because Meerut being a small town, there would be no public demonstration there and also because trial by jury does not obtain there. There were three Englishmen among them and probably because of this, the case roused great interest and sympathy among British Labour circles of all shades of opinion. The trial dragged on for nearly four years and during this period, bail was refused to the accused, though repeatedly asked for. The prosecution case was that the accused had conspired to deprive the King of the sovereignty of India and with the help of the Communist International had endeavoured to set up a government on the Soviet model. On January 16th, 1933, judgment was delivered. Three of the accused were acquitted and the rest (excluding one who had died during the course of trial) were sentenced to various terms of imprisonment—from three years' imprisonment to transportation for life.

The Meerut arrests were made when the Conservative Party was in power but in June, as a result of the General Election, the Labour Party came into office with Captain Wedgwood-Benn as the Secretary of State for India. It was expected that the Labour Party would do something for the Meerut prisoners but actually nothing was done. Nevertheless, another move was taken by the Labour Cabinet in order to placate Indian Labour circles. As the Labour counterpart of the Simon Commission, a Royal Commission on Labour was appointed, with Mr. Whitely as the Chairman. The Commission was to report on labour conditions in India and the possible lines of amelioration. Having gathered experience from the boycott of the Simon Commission, the Labour Government offered two seats to Indian trade-union leaders—to Mr. N. M. Joshi (Bombay) and Mr. Chamanlal (Lahore). Both of them who belonged to the Right Wing of the Labour Movement accepted the offer and that decision at once created a split among Indian trade-unionists. When the Congress met at Nagpur in November with Pandit Jawaharlal Nehru as the President, it was found that the majority were for the boycott of the Labour Commission (called the Whitley Commission). Several factors accounted for this. Boycott was then in the air. Moreover, the Labour Cabinet having failed to do anything for the Meerut prisoners, it was felt that a Commission appointed by them would be of no benefit to India. Thirdly, the sweeping arrests made in March last all over India had created sympathy in trade union circles for the Left Wingers. When the boycott resolution was carried, there were shouts of 'Down with Chamanlal,' 'Down with Joshi', etc., and placards were also displayed to that effect. These demonstrations against Mr. Joshi who had done so much for the Indian Labour Movement and may be justly regarded as one of the fathers of that movement—greatly offended the Right Wingers who walked out of the Congress. Thereafter, they set up an organisation of their own under the name of the 'All-India Trade Union Federation'. The reason generally given for the secession was that the Trade Union Congress had affiliated itself to the League against Imperialism and the Pan-Pacific Trade Union Secretariat—both of which were Communist organisations. But the real reason was the boycott of the Whitley Commission which if given effect to, would have entailed the resignation of Messrs. Joshi and Chamanlal from that body. As for the affiliation to the League against Imperialism, it should be noted that it was done at the Jharia session of

## SIGNS OF COMING UPHEAVAL (1929)

the Trade Union Congress in 1928—but at that time the Right-Wing Trade-Unionists were able to swallow the resolution because they were still strong enough to keep the Secretariat in their hands. As a matter of fact, the Right Wingers were defeated over the question of the Whitely Commission, not because the Communists were in a majority but because the Centre Party who were not Communists, sided with them on that question. Consequently, if the Right Wingers had not seceded from the Trade Union Congress at Nagpur, they would still have played an important role. But they would have to suffer one disadvantage—which probably they were not prepared to do—namely, to forgo the annual trip to Geneva on the occasion of the International Labour Conference. The Trade Union Congress passed a resolution boycotting the International Labour Conference at Geneva because the Conference had been of little help to the Indian workers and the Indian representatives to that Conference were appointed by the Government of India and not by the All-India Trade Union Congress. This resolution, like the one boycotting the Whitley Commission, was unacceptable to the Right Wingers and proved to be the proverbial last straw.

It would have been in the fitness of things if a political campaign had been launched in 1929. It would have then synchronised with a movement in other spheres as well. But that was not to be. So there was only marking time in political circles. In Bengal, the Congress Party was able to turn out the Ministers repeatedly. Disgusted with the Party's tactics, the Governor dissolved the Legislative Council in May and ordered a fresh election at once. The result was that the Congress Party came back with added strength and the Nationalist Moslems regained some of the seats they had lost at the last election. Just before the election, judgment was delivered in a suit brought against the Nationalist paper, *Forward,* by the East Indian Railway[1] for defamation for publishing reports damaging to the Company about a railway accident near Calcutta. The court

[1] The East Indian Railway is a State-owned Railway and the most important Railway in India.

gave exemplary damages to the tune of Rs. 150,000 (Rs. 13½=£1 approximately), and it was expected that this would force the paper to close down. However, the next day *Forward* ceased to appear, but in its place another daily paper called *Liberty* was born. The Congress Party did not therefore have to suffer any inconvenience for want of an organ.

In June, the Labour Party came into power and Lord Irwin, the Viceroy, was invited to London for consultation, where he remained for some months. While he was there, a sudden change came over the Mahatma. At a meeting of the Congress Working Committee in July, a resolution was passed calling upon Congressmen to resign their seats in the Legislatures. No notice was given to the Congress Parties in the different Legislatures, nor was their opinion invited and the most surprising thing was the acquiescence of Pandit Motilal Nehru, who had been leading the Congress Party in the Assembly. The Pandit had in the month of May encouraged the Bengal Congress Party to fight the elections and had especially enjoined on them to recapture some of the Moslem seats. When a meeting of the All-India Congress Committee[1] was held at Allahabad the same month, a strenuous opposition was put forward by the late Mr. J. M. Sengupta and the writer, both of whom were members of the Congress Working Committee. As a result of this opposition and also of the dissatisfaction expressed by the Congress Parties in the different Legislatures, the resolution regarding resignation from the Legislatures was rescinded and the whole matter was adjourned till the Lahore Congress in December. Up till now it is a puzzle to many as to what happened between May and July to make Pandit Motilal Nehru change his front. Was he suddenly disappointed at the work put in by the Congress Parties in the Legislatures ? Was he faced with a revolt or a faction in his own Party in the Assembly and therefore wanted to dissolve it ? Or did he want to put up a united

---

[1] The All-India Congress Committee is a body of about 350 members representing the different provinces of India. Every year it elects an Executive of 15 members, called the Working Committee.

front against the Left Wingers who were growing more powerful, and for that reason wanted to placate the Mahatma by agreeing to his pet theory of Council-boycott? In any case, there is no doubt that without the support of Pandit Motilal Nehru, the Mahatma would never have forced his views on the Congress. And one has to remark with great regret that Pandit Motilal Nehru who was the only man who could influence the Mahatma either way at that time, did a positive disservice to his country by actively supporting the Mahatma in his policy of reviving the boycott of the Legislatures. The harmful effect of this boycott became more and more evident in the years to come. To say the least, it was tactically a great blunder to boycott the Legislatures when the new Constitution was under consideration, especially when it had been demonstrated the year before, that because of the presence of Congressmen in the Assembly, that body had been able to repudiate the Simon Commission. The writer was among the few men who fought against the proposed boycott till the very last —but with the support of Pandit Motilal Nehru and subsequently of the late Mr. J. M. Sengupta, the Mahatma could easily carry the Congress with him and even Bengal could not put up an undivided opposition, as had been possible at the Allahabad meeting of the All-India Congress Committee in July, before the breach between the late Mr. Sengupta and the writer took place.

In August, a special meeting of the All-India Congress Committee was called to decide who should preside over the ensuing Congress. In accordance with the Congress Constitution, the vast majority of the Provincial Congress Committee had nominated Mahatma Gandhi, but he declined to accept the nomination. The general feeling in Congress circles was that the honour should go to Sardar Vallabhbhai Patel. But the Mahatma decided to back the candidature of Pandit Jawaharlal Nehru. For the Mahatma the choice was a prudent one, but for the Congress Left Wing it proved to be unfortunate, because that event marked the beginning of a political rapprochement between the Mahatma and Pandit Jawaharlal Nehru and a consequent alienation between the latter and the Congress Left Wing. Since 1920, Pandit Jawaharlal Nehru had been a close adherent of the policy advocated by the Mahatma and his personal relations with the latter had been always friendly. Nevertheless, since his return from Europe in December 1927, Pandit Jawaharlal Nehru began to call himself a Socialist and give expression to views hostile towards Mahatma Gandhi and the older leaders and to ally himself in his public activities with the Left Wing opposition within the Congress. But for his strenuous advocacy, it would not have been possible for the Independence Lague to attain the importance that it did. Therefore, for the Mahatma it was essential that he should win over Pandit Jawaharlal Nehru if he wanted to beat down the Left Wing opposition and regain his former undisputed supremacy over the Congress. The Left Wingers did not like the idea that one of their most outstanding spokesmen should accept the Presidentship of the Lahore Congress, because it was clear that the Congress would be dominated by the Mahatma and the President would be a mere dummy. They were of opinion that a Left Wing leader should accept the Presidentship only when he was in a position to have his programme adopted by the Congress. But the Mahatma took a clever step in supporting the candidature of Pandit Jawaharlal Nehru and his election as President opened a new chapter in his public career. Since then, Pandit J. L. Nehru has been a consistent and unfailing supporter of the Mahatma.

In the meantime the Simon Commission had been busy with its own work and on October 16th, 1929, after some sort of prearrangement, Sir John Simon wrote to the Prime Minister, Mr. Ramsay Macdonald, asking for an extension of the terms of reference in order to enable him to examine the methods whereby the future relations between the Indian States and the British Indian provinces could be readjusted. He also suggested that after the publication of the Commission's Report, a conference should be arranged between the representatives of His Majesty's Government and representatives of British India and the States. To both these suggestions the Cabinet agreed. The same month Lord

Irwin returned to India and soon after his arrival, he issued a statement on October 31st, 1929, saying that he had been 'authorised by His Majesty's Government to state clearly that in their judgment, it is implicit in the Declaration of 1917 that the natural issue of India's constitutional progress, as there contemplated, is the attainment of Dominion Status'. He further stated that a Round Table Conference would be held in London after the publication of the report of the Simon Commission as had been suggested by Sir John Simon himself.

The situation created by this new attitude on the part of the British Cabinet and the Viceroy did not remain unnoticed or unutilised. In the absence of Deshabandhu Das, there was at least one personality who could seize the opportunity at once and, fortunately for him, he then occupied a strategic position as an intermediary between the Viceroy and the people's representatives. That man was Mr. Vithalbhai Patel who, though a veteran Congressman, had been elected to the Presidential chair of the Assembly in 1925. President Patel had had a remarkable public career. An advocate by profession, he had made politics his first love. Through thick and thin, he had been with the Congress for a long period and at times he had been the General Secretary of the All-India Congress Committee. In that capacity he had been a member of the Congress deputation which visited England before the Reforms of 1919. He was a close student of Constitutional Law and an expert in parliamentary procedure and especially in obstructive tactics. People used to say of him: 'Give Vithalbhai the most perfect constitution in the world and he will tear it to pieces.' So great was his success as a President, that in 1927 he was re-elected unopposed, following the procedure in the British House of Commons. Without causing undue annoyance to the Government, he was able to conduct the affairs of the Assembly in a manner which would do credit to any popular President. In 1929 when a bomb was thrown in the Assembly, the Government wanted to use the opportunity for taking over the entire control of the guards in the Assembly premises and it was a tough fight that the President had to wage in order to thwart the Government. He had also to fight hard in order to bring under his control the Secretariat of the Assembly, that was formerly under Government of India. But in all fights he conducted himself with such a tact and adhered so scrupulously to constitutional procedure, that he was able to win the respect of Viceroy, Lord Irwin.

Mr. Vithalbhai Patel persuaded the Viceroy that he should personally meet the Congress leaders, Mahatma Gandhi and Pandit Motilal Nehru, and attempt an understanding with them. To this the Viceroy agreed and the interview took place in December. But before that, he had to prepare the ground by arranging for a gesture to be made on behalf of the leaders as a reply. Thus there met at Delhi in November the conference of leaders of all parties. The conference by an overwhelming majority decided to issue a manifesto appreciating the sincerity underlying the Viceroy's pronouncement and tendering co-operation to His Majesty's Government in their effort to evolve a Dominion Constitution for India. The signatories further hoped that the Round Table Conference proposed 'not to discuss when Dominion Status is to be established but to frame a scheme of Dominion Constitution for India'. They also urged that the Round Table Conference should be preceded by a general amnesty. The manifesto was signed by Mahatma Gandhi, Messrs. Nehru (father and son), Pandit M. M. Malaviya, Dr. Ansari, Dr. Moonje, Sardar Vallabhbhai Patel, and the Right Hon. V. S. Sastri, Sir Tej Bahadur Sapru, Mrs. Besant, Mrs. Naidu and others. Pandit Jawaharlal Nehru did not at first agree with the other leaders and intended issuing a contrary manifesto together with the writer. But towards the end of the meeting, Mahatma Gandhi prevailed upon him to sign the leaders' manifesto on the ground that he was the President-elect of the Lahore Congress, and the manifesto would lose much of its value if his signature did not appear on it. Thereafter Dr. S. Kitchlew (Lahore), Mr. Abdul Bari (Patna) and the writer issued a separate manifesto opposing the acceptance of Dominion Status and also the idea of participating in the so-called Round Table Conference. The manifesto pointed out that in a real Round Table Conference only the belligerent parties should be represented and the Indian representatives should be selected not by the British Government as had been intended, but by the Indian people. It also warned the Indian people that the Viceroy's pronouncement was a trap laid by the British Government. It was reminiscent of a similar move made by the British Government some years ago in the case of Ireland when the Prime Minister, Mr. Lloyd George, suggested that an Irish Convention consisting of all parties should be held for framing a Constitution for Ireland—but the Sinn Fein Party were clever enough to see through the game and boycott the convention. The leaders' manifesto drew public attention and a large measure of public support as well. The contrary manifesto, however, was welcomed only by Left Wing Congressmen and by the youths in general.

The same month—in November—the annual meeting of the Bengal Congress Committee was held for electing officer-bearers, etc. At that meeting it was found that two groups had formed within the Committee, one following the leadership of the late Mr. Sengupta and the other of the writer. There was a keen contest and the latter party ultimately won by a narrow magin. This was the beginning of the Bengal dispute and the split in the Congress Committee led to a split among the youths and students as well. The breach had begun at the time of the Calcutta Congress when the late Mr. Sengupta supported the Mahatma and wanted the writer to do so. Since then a separate party had grown up in Bengal under the leadership of the late Mr. Sengupta which stood for unquestioning obedience to the Mahatma and his policy. The majority party in Bengal did not bind itself to the Mahatma in that way and in its outlook and programme it was allied with the Left Wing opposition to the Mahatma in the Congress.

The Congress leaders, Mahatma Gandhi and Pandit Motilal Nehru, were to meet the Viceroy in December. On the eve of that interview an unfortunate event took place. There was an attempt to wreck the Viceroy's train, but fortunately nothing serious happened and Lord Irwin had a providential escape. The longed for interview took place but it proved abortive. The Congress leaders wanted an assurance from the British Government, or at least from the Viceroy, that Dominion Status would be granted to India, but that assurance was not forthcoming. They had therefore to leave the Viceroy disappointed and come to the Lahore Congress with empty hands.[1] The general atmosphere in the country was in favour of an extremist policy. Throughout the year there had been unrest. In Punjab, following the arrest of Sardar Bhagat Singh and his comrades, the Naujawan Bharat Sabha had done a lot of propaganda on their behalf. The self-immolation of Jatin Das had further electrified the atmosphere. On the other hand, the leaders who had cried halt at the Calcutta Congress had not been able to achieve anything. The Mahatma had further compromised himself by making statements to the effect that if there was no response from the Government by December 31st, 1929, he would be an 'independence-wallah' on January 1st, 1930. His orthodox followers like himself, had all along been advocates of Dominion Home Rule and they did not like to depart from that attitude. But the Mahatma felt that in the atmosphere then prevailing in the country, a resolution on independence would be carried in spite of his opposition and it was therefore much better for him to move it.

The Congress met under the Presidentship of Pandit J. L. Nehru at Lahore. As had been anticipated, the President was a figurehead and the entire proceedings were dominated by Mahatma Gandhi, who by advocating independence, was able to win over some of the Left Wing elements as well. The Madras Congress in 1927, though it passed a resolution on independence, had not altered the goal as defined in the Congress Constitution, and this was done at Lahore. There was considerable excitement

---

[1] It is generally believed that neither the British Government nor Lord Irwin could give any assurance to Mahatma Gandhi because of the opposition raised in England by Mr. Churchill, Lord Birkenhead, Lord Reading and others, soon after the Viceregal pronouncement of October 31st, 1929.

over a clause in the resolution moved by the Mahatma, which congratulated the Viceroy on his providential escape when his train was bombed. The feeling in the Congress was that that clause was uncalled for in a political resolution, but the Mahatma insisted on retaining it, probably because he wanted to placate Lord Irwin and prepare the ground for a rapprochement in future. Be that as it may, the Mahatma made it a question of confidence and by a narrow margin he won. Next came the question of the plan of campaign for the coming year. Here the Mahatma was quite unprepared. A resolution was passed by the Congress calling upon Congressmen to resign their seats in the Legislatures and thereby the victory of the Swarajists in 1923 was avenged in 1929. As for the positive part of his plan, the Working Committee adopted a resolution, at the instance of the Mahatma, recommending that autonomous boards, like All-India Spinners' Association, should be organised for carrying on propaganda for the removal of untouchability, for the promotion of temperance and suppression of the drink and drug traffic, etc. The question was therefore raised by everyone as to what work would be left for Congressmen and for Congress organisations in the country. When the resolution regarding the constitution of autonomous boards came up before the Subjects Committee, there was considerable opposition, the feeling being that that work should be done by the Congress organisations and not by *ad hoc* bodies as proposed by the Mahatma. The resolution was thereupon defeated. On behalf of the Left Wing, a resolution was moved, by the writer, to the effect that the Congress should aim at setting up a parallel Government in the country and to that end, should take in hand the task of organising the workers, peasants and youths. This resolution was also defeated, with the result that though the Congress accepted the goal of complete independence as its objective, no plan was laid down for reaching that goal—nor was any programme of work adopted for the coming year. A more ridiculous state of affairs could not be imagined, but in public affairs, we are sometimes inclined to lose not only our sense of reality but our common sense as well. When the time came for electing the working Committee for the coming year, the Mahatma came forward with a list of fifteen names, from which the names of Mr. Srinivasa Iyengar, the writer, and other Left Wingers had been deliberately omitted. There was a strong feeling in the All-India Congress Committee that at least the names of Mr. Iyengar and the writer should be retained. But the Mahatma would not listen. He said openly that he wanted a committee that would be completely of one mind and he wanted his list to be passed in its entirety. Once again it became a question of confidence in the Mahatma and as the House did not want to repudiate him, it had no option but to give in to his demand.

Altogether the Lahore Congress was a victory for the Mahatma. Pandit Jawaharlal Nehru, one of the most prominent spokesmen of the Left Wing, was won over by him and the others were excluded from the Working Committee. The Mahatma could henceforward proceed with his own plans without fear of opposition within his Cabinet, and whenever any opposition was raised outside his Cabinet, he could always coerce the public by threatening to retire from the Congress or to fast unto death. From his personal point of view, it was the cleverest move. With a subservient Cabinet, it was possible for him to conclude the pact with Lord Irwin in March 1931, to have himself appointed as the sole representative to the Round Table Conference, to conclude the Poona Agreement in September 1932—and do other acts which have done considerable disservice to the public cause.

For the general public, unacquainted with the intricacies of politics or with the differences in the inner councils of the Congress, the Lahore Congress was a great inspiration. After the midnight of December 31st, the President of the Congress came out to hoist the flag of independence. In spite of the biting cold of a Lahore winter, there was a mammoth gathering and as the flag went up, a thrill went through the vast audience. When the Congress was dissolved, there was a light on the horizon and the members of the great Assembly departed with a new hope and with the torch of a new message.

## CHAPTER X

## STORMY 1930

With the dawn of the new year there was hope and confidence in every heart. People anxiously looked to the Working Committee for instructions as to what they were required to do for the early attainment of independence. The Mahatma sensed the atmosphere correctly and he stated : 'Civil Disobedience alone can save the country from impending lawlessness and secret crime, since there is a party of violence in the country which will not listen to speeches, resolutions, or conferences, but believes only in direct action.' He therefore resolved to place himself at the head of the national struggle in order to keep it within the limits of non-violence. Early in January the first order went out. January 26th should be observed all over India as the day of independence. On that day a manifesto, prepared by the Mahatma and adopted by the Working Committee of the Congress, was to be read from every platform and accepted by the people. The manifesto which is set forth below, was at once a declaration of independence and a pledge of loyalty to the Indian National Congress and to the sacred fight for India's liberty.

'We believe that it is the inalienable right of the Indian people as of any other people, to have freedom and to enjoy the fruits of their toil and have the necessities of life so that they may have full opportunities of growth. We believe also that if any Government deprives the people of these rights and oppresses them, the people have a further right to alter it or to abolish it. The British Government in India has not only deprived the Indian people of their freedom but has based itself on the exploitation of the masses, and has ruined India economically, politically, culturally and spiritually. We believe therefore that India must sever the British connection and attain Purna Swaraj or complete independence.

'India has been ruined economically. The revenue derived from our people is out of all proportion to our income. Our average income is seven pice (less than twopence) per day, and of the heavy taxes we pay, 20 per cent are raised from the land revenue derived from the peasantry, and 3 per cent from the Salt Tax which falls most heavily on the poor.

'Village industries, such as hand-spinning, have been destroyed, leaving the peasantry idle for at least four months in the year, and dulling their intellect for want of handicrafts; and nothing has been substituted, as in other countries, for the crafts thus destroyed.

'Customs and currency have been so manipulated as to heap further burdens on the peasantry. The British manufactured goods constitute the bulk of our imports. Customs duties betray clear partiality for British manufactures, and revenue from them is used not to lessen the burden on the masses but for sustaining a highly-extravagant administration. Still more arbitrary has been the manipulation of the exchange ratio, which has resulted in millions being drained away from the country.

'Politically, India's status has never been so reduced as under the British regime. No reforms have given real political power to the people. The tallest of us have to bend before foreign authority. The rights of free expression of opinion and free association have been denied to us, and many of our countrymen are compelled to live in exile abroad and cannot return to their homes. All administrative talent is killed, and the masses have to be satisfied with petty village offices and clerkships.

'Culturally, the system of education has torn us from our moorings and our training has made us hug the very chains that bind us.

'Spiritually, compulsory disarmament has made us unmanly, and the presence of an alien army of occupation, employed with deadly effect to crush in us the spirit of resistance, has made us think that we cannot look after ourselves or put up a defence against foreign aggression, or even defend our homes and families from the attacks of thieves, robbers and miscreants.

'We hold it to be a crime against man and God to submit any longer to a rule that has caused this fourfold disaster to our country. We recognise, however, that the most effective way of gaining our freedom is not through violence. We will therefore prepare ourselves by withdrawing, so far as we can, all voluntary association from the British Government, and will prepare for civil disobedience, including non-payment of taxes. We are convinced that if we can but withdraw our voluntary help and stop payment of taxes without doing violence even under provocation, the end of this inhuman rule is assured. We therefore hereby solemnly resolve to carry out the Congress instructions issued from time to time for the purpose of establishing Purna Swaraj.'

The reports from different parts of the country showed that the Independence Day celebrations were a great success. Unprecedented enthusiasm was exhibited everywhere and the Mahatma felt that he could go ahead with a dynamic programme. But just at this moment the practical politician in him asserted itself. While starting the civil-disobedience campaign he wanted to leave the door open for a compromise and he realised that the independence resolution of the Congress might prove to be a stumbling block. He also felt that some of his wealthy supporters—the Indian capitalists—were alarmed at the resolutions of the Lahore Congress. Some sort of explaining away was therefore necessary, particularly in view of the fact that the word 'independence' implied severance of the British connection. On January 30th he issued a statement in his paper, *Young India,* saying that he would be content with the 'substance of independence' and he mentioned eleven points to explain what he meant by that expression. At the same time he virtually gave up the use of the word 'independence' and substituted in its place the more elastic expression, 'substance of independence', or another expression especially coined by him—namely, 'Purna Swaraj', which he could interpret in his own way. The eleven points enunciated by him had a reassuring effect on all circles that had been alarmed by the idea of independence and they paved the way for lengthy negotiations in the months to follow. The eleven points were as follows:

1. Total prohibition.
2. Reduction of the ratio (of the rupee to the pound sterling) from 1s. 6d. to 1s. 4d.
3. Reduction of the land revenue to at least 50 per cent and making it subject to legislative control.
4. Abolition of the Salt Tax.
5. Reduction of the military expenditure to at least 50 per cent to begin with.
6. Reduction of the salaries of the higher graded services to one half or less so as to suit the reduced revenue.
7. Protective tariff on foreign cloth.
8. The passage of the Coastal Traffic Reservation Bill (reserving to Indian ships the coastal traffic of India).
9. Discharge of all political prisoners save those condemned for murder, or the attempt thereat, by the ordinary judicial tribunal; withdrawal of all political prosecutions; abrogation of Section 124a (Indian Penal Code), the Regulations of 1818 and the like; and permission to all the Indian exiles to return.
10. Abolition of the C.I.D. (Criminal Investigation Department) or its popular control.
11. Issue of licences to use fire-arms for self-defence, subject to popular control.

By the beginning of February, the situation was favourable for the Mahatma. The Working Committee had vested him with dictatorial powers for conducting the civil-disobedience campaign. Besides the warm response given by the country on Independence Day, the members of the different Legislatures belonging to the Congress Party had submitted their resignations out of deference to the mandate of the Lahore Congress. A large section of the Moslems was of course opposed to the idea of Satyagraha and civil disobedience, and the Ali brothers openly appealed to their co-religionists not to heed the Congress appeal. Nevertheless, the Nationalist Moslems, who were by no means negligible, were wholeheartedly with the Congress and the North-West Frontier Province, a predominantly Moslem province, was going to give solid support to the coming campaign. After much searching of heart, on February 27th, the Mahatma announced his plan of campaign. The next few moves taken by him will stand out for all time as some of the most brilliant achievements of his leadership and they reveal the height to which his statesmanship can ascend in times of crises. Writing in *Young India* on February 27th, 1930, he said :

'This time on my arrest, there is to be no mute passive non-violence, but non-violence of the most active type should be set in motion so that not a single believer in non-violence as an article of faith for the purpose of achieving India's goal, should find himself free or alive at the end of the effort.... So far as I am concerned, my intention is to start the movement only through the inmates of the Ashrama (meaning—his own Ashrama) and those who have submitted to its discipline and assimilated the spirit of its methods.' Referring to the possibility of a suspension of civil disobedience in the event of an outbreak of violence, as in 1922, the Mahatma wrote : 'Whilst, therefore, every effort imaginable and possible should be made to restrain the forces of violence, civil disobedience once begun this time cannot be stopped and must not be stopped so long there is a single civil resister left free or alive.' The last statement helped to reassure all those people who had taken strong exception to the Bardoli retreat in 1922 following the manifestation of mob violence at Chauri-Chaura.

The Mahatma further announced his intention of defying the Salt Law along with seventy-eight of his chosen followers—the members of his Ashrama. He would commence a march from Ahmedabad to the sea-coast—his pilgrimage to the sea—on March 12th and after arriving there, would launch the civil-disobedience campaign. That would be the signal for the whole country to take up the movement. The Mahatma decided to start this particular campaign, because it would appeal to the country as a whole, and especially to the poor. From time immemorial the people had been accustomed to manufacture salt from sea-water or from the soil. That right had been taken away from the people by the British Government. Now the Salt Law as administered is doubly iniquitous. It prohibits the people from utilising the salt which has been given by nature and forces them to import it from abroad. Moreover, the imposition of the Salt Tax serves to enhance the price of the salt which even the poorest of the poor has to buy. Explaining this point to the Viceroy in a letter dated March 2nd, he wrote:

'If you cannot see your way to deal with these evils and my letter makes no appeal to your heart, then on the twelfth day of this month I shall proceed with such co-workers of the Ashrama as I can take, to disregard the provisions of the Salt Laws. I regard this (Salt) Tax to be the most iniquitous of all from the poor man's standpoint. As the independence movement is essentially for the poorest in the land, the beginning will be made with this evil. The wonder is that we have submitted to the cruel (Salt) monopoly for so long.'

In the same letter which was a lengthy document, the Mahatma tried to explain to the Viceroy why he was being forced to resort to civil disobedience. Making it clear that the letter was not intended as a threat but was a simple and sacred duty peremptory on a civil resister, the Mahatma wrote: 'In common with many of my countrymen I had hugged the fond hope that the proposed Round Table Conference might furnish a solution. But when you said plainly that you could not give any assurance that you or the British Cabinet would pledge yourselves to support a scheme of full dominion status, the Round Table Conference could not possibly furnish the solution for which vocal India is consciously, and the dumb millions are unconsciously, thirsting. Needless to say there never was any question of

Parliament's verdict being anticipated. Instances are not wanting, of the British Cabinet, in anticipation of the Parliamentary verdict, having pledged itself to a particular policy. The Delhi interview having miscarried, there was no option for Pandit Motilal Nehru and myself but to take steps to carry out the solemn resolution of the Congress arrived at in Calcutta at its session in 1928.' In order to keep the door open for a compromise, in spite of the launching of the civil-disobedience campaign, the Mahatma continued : 'But the resolution of independence should cause no alarm if the word Dominion Status mentioned in your announcement had been used in its accepted sense. For has it not been admitted by responsible British statesmen that Dominion Status is virtual independence ?'

To this letter—or ultimatum—of Mahatma Gandhi, the Viceroy sent a brief reply regretting that Mr. Gandhi intended to contravene the law. So, true to his announced programme, the Mahatma commenced his three weeks' macrh to Dandi, the sea-coast village, where the disobedience of the Salt Law was to begin. At that time the Government were sceptical about the effect that the march would produce and they were not inclined to take him seriously. The Anglo-Indian papers began to write taunting articles and the *Statesman* of Calcutta in a leading article wrote to the effect that the Mahatma could go on boiling sea-water till Dominion Status was attained. This scepticism was also shared by a section of Congressmen. Nevertheless, the march to Dandi was an event of historical importance which will rank on the same level with Napoleon's march to Paris on his return from Elba or Mussolini's march to Rome when he wanted to seize political power. Fortunately for the Mahatma, he had a wonderfully good Press within India and outside. In India, for days and days, every detail connected with the march found the widest publicity. The march on foot enabled him to rouse the entire countryside through which he passed and it also gave him time to work up the feelings of the country as a whole. If, on the other hand, he had taken the train to Delhi from Ahmedabad, arriving there the next day, he would neither have been able to rouse the people of Gujerat, nor would he have had enough time to work up the entire nation. While the Mahatma was marching from village to village, an intense propaganda was carried on in the neighbourhood asking the people to give up service under the Crown and to prepare for the non-payment of taxes, which would be started before long. At every step the Mahatma received an unexpectedly warm welcome and that made the Government realise that the coming campaign would be a much more serious affair than they had thought at first.

On April 6th, after a purificatory bath in the sea, the Mahatma started civil disobedience by appropriating pieces of salt lying on the beach. Almost simultaneously, illegal salt manufacture was begun all over the country. Where natural conditions precluded any such campaign, disobedience of other laws was attempted. In Calcutta, for instance, the Mayor, the late Mr. J. M. Sengupta, started disobedience of the Law of Sedition by openly reading seditious literature in a public meeting. Boycott of foreign cloth was begun on an extensive scale and along with that, another campaign grew up for the boycott of British goods of all sorts. There was also an intensive campaign for the boycott of liquor and of intoxicating drugs. To enforce the boycott, picketing by Congress volunteers was organised all over India. A few weeks after the march began, the Mahatma addressed a special appeal to the women of India (*Young India*, April 10th, 1930). Therein he said: 'The impatience of some sisters to join the good fight is to me a healthy sign.... In this non-violent warfare, their contribution should be much greater than men's. To call women the weaker sex is a libel.... If by strength is meant moral power, then woman is immeasurably man's superior.' Proceeding, the Mahatma appealed to them to take up the picketing of liquor shops and foreign-cloth shops. The prohibition of intoxicating drugs and drinks would reduce the Government revenue by 250 millions of rupees (Rs. 13½ = £ 1 roughly)—while the boycott of foreign cloth would stop an annual drain of nearly 600 millions of rupees. He further appealed to women to devote their spare hours to spinning with a view to stimulating the production of Khadi. In conclusion he said : 'But there is no excitement and adventure in the liquor and foreign-cloth picketing, some sisters may retort. Well, if they will put their whole heart into this agitation, they will find more than enough excitement and adventure. Before they have done with the agitation, they might even find themselves in prison. It is not improbable that they may be insulted and even injured bodily. To suffer such insult and injury would be their pride. Such suffering, if it comes to them, will hasten the end.'

The appeal was transmitted all over the country and it had a magic effect. Even the women of the most orthodox and aristocratic families were moved.[1] Everywhere women came out in their thousands to carry out the Congress mandate. Not only the Government but the people of the country as well, were taken by surprise at the manifestation. Temperance workers like Miss Mary Campbell,[2] who had worked for forty years in India, were amazed at the phenomenon. Well might foreign observers like Mr. H. N. Brailsford and Mr. George Slocombe say that if the civil-disobedience campaign had accomplished nothing else but the emancipation of the women of India, it would have fully justified itself. The energy and enthusiasm of the women stirred the men to greater effort and sacrifice. Within three weeks of the commencement of the campaign, the Government resolved to strike. On April 27th, the first emergency ordinance was promulgated called the Press Ordinance, which brought the papers under the full control of the officials. Most of the Nationalist papers ceased publication for a long period as a protest. Other ordinances followed, aiming at the suppression of the different activities of the Congress. Congress organisations were declared unlawful all over the country and an ordinance was

---

[1] E.g., women belonging to the family of such an orthodox and highly respected Brahmin as Pandit Madan Mohan Malaviya went to prison without fear or hesitation.
[2] *Manchester Guardian* of June 22nd, 1931, contains her description of the awakening among the women in Delhi where alone, 1.600 women were imprisoned

issued, enabling the Government to confiscate the property belonging to them. The result of these ordinances was that the Congress could no longer function openly and many of its activities, like raising funds, recruiting volunteers, etc., had to be conducted in an underground manner. Nevertheless, the activities of the Congress instead of being paralysed by the ordinances, were further stimulated. As meetings and processions were banned everywhere, they continued to be held in defiance of the official ban. Newspapers, bulletins, leaflets were printed and distributed by Congress agencies in spite of official prohibition. In some places as in Bombay, Congress propaganda was conducted by means of the radio and the police were not able to find out from where the messages were being transmitted.

Faced by a non-violent rebellion, the Government first proceeded to make arrests. But that was of no avail. According to official figures,[1] more than sixty thousand civil resisters were cast in prison. Special prisons had to be improvised at short notice but these were filled up in no time. Besides the activities described above, which were more or less common to the whole of India, there were special activities in certain provinces. For instance, in the Central Provinces and a part of the Bombay Presidency, disobedience of forest laws was started and people began to cut down timber at will. In Gujerat, the United Provinces and certain districts of Bengal, particularly Midnapore district, non-payment of taxes and of land revenue was launched. In the North-West Frontier Province, thanks to the efforts of Khan Abdul Gaffar Khan, better known as Frontier Gandhi, an intensive anti-Government movement was on foot, including the non-payment of taxes. In spite of the warlike traditions of the people there, the movement was entirely non-violent. The Frontier Gandhi had organised a corps of volunteers dressed in red uniform who were

---

[1] The official figures are an underestimate. The writer knows from personal experience that many people were sentenced on charges like stealing, exercising intimidation, rioting, etc., though they were full-fledged Satyagrahis. As the Satyagrahis did not take any part in Court proceedings, these charges were never challenged. The official figures are based on the returns for purely political offences.

called 'Khoda-i-Khidmadgar' or 'Servants of God'. The red shirt volunteers were an eyesore to the Government, because their campaign was affecting the loyalty of the people who had formerly contributed some of the finest regiments to the Indian Army. Moreover, because of the strategic position of the Frontier Province, a political movement in that part of the country was exceedingly unwelcome to the Government.

As soon as the Government realised the serious proportions which the campaign had assumed, they became entirely ruthless and brutal in their attempts at suppression. It is not possible to describe the atrocities committed by the forces of the Crown—including both the police and the military—in this connection. It is difficult to say which province suffered most, for each province had its tale of woe. In Bengal, the Midnapore district suffered most and the sufferings of the people gave birth to a terrorist movement for organising reprisals against officials. Parts of the United Provinces where the no-rent campaign was very strong, also suffered badly. In Gujerat, when the sufferings of the peasantry became unbearable, they left their homes and migrated to the neighbouring state of Baroda. Indiscriminate and brutal use of force, attack on women and wanton destruction of property—constituted some of the features of the 'illegal' measures adopted by agents of the Crown towards a people who had, on the whole, remained strictly non-violent. The usual method of attacking Satyagrahis and unarmed citizens, including women, was with the help of powerful sticks, which being iron-shod or covered with leather, could split human skulls with ease.[1] Attacks were made on helpless Satyagrahi prisoners as well.[2] Where

---

[1] In most provinces the Congress agencies had to set up hospitals and to organise Ambulance Services for taking care of the injured Satyagrahis. The finest and most-equipped hospitals were in Bombay City where the number of injured Satyagrahis was the largest of all the Indian cities.

[2] Such an attack was made in the Alipore Central Jail in Calcutta in April, 1930. Among those who were attacked were the late Mr. Sengupta, then Mayor of Calcutta, Mr. Kiron Sankar Roy, Secretary, Bengal Congress Committee, Prof. N. C. Bannerji, Mr. S. R. Bakshi, Editor of *Liberty*, the writer and a large number of fellow-prisoners. The writer, who was in the front rank, was, during the course of the attack thrown

these were not sufficient for striking terror, shooting was occasionally resorted to. In most provinces such shooting incidents occurred occasionally, but the most diabolical incident took place at Peshawar (the capital of the North-West Frontier Province) on April 23rd, where the number of people shot and killed on one day went up to several hundreds. The facts are roughly these. There was a peaceful demonstration following the arrests of some local leaders. The authorities lost their heads and sent some armoured cars to disperse the crowd that was by that time moving homewards. The armoured cars, full of soldiers, rushed full tilt into the crowd without warning from behind, killing three people on the spot and wounding a large number. Thereupon the crowd is reported to have set fire to the cars. Soldiers were at once rushed to the spot and ordered to open fire. But the crowd did not run away; hundreds of them stood their ground and faced the bullets. When the facts became known, the public demanded an inquiry which the Government refused. Then the Working Committee of the Congress appointed a Committee with Mr. Vithalbhai Patel (who by then had resigned the Presidentship of the Assembly) as Chairman to inquire into and report on the facts. This Committee was not allowed to proceed to the Frontier Province. It had therefore to assemble in Punjab at a place nearest to the Frontier Province and collect evidence there. As soon as the report of the Committee was published, it was banned by the Government. Nevertheless, through the efforts of Congress organisations, wide publicity was given to it.

The only redeeming feature of the Peshawar episode was the refusal of a company of Garhwali[1] soldiers to open fire on the unarmed crowd. After their refusal they were

down and rendered unconscious for more than one hour. The public demanded an inquiry which the Government refused. At the end, Government appointed a Medical Board consisting of Dr. B. C. Roy and Lt.-Col. Denham White who examined the injured prisoners and issued a report on their physical condition.

[1] The Garhwalis are recruited from the mountainous portion of the United Provinces bordering on the Himalayas. Together with the Gurkhas of Nepal, the Sikhs of the Punjab and the Pathans of the Frontier Provinces —they form the pick of the Indian Army.

at once disarmed, placed before a court-martial and sentenced to long terms of imprisonment. In most of the provinces where atrocities were perpetrated, local committees were appointed by the public to inquire into and report on those incidents. To publish those reports would require a big volume and would be outside the scope of this book. It would not, however, be out of place to quote some lines from the second letter [1] addressed by the Mahatma to the Viceroy early in May on the eve of his arrest, which was published in *Young India* on May 8th, 1930.

'I had hoped that the Government would fight the civil resisters in a civilised manner. I could have had nothing to say if in dealing with the civil resisters the Government had satisfied itself with applying the ordinary process of law. Instead, whilst the known leaders have been dealt with more or less according to the legal formality, the rank and file have been often savagely and in some cases, even indecently assaulted. Had these been isolated cases, they might have been overlooked. But accounts have come to me from Bengal, Bihar, Utkal, the United Provinces, Delhi and Bombay, confirming the experiences of Gujerat, of which I have ample evidence at my disposal. In Karachi, Peshawar and Madras the firing would appear to have been unprovoked and unnecessary. Bones have been broken, private parts have been squeezed, for the purpose of making volunteers give up salt which is valueless to the Government but precious to the volunteers. At Mathura an Assistant Magistrate is said to have snatched the National flag from a ten-year-old boy. The crowd that demanded restoration of the flag, thus illegally seized, is reported to have been mercilessly beaten back. That the flag was subsequently restored, betrayed a guilty conscience. In Bengal, there seem to have been only a few prosecutions and assaults about salt, but unthinkable cruelties are said to have been practised in the act of snatching flags from volunteers. Paddy fields are reported to have been burnt, eatables

---

[1] It is not quite sure if this letter actually reached the hands of the Viceroy.

forcibly taken. A vegetable market in Gujerat has been raided because the dealers would not sell vegetables to officials. These acts have taken place in front of crowds who have submitted without retaliation in pursuance of the Congress mandate. Yet this is only the fifth week of the struggle!'

An English disciple of Mahatma Gandhi, Miss Madeleine Slade, paid a visit to Bulsar in Gujerat on June 6th to see with her own eyes how the Satyagrahi volunteers engaged in the non-violent raid on the Dharsana Salt Depot were being treated by the police. She published her report in *Young India* in the issue of June 12th, 1930. Therein she stated that she had found evidence of the following injuries perpetrated on the Satyagrahi volunteers:

1. Lathi[1] blown on head, chest, stomach and joints.
2. Thrusts with lathis in private parts, abdominal regions.
3. Stripping of men naked before beating.
4. Tearing off loin cloths and thrusting of sticks into anus.
5. Pressing and squeezing of the testicles till a man becomes unconscious.
6. Dragging of wounded men by legs and arms, often beating them the while.
7. Throwing of wounded men into thorn hedges or into salt water.
8. Riding of horses over men as they lie or sit on the ground.
9. Thrusting of pins and thorns into men's bodies, sometimes even when they are unconscious.
10. Beating of men after they have become unconscious, and other vile things too many to relate, besides foul language and blasphemy, calculated to hurt as much as possible the most sacred feelings of the Satyagrahis.

To turn now to other events. April 1930 was a month bristling with sensational incidents. Every day seemed to

---

[1] A lathi is an iron-shod heavy stick.

bring forth some new development and no part of the country was free from it. The Indian Legislative Assembly did not have a quiet time either, though the Congress members were out of it. Pandit Madan Mohan Malaviya who was leading the Independent Party there, assumed the leadership of the opposition. Early in April, he walked out of the Assembly together with his followers, as a protest against the manner in which the Government had forced on the Assembly the principle of Imperial Preference in connection with the Cotton Tariff Bill. Two days later he resigned from the Assembly together with some other members of his Party. This was followed by the resignation of the President of the Assembly, Mr. V. J. Patel. He addressed two letters to the Viceroy in which he stated that after the resignation of the Congress Party and of Pandit Malaviya's Independent Party, the Assembly had lost its representative character and in the circumstances, he felt that his place was with his people. He also protested against what seemed to him a change of front on the part of the Government on the constitutional question.

Another incident of a totally different character took place in April in the easternmost part of the country. That was the Armoury Raid in Chittagong in East Bengal. A number of young men belonging to a local revolutionary party led by Mr. Surjya Kumar Sen, raided the Chittagong Armoury. They shot dead the guards on duty, took possession of the premises, removed what weapons they could and destroyed the rest. Thereafter they retired to the hills and continued guerrilla warfare for some days. Ultimately they were overpowered, the majority of them being killed and the rest forced to fly for their safety. Members of this party who were at large, continued terroristic activities for a long time.[1] About this time the Afridi tribes on the North-West Frontier grew restless and began to give trouble

[1] The first batch of young men arrested after the raid were sent up for trial in what is known as the Chittagong Armoury Raid Case and after a long trial, the majority of them were sentenced to transportation for life and sent over to the Andamans Islands in the Bay of Bengal. The leader of the group, Surjya Kumar Sen, evaded arrest for a long time but was subsequently arrested and hanged after trial. Chittagong has since 1930 been under a form of martial law.

to the British Government.

Early in May, the Mahatma wrote his second letter to the Viceroy (part of which has been quoted above), in which he said:

'Dear Friend,

'God willing it is my intention to set out for and reach there with my companions on.... and demand possession of the Salt Works.... It is possible for you to prevent this "raid", as it has been playfully and mischievously called, in three ways:
1. By removing the Salt Tax.
2. By arresting me and my party unless the country can, as I hope it will, replace every one taken away.
3. By sheer goondaism (i.e. terrorism) unless every head broken is replaced, as I hope it will be....'

*Young India*, May 8th, 1930.

But before the Mahatma could carry out his intention he was seized by the custodians of law on May 5th, 1930 and cast in prison without trial under an old regulation, called Bombay Regulation XXV of 1827.

The arrest of Mahatma Gandhi caused public excitement all over India, but there was no outbreak of violence except in one town, viz. Sholapur in Bombay Presidency. In that town with a large industrial population, the people rose in revolt and overpowered the local police. They took possession of the town, hoisted the national flag and declared their independence. They held the town for some time but troops were rushed in from Bombay and the authority of the British Raj was once again restored. Martial law was then established and this was followed by a reign of terror. During the martial law regime, various restrictions and humiliations were inflicted on the people. For instance, people were not allowed to wear Gandhi caps[1]

---

[1] White caps made of Khadi are called Gandhi caps. They are generally worn by members of the Congress Party.

in public, the national flag was pulled down wherever it was seen, etc. Those who were suspected of taking a leading part in the disturbance were sent up for trial. Some of them were hanged and others sentenced to long terms of imprisonment.

While these stirring events were taking place and the people were thinking in terms of independence, the 1927 programme of the Government was being translated into action. The Reports of the Provincial Committees and of the Indian Central Committee, appointed to assist the Simon Commission, had been published before the end of 1929. An auxiliary committee of the Simon Commission presided over by Sir Philip Hartog that had been appointed to report on the growth of education in India, had also issued its report in October 1929. Only the report of the Simon Commission had been held up, possibly because of the Labour Party coming into power in June 1929. However, on June 7th, 1930, the report of the Commission was issued. The report met with vehement opposition from all quarters, so reactionary were its recommendations. Even the Indian Liberals demanded that the Simon Report should not form the basis of discussion at the Round Table Conference. And since the Indian Legislative Assembly rejected the Simon Report *in toto*, even in the absence of the Nationalist members—the Government had no option but to agree to the demand. At a time when the breach between the Government and the Congress appeared to be beyond repair, an enterprising British journalist arrived on the scene to try his wits. By clever manœuvring, Mr. George Slocombe, representative of the *Daily Herald*, managed to get permission to interview Mahatma Gandhi in Yervada Prison in Poona on May 19th and 20th, 1930, with a view to ascertaining from him the conditions on which he would be prepared to call off the civil-disobedience movement. The Mahatma said that the movement could not be stopped without a definite guarantee of the 'substance of independence'. He mentioned four points as a prerequisite to suspension of civil disobedience and participation in the Round Table Conference :

1. The terms of reference to the Round Table Conference to include the framing of a Constitution giving India the substance of independence.
2. Satisfaction to be granted to the demand for the repeal of the Salt Tax, the prohibition of liquor and opium and ban on foreign cloth.
3. An amnesty for political prisoners to coincide with the end of the civil-disobedience campaign.
4. The remaining points raised in the Mahatma's letter to the Viceroy to be left for future discussion.

On June 20th, Mr. Slocombe interviewed Pandit Motilal Nehru, the Acting President of the Congress, on the eve of his arrest. The Pandit substantially confirmed what the Mahatma had told Mr. Slocombe. On June 25th, Mr. Slocombe drafted a statement outlining the basis for negotiations between the Government and the Congress and his statement was approved by the Pandit. The statement ran thus :

'If in certain circumstances the British Government and the Government of India, although unable to anticipate the recommendations that may in perfect freedom be made by the Round Table Conference or the attitude which the British Government may reserve for such recommendations, would nevertheless be willing to give a private assurance that they would support the demand for full responsible government for India, subject to such mutual adjustments and terms of transfer as are required by the special needs and conditions of India and by her long association with Great Britain and as may be decided by the Round Table Conference, Pandit Motilal Nehru would undertake to take personally such an assurance—or the indication received from a responsible third party, that such an assurance would be forthcoming—to Mr. Gandhi and to Pandit Jawaharlal Nehru. If such an assurance were offered and accepted, it would render possible a general measure of conciliation which would entail simultaneous calling off of the civil-disobedience movement, the cessation of the Government's present repressive policy and a generous measure of amnesty for political prisoners, and would be followed by the participation of the Congress in the Round Table Conference on terms to be mutually agreed upon.'

This statement was sent by Mr. Slocombe to Sir Tej Bahadur Sapru and Mr. M. R. Jayakar, with a view to interesting them in the cause of peace. Both of them took up the matter enthusiastically and waited upon Lord Irwin for the purpose in the early part of July. They obtained permission to interview Mahatma Gandhi and Pandit Motilal and Pandit Jawaharlal Nehru in prison. On July 23rd and 24th they met the Mahatma in Yervada Prison and with his memorandum, they met the two Pandits in Naini Prison near Allahabad on July 28th. The Pandits said among other things that no final word could be given without personal consultation with Mahatma Gandhi. With the Nehrus' memorandum, Mr. Jayakar again saw the Mahatma on July 31st. Orders were then given for the Pandits to be taken from Naini Prison to Yervada Prison. On August 13th, 14th, 15th, consultations took place in Yervada Prison at which were present the two peacemakers, Mahatma Gandhi, Pandit Motilal and Pandit Jawaharlal Nehru, Mrs. Sarojini Naidu and Sardar Vallabhbhai Patel. A joint statement was issued by the Congress leaders on August 15th, stating that no solution would be acceptable to them or to the Congress which did not guarantee the following points :

1. India's right to secede at will.
2. Grant of a national government responsible to the people including control of defence and finance.
3. India's right to submit to an impartial scrutiny of the so-called public debt of India.

This statement was duly communicated to the Viceroy and on August 28th, 1930, Lord Irwin sent a reply to the two peacemakers saying that he felt that it was impossible to hold any discussion on the basis of the joint statement of August 15th. Thus the peace negotiations failed. The peacemakers made a further attempt by interviewing the leaders in Naini and Yervada Prisons, but the leaders opined that there was an unbridgeable gulf between the Government and the Congress.

Soon after the final break in the negotiations, Pandit Motilal Nehru was suddenly released from prison on September 8th, because he had fallen seriously ill. He remained alive for five months only, but during this period, in spite of extreme ill-health, he spent the greater part of his time and energy in trying to stiffen the movement throughout the country. During his stay in Calcutta, he also devoted much of his time to a settlement of the Bengal dispute. Immediately after the Lahore Congress, he had visited Calcutta in order to inquire into the election complaints preferred against the Executive of the Bengal Congress Committee (of which the writer was the President), by the party of the late Mr. J. M. Sengupta. He had given his verdict in favour of the former, but after his departure, differences broke out again, with the result that at the elections to the Calcutta Municipality, the two Congress groups put forward two separate sets of candidates. When the civil-disobedience movement was started, two separate committees came into existence for conducting the civil-disobedience campaign in Bengal. A few months later when the election of the Mayor of Calcutta was to take place, one party put up the outgoing Mayor, the late Mr. Sengupta, while the other party put up the writer—and the latter won. These dissensions lowered the prestige of the Congress to a large extent. However, through Pandit Motilal Nehru's influence, the two civil-disobedience committees were amalgamated and other differences were patched up—so that when he left Bengal in December, the prestige and strength of the Congress were restored to some extent.

While the above events were taking place, the bureaucracy were pursuing their own plan. In June, the report of the Simon Commission was published and on September 20th, the Government sent their despatch to London, as a preliminary to the discussions of the Round Table Conference. Some of the principal points in the recommendations of the Commission were as follows :

1. The new Constitution should, as far as possible, contain within itself provision for its own development.
2. The ultimate Constitution of India must be federal.
3. Burma should be excluded from the new Constitution.
4. There should be full autonomy in the provinces including the department of Law and Order—but the Governor should, on the administrative side, be given overriding powers in certain matters like internal security, safeguarding of all communities, etc.
5. The presence of British troops and British officers in Indian regiments will be essential for many years. The Commander-in-chief should not be a member of the Viceroy's Executive Council and he should not sit in the Legislature.
6. The Provincial Legislative Councils should be enlarged.
7. The Lower House of the Central Legislature should be called the Federal Assembly. It should be enlarged and be elected by the Provincial Councils. The Upper House—the Council of State, should remain much as it is at present.
8. A Provincial Fund should be constituted for ensuring adequate resources to the provinces without infringing their autonomy.
9. The Governor-General should select and appoint the members of his Cabinet. He should be the actual and active head of the Government and in some matters his powers should be enlarged. (The Commission did not recommend the introduction of responsibility at the centre.)
10. The High Courts should be under the administrative control of the Government of India.
11. The functions and membership of the Council of the Secretary of State for India should be reduced.

Some of the main points in the Government of India's Despatch were as follows:

1. The following subjects should be under the control of the British Parliament: defence, foreign relations, internal security, financial obligations, financial stability, protection of minorities and of the rights of services recruited by the Secretary of State, the prevention of unfair economic and commercial discrimination.
2. The proposal of the Statutory Commission for the abolition of diarchy and the introduction of responsible government (including the department of law and order) in provinces was approved.
3. The Governor should be given the discretion to appoint officials as Ministers.
4. In Madras, Bombay, Punjab, Central Provinces and Assam, the Legislature should have a single chamber. In Bengal, the United Provinces and Bihar and Orissa there should be two chambers.
5. The separation of Burma was approved in principle.
6. The members of the Governor-General's Executive Council should be appointed by the Governor-General himself. The Governor-General's Cabinet while being of a 'unitary' character and not responsible to the Legislature, should consist of some elected members of the Legislature who could command some support from that body.

On November 12th, 1930, the first session of the Round Table Conference was held in London under the Chairmanship of Mr. Ramsay Macdonald, the Prime Minister. It consisted of eighty-nine members, sixteen from the British parties, sixteen from the Indian States and fifty-seven from British India. The Congress Party was of course unrepresented. After the preliminary sittings of the Conference, several committees were appointed to consider the problems in detail. There was the Federal Structure Committee with Lord Sankey as Chairman, the Franchise and Services Committee with Sr William Jowitt as Chairman, the Burma Committee with Earl Russell as Chairman, the Defence Committee with Mr. J. H. Thomas as Chairman, the Minorities Committee with Mr. Ramsay Macdonald as Chairman etc. The fact that the representatives of the Indian States were invited to the Conference made it evident at the very outset that the British Government were anxious to bring the Indian States within the future Indian Constitution. The first step in that connection had been taken by Sir John Simon when he wrote to the British Prime Minister for an enlargement of the terms of reference with a view to including the question of the relations between British India and the Indian States. The Simon Commission also reported that the ultimate Constitution of India must be a federal one. The only question that remained undecided was as to when it would be possible to bring about a federation of British India and the Indian States. In the circumstances it was no surprise when on November 17th, at a sitting of the Round Table Conference, His Highness the Maharaja of Bikaneer, welcomed such a federation. The whole idea had been talked over and discussed, months before the Round Table Conference met. The proposal of federation was one of the cleverest moves adopted by the British Government at this stage, and it is a pity that elderly politicians like Sir Tej Bahadur Sapru and Mr. M. R. Jayakar did not see through the game at once, though Mr. Srinivasa Sastri and Mr. M. A. Jinnah did feel suspicious towards the idea at the beginning. The Government of India in their despatch of September 20th, had merely mentioned the safeguards—that is, the subjects that should be retained under the control of His Majesty's Government and the British Parliament. But what about the subjects that were to be within the purview of the Indian Legislature? British interests demanded that there should be a Conservative element in that body that could be trusted to checkmate the radical forces in British India. And what could be better than to bring the Indian Princes in, so that they might act as a dead weight in the Central Legislature? This rapprochement between the British Government and the Indian Princes had begun as early as 1922, as we have already seen in Chapter II, following the visit of H.R.H. the Prince of Wales to India. Faced with a Nationalist upheaval in British India, the British Government turned to the Indian Princes for sympathy and assistance. The Princes, on their side, were also faced with a democratic movement within their territories which had the support of the people of British India and they wanted the help of the British Government to hold in check the popular revolt. It was in pursuance of this demand that the Indian States Bill was introduced by the Government in the Indian Legislative Assembly in September 1922, and when thrown out by the Legislature, was certified as law by the Viceroy. The culmination of this friendship was the idea of federation—an unholy alliance between the British Government and the Indian Princes, in order to thwart the mass awakening in India.

The net result of the first session of the Round Table Conference was the offer to India of two bitter pills—Safeguards and Federation. To make these pills eatable, they were sugar-coated with 'Responsibility'. Liberal politicians felt quite happy when the Prime Minister announced in his closing speech on January 19th, 1931, that they would be given responsible Government at the centre, if they agreed to Safeguards and Federation and they never stopped to inquire what would remain of real 'Responsibility' after Safeguards and Federation had been conceded. To make matters worse, the anti-Nationalist Moslems who were present at the Round Table Conference declared that they would agree to responsible Government with Federation and Safeguards, only if the communal question was decided to their satisfaction. On January 19th, 1931, the Round Table Conference was adjourned *sine die*. The Liberal politicians seemed to be in high spirits, so satisfied they were at their own achievements in London. For the layman, the only thing they brought from across the seas was the assurance given by the Prime Minister that 'steps would be taken to enlist the co-operation of those sections of public opinion which had held aloof from the Conference'.

CHAPTER XI

## THE GANDHI-IRWIN PACT AND AFTER
## (1931)

Towards the end of 1930 and the beginning of 1931, the atmosphere was once again favourable for an understanding between the Government and the Congress. In the first place, the Labour Party was in power and Capt. Wedgwood Benn was at the India Office. Secondly, Mahatma Gandhi by his very absence had exerted a great influence on the Round Table Conference. Talking and discussing with nondescripts and self-appointed leaders while the only representative party in India was engaged in a bitter struggle with their Government, the British politicians had felt the unreality of the first Round Table Conference. Hence the determination of the Labour politicians to come to a compromise with the Congress, if only the latter would not ask for too much. Thirdly, Lord Irwin was the Viceroy and Governor-General of India and he was farsighted enough to realise that if an understanding was to be arrived at between the Government and the Congress, it was desirable to do so while the Mahatma was the leader of the latter body, for according to sane Britishers, 'Gandhi was the best policeman the Britisher had in India'.[1] The third factor was undoubtedly the most important. If there had been an intransigent Viceroy at the helm of affairs in India, no understanding with the Congress would have been possible, however sympathetic might have been the attitude of Whitehall at the time.

But why was Lord Irwin so agreeable to an understanding with the Congress? No doubt his vision was broader than that of the average British politician and he had an innate sense of fairness and justice, so characteristically

[1] This was the opinion expressed by Miss Ellen Wilkinson, Ex-M.P. after her visit to India in 1932 as a member of the India League Deputation.

lacking in the latter. The late Moulana Mohammed Ali had once described him as 'that tall thin Christian'. A true Christian he undoubtedly was. Nevertheless, Lord Irwin would never have been able to carry with him either the 'steel frame' in India or Mr. Baldwin and the Conservative leaders in England, but for the serious developments in India. Bombay, the gateway of India, was the storm centre of the movement. The no-tax campaign was very strong in Gujerat, the United Provinces and parts of Bengal. Throughout India the boycott of British goods was effective and civil disobedience in some form or other was going on in every province. In Bengal, terrorist activities had become a serious menace. Last but not least, in the North-West Frontier Province, the situation was alarming—and the situation in that province was affecting seriously the attitude of the frontier tribes, who ordinarily are quite indifferent to political developments in India. Several of these tribes had told the British authorities that they would make peace with them if only the latter would release the naked fakir (meaning Mahatma Gandhi) and Khan Abdul Gaffar Khan (the leader of the Frontier Province) and concede Swaraj to India. Though the abdication of King Amanulla in Afghanistan had eased the situation there, by ushering in a Government more friendly to Great Britain, the Government had not forgotten how the Afghan King had taken advantage of their preoccupations in 1919 by declaring war on them and had succeeded in extracting a favourable treaty. The Government were therefore feeling uneasy over the attitude adopted by the frontier tribes towards the developments in India.

On the day that the Prime Minister, Mr. Ramsay MacDonald, delivered his closing speech at the Round Table Conference, the Viceroy made a public appeal for the co-operation of the Congress in his address before the Indian Legislative Assembly. Within a week of this appeal, Mahatma Gandhi and the other members of the Working Committee were unconditionally released in order to give them an opportunity to consider the Premier's statement at the Round Table Conference. The Premier, after referring to the offer of responsibility with Federation and Safeguards, had ended with the following words : 'Finally I hope and I trust and I pray that by our labours together, India will come to possess the only thing which she now lacks to give her the status of a Dominion amongst the British Commonwealth of Nations—what she now lacks for that—the responsibilities and the cares, the burdens and the difficulties, but the pride and the honour of responsible government.' The Indian Liberal leaders who were on their way to India, sent a cablegram requesting Mahatma Gandhi not to come to a final decision about the Government's offer without giving them a hearing and they were evidently afraid that the Working Committee would summarily reject the Premier's offer. Their apprehension was not unfounded. The members of the Working Committee, soon after their release, met at Allahabad, where Pandit Motilal Nehru was lying seriously ill. The first reactions to the offer were anything but favourable. On February 6th, the Liberal leaders, Sir Tej Bahadur Sapru and the Right Hon. V. S. Sastri and Mr. M. R. Jayakar arrived and proceeded straight to Allahabad. Pandit Motilal Nehru, in spite of his failing health, had taken up a strong attitude, but the Liberal leaders persuaded the Mahatma not to reject finally the offer without having a talk with the Viceroy who made a generous gesture. Allahabad, at that time, was full of peacemakers and sensation-mongers, some of whom had no other business but to carry tales from one side to the other. On February 14th, the Mahatma applied for an interview with Lord Irwin and then proceeded to Delhi to meet him. Most of the members of the Working Committee accompanied him but Pandit Motilal Nehru could not, as he was too ill. This was a great misfortune.

At Delhi, the Mahatma was surrounded by wealthy aristocrats and by politicians who were dying for a settlement and on the side of the Working Committee there was no one with sufficient personality who could force his views on the Mahatma. Even Pandit Jawaharlal Nehru, who could have done so, failed on this occasion and as for the other members of the Working Committee, most, if not all, of them were more anxious for a settlement than the Mahatma himself. The negotiations between the Viceroy and the Mahatma dragged on from day to day and the Mahatma kept the Working Committee informed of all the developments. On March 4th, the negotiations came to an end and when the Mahatma put before the Working Committee the terms of the Pact, he made it quite clear that he would not proceed one step further without their unanimous support. At this juncture the responsibility of Pandit Jawaharlal Nehru was very great. Besides being the President of the Congress, he was the only member of the Working Committee who could be expected to understand and advocate the Left Wing point of view and his refusal would have been sufficient to prevent the final acceptance of the Pact by the Mahatma and the Working Committee. Unfortunately he gave in and so the Pact was approved by the Working Committee and the next day, March 5th, the Mahatma and Lord Irwin put their signature to it. When the publication of the Pact created an uproar in the country, Pandit Jawaharlal came out with the statement that he did not approve of some of the terms of the Pact—but as an obedient soldier he had to submit to the leader. But the country had regarded him as something more than an obedient soldier.

The Pact—called the Delhi Pact or the Gandhi-Irwin Pact—was published the next morning in all the papers. It was a lengthy document and from the Congress point of view the drafting was faulty, because it did not give the impression that the Congress had scored a victory. The perusal of the terms of the Pact had a damping effect on all 'Congressite' readers. The writer was in the Alipore Central Jail in Calcutta at the time. For days the papers had published substantially correct forecasts of the terms of the coming Pact. Even the blind followers of the Mahatma, when they read the forecasts, invariably remarked that it was unthinkable that their leader—meaning the Mahatma—would agree to those terms. Nevertheless, what was unthinkable came to be actual. The Mahatma was not blind to the realities of the situation, and in a Press statement issued simultaneously with the Pact, he stressed the point that the settlement did not imply a victory for either party and that he would strain every nerve to make final what was provisional, so that the Pact would prove to be a precursor of the goal, to attain which the Congress had been striving. The terms of the Pact were briefly as follows: Mahatma Gandhi on behalf of the Congress agreed:

1. To suspend the Civil-Disobedience Movement.
2. To participate in the deliberations of the forthcoming Round Table Conference for drafting a Constitution for India on the basis of (a) Federation; (b) Responsibility and (c) adjustments and safeguards that may be necessary in the interests of India.
3. To forge the demand for an investigation into the allegations of police atrocities in different parts of India.

The Viceroy on behalf of the Government agreed:

1. To release simultaneously all political prisoners incarcerated in connection with the non-violent movement.
2. To restore confiscated property and land to the owners where it had not been already sold or auctioned by the Government.
3. To withdraw the emergency ordinances.
4. To permit people who live within a certain distance of the seashore to collect or manufacture salt free of duty.
5. To permit peaceful picketing of liquor, opium and foreign-cloth shops, the last item designed not as a discrimination against British goods but as an encouragement to the Swadesi movement (i.e. indigenous industries).

The politically trained section of the people could analyse the terms of the Pact and to them it was a great disappointment. Youth organisations in the country, taken as a whole, were also dissatisfied. But to the mass of the people, it appeared as a great victory for the Congress. Only in Bengal was there no public enthusiasm and for reasons which will be presently explained. With the announcement of the armistice, the official machinery of the Congress began to work expeditiously and with great efficiency. The Working Committee decided to hold the annual session of the Congress at Karachi and suspending the constitutional procedure for the election of the President, it elected Sardar Vallabhbhai Patel, than whom a stauncher follower of the Mahatma it was difficult to find, as the President. Every member of the Working Committee felt that his prestige was at stake and strained every nerve to get the largest number of supporters from his province to attend the Karachi Congress. Besides the members of the Working Committee, all the leaders of the Right Wing felt called upon to exert themselves in order to secure the ratification of the Pact at the Karachi Congress. All the monied interests also desired to see the armistice followed up by a permanent peace, so that they could settle down to business peacefully. Consequently, there was no dearth of funds for those who wanted to go to Karachi to support the Mahatma. On the other hand, the oppositionists were at a great disadvantage. Many of their adherents were still in prison and did not get the benefit of the amnesty which the Pact had promised. Defections among their leaders had weakened their position in the country and even those who were in a position to attend the Karachi Congress, were handicapped by want of necessary funds. After the Lahore Congress, Mr. Srinivasa Iyengar had retired from public activity. Along with other Left Wing leaders, he had been treated shabbily by the President of the Lahore Congress and by the Mahatma, who was instrumental in excluding him from the Working Committee, though he was the most outstanding leader from Madras and was an ex-President of the Congress. This insult he had taken to heart so much that he had vowed he would have nothing to do with the Congress so long as Mahatma Gandhi remained the leader. Besides Mr. Srinivasa Iyengar, there was another defection in the person of Dr. Mohammed Alam of Lahore who had played a prominent part at the Lahore Congress, but who became a supporter of the Mahatma after the Gandhi-Irwin Pact. Of all the Provinces, Bengal was most hostile to the Pact but even there, there was a party led by the late Mr. Sengupta pledged to support the Mahatma.

In these circumstances, what could the Left Wingers do? Before my release from prison on March 8th, I ascertained that the political prisoners, as a rule, were hostile to the Pact, and I naturally shared their feelings. But after coming out, I realised that the Pact was a settled fact and there was no possibility of preventing its ratification at the Karachi Congress. The only question that we had to decide was whether we should put up an insignificant opposition at Karachi, or whether we should refrain from dividing the House while disapproving of the Pact. Before coming to a decision, I considered it advisable to meet the Mahatma personally. I therefore undertook a journey to Bombay which also enabled me to gauge public feeling in the provinces through which I passed. At Bombay I had long conversations with the Mahatma. After criticising the Pact, the point that I urged was that we would be prepared to support him as long as he stood for independence—but the moment he gave up that stand, we would consider it our duty to fight him. At the end, the Mahatma gave the following assurances : [1]

1. He would ask the Karachi Congress for a mandate to bind the hands of the Congress Deputation to the Round Table Conference.
2. That mandate would contain nothing that was not consistent with the status of independence for which the Lahore Congress had declared.
3. He would use all his influence and strain every nerve to secure amnesty for those who had been left out in the Pact.

From Bombay the Mahatma left for Delhi and I travelled in the same train with him. This gave me a further

---

[1] I also learnt from the Mahatma that he had voluntarily withdrawn the demand for an inquiry into the police atrocities.

opportunity not only of supplementing our talks at Bombay but also of observing how the public were reacting to the Pact. From the ovation he received everywhere, it was quite apparent that his popularity had reached the high watermark. It had surpassed even the record of 1921. At Delhi, no sooner did we arrive than we received a bombshell in the shape of news, to the effect that the Government had decided to execute Sardar Bhagat Singh and two of his comrades in the Lahore Conspiracy Case. Pressure was brought to bear upon the Mahatma to try to save the lives of these young men and it must be admitted that he did try his very best. On this occasion, I ventured the suggestion that he should, if necessary, break with the Viceroy on the question, because the execution was against the spirit, if not the letter, of the Delhi Pact. I was reminded of a similar incident during the armistice between the Sinn Fein Party and the British Government, when the strong attitude adopted by the former, had secured the release of an Irish political prisoner sentenced to the gallows. But the Mahatma who did not want to identify himself with the revolutionary prisoners, would not go so far and it naturally made a great difference when the Viceroy realised that the Mahatma would not break on that question. However, at that time, Lord Irwin told the Mahatma that he had received a largely-signed petition asking for the commutation of the death-sentence passed on the three Lahore prisoners. He would postpone their execution for the time being and give serious consideration to the matter, but beyond that he did not want to be pressed at the moment. The conclusion which the Mahatma and everybody else drew from this attitude of the Viceroy, was that the execution would be finally cancelled and there was a jubilation all over the country and especially in Bengal, where some revolutionary prisoners were also going to be executed.

About ten days after this incident the Congress was to meet at Karachi. The general expectation being that the execution would be cancelled, it was a most painful and unexpected surprise when on March 24th, while we were on our way to Karachi from Calcutta, the news was received that Sardar Bhagat Singh and his comrades had been hanged the night before. Gruesome reports were also afloat in the Punjab about the manner in which their dead bodies had been disposed of. It is impossible to understand at this distant date the poignant grief which stirred the country from one end to the other. Somehow or other, Bhagat Singh had become the symbol of the new awakening among the youths. People did not stop to inquire if he was really guilty of the murder charge brought against him. It was enough for them to know that he was the father of the Naujawan Bharat Sabha (the Youth Movement) in the Punjab—that one of his comrades, Jatin Das, had died the death of a martyr and that he and his comrades had maintained a fearless attitude while they were in the dock. Every one felt that the Congress was meeting under the shadow of a bereavement. The President-elect, Sardar Vallabhbhai Patel, gave orders that the usual festivities on the first day of the Congress would be suspended. Nevertheless, when the Mahatma alighted near Karachi, there was a hostile demonstration, and several young men received him with black flowers and black garlands. The feeling among a considerable section of the youths was that the Mahatma had betrayed the cause of Bhagat Singh and his comrades.

The All-India Congress Committee was to meet on March 26th and the plenary session of the Congress on the 29th. The execution having taken place on March 23rd, caused a great deal of nervousness among the supporters of the Pact and they apprehended an open split in the Congress. But the official party machinery had worked with great thoroughness and from all the provinces supporters of the Pact had been elected as delegates in large numbers. The Left Wing, to which I belonged, had resolved previously to come to Karachi, survey the situation there, consider carefully what the Mahatma had communicated to me in Bombay as to his future attitude and then make their final decision. At Karachi it was quite clear that they would not have much support from the elected delegates who alone could vote at the Congress—though among the general public and particularly the youths—they had larger support. There was another factor which had to be considered. If we were consistent and honest, it would not do to merely oppose the Pact and then go back home. We would have to give notice to the Government and start the movement again. What support would we get if we did so? There was no doubt that the response in men and money would be disappointing. There was therefore no possibility that if we continued the fight, we would achieve better results than the Mahatma had done. In the circumstances, what would we gain by dividing the House? If we were defeated, as we were sure to be, our opposition would be futile. If we succeeded in throwing out the Pact—which was unlikely in the circumstances—but failed to carry on a more vigorous campaign, the country would not gain by our opposition. Moreover, the execution of Sardar Bhagat Singh and his comrades had to be considered. The Government had sufficient cognisance of the situation in the country to realise that the execution on the eve of the Congress was likely to create a split in the Congress and would considerably strengthen the position of the anti-Pact Party. If the Government were so anxious to create a split, there was something to be said in favour of avoiding it. In times of crises, a party has sometimes to stand by its leaders even when it is known that they are committing a blunder. This was the first occasion for an agreement between the Nationalist leaders and the Government. If the rank and file of the Party repudiated the leaders after they had entered into an agreemnt, that would be damaging to the prestige not only of the leaders, but also of the Party itself. The Government would in future be able to say that it is of no use to have any negotiations with the leaders because they are likely to be repudiated by their followers. After duly weighing all these considerations, we decided that a statement should be made to the effect that the Left Wing of the Congress did not approve of the Gandhi-Irwin Pact, but that in view of the circumstances prevailing at the time, they would refrain from dividing the House. This statement was made by me before the Subjects Committee of the Congress and was received with great jubilation by the supporters of the

Pact, while it caused disappointment to our more enthusiastic supporters.

Sardar Vallabhbhai Patel presided over the Congress. In his opening speech he gave the go-by to the Lahore resolution on Independence and advocated Dominion Status for India. Much of his speech was devoted to agrarian grievances and to social and economic reforms, necessary for the uplift of the country. Among the resolutions adopted at the Congress was one appreciating the courage and self-sacrifice of Sardar Bhagat Singh and his comrades, while condemning all acts of violence. This resolution was on the same lines as the 'Gopinath Saha resolution' adopted by the Bengal Provincial Conference in 1924, of which the Mahatma had strongly disapproved. The circumstances at Karachi were such that this resolution had to be swallowed by people who, under ordinary circumstances, would not have come within miles of it. So far as the Mahatma was concerned, he had to make his conscience somewhat elastic. But that was not enough. To perfect the stage-management, Sardar Kishen Singh, the father of the late Sardar Bhagat Singh, was brought to the rostrum and made to speak in support of the Congress leaders. The tactics of the official party were superb. The other resolutions passed at the Congress referred to :

1. The ratification of the Gandhi-Irwin Pact.
2. The mandate given to the Congress delegation to the Round Table Conference; and
3. The fundamental rights of the Indian people for which the Congress would strive.

The mandate given to the Congress delegation was in keeping with the assurance given by the Mahatma to the writer in Bombay. The 'fundamental rights resolution' was meant to placate the Socialist elements in the Congress. As for the personnel of the Congress delegation, the Working Committee was empowered to make the selection. Towards the end of the session, the Working Committee for the next year was chosen and, as at the Lahore Congress, only such men were selected as would be inclined to follow the Mahatma blindly. During the Congress session, the Mahatma used to hold a public prayer in the morning and unprecedented crowds attended it. No propaganda could be more effective in drawing public support.

Simultaneously with the Congress, a session of the All-India Naujawan Bharat Sabha (All-India Youth Congress) was held in Karachi over which the writer was called upon to preside. At that time there was a distinct tendency among the youths in Punjab and Sindh to break away from the Indian National Congress and run a separate organisation. I pleaded strongly against this viewpoint and urged the capture of the official Congress machinery in place of boycott. With regard to the Gandhi-Irwin Pact I made the following criticism:

1. The Pact had gone into many petty and unnecessary details but had avoided the main issue of Swaraj.
2. The Conference was really no Round Table Conference because there was no finality about the decisions of the Conference and the whole matter would be considered *de novo* by the British Parliament. In a real Round Table Conference, as the South Africans and the Irish had, the decisions are always final and binding on both parties. The name Round Table Conference had been used only to hoodwink foolish Indian politicians.
3. The Indian delegates to the Round Table Conference would be selected not by the Indian people but by the British Government.
4. The Conference would not be confined to the representatives of the two belligerent parties. Non-descripts of all kinds who had nothing to do with the fight for Swaraj, would be there to throw obstacles in the path of the real nationalists.
5. The proposal of a Federation between nationalist British India and the autocratic Indian Princes was an absurd one. The Princes or their nominees would act as a dead weight against the national forces.

6. 'Safeguards' take away what 'responsibility' gives. It was a gross error on the part of the Mahatma to talk of 'Safeguards' in the interests of India. The only safeguard that the Indians want is liberty. The actual 'safeguards' are demanded by Britishers and are against the interests of Indians. It is wrong to induce the Indian people to accept such safeguards by saying that they are in the interests of India.
7. The amnesty provided under the Pact was inadequate because the following classes of political prisoners were excluded :

   (a) The state prisoners and 'detenus' imprisoned without trial, of whom there were about one thousand in Bengal alone.
   (b) Prisoners convicted of revolutionary offences.
   (c) Prisoners under trial for alleged revolutionary offences.
   (d) The under-trial prisoners in the Meerut Conspiracy Case.
   (e) Prisoners incarcerated in connection with labour strikes and other labour disputes.
   (f) The Garhwali soldiers who had been court-martialled and given heavy sentences for refusing to fire on unarmed citizens.
   (g) Prisoners sentenced in connection with the civil-disobedience movement, the charges against whom referred to violence of some sort.

8. The demand originally made by Mahatma Gandhi for an inquiry into police atrocities during the period of the civil-disobedience movement was excluded from the Pact.

The above criticism met with general approval at the Youth Congress and a resolution was adopted condemning the Delhi Pact.

The Delhi Pact, as we shall see later on, proved to be not a blessing but a curse. The time was not opportune for an understanding of the sort attempted. The struggle should have been continued for some time longer. The Pact, as drafted, contained nothing of value. Ever since the negotiations started in 1929, the Congress leaders had always insisted on an assurance from the Government, regarding the grant of Dominion Status. Because that assurance was not forthcoming, the fight had to be launched in 1930. For the same reason, the peace-negotiations prior to the First Round Table Conference in 1930, had proved abortive. How the fight could be suspended without such an assurance, passes one's comprehension. The only reason one can suggest is that there was no one in the Working Committee to point out the correct thing to the Mahatma and with the lamented death of Pandit Motilal Nehru, the last intellectual stalwart of the Congress had disappeared. Though he lacked the emotional appeal necessary in a front-rank leader, the Pandit was nevertheless a leader among men. He towered head and shoulders above his contemporaries and in 1931, he was the one man in the Congress Working Committee who could have influenced the Mahatma for good. It was therefore a misfortune that at the time of the Delhi negotiations he was on his deathbed and it was nothing short of a national calamity that he passed away early in March 1931.

Inopportune as the Pact was, lack of diplomacy was also responsible for some of its shortcomings. For instance, on the demand for an inquiry into the police atrocities, the Mahatma had been informed that if he stuck to it till the breaking-point, the Government would yield. Nevertheless, he voluntarily gave up the demand on an appeal from the Viceroy. With better bargaining, even in March 1931, one could have extracted more from the Government, because they were really anxious for a settlement. But men with fixed ideas are not well-qualified for political bargaining. So far as the Mahatma is concerned, he alternates between obstinacy and leniency and moreover, he is too susceptible to personal appeals—and with such habits of mind, it is difficult to get the better of one's opponent in political bargaining. The Delhi truce was a great help to the Government. It gave them time to inquire more deeply into the tactics of the Congress and thereafter to perfect their machinery for dealing with that body in future. In the case of the Congress, the Pact had a soporific effect. The enthusiasm of the people began to evaporate and it is out of public enthusiasm that one gets men and money for a non-violent mass movement. While the Government could resume their activity at any time because they had no dearth of men or money, the Congress would have to wait till public enthusiasm could be worked up once again. During the period of the Delhi truce while the Round Table Conference was sitting in London, the Government were perfecting their plans for striking at the Congress. For instance, by October 1931, the emergency ordinances for the next year had been already prepared. Dr. M. A. Ansari, the Nationalist Moslem leader of Delhi, had unquestionable proofs of this and he duly passed them on to the Congress President, Sardar Vallabhbhai Patel. It was easy for the Government to prophesy future developments because they knew that nothing substantial would be offered to the Congress. But the Congress guided by the honest and straightforward policy of the Mahatma made no preparations for the coming fight. In fact, before he left for London, the Mahatma assured Lord Irwin that he would try his level best for a settlement there and when he left London, he assured the Premier, Mr. Ramsay Macdonald, that he would endeavour till the last to avoid a resumption of hostilities and if that was impossible, he would at least strive to avoid bitterness as far as possible.[1] Further, the day before Mahatma Gandhi landed in Bombay, he sent by radio an exceedingly conciliatory message which was immediately published in all the papers. But that had no effect on the new Viceroy, Lord Willingdon, who had already perfected his arrangements and was spoiling for a fight in order to avenge himself for the slight humiliation which the Government had to face in agreeing to an armistice with the Congress.

In spite of the inadequate provisions of the Pact, if it

[1] True to his assurance, on the eve of his arrest under Regulation 25 of 1827 on January 4th, 1932, the Mahatma issued an appeal in which he said, 'Discard every trace of violence from your heart; give absolute protection to every English man, woman and child.'

had provided for an inquiry into the alleged atrocities, it would have had a very healthy check on such misdeeds in future. During the preceding twelve months there had been excesses committed by the police and the military in Peshawar, Gujerat, the United Provinces and the Midnapore district in Bengal, in connection with which the public had demanded redress. We have already referred to the shooting in Peshawar. In Gujerat, the United Provinces and Midnapore, excesses had been committed by the forces of the Crown in trying to suppress the no-tax campaign and in the United Provinces there had been allegations of assault on women of a revolting description. In addition to these, a recent incident which was still fresh in the public mind was the assault by the police on a peaceful procession in Calcutta on Independence Day (January 26th, 1931). This procession which was being led by the writer who was then the Mayor of Calcutta, was suddenly attacked without warning by British mounted police armed with lathis (powerful sticks covered with leather) and mercilessly belaboured. The writer and a number of other processionists, including Mr. Chattopadhyaya, the Education Officer, and Mr. Ghoshal, the Deputy Licence Officer of the Calcutta Municipality, were seriously injured in the assault, though the procession remained peaceful and non-violent till the end. The next day the writer was sentenced to six months' imprisonment for rioting,[1] by the Chief Presidency Magistrate of Calcutta. That the Mayor of the first city in India could be treated by the police in this fashion was something which even the Indian public could not stand. The police, on the other hand, felt that they could do just as they liked because they would never be called upon to appear before the bar of public opinion.

[2] On this occasion the writer had to spend 24 hours in the Lalbazar Central Police Station without food and drink and without change. There was only a small quantity of Tincture of Iodine available at the station for application to his injuries. This was soon exhausted and when he asked for more, he did not get any. The next day he had to appear in Court with his clothes covered with blood and his arm in a sling. He made a statement before the Magistrate regarding his treatment in the Police Station which was duly recorded. After his removal to prison he was X-rayed and it was then found that two of the fingers in his right hand had been fractured.

The restricted scope of the amnesty promised under the Pact, caused considerable disappointment among certain sections of the people and alienated the Mahatma still more from the revolutionaries and from trade-union circles, including the friends and followers of the Meerut prisoners. If the Mahatma could have secured amnesty for all these classes of prisoners, he would have stood out not only as the representative of the Nationalists but also of the trade-unionists and the revolutionaries, and he could have exerted his influence on them for good. The Government, too, if they had taken courage in both hands and opened wide the gates of the prison-house, would have made a magnanimous gesture which would have gone straight into the hearts of the people. And they would have lost nothing thereby—because if anyone happened to abuse his liberty, he could again be put back in prison through the help of the Regulation and the Ordinances. Since the Mahatma confined himself to the cause of the Satyagrahis, the revolutionaries in prison addressed a letter to Lord Irwin stating that a settlement with Mahatma Gandhi would not necessarily be binding on them and that if His Excellency desired a real settlement of the Indian question, the Government should come to a separate understanding with the Revolutionary Party. This letter reached the Viceroy's hands through a prominent Indian politician.[1]

This representation was not altogether useless, because a few months later, the Governor of Bengal, Sir Stanley Jackson, made an effort to come to an understanding with the revolutionaries. At his instance the late Mr. J. M. Sengupta went to Buxa Detention Camp in North Bengal and interviewed some of the leaders. The result was not unsatisfactory. The interviewed prisoners said that they were prepared to discuss terms, but they insisted that the negotiations should be carried on direct with the Government and not through any police-officer. They also gave a preliminary outline of the terms which the late Mr. Sengupta duly conveyed to the Governor. Thereafter, a reference was

---

[1] I came to know these facts after my release from prison in March 1931.

made by the Government to the prisoners through the Superintendent of the Camp, who was a police-officer. But they refused to move further in the matter, if the negotiations were not carried on direct with them. As the Government were not agreeable to that, the negotiations fell through.

In spite of all that has been written above, to the unsophisticated masses, the Delhi Pact appeared to be a victory for the Mahatma. Only with the lapse of time were they to be gradually disillusioned. Many intelligent people seriously believed that besides the written, there were other unwritten terms which would be disclosed later on and many of those who were against the Pact maintained that the Mahatma should be given a free hand till the end of the Second Round Table Conference. The Karachi Congress undoubtedly represented the pinnacle of the Mahatma's popularity and prestige. I travelled with him for some days and was able to observe the unprecedented crowds that greeted him everywhere. I wonder if such a spontaneous ovation was ever given to a leader anywhere else. He stood out before the people not merely as a Mahatma but as the hero of a political fight. The question that stirred me at the time was as to how he would utilise the unique position he had been able to attain. Would he be able to move from one victory to another, or would the anti-climax begin? The first shock came when the news was announced that the Working Committee on April 2nd, had selected Mahatma Gandhi as the sole representative of the Congress at the Round Table Conference and that he had accepted that decision. What really was behind that decision I have never been able to understand. Was it due to the vanity of the Mahatma who wanted to appear before the world as the sole representative of the dumb millions of India? Or was it merely one more error of judgment on the part of the Working Committee? Or was there some other motive behind the decision? It is impossible to accept the first explanation. Whatever the real explanation may be, the decision itself was a thoroughly wrong one. Alone in an assembly of about one hundred men, with all kinds of nondescripts, flunkeys and self-appointed leaders arrayed against him like a solid phalanx, he would be at a great disadvantage. Moreover, he would have nobody at his side to back him up in the fight that he would have with the reactionary Moslem leaders. But there was no help for it. The blind followers of the Mahatma could not be expected to criticise him and those who were not his orthodox followers had no influence on him regardless of their character, wisdom, or experience.

While the first move of the Mahatma after the Karachi Congress was not a wise one, the second move was a positive blunder. In private and in public, he began to say that his going to the Round Table Conference depended on his ability to solve the Hindu-Moslem question beforehand. Along with this statement he also began to say that if the Moslems made a united demand on the question of representation, electorate etc., in the new Constitution, he would accept the demand. The effect of these statements was a most tragic one. After the Delhi Pact, the reactionary Moslems had been somewhat overawed by the strength and power of the Congress and they were in a mood to come to terms wiith that body on a reasonable basis. The first statement of the Mahatma immediately changed that mood and made them feel that they held the key position, since if they refused to come to an understanding with him, they could prevent his attending the Round Table Conference. The second statement of the Mahatma made the reactionary Moslems feel that if only they would remain firm and secure the support of the Nationalist Moslems, the Mahatma could be forced to accept all their extreme demands. After the above statements had been made, the Mahatma had a conference with some reactionary Moslem leaders in Delhi in April. I was in Delhi at the time and I went to see him the same evening, after the conference. He seemed to be in a depressed mood, because they had presented him with the fourteen demands made by Mr. Jinnah (known in India as Jinnah's fourteen points) and he felt that an agreement would not be possible on that basis. Thereupon I remarked that the Congress should only care for an agreement between Nationalist Hindus and Nationalist Moslems and that the agreed solution should be placed before the Round Table Conference as the Nationalist demand and that the Congress need not bother what other anti-Nationalist elements thought or said. The Mahatma then asked me if I had any objection to separate electorates since it could be argued that in the absence of the third party the different communities would live and work in concord. To this I replied that separate electorates were against the fundamental principles of Nationalism and that I felt so strongly on the subject that even Swaraj on the basis of separate electorates was, in my opinion, not worth having. While we were engaged in this discussion, Dr. Ansari and some of the Nationalist Moslem leaders including Mr. Sherwani, arrived on the scene and joined in the discussion. They said that if for any reason the Mahatma gave up the demand for a common electorate for both Hindus and Moslems and accepted the demand of the reactionaries for a separate electorate for each community, they would oppose the reactionary moslems and also the Mahatma, because they were convinced that separate electorates were bad not only for the country as a whole, but also for the different communities. The strong attitude of the Nationalist Moslems on this occasion was largely responsible for preventing the Mahatma from agreeing to separate electorates, and forced him to wriggle out of the uncomfortable situation in which he had placed himself.[1] Soon after this, the Mahatma issued a public statement saying that he could not accept the demands made by the communalist Moslem leaders, since the Nationalist Moslems were opposed to them.

The atmosphere in Delhi was then (i.e. in April 1931) full of intrigue. Though Lord Irwin was inspired by a sincere desire for a settlement, there were many officials who were against it. These diehard elements were encouraged by the impending departure of Lord Irwin from India and the advent of Lord Willingdon, who had the reputation of being a strong man. While we were in Delhi, information reached us from a reliable source as to the

---

[1] In the light of these facts, the attitude of the Nationalist Moslems in 1934 to the Prime Minister's Communal Award is inexplicable.

tactics that the British Government would follow at the Round Table Conference. We were told that every effort would be made to drag Mahatma Gandhi at the very outset into minor issues with a view to getting the Indians to fight among themselves, so that they would not be able to combine against the British Government over the major issues. I duly conveyed to the Mahatma this information for what it was worth. He said in reply that his plan was to meet the authorities concerned soon after his arrival in London and try to obtain satisfaction from them on the major issues. If he felt satisfied, he would go into the minor issues—otherwise his work in England would end there and then. Unfortunately, when Mahatma Gandhi was in England, the minorities problem assumed the greatest importance and all the major problems were put aside. Events took place exactly as it had been prophesied in April at Delhi.

On April 18th, Lord Irwin's tenure of office came to an end. Before leaving Delhi he made an exceedingly conciliatory speech at the Chelmsford Club. Though a prominent member of the Conservative Party, he had proved himself to be a well-wisher of India. After Lord Ripon, no Viceroy had adopted such a friendly attitude towards the Indian people as he had. That he could not do more for India was due to the reactionary forces that were working against him both in India and in England. With the arrival of Lord Willingdon, the official attitude began to stiffen. Effect was not given to the Pact by officials in different provinces. In Gujerat the peasantry had great difficulty in getting back their confiscated lands and the Mahatma had to spend practically the whole of his time between the Karachi Congress and his departure for London in attending to their grievances. In the United Provinces, though the civil-disobedience movement was suspended, the peasants said that they were made unable to pay the rent. Even the Mahatma's advice that they should pay 50 per cent of their dues—they could not give effect to. The situation was, however, worst in Bengal. In spite of the Pact, imprisonment without trial continued from day to day on the plea that there was a revolutionary movement afoot. Out of nearly thousand state prisoners incarcerated without trial, not a single soul was released. The Conspiracy Cases then going on in the province were continued as usual. From time to time terrorist activities took place by way of retaliation against official oppression. No change in the official attitude was visible at all in Bengal after the truce and in India, as a whole, signs of goodwill on the official side were lacking.

By July, the Congress headquarters had unmistakable proofs that the provisions of the Pact were not being given effect to. A 'charge sheet' containing allegations of breaches of the Pact on the official side were handed over to the Home Secretary to the Government of India at Simla by the Mahatma personally. The air was thick with rumours that the Mahatma would decline to go to London. The authorities in London grew anxious as they wanted the Mahatma to come at any cost. Pressure was brought to bear on the Viceroy to see that everything possible was done to facilitate his going to London. In August, the Mahatma had long talks with the new Viceroy as a result of which the tension was considerably eased. The Mahatma wanted an arbitrator to inquire into complaints about the non-fulfilment of the Pact, but to this the Viceroy would not agree. He however promised inquiries into the specific allegations made by the Mahatma. An eleventh-hour agreement between the Congress leader and the Viceroy was somehow arrived at. The Mahatma took a special train to Bombay and was just in time for the outgoing boat, S. S. *Rajputana*. On September 11th, 1931, the Mahatma set foot on French soil. The next day he was in London.

CHAPTER XII

## MAHATMA GANDHI IN EUROPE (1931)

Dressed in loin-cloth and sandals and with but a shawl to protect him from the inclement weather, the Mahatma landed in Marseilles on September 11th, 1931. A select group of British and Indian friends and admirers met him there and accompanied him to London. On arriving there, he was taken straight to a reception at the Friends' House. In reply to the address of welcome, referring to the British Government, he humorously remarked: 'You cannot honestly balance the Budget without first balancing the relations between India and England.'

The writer was one of those who at one time felt misgivings as to whether the Mahatma would be well-advised to visit Europe in his characteristic loin-cloth. On his former visits to Europe, he was, of course, clothed differently. But on this occasion he did the right thing in adhering to his favourite dress. Questioned by a reporter about his dress, the Mahatma once jocosely remarked: 'You people wear plus-fours, mine are minus-fours.' Then changing to a more serious vein, he said: 'If I came here to live and work like an English citizen, then I should conform to the customs of the country and should wear the dress of an Englishman. But I am here on a great and special mission, and my loin-cloth, if you choose so to describe it, is the dress of my principals, the people of India.' His countrymen today feel proud that he stuck to the dress of his principals and even attended the Buckingham Palace party in the same dress.

During his stay in London, between September 12th and December 1st, the Mahatma spoke twelve times at the Round Table Conference[1]—twice before the plenary session

---

[1] The second Round Table Conference consisted of 107 members. Of these, 65 were from British India, 22 from the Indian States and 20 from the three British Parties. The Minorities Committee of the Con-

of the Conference on November 30th and December 1st, eight times before the Federal Structure Committee and twice before the Minorities Committee. In his maiden speech before the Federal Structure Committee on September 15th, 1931, he explained the position of the Indian National Congress and the mandate given by the Karachi Congress and went on to say: 'Time was when I prided myself on being called a British subject. I have ceased for many years to call myself a British subject; I would far rather be called a rebel than a subject. But I have now aspired—and I still aspire—to be a citizen, not in the Empire but in a Commonwealth, in a partnership if possible, if God wills it, an indissoluble partnership but not a partnership superimposed upon one nation by another.' (It is clear from this speech that in spite of the Lahore resolution on independence, the Mahatma was striving for a settlement with Britain on the basis of Dominion Status.)

In the Press interview which the Mahatma had granted on board S. S. *Rajputana*, it was evident that he was full of optimism. But before the second meeting of the Federal structure Committee which took place on September 17th, disllusionment began to creep in. He began to realise of what stuff the members of the Round Table Conference were made. Therefore at the outset of his speech on September 17th, he said: 'I have endeavoured to study, as I had not done before, the list of the delegates; and the first feeling of oppression that has been coming upon me is that we are not the chosen ones of the nation which we should be representing, but we are the chosen ones of the Government. Furthermore, knowing well the different parties and groups in India from experience, as I study the list of delegates I see some very noticeable gaps,[1] and so I am oppressed with a sense of unreality in connection with our

ference was composed of 6 Britishers, 13 Moslems, 10 Hindus. 2 from the depressed classes, 2 from Labour, 2 Sikhs, 1 Parsi, 2 Indian Christians, 2 Britishers domiciled in India, 1 Anglo-Indian and 3 women—total 44. The Moslems who are a quarter of the Indian population had the largest representation and there was only one Nationalist Moslem among them.

[1] This reference was to the Nationalist Moslems, among others, whose absence the Mahatma now began to feel. The discovery of the Mahatma, one cannot help feeling, was rather belated.

composition.' The Mahatma began to see through the game of the British politicians—hence in order to turn the tables on them he called upon them to make concrete proposals. (In reply to that move, the Government sought to turn the tables on him by summoning the Minorities Committee which would form the battle-ground for the Indian delegates.) In the same meeting, replying to an attack levelled against the Congress, the Mahatma said: 'Though the Government of the day has accused us of insolently setting up a parallel Government, I would like to subscribe to that charge in my own fashion. Though we have not set up any parallel Government,[1] we certainly aspire some day or other to displace the existing Government and in due course, in the course of evolution, also to take charge of that Government.'

Mahatma Gandhi's first speech before the Minorities Committee was delivered on October 8th, 1931. The apprehension that he had hinted at on September 17th, had been realised by then and all attempts to arrive at a settlement of the communal question had ended in failure. No wonder, when the members were the chosen ones of Government! This result had been clearly indicated in the manifesto issued by the writer and others in opposition to the leaders' Delhi manifesto in November 1929. On October 8th, 1931, the Mahatma said: 'It is with deep sorrow and deeper humiliation that I have to announce utter failure on my part to secure an agreed solution of the communal question through informal conversation among and with the representatives of different groups.... But to say that the conversations have to our utter shame failed is not to say the whole truth. Causes of failure were inherent in the composition of the Indian delegation. We are almost all not elected representatives of the parties or groups we are presumed to represent—we are here by nomination of the Government. Nor are those whose presence was absolutely necessary for an agreed solution to be found here.

---

[1] The writer moved a resolution at the Lahore Congress in 1929 to the effect that the Congress should aim at setting up a parallel Government. This resolution was defeated, all the followers of the Mahatma voting against it.

Further you will allow me to say that this was hardly the time to summon the Minorities Committee. It lacks the sense of reality in that we do not know what it is that we are going to get.... I therefore venture to suggest that the Minorities Committee be adjourned *sine die* and that the fundamentals of the Constitution be hammered into shape as quickly as possible.... Should all efforts at agreement fail even when the Round Table Conference reaches the end of its labours, I would suggest the addition of a clause to the expected Constitution appointing a judicial tribunal that would examine all claims and give its final decision on all the points that may be left unsettled.' Going through this speech, one cannot help thinking what a change it would have made if the Mahatma had come to London with a full contingent of Nationalist representatives of Moslems and other minority communities to counteract the mischievous moves of 'the chosen ones of the Government'. It is also to be regretted that despite the warning he had received at Delhi, soon after the Karachi Congress, the Mahatma did not realise that the main function of the Minorities Committee would be to create confusion among the Indian members and shelve the main political issues. It was certainly another blunder for Mahatma to suggest a judicial tribunal which would of course be appointed by the British Government and would in all probability have produced the same document as the Prime Minister's Communal Award. If the British Government had taken the Mahatma at his word and appointed a judicial tribunal, what would have been the Mahatma's position today?

Before the next meeting of the Minorities Committee was held in November 13th, 1931, an interesting development had taken place. The so-called representatives of the minority communities had concluded a Pact themselves as a solution of the communal question. This Pact—called the Minorities Pact—vouchsafed to them a very large share of the loaves and fishes of the Constitution. The Pact was made with the full approval of the Government and the British members of the Conference coming from India had taken a leading part in it. The Sikhs did not, however, join this Pact. Before entering into this Pact, Dr. Ambedkar, the nominated representative of the Depressed Classes, wanted to come to an agreement with the Mahatma whereby a certain number of seats would be reserved in the Legislatures for the Depressed Classes on the basis of a Common Electorate for all sections of the Hindus. At that time, the Mahatma would not think of any such compromise. When Dr. Ambedkar joined the Minorities Pact, he was assured not only of a number of seats for the Depressed Classes, but also of a separate electorate for them. There is no doubt that if a settlement had then been made with Dr. Ambedkar, the terms would have been much better than the terms of the Poona Pact concluded in September 1932, after the historic fast of the Mahatma.

At the meeting of the Minorities Committee held on November 13th, 1931, the Chairman, Mr. Ramsay Macdonald, referring to the Minorities Pact, claimed that it was acceptable to well over 115 million people in India. He also replied to the Mahatma's attack at the previous meeting and urged on the contrary, that inability to solve the communal question was hampering the progress of Constitution-building. In his speech the Mahatma emphatically challenged both these assertions and with reference to the first, he claimed that the Congress represented 85 per cent of the population not merely of British India but of the whole of India. In the same speech the Mahatma made one significant assertion: 'I would like to repeat what I have said before—that while it will always accept any solution that may be acceptable to the Hindus, Mussalmans and Sikhs, the Congress will be no party to special reservation or special electorates for any other minorities.'[1] The Mahatma once again urged the appointment by the Government of a judicial tribunal to give a final decision on the communal question.

---

[1] In the light of this statement the Mahatma's endorsement of the Poona Pact in September 1932, is inexplicable, since the Poona Pact provided for reservation of seats for the Depressed Classes.

Before the Federal Structure Committee on October 23rd, 1931, Mahatma Gandhi put forward with due emphasis the Congress view regarding a Supreme Court for India. He urged that this Federal Court should be a court of the widest jurisdiction possible and not one to decide only those cases that arise from the administration of Federal laws. He opposed the idea of having two Supreme Courts, one to deal merely with Federal Law and the other to deal with all the other matters not covered by the Federal Administration or the Federal Government. On November 17th, 1931, the Mahatma spoke on the Congress demand for complete control over the army and over external affairs. He said that the present army, whether Indian or British, was an army of occupation. 'I would say emphatically that the whole of this army should be disbanded if it does not pass under my control before I could possibly shoulder the burden of running the Government of India under the terrible handicaps under which we are labouring as a legacy of alien rule.... If the British people think that we shall require a century before that can be done, then for that century the Congress will wander in the wilderness and the Congress must go through that terrible fiery ordeal.... and if it becomes necessary and if it is God's will—a shower of bullets.'

On November 19th, 1931, before the Federal Structure Committee, the Mahatma opposed the resolution on commercial safeguards for Britishers passed by the first Round Table Conference as being detrimental to the interests of the Indian people. He agreed that there should be no racial discrimination against foreigners as such. He also agreed that 'no existing interest legitimately acquired and not being in conflict with the best interests of the nation in general, shall be interfered with except in accordance with the law applicable to such interests'. But he made it clear that the National Government of the future might find it necessary to dispossess the 'haves' in the interests of the 'have-nots', i.e. the famished millions of India. Existing interests should be subjected to judicial scrutiny when necessary—but no racial question would be involved therein. He further opposed the existing rights[1] of the European community in India in regard to criminal trials. In his next speech at the Round Table Conference on November 25th, he maintained that the obligations to be taken over by the future National Government of India should be subject to audit and impartial examination.[2] He condemned the fixing of the currency ratio at 1s. 6d. instead of at 1s. 4d., as the Indian people had demanded. Continuing, he said : 'I would want complete control of the Indian finance if India was really to have responsibility at the centre. In my opinion, unless we have control over our own purse, absolutely unrestricted, we shall not be able to shoulder the responsibility nor will it be a responsibility worth the name.' In another speech, the same day, he maintained that after mature consideration he had come to the conclusion that provincial autonomy and central responsibility must go together. 'A strong centre governed and administered by an alien authority and a strong autonomy (for the provinces) are a contradiction in terms.' Speaking of central responsibility, he said : 'I want that responsibility at the centre that will give me, as you all know, control of the army and finance. I know that I am not going to get that here and now and I know there is not a British man ready for that. Therefore, I know I must go back and yet invite the nation to a course of suffering.'

Mahatma Gandhi's first speech at the plenary session of the Round Table Conference on November 30th, is a priceless document, though it affords painful reading, being a record of disillusionment complete. He started by saying : 'All the other parties at this meeting represent sectional interests. The Congress alone claims to represent the whole of India and all interests.... And yet here I see that the Congress is treated as one of the parties.... I wish I could convince all the British public men, the British Ministers that the Congress is capable of delivering the

---

[1] For instance the right to have a European judge or a European jury in the trial.
[2] In this connection he referred to the Report of the Public Debt Enquiry Committee appointed by the Karachi Congress in 1931.

goods.... But no, although you have invited the Congress you distrust the Congress. Although you have invited the Congress, you reject its claim to represent the whole of India.' Referring to the communal question, he told the unpleasant truth 'that so long as the wedge in the shape of foreign rule divides community from community and class from class, there will be no real living solution, there will be no living friendship between these communities'. On the question of the national demand he said: 'Call it by any name you like, a rose will smell as sweet by any other name, but it must be the rose of liberty that I want and not the artificial product.' Then in order to soften his demand for independence he appealed in these words: 'I want to become a partner with the English people; but I want to enjoy precisely the same liberty that your people enjoy and I want to seek this partnership not merely for India and not merely for mutual benefit.' Then finding that all appeals were useless, he flared up and said: 'Will you not see the writing that these terrorists are writing with their blood?' And then he said: 'I shall hope against hope, I shall strain every nerve to achieve an honourable settlement for my country.... It can be a matter of no joy and comfort to me to lead them again to a fight of that character, but if a further ordeal of fire has to be our lot, I shall approach that with the greatest joy and with the greatest consolation that I was doing what I felt to be right, that the country was doing what it felt to be right.'

At the last sitting of the plenary session of the Round Table Conference on December 1st, 1931, the Prime Minister, Mr. Ramsay Macdonald, made the following declaration:

> 'At the beginning of the year (1931) I made a declaration of the policy of the then Government and I am authorised by the present one to give you and India specific assurance that it remains its policy. I shall repeat the salient sentences of that declaration.
> 'The view of His Majesty's Government is that responsibility for the Government of India should be plac-

ed upon the Legislatures, Central and Provincial, with such provisions as may be necessary to guarantee during the period of transition the observance of certain obligations and to meet other special circumstances and also with such guarantees as are required by the minorities to protect their political rights. In such statutory safeguards as may be made for meeting the needs of the transitional period, it will be the primary concern of His Majesty's Government to see the reserved powers so framed and exercised as not to prejudice the advance of India through the new Constitution to full responsibility for her own Government. 'Regardiing the Central Government it made it plain that, subject to defined conditions, His Majesty's late Government was prepared to recognize the principle of responsibility of the executive to the Legislature if both were constituted on an All-India Federal basis.
'The principle of responsibility was to be subject to the qualification that in the existing circumstances, defence and external affairs must be reserved to the Governor-General and that regarding finance, such conditions must apply as would insure the fulfilment of the obligations incurred under the authority of the Secretary of State (for India) and the maintenance unimpaired of the financial stability and credit of India. 'Finally, it was our view that the Governor-General must be granted the necessary powers to enable him to fulfil his responsibility for securing the observance of the constitutional rights of the minorities and for ultimately maintaining the tranquillity of the State.'

Moving a vote of thanks to the Premier the Mahatma said that in all probability he had come to the parting of the ways but he hoped that if a fight was unavoidable, it would be conducted without malice on either side. Three days later the Mahatma said good-bye to the Premier and left London. Before leaving London in an interview to the Press he stated that an immediate nationwide resumption of civil disobedience was out of the question—but he did foresee the possbility of local civil disobedience being launched as a protest against specific acts of injustice and tyranny, as for example the ordinances promulgated in Bengal, the United Provinces and the Frontier Province.

During his stay of nearly three months in England, the Mahatma had an exceedingly busy time. A glance at his daily routine would show that he was overstraining himself —sometimes not allowing himself to have more than two hours' sleep for days together. He met all sorts of people there—M.P.s, politicians, journalists, missionaries, society ladies, social workers, litterateurs, artists, students, and what not. During week-ends he would undertake tours to Cambridge or Oxford or Lancashire, in order to awaken interest in and sympathy for India. But it seems that there was lack of co-ordination and unity of purpose in all his activities. Indian members of the Round Table Conference complained that it was difficult to get at the Mahatma when they wanted him. Indian Liberal members of the Round Table Conference complained that instead of playing a lone hand, he could have rallied all the anti-communal forces and become the leader of a united Nationalist Party.[1] Whatever the truth of these criticisms may be, there is no doubt that the Mahatma's visit to England was badly planned— if there was any plan at all—and his personal entourage did not consist of any advisers worth the name. His indecision, till the eleventh hour, about attending the London Conference was largely responsible for his lack of plan and for his late arrival in London which considerably handicapped him. As contrasted with him, the Government had made elaborate arrangements and all their plans had been carefully worked out in advance. It was only in London that he realised what it meant to have a conference with members chosen by the Government, with the Congress as one of the several parties present there and with himself as the only representative of the Congress. The wonder of it is that such a shrewd politician as the Mahatma made such a belated discovery in spite of the warnings given by

---

[1] This was the view expressed by the Right Hon. V. S. Sastri in the *Indian Review* of January 1932.

lesser folk in India.

But the causes of the Mahatma's failure in London go much deeper. If the Mahatma meant to co-operate with the Round Table Conference, he should have gone there in 1930. The terms which he got in March 1931—he could have easily got in August 1930. The assurance regarding Dominion Status which he had demanded in 1929 and 1930 —he could not get even in 1931 and as for the other concessions in the Gandhi-Irwin Pact, Lord Irwin would in all probability have agreed to them at any time. In 1930, the Congress could easily have got half the number of seats at the Conference. By going there in 1931, alone and unfriended, the Mahatma had the tactical disadvantage of having to meet a conference which had come into existence without the participation of the Congress and of having to build on sectarian foundations laid by communalist members. With the Labour Cabinet in power in England in 1930 and Lord Irwin in Delhi, the Congress could have given a different turn to the Conference. In 1931 the situation was altered completely. The Labour Cabinet was replaced by a virtually Conservative Cabinet; Lord Irwin made room for Lord Willingdon, while Sir Samuel Hoare succeeded Capt. Wedgwood-Benn at the India Office. The last flickering hope died out when the General Election in October brought the Conservatives into power (under the name of the National Government) with a thumping majority.

In spite of these unfavourable circumstances when the Mahatma did go to England, he should have concentrated entirely on the work of the Conference, with a view to counteracting all the mischievous moves of the Government. Probably under the influence of pro-Indian Britishers like Mr. C. F. Andrews, he unfortunately took it into his head that he should go about rousing sympathy for India among Britishers. That was not the purpose for which he had come to England nor was it possible for him to do so within the short time and with the limited energy at his disposal. Going over the list of persons whom the Mahatma met, one cannot help feeling that for the purpose for which he had come to England, most of the engagements were unnecessary, if not useless. If he had come on an ordinary propaganda tour, a programme such as he had, would have been quite helpful and in order.

There was another deepr cause which accounted for the Mahatma's failure. During his stay in England he had to play two roles in one person, the role of a political leader and that of a world-teacher. Sometimes he conducted himself not as a political leader who had come to negotiate with the enemy, but as a master who had come to preach a new faith—that of non-violence and world-peace. Because of his second role, he had to spend much of his time with people who were quite useless in promoting his political mission. In the absence of advisers from his own party, the place was filled by some of his British admirers. From the moment of his landing in Europe till the moment of his departure, he was surrounded by them. In order to demonstrate his fairness and universal love, he accepted as his hostess an English lady. As contrasted with the Mahatma, the Irish Sinn Fein delegation to London in 1921 had lived a different life. They used to live entirely among themselves and avoid all social engagements with Britishers, though attempts were made to drag the delegation into them. This aloofness and indifference had impressed British politicians much more than the Mahatma's friendliness did. But being a world-teacher, the Mahatma had his own code of ethics.

There is no doubt that in 1930, when the Mahatma was in prison, he had exerted a much greater influence on the Round Table Conference. At the Conference, the Indian Liberal politicians had fully exploited his influence. But when he appeared in person and all alone, he lost much of the glamour and the halo that had attached to his name. He was at a physical disadvantage, being a single frail individual in a group of 107. If he had accepted the offer made by the Government, of fifteen or sixteen seats for the Congress Delegation, his position would have been stronger. His colleagues would have been of great help to him in meeting, and crossing swords with, a solid phalanx of reactionaries. Moreover, the Mahatma did not seem to be cut out for the role of a bargainer. He therefore met the fate which overtook President Wilson at the time of the Versailles Treaty. The Professor-President of America was no match for the Welsh wizard, Mr. Lloyd George—nor was the saint-politician from India any match for the wily Mr. Ramsay Macdonald. On the British side, the Mahatma was handled very tactfully. He had on the whole a very friendly welcome in England which he recognised publicly before he left the country. Special facilities were afforded him while moving about in London. On the plea of guarding his person, two stalwarts from Scotland Yard were detailed to be near him—so that the authorities had not the slightest difficulty in knowing everything about his daily routine and engagements. I have not been able to understand why the Mahatma accepted this escort from Scotland Yard. If an escort was really necessary, his numerous admirers and followers in London could have easily served the purpose.

It has been already remarked that the last hope of a settlement faded away when the Conservatives were returned to power. Their estimate of the Indian situation as also of the Indian leader, was quite different from that of the Labourites. His goodness, his frankness, his humble ways, his profound consideration for his opponents—not only did not impress John Bull, but was construed as weakness. His habit of putting all his cards on the table was all right for India and the Indians, but damaged his prestige among British politicians. His proneness to confess his ignorance on intricate questions of finance or law would have been all right in the company of truth-seeking philosophers, but lowered him in the estimation of the British public who were accustomed to see their leaders looking more wise than they really were. His repeated offer of wholehearted cooperation at the Round Table Conference had a most tragic effect and made them think—'Gandhi is on his last legs'. What impression could such a statement make on a veteran politician in England? 'I shall be here as long as I am required, because I do not want to revive civil disobedience. I want to turn the truce that was arrived at at Delhi into a permanent settlement. But for heaven's sake give me, a frail man sixtytwo years gone, a little bit of chance. Find a little corner[1] for him and the organisation that he represents.'[2] If, on the contrary, the Mahatma had spoken in the language of Dictator Stalin, or II Duce Mussolini or Fuehrer Hitler—John Bull would have understood and would have bowed his head in respect. As it was, the Conservative politicians began to think: 'Is this frail man in loin-cloth so formidable that the powerful British Government should yield to him? India was being ruled by a man who was fit to be a bishop and so we had so much trouble. If only we had a strong man at Delhi and at the India Office—everything would be all right.' This is how the Indian situation was summed up after the General Election of October 1931. And all his propaganda among Church dignitaries, professors and cranks was of no use to India. The secret of political bargaining is to look more strong than you really are. Indian politicians, if they want to match themselves successfully against their British opponents, will have to learn many things which they do not know and unlearn many things which they have learnt.

Going through the speeches of the Mahatma at the Round Table Conference, one is pained at every step. That from the very beginning he had to speak at length on the status of the Congress as contrasted with other parties and had to repeat his remarks over and over again—only shows that a conspiracy had been hatched in advance to ignore the Congress completely. At the Conference the Mahatma remarked that in the reports submitted by the different committees, the views of the so-called majority were given prominence,—while his dissentient note was condemned to insignificance, as if it reflected the opinion of just one individual. Some weeks after his arrival in London, the Mahatma did realise the hopelessness of the situatiion. If he had any political diplomacy, he should have sought a convenient opportunity of getting out of the Conference as soon as

---

[1] It is to be regretted that they cornered him successfully.
[2] The Mahatma's speech at the plenary session of the Round Table Conference on November 30th, 1931.

possible and then should have made an extensive tour in America and on the Continent to expose the unreality of the Conference and to popularise the Indian cause. By sticking to the Conference till the end, he unnecessarily lent prestige to a body that should have been exposed before the bar of world-opinion.

The Mahatma after leaving England spent a few days in Paris. There he had a group of friends and admirers, who were however more interested in his non-violence as a message to the world, than in his struggle for India's freedom. His brief stay in Paris was well utilised, but unfortunately no attempt was made to get into touch with politicians—or with the people who really count in the modern political world. Nor was any attempt made by him to raise the Indian issue as an international political issue. From Paris he went to Geneva. There also he had a group of friends many of whom were interested more in his philosophy than in his politics. Though he visited Geneva, no serious attempt was made to bring him into touch with the people who count in the organisation of the League of Nations. He paid a visit to the International Labour Office and that was about all. However, the most useful part of his time in Switzerland was spent in the company of that great man and thinker—that great friend of India and India's culture, M. Romain Rolland. India today has not a warmer friend outside her shores than this great soul, and therefore the Mahatma rendered a great public service to India by spending some of his time in the company of the French savant. From Switzerland the Mahatma travelled to Italy. He was given a warm reception by the Government and the people of Italy, and was received in audience by the head of the Government, Signor Mussolini. That meeting was certainly an historic one. The Dictator of Italy conveyed his best wishes for the success of the Mahatma's efforts. It was the only occasion on the Continent that the Mahatma came into contact with a man who really counts in the politics of modern Europe. The Mahatma's attitude towards the Fascist authorities, including his attendance at a demonstration of the Fascist boys (the Balilla) was severely criticised in anti-Fascist circles. But there is no doubt that from the point of view of India, the Mahatma rendered great public service by his visit to Italy. The only regret is that he did not stay there longer and did not cultivate more personal contacts.

Reviewing the Mahatma's visit to Europe as a whole, one must say that it is to be regretted that he spent so much of his time in England and so little on the Continent. Even on the Continent he did not devote sufficient time or attention to politicians, industrial magnates and other people who really count in present-day politics. There were many countries on the Continent eagerly expecting a visit from him and where he would have received a most cordial reception. If he had desired, he could without difficulty, have come in touch with the most important individuals and organisations in Europe—to the great benefit of India. But may be, that did not interest him so much. Outside India he had another role to play besides that of a politician and it is not always easy to play two roles in one person.

CHAPTER XIII

## THE FIGHT RESUMED (1932)

True to his habit of travelling by the lowest class available, the Mahatma arrived in Bombay as a deck-passenger by S. S. *Pilsna* on December 28th, 1931. Elaborate arrangements had been made by the Bombay Congress Committee to accord him a right royal reception. Thanks to the propaganda of the Congress, the failure of the Mahatma to achieve something tangible for his country at the London Conference had not produced any depressing effect. And judging from the warmth, cordiality and affection displayed at the reception, one would think that the Mahatma had returned with Swaraj in the hollow of his hand. The same evening he spoke at a mass meeting of 200,000 pople at Azad Maidan. Only with the help of loudspeakers could his voice be audible to that vast gathering. The festivity over, the Mahatma settled down to business. Reports from different parts of the country were duly placed before him. It was soon evident that the situation was materially different from what it was when he had sailed from Bombay towards the end of August. It looked as if the Government had been waiting till Mahatma Gandhi sailed from Bombay in order to start a policy of ruthless repression. The two authors of the Delhi Pact being away from India, the Government could treat that document as a scrap of paper.

It is necessary to recapitulate briefly the events of 1931 which led to a crisis at the end of the year rendering imperative a resumption of the civil-disobedience campaign. After the Karachi Congress, youth and labour circles continued to condemn the Delhi Pact. The Provincial Youth Conference (Naujawan Bharat Sabha) of the United Provinces, held at Muttra in May and presided over by the writer, passed a resolution of disapproval. In July a session of the All-India Trade Union Congress was held in Calcutta under the Presidency of the writer, where a similar resolution was passed. The Right Wing trade unions had seceded in the meantime, but all the unions joined the Congress.

Trouble arose from the very beginning over the question of credentials. After the Nagpur session of the Trade Union Congress held in 1929, a split had occurred among those trade unionists who were generally regarded as Communists. Mr. M. N. Roy, the erstwhile representative of India on the Communist International, was expelled from that body. Following this incident, a split occurred among the pisoners in the Meerut Conspiracy Case and also among their followers in Bombay. One group was reported to follow the lead of the official Communist Party and the other of Mr. M. N. Roy. The Girni-Kamgar Union (Textile Workers' Union) of Bombay, formerly controlled jointly by members of both the groups, was the scene of a split and the Credentials Committee of the Trade Union Congress reported that the Roy group was in possession of the union and was therefore entitled to be represented on the Trade Union Congress. This was resented by the other group, who thereupon resorted to constitutional obstruction culminating in a motion of no-confidence in the President. This motion being defeated, the anti-Roy group withdrew from the Congress after creating a lot of disturbance and set up a Red Trade Union Congress.[1] After the defection, the Congress continued its deliberations. It resolved not to affiliate with any international body but to continue unaided the struggle for the rights of the Indian workers. Mr. Ruikar, President of the Nagpur Textile Workers' Union, was elected President for the coming year, and Mr. S. Mukundalal of Calcutta was elected the Secretary. In spite of the internal dissensions in the Trade Union Movement, barring the Right Wingers, all other trade-unionists were opposed to the Delhi Pact. The Pact contained no clause benefiting the workers in any way and neither the undertrial prisoners nor those convicted in connection with industrial strikes, were granted amnesty. Two Right Wing leaders, Mr. V. V. Giri and Mr. Shiva Rao, were, however, nominated by the

---

[1] From the beginning the Red Trade Union Congress has not shown much sign of activity except occasionally in Bombay and in Calcutta.

Government as members of the second Round Table Conference.

While trade union circles merely kept up vocal opposition to the Delhi Pact, the revolutionaries in Bengal, exasperated by the repressive policy of the Government, created a serious crisis in the province. The Armoury Raid in Chittagong in April 1930, was an aggressive act, but it was on the whole an isolated one. The subsequent acts of terrorism in other parts of Bengal were acts of retaliation or reprisal rather than acts of aggression. In Dacca, the principal city of East Bengal, in August 1930, Mr. Lowman, the head of the Intelligence Branch of the Police was seriously wounded. But prior to that, there had been Hindu-Moslem riots in Dacca and Mymensingh districts, in connection with which the conduct of the police had been open to serious question. Moreover the Dacca police had been harsh and brutal in dealing with Satyagrahi volunteers engaged in peaceful picketing of foreign cloth and liquor shops and in other non-violent activities. Towards the end of 1930, the Inspector-General of Prisons, Bengal, Lieut-Col. Simpson, was assassinated in his office in the Government Secretariat buildings in Calcutta. But prior to that there had been indescribable ill-treatment of political prisoners in many prisons in Bengal and all appeals made to the Government for redress had been of no avail. The murder of Mr. Peddie, Magistrate of Midnapore, in 1931, and subsequently of two of his successors, was the result of the untold atrocities committed by the forces of the Crown in Midnapore district in the attempt to suppress the non-violent no-tax campaign. The public of Calcutta had appointed an impartial committee consisting mostly of Moderate men to inquire into and report on some of the atrocities committed in that district. The report was duly published and the facts brought to the notice of the Government. But no redress followed. It was then that in a fit of exasperation people took to terrorism by way of reprisal.

These acts of terrorism served to stiffen the attitude of the Government and a stronger dose of repression was administered. A golden opportunity of putting an end to the regrettable state of affairs arose in March 1931, when the Delhi Pact was concluded. But instead of turning over a new leaf, the authorities decided to copy the Black and Tan methods that had been employed in Ireland. Between June and October 1931, three rgrettable incidents took place successively—at Chittagong, at Hijli Detention Camp, seventy miles from Calcutta, and at Dacca. At Chittagong an Indian police officer was murdered. The next morning, hooligans were let loose on the town and while the police remained inactive, looting went on in broad daylight. The idea was to teach the people of Chittagong a 'moral' lesson. An inquiry committee appointd by the Calcutta public came to the conclusion after investigation that the conduct of some local officials was open to serious question and the late Mr. J. M. Sengupta openly made the allegation in a public meeting in Calcutta. On the report of the divisional Commissioner, official action against some officers was taken after a very long time. At the Hijli Camp there was some misunderstanding between the state-prisoners and the armed guards. Following this, one night the armed warders made a surprise attack on the state-prisoners' barracks and, after firing indiscriminately at the barracks, attacked the state-prisoners with the butt-end of their rifles. During the firing, two of the state-prisoners, Santosh Mitra and Tarakeswar Sen, were killed and twenty seriously injured. An official committee appointed by the Government consisting of a judge of the High Court came to the conclusion after an open inquiry that the firing was altogether unjustified. At Dacca, there was an unsuccessful attempt to murder the District Magistrate. The same night, four parties of policemen went out to different parts of the city, raided the houses of respectable citizens, destroyed furniture and other articles, assaulted people and carried away whatever valuables they could besides making a large number of indiscriminate arrests. The Calcutta public sent a Committee of Inquiry,[1] which after due inquiry, corroborated

---

[1] The writer was a member of this Committee, but when he arrived near Dacca, he was removed from the district by sheer physical force by police officers. The moment he was free he started for Dacca again when

all the above facts.

In November a new ordinance was promulgated by the Government which introduced a veiled form of martial law in the district of Chittagong. Under this ordinance, hardship and penalty were imposed on the people as one would expect under martial law. The curfew order was introduced, people were ordered to carry identification cards, young men were prohibited to use bicycles, political suspects were ordered to remain indoors for weeks at a stretch, collective fines were imposed on villages which were suspected to be frequented by revolutionaries. Moreover, soldiers were made to march through the villages as a display and people were ordered, on pain of penalty, to come out and receive them. Many of these orders were issued subsequently in Midnapore and Dacca districts. While this double dose of repression was being administered, no steps were taken to punish the officials responsible for the happenings at Chittagong, Hijli and Dacca, nor was any compensation or relief given to the sufferers. To add to the unrest, during the period of truce, some revolutionary prisoners were condemned to death and hanged. The vicious circles of official repression—revolutionary terrorism[1]—official counter-terrorism—thus went on. A further complication arose when the Calcutta Municipal Corporation passed a resolution[2] expressing grief at the execution of one of the revolutionary prisoners, Dinesh Chandra Gupta. In the midst of this turmoil the position of the Congress in Bengal was unenviable. Theoretically there was peace between the Government and the people, but in reality the relations were strained and there were 'hostilities' on both sides. To consider the situation a special session of the Bengal Provincial Conference was held at Berhampore in December. The Conference resolved that the Government had virtually violated the Delhi Pact and the Congress should, therefore,

he was put in prison. He was subsequently released and could then continue the inquiry.
  [1] In December 1931, two schoolgirls, named Shanti and Suniti, shot dead the Magistrate of Comilla.
  [2] This resolution was resented by the Government as well as by all Britishers.

formally give notice to the Government and revive the civil-disobedience campaign, emphasis being laid on the boycott of British goods. It was hoped that the revival of the civil-disobedience movement would divert the energy of the youths and thereby help to stop the terrorist campaign in the province.

But the trouble was not only in Bengal. During the absence of the Mahatma from India a crisis had arisen in the Frontier Province, and also in the United Provinces. The official complaint was that the Red Shirt Volunteers [1] of the Frontier leader, Khan Abdul Gaffar Khan, were engaged in subversive activities, though as a matter of fact they were perfectly non-violent. No notice was sent to the Congress headquarters about this complaint. Suddenly an ordinance was issued declaring the Red Shirt Volunteers an illegal body. Simultaneously Khan Abdul Gaffar Khan, the Frontier Gandhi, and his brother, along with some other leaders, were put under arrest and taken to distant prisons. Several hundred Red Shirts were immediately cast into prison, and within a few months their number arose to several thousands. Thereafter troops were sent into the remotest villages in order to terrorise the people and break up the Red Shirt organisation.

In the United Provinces there had been an acute economic crisis for some time past. In November 1930, Mr. H. N. Brailsford, the wellknown Socialist writer, who was an altogether independent observer, told the writer in Calcutta that the conditions in the United Provinces were verging on an agrarian revolution. About this time the no-rent campaign was started by the Congress in the province. After the Delhi truce, when the no-tax campaign was suspended, the peasants being in the same condition as in 1930, could not pay their rent. In May, the Mahatma tried to mediate in the matter and advised the peasants to pay 50 per cent of their dues—but that also they could not. Thereupon the Government remitted a portion of the land

---

[1] These volunteers were so called from the colour of their uniform. They were Congress volunteers and had nothing to do with the Communist Party.

revenue and maintained that that was enough. The peasants thought otherwise and, on their behalf, the Provincial Congress Committee tried to carry on negotiations with the Government. In November matters reached a crisis. The Government demanded that the peasants should pay up their dues pending negotiations. The peasants demanded, on the contrary, that pending negotiation, the collection should be suspended. At this stage the Provincial Congress Committee approached Sardar V. Patel, the Congress President, and Mahatma Gandhi, who was then in Europe, for advice. The Mahatma left it to the Committee to do as they thought best. The Peasants' League (Kisan League) of the United Provinces then took the matter in hand and informed the Congress Committee that if they did not start the no-rent campaign, it would be launched by the Kisan League. Faced with the possibility of losing its hold on the masses, the Provincial Congress Committee decided to commence the no-rent campaign. Immediately this was done, an ordinance was issued for suppressing that campaign. A large number of arrests was made under the ordinance and about the middle of December when Pandit Jawaharlal Nehru and Mr. Sherwani were leaving Allahabad for Bombay to make preparations for the reception of the Mahatma, they were arrested in the train.

As has been stated at the beginning of this chapter, on December 28th, 1931, Bombay city was *en fete* for the reception of India's beloved leader. Never was a king or a victorious general given a warmer welcome. A hostile demonstration was attempted by the followers of Dr. Ambedkar as also by the local Communist Party, but the smallness of it only served to throw into bolder relief the tremendous hold which the Mahatma had over the masses. The next day the Congress Working Committee met and authorised Mahatma Gandhi to apply for an interview[1] with the Viceroy and accordingly he sent the following telegram:

---

[1] The writer, who was one of those invited to attend this meeting of the Working Committee, expressed the opinion that in the circumstances it would be humiliating for the Mahatma to apply for an interview. But all the others present thought differently.

'I was unprepared on landing yesterday to find the Frontier and the U. P. Ordinances, shootings in the Frontier and arrests of valued comrades in both and on the top, the Bengal Ordinance awaiting me. I do not know whether I am to regard these as an indication that friendly relations between us are closed or whether you expect me still to see and receive guidance from you as to the course I am to pursue in advising the Congress.'

The Viceroy sent a long reply on December 31st and stated at the end : 'His Excellency feels bound to emphasise that he will not be prepared to discuss with you any measures which the Government of India, with the fullest approval of His Majesty's Government, found it necessary to adopt in Bengal, the United Provinces and the North-West Frontier Province.'

Soon after receipt of this telegram the Working Committee met on January 1st, 1932, and adopted the following resolution :

'....The Committee rgards the Premier's declaration as wholly unsatisfactory and inadequate, and in terms of the Congress demands, opines that nothing short of complete independence, carrying full control of defence, external affairs and finance, with such safeguards as may be demonstrably necessary in the interest of the nation, can be regarded by the Congress as satisfactory. The Committee notes that the British Government was not prepared to regard the Congress at the Round Table Conference as entitled to speak on behalf of the nation as a whole. At the same time the Committee recognises with sorrow that communal harmony could not be attained at the said Conference. The Committee invites the nation, therefore, to make ceaseless efforts to demonstrate the capacity of the Congress to represent the nation as a whole and promote an atmosphere that would make the Constitution, framed purely on a national basis, acceptable to the various communities composing the nation. Meanwhile, the

Committee is prepared to render co-operation to Government, provided the Viceroy reconsiders his Thursday's telegram to Mahatma Gandhi, adequate relief is granted in respect of the ordinances and its recent acts, a free scope is left to the Congress in any future negotiations and consultations to prosecute the Congress's claim for complete independence, and administration of the country is carried on with popular representatives pending the attainment of such independence.

'In the absence of a satisfactory response from Government in terms of the foregoing paragraph, the Working Committee will regard it as an indication on the part of the Government that it has reduced to nullity the Delhi Pact.

'In the event of a satisfactory response not forthcoming, the Committee calls upon the nation to resume civil disobedience.'

The same day the Mahatma sent a long rejoinder to the Viceroy asking him to reconsider his decision and grant an interview without imposing any conditions as to the scope of discussion. He enclosed a copy of the Working Committee's resolution and added: 'If His Excellency thinks it worth while to see me, the operation of the resolution will be suspended pending our discussion, in the hope that it may result in the resolution being finally given up.'

On January 2nd, 1932, the Viceroy informed Mahatma Gandhi that an interview under the threat of civil disobedience was out of the question. The Mahatma replied as follows : '....Surely it is wrong to describe an honest expression of opinion as a threat. May I remind the Government that the Delhi negotiations were opened and carried on whilst civil disobedience was on and that when the Pact was made, civil disobedience was not given up but only discontinued. This position was reasserted and accepted by His Excellency and his Government last year prior to my departure for London....Meanwhile I wish to assure the Government that every endeavour will be made on the part of the Congress to carry on the struggle without malice and in a strictly non-violent manner....'

That was the end of the negotiations. On January, 4th, the Government of India issued a statement justifying their attitude and conduct. Simultaneously orders were issued to local authorities throughout India to strike at the Congress organisations at once. The ordinances carefully prepared by the Government of India in 1931 during the period of the truce were at once put into operation. According to lists previously prepared by the local authorities, sweeping arrests of Congress leaders were made before they could find time to launch the civil-disobedience campaign. Within a week almost everybody who was somebody in the Congress Party was in prison. Nevertheless, the campaign began to gain in strength and volume without any direction from headquarters. According to official statistics, 14,800 arrests were made in January and 17,800 in February. The Government soon realised that if arrests were continued at that rate it would be impossible to deal with the large prison population. In March, tactics were therefore changed and, instead of making arrests, force was used in dealing with Congressmen and their demonstrations. Under the ordinances, the following steps among others were taken by the local authorities all over India: orders were issued prohibiting meetings and processions; Congress organisations were declared illegal and Congress offices were taken possession of; Congress funds were seized; orders were served on people not to help the Congress in any way nor to harbour Congres volunteers, on pain of punishmnt; land and property were seized for not paying land revenue or other taxes; National literature was banned; the Nationalist Press was gagged; shop-keepers were ordered not to close their shops when asked by the Congress to do so; 'lathi charges' and even firing were resorted to for dispersing Congress demonstrations.

Despite all these restrictions, the civil-disobedience campaign was in full swing. The following were some of the activities of the Congress: holding meetings and conferences in spite of Government prohibition; organising processions in defiance of police orders; picketing foreign cloth and liquor shops; picketing British goods, banks, insurance companies, etc.; publishing unauthorised bulletins, newspapers, etc.; saluting the national flag in public and hoisting it over Government buildings; manufacturing salt; attempting to reoccupy buildings seized by the Government; withholding of land revenue and taxes. Besides these activities, during the first six months of the year, special campaigns were conducted on an all-India basis under the orders of the Congress Working Committee or of the Congress President. From April 6th to April 13th, the national week was observed in commemoration of the Amritsar massacre of 1919. This was followed by the holding of the 47th session of the Congress at Delhi on April 24th, in spite of the severest police restrictions. The Delhi Congress was followed up by a series of provincial, district and sub-divisional political conferences held throughout India in defiance of the police ban. A raid on the Wadala Salt Depot was attempted on May 15th. An All-India Swadeshi Day was observed on May 29th, to stimulate the Swadeshi[1] (i.e. national industry) movement and an All-India Prisoners' Day was observed on July 4th, to express sympathy for political prisoners. On April 8th, during the National Week Celebration at Allahabad, the police attempted to disperse by force a Congress procession led by the revered widow of Pandit Motilal Nehru. Among those who were seriously injured during the police attack was Mrs. Motilal Nehru herself. This event sent a thrill of horror and indignation throughout the country.[2] The Delhi Congress was carefully planned. Though the President-elect, Pandit Madan Mohan Malaviya, was arrested on his way to Delhi, the police could not prevent a large number of delegates from arriving there for participating in the Congress. The Congress session having been banned by the Government, in the absence of a better arrangement, it was

---

[1] After the Congress was banned, 'Buy Indian' Leagues were organised within the ambit of the Law.
[2] The medical officer who attended on Mrs. Nehru reported as follows: 'Her injuries were caused by something like a lathi. She has received half a dozen injuries, including a bad cut on her head which caused profuse bleeding.'

held near the Clock Tower in the Chandni Chowk and Mr. Ranchoddas Amritlal of Ahmedabad presided. There was a short session and the resolutions adopted by the Subjects Committee, which had been printed beforehand, were distributed among the public. The Congress reiterated the resolution on independence, approved of the decision of the Working Committee to revive the civil-disobedience movement, and reaffirmed its faith in the leadership of Mahatma Gandhi. Soon after, the police arrived on the scene, dispersed the gathering by force, and made a large number of arrests.

Reviewing the Congress movement during the first four months, Pandit M. M. Malaviya in a public statement, issued on May 2nd, 1932, declared:

'During these four months up to April 20th last, according to the reports published in the Press, 66,646 persons, among whom were included 5,325 women and many children, have been arrested, imprisoned and humiliated. This could not possibly include arrests in the far-off villages in the interior of the country and, therefore, the Congress estimates the total arrests to be over 80,000 up to that date. The jails are overcrowded and ordinary prisoners are being released before their time to make room for political prisoners. To this has to be added the number of arrests made during the last ten days, including those of the delegates to the Delhi Congress. According to the reports in the Press, firing has been rsorted to in at least 29 cases with considerable loss of life. There have been lathi charges on unarmed crowds at 325 places. There have been 633 cases of house searches and 102 cases of confiscation of property. A general policy has been pursued of imposing extraordinarily heavy fines on persons who have been convicted in connection with the movement and property far in excess of what was necessary for realising the amount of the fines has been attached and sold. The Press has been gagged as it has never been gagged before. 163 cases have been reported where the newspapers and public presses have been rgulated by orders for confiscation, demands for security and consequent closing down of the presses, warnings, searches and arrests of editors, printers or keepers. Numerous public meetings and processions of non-violent men and women have been dispersed by lathi charges, and sometimes by firing.' (*Indian Recorder*, Calcutta p. 271).

In connection with the above report, it may be noted, that during the period under review, political prisoners in Karachi Jail and in Haripur Jail in the Frontier Provinces were subjected to whipping. In Rajashahi Jail in Bengal, political prisoners were subjected to numerous humiliating punishments like bar-fetters, night handcuffs, gunny clothing, etc. In Suri Jail in Bengal, women prisoners went on hunger-strike as a protest against ill-treatment.[1]

On the whole the activities of the Congress in 1932 did not compare unfavourably with those of 1930. Nevertheless, every Congressman could feel one difference. In 1930 the Congress had taken the offensive, while the Government was on the defensive. In 1932 it was just the reverse. There is no doubt that in spite of the manifold defects of the Delhi Pact, diehards in England and in India took it as a defeat or a humiliation for the all-powerful British Government. They were smarting under a sense of defeat and wanted to avenge themselves. The overwhelming majority gained by the Conservatives at the General Election in October 1931, encouraged them greatly. Moreover, the attitude of Mahatma Gandhi and the statements made by him in England, gave them the impression that he was unwilling or unprepared to face a fight again. That the Mahatma was honestly pursuing a peaceful policy has to be admitted on all hands and his very unpreparedness can be regarded as

[1] In many other prisons similar incidents took place. In Rajmundry Jail, a prisoner belonging to the Lahore Conspiracy Case was flogged. In Bellary Jail, political prisoners were attacked by warders with sticks (lathis). In the Deoli Detention Camp for Bengal state-prisoners near Ajmer, the state-prisoners were assaulted by the guards and seriously injured. In all such cases the usual charge against the prisoners was one of insubordination.

a proof of his sincerity of purpose. In fact, the Mahatma carried his peaceful intentions so far that he neglected to keep his 'powder dry'. He was in reality dragged into a fight in 1932 because of the *non possumus* attitude of the Viceroy on the one hand and the rising temper of the public on the other. In this connection it is significant that the aggressive steps taken by the Government of India during the absence of the Mahatma had the full approval of His Majesty's Government. Apart from the Government's attitude there were two other factors that forced the Mahatma to resume the fight: the general temper of the public and the influence of the Left Wing. As for the first, in none of the major provinces was the public satisfied at the attitude of the Government. Those who had given in to the Mahatma hoping that something tangible would come out of the Round Table Conference were disillusioned. Further, the steady propaganda carried on by Left Wing Congressmen, youth-leaguers [1] and Left Wing Labourites also had its effect. While in England the Mahatma did feel now and again that another fight was unavoidable but the pity of it is that no preparations were made by the Congress for the campaign and no plans were prepared in advance. The campaign of 1932 was an imitation of that of 1930 and the Government had prepared effective counter-measures for dealing with a campaign of that sort. If the Congress wanted to be successful in 1932 as well, it should have devised new tactics to take the Government by surprise.

It is not generally understood why the Congress was unsuccessful in 1932, though the same tactics had been successful in 1930. The reason is that in 1930 the tactics of the Congress had taken the Government by surprise. No doubt, the same tactics had been employed in 1921 and 1922, but owing to the sudden termination of the campaign in February 1922, the Congress did not have to disclose all its secrets. Moreover, eight years had elapsed since that campaign and most of the men who had dealt with that

---

[1] On December 22nd, 1931, the Maharashtra Youth Conference met at Poona with the writer in the chair and passed a resolution calling upon the Congress Working Committee to resume the civil-disobedience campaign.

campaign were no longer in the service of the Government. Consequently, the 1930 campaign was to all intents and purposes a novel campaign and it took the Government some time to comprehend it and to develop counter-tactics thereafter to cope with it. The Delhi Truce gave the Government time to do this work and on January 1st, 1932, when the Working Committee resolved to resume the civil-disobedience campaign, the Government forces were in complete readiness to strike immediately and ruthlessly. And they were not content with striking at those who worked in the open, but made a clean sweep of the brains and financiers of the movement as well.[1]

During the first eight months of the year the fight went on with unabated zeal. The declaration of the Government that the Congress would soon be down and out was falsified. The Congress was still alive and kicking, and there was no sign that it would meet with an early death. In March the movement was further strengthened because the Jamiat-ul-ulema, the all-India organisation of the Moslem priests and divines, under the leadership of Mufti Kifayetullah, declared for non-co-operation and the leaders of the Jamiat soon found themselves in prison. This decision of the Jamiat considerably strengthened the position of the Nationalist Moslems, who had all along been an integral part of the Congress, and of the Moslems of the Frontier Province, who were going through the worst form of official repression. Nevertheless, the odds were against the Congress. In Bombay, which had been the storm centre in 1930, Hindu-Moslem riots broke out in May and dragged on for nearly six weeks. Owing to this outbreak, the Congress campaign in Bombay suffered a terrible setback from which it could not recover. In Gujerat, the harassed, persecuted and impoverished peasantry could no longer wage the brave fight of which they could boast in 1930. In the United Provinces, after some months, the no-rent campaign could not make further head-

[1] Among those imprisoned in this way were Mr. Bhulabhai Desai, former Advocate-General of Bombay and Mr. Sarat C. Bose, a prominent advocate of Calcutta and a front-rank Congressman who was an Alderman of the Calcutta Municipality. At present (November 1934) the latter is still in detention.

way in the face of official repression. In Bengal, more serious than the civil-disobedience movement was the terrorist campaign of the revolutionaries. But though terrorism was a thorn to the Government, it brought untold hardship on the people, since several districts like Chittagong, Midnapore and Dacca were virtually handed over to martial law and the innocent villagers were subjected to heavy collective fines for the misdeeds committed by unknown people. During the year a liberal use was made of firearms for dispersing Congress demonstrations. Replying to a question in the Indian Legislative Assembly, the Home Member to the Government of India, Mr. (now Sir) H. G. Haig stated that in dispersing assemblies, firing was resorted to seventeen times in Bengal, seven times in the United Provinces, three times in Bihar and Orissa, once in Madras Presidency, once in the Frontier Province—while in Bombay Presidency the casualties from shooting were thirty-four killed and ninety-one wounded. In this situation, when the Congress was engaged in a life and death struggle, an unexpected development took place which led to a complete sidetracking of the civil-disobedience movement in the country. That was the fast of Mahatma Gandhi on September 20th, 1932.

On March 11th, the Mahatma had written to Sir Samuel Hoare informing him that in keeping with what he had stated at the Round Table Conference in London on November 13th, 1931, if the depressed classes were torn away from the main body of Hindus by the grant of separate electorate, he would resist it with his life and in pursuance of that resolve, he would fast unto death. On April 13th, Sir Samuel Hoare had replied in a non-committal way, saying that the Government would give the matter their fullest consideration before coming to a decision. The 'Communal Award'[1] of the Prime Minister, Mr. Ramsay Macdonald, was thereafter announced on August 17th. It provided for

---

[1] As the members nominated by the British Government to the Second Round Table Conference in 1931 could not come to an agreement on the question of representation, electorate, etc. for the legislatures under the New Constitution, the British Prime Minister announced the Government's decision. This decision is known as the Communal Award.

a certain number of seats for the depressed classes in the Provincial Legislatures which would be filled up on the basis of a separate electorate. In addition to this, members of the depressed classes would be entitled to stand for election from the general constituencies earmarked for Hindus and would be registered in a common electoral role along with other Hindus. The award further provided that if His Majesty's Government were satisfied that the communities concerned were mutually agreed upon a practicable alternative scheme, either in respect of one or more of the Governor's provinces or in respect of the whole of British India, before the new Government of India Bill was passed into law, they would be prepared to recommend to Parliament that the alternative should be substituted for the provisions now outlined. On August 18th, the Mahatma addressed a letter to the Premier informing him that in accordance with what he had written to Sir Samuel Hoare on March 11th, he had resolved to commence fast unto death at noon on September 20th. 'The fast will cease if during its progress, the British Government, of its own motion or under pressure of public opinion, revise their decision and withdraw their scheme of communal electorates for the depressed classes whose representatives should be elected by general electorate under common franchise, no matter how wide it is.' The Mahatma further asked that the entire correspondence be given immediate and full publicity. The Premier replied on September 8th regretting the decision of the Mahatma but affirming that the provisions of the award could not be altered except on the condition stated therein. The Mahatma received this communication the next day and immediately replied saying that he felt compelled reuctantly to adhere to the decision he had already conveyed.

Words cannot describe the anxiety and alarm that passed from one end of the country to the other when the news about the impending fast was published on September 13th. Frantic appeals were made to the Mahatma to desist but the appeals proved ineffective. Government offered to release him under certain conditions but he declined conditional release. It was therefore decided to leave him undisturbed in Poona Prison, but to remove all restrictions regarding interviews and correspondence. On an appeal from Pandit M. M. Malaviya, a conference of Hindu leaders met at Bombay on September 19th, in order to deliberate how the Mahatma's life could be saved. After a preliminary discussion there, the leaders adjourned to Poona in order to be in constant touch with the Mahatma. After prolonged discussions, an agreement was arrived at between Hindu leaders on September 24th, which virtually did away with separate electorate for the depressed classes. This agreement hereafter known as the Poona Agreement,[1] was ratified by the Hindu leaders' conference and by the Hindu Mahasabha on September 25th, and was cabled to the Government of India and to the Prime Minister. On September 26th, His Majesty's Government announced that they were prepared to recommend to Parliament to endorse the Poona Agreement. The whole country breathed a sigh of relief. Prayers went up to heaven that the Mahatma's life had been saved.

The Poona Agreement provided for a certain number of reserved seats for members of the depressed classes in the Legislatures on the basis of a common electorate for all classes of Hindus. There was, however, one qualification. The members of the depressed classes registered in the general electoral roll in a constituency would form an electoral college which would elect a panel of four candidates belonging to the depressed classes for each of such reserved seats by the method of the single vote. The provision for a primary election, to be in operation for ten years, was insisted on by Dr. Ambedkar (who had been nominated by the Government to the Round Table Conference), though before the Simon Commission and at the first Round Table Conference he had demanded reservation of seats for the depressed classes on the basis of a common electorate for all Hindus. Mr. M. C. Rajah, a prominent leader of the depressed classes had, on the contrary, consistently stood for reservation of seats for his commu-

---

[1] Also called the Poona Pact.

nity on the basis of a common electorate. Earlier in the year he had entered into a pact with Dr. Moonje, President of the Hindu Mahasabha, on this basis. This pact, known as the Rajah-Moonje Pact, was, however, opposed by Dr. Ambedkar and his followers and on that ground it was not accepted by the British Government.

As long as the Mahatma was on fast, rational thinking was completely suspended and the one thought of his countrymen was how to save his life. Once he was out of danger, people began to examine the Poona Agreement in the cold light of reason. Then it was realised that while the Communal Award provided 71 seats in the Provincial Legislatures for the depressed classes, the Poona Agreement had provided 148. These additional seats would be given them at the expense of the rest of the Hindu community. In provinces like Bengal, where Hindus had already been unjustly treated in the award, the Poona Agreement was regarded as a further injustice by the rest of the Hindu community—particularly in view of the fact that the depressed classes problem hardly existed there. Moreover, it was realised that the Poona agreement had not done away with separate electorate altogether. People began to ask seriously if, after all, it was worth while for Mahatma Gandhi to have staked his life for such an issue, especially when the Communal Award was from start to finish an objectionable document.

But whatever may be the permanent value of the Poona Agreement, there is no doubt that the fast of Mahatma Gandhi had a permanent and far-reaching effect in rousing the conscience of the Hindu community. It was a unique spectacle to see how the heart of the entire nation throbbed for one man. All sections of the Hindus were stirred to activity as they had never been before. The most important result of the 'epic fast' was to give a powerful impetus to the movement for the eradication of untouchability. During the fast such a colossal amount of sympathy had been generated not only for the Mahatma personally but for the cause of the depressed classes as well, that it would have been a great pity if that sympathy had not been harnessed into permanent channels of activity through the organisation of the All-India Anti-Untouchability League.

While the Mahatma's fast had a remarkable effect on his countrymen, in the international sphere it did not prove to be an unmixed blessing. It served to advertise to a disproportionate degree the issue of the depressed classes. Hitherto the world had known only one issue relating to India, the political issue—India's grievance against England. Now the leader of the Nationalist movement himself announced to the world that there was another issue—the internal isue—of such vital importance to India that he was prepared to stake his life for it. And British propagandists were not slow to take advantage of the opportunity. In September 1932, the whole of Europe was told that the Mahatma was fasting because he was against granting certain rights to the untouchables.[1] Ever since then the European public have been constantly fed with stories that India is a land full of internal dissensions where not only Hindus and Moslems, but Hindus themselves, are perpetually fighting with one another and only the strong hand of Britain is able to maintain peace and order.

The fast had another unfortunate effect which proved to be more serious. It served to sidetrack the political movement at a time when all possible attention should have been devoted to it. If with termination of the fast the Mahatma had handed over the anti-untouchability work to friends outside, the effect of the fast would not have been so harmful. But when the leader himself began to conduct the anti-untouchability campaign from behind the prison-walls, what could his followers do? The Mahatma had all along held that a Satyagraha prisoner should regard himself as 'civilly dead' and should not bother about the work outside prison. But on this occasion he did not stick to his usual principle. To make matters worse, when questions were put to him at this time as to whether political work should be done or social work, he gave replies that were

---

[1] In many countries in Europe the writer has heard this remark made by people generally interested in Indian affairs. At first he did not realise the significance of this remark—but later on he found out that in September 1932, this story had been told all over Europe.

rather confusing or he did not reply at all, which led people to think that he preferred social work to political. This lead of the Mahatma was naturally followed more by his blind followers and by those who were tired of repeated suffering and imprisonment and wanted a convenient excuse for giving up the political fight.

Another theory has been put forward to explain the Mahatma's conduct. It is advanced that he realised the ultimate failure of the movement and therefore wanted to create out of it another movement which would be of benefit to his countrymen. This theory cannot be accepted since in November 1931, in London, the Mahatma had spoken of his determination to resist with his life, special electorate for the depressed classes. One feels inclined to think that this sidetracking of the civil-disobedience movement was the result of that subjectivism which seizes him at times and makes him utterly blind to and oblivious of objective realities. Ever since the Round Table Conference, he had begun to ponder so deeply over the depressed classes problem that the other problems receded to the background for the time being. Whatever the real explanation may be, there is no doubt that the fast served to sidetrack the civil-disobedience movement and cause a diversion of men, money and public enthusiasm to the anti-untouchability (or 'Harijan') [1] campaign at a time when the position of the Congress, vis-a-vis the Government, was none too strong. The effect was the same as it would be if in the middle of a battle a general gave the order to his troops to start excavating a canal in order to supply water to the thirsty people of the countryside.

In response to the appeal made by the Mahatma on September 26th, temples and public wells throughout India began to be thrown open to the untouchables. In fact so rapid was the march of progress, that it looked as if the demon of untouchability would be laid low in no time. However, a resistance was met with at Guruvayur in South India where the Zamorin, the trustee of the temple, refused

---

[1] The word 'Harijan' (literally, 'a man of God') was coined by the Mahatma to denote a member of the depressed classes or untouchables.

to throw it open to the untouchables on the plea of tradition and legal difficulties. Thereupon, Mr. Kelappan, a well-known and highly-esteemed Congress worker, commenced a fast as a protest against the exclusion of untouchables from the temple. When his condition became critical, the Mahatma was prevailed upon to intervene and save his life. At the request of the Mahatma who undertook to continue the fight, Kelappan gave up the fast. About this time it was found that in many places the authorities or trustees of several temples were raising legal obstacles in the way of throwing open the temples to untouchables. It was therefore considered desirable to introduce legislation in the Madras Legislative Council and in the Indian Legislative Assembly to remove such legal difficulties once for all. The Bill drafted for the Madras Council was refused sanction by the Viceroy. Permission for introduction of the Bill drafted for the Indian Legislative Assembly was granted by the Viceroy on January 23rd, 1933, but it was made clear that the Government would not commit itself in any way with regard to the Bill and would afford full opportunity for public opinion to express itself on the question. A special request was made to the Government of India for affording facilities for the speedy passage of the Temple Entry Bill, but the Viceroy declined to offer any such facilities and, thanks to the dilatory tactics of the Government, the Bill is still hanging fire. To strengthen the demand for temple entry for untouchables, plebiscite of temple-goers was taken at Guruvayur on December 25th, 1932. Though Guruvayur is regarded to be a socially backward place, out of 20,163 votes recorded, 77 per cent were in favour of temple entry, 13 per cent were against, while 10 per cent were neutral.

Another beneficial result followed from the appeal of the Mahatma made on September 26th to settle Hindu-Moslem differences. A Unity Conference was convened at Allahabad in which Pandit Malaviya and Moulana Shaukat Ali took leading part. The Conference met on November 1st, under the presidentship of Mr. Vijayaraghav Achariar, ex-President of the Congress, and a large number of representative Hindus and Moslems attended. The atmosphere was one of perfect cordiality. A great deal of progress was made in the negotiations for a Hindu-Moslem settlement. But ultimately two obstacles arose. On one side, the leaders of the communalist section of the Moslems condemned the unity efforts. On the other side, the Bengal problem proved insoluble, since the Europeans would not surrender any seat allowed them under the Communal Award and the Moslems would not be content with less than 51 per cent of the total number of seats. Though the Conference did not come to a successful conclusion, it had a moral value and it helped to clear the atmosphere considerably.

We may now review the actions of the Government during the year 1932. While taking the severest measures against the Congress, the Viceroy constantly urged that the Government would simultaneously push on the work of constitution-making. About the middle of January, the Consultative Committee was appointed for keeping the Government in close touch with all the leaders of the other parties, barring the Congress, through the Viceroy and especially for considering the recommendations of the Franchise, Federal Finance and Indian States Inquiry Committee as a preliminary to their consideration by His Majesty's Government. Owing to the delay in issuing the Communal Award, the Consultative Committee was twice postponed on the insistence of the Moslem members. On June 27th, an announcement was made by the Government to the effect that they had decided to provide for Provincial Autonomy and Federation in a single Bill and that they would abandon the Third Session of the Round Table Conference. The Indian Liberal leaders immediately lodged a strong protest against the abandonment of the Round Table Conference and following this Messrs. Sastri, Jayakar, Joshi and Sir Tej Bahadur Sapru resigned from the Consultative Committee. This made the Government climb down a bit, and on July 7th, Sir Samuel Hoare, in a speech before the Central Asian Society, explained that the change of procedure did not imply a change of policy. He further stated that when the Joint Parliamentary Committee met to consider the Government proposals, Indians would be enabled to appear not only as witnesses but also to participate in the discussions of the Committee. The explanation of the Secretary of State for India was not considered adequate by the Liberal leaders who persisted in their opposition. On September 5th, a fresh announcement was made by the Viceroy before the Indian Legislative Assembly to the effect that since the Consultative Committee would not be able to make the contribution anticipated from it, it had been decided to hold further discussions in London. A small body of representatives from British India and from the Indian States would therefore meet in London about the middle of November. The work would be in accordance with a fixed agenda and there would be no public session. The Liberal leaders now felt satisfied that their trip to London was restored. The Third Round Table Conference commenced work on November 17th and ended on December 24th, the final session being open to the public. The Labour Party did not participate in this Conference on the ground that the Government had gone back on the policy of conciliation. They also wanted that the Indian members should keep aloof, but that desire was not complied with. Sir Samuel Hoare summed up the results of the Conference at the close of the session. The following are some of the decisions made by the Government to which he referred:

1. The Moslem community would have a representation of 33⅓ per cent in the Federal Legislature so far as British India was concerned.
2. It was not possible to give any definite date as to when the Federation would be in operation.
3. Sindh and Orissa would be separate provinces.
4. The Defence Budget would be non-votable.
5. For employing Indian troops outside India for purposes other than Indian, the decision of the Federal Ministry and the Federal Legislature would be taken but the Crown would have full authority when Indian troops were to be employed outside India

in the defence of India.

Finally, in response to an appeal for co-operation made by Sir Tej Bahadur Sapru, Sir Samuel Hoare said that he wanted to see no empty chairs at the Round Table Conference of the Joint Select Committee. During the year the revolutionary movement was strong in the province of Bengal. Special powers were given to the Bengal Government by the Viceroy, in addition to the Viceregal Ordinances. The Viceregal Ordinances, four in number, designed mainly for coping with the civil-disobedience movement, were issued on January 4th, 1932. On June 30th, before these Ordinances were due to lapse, a fresh but comprehensive Ordinance, called the Special Powers Ordinance 1932, was promulgated by the Government of India. In addition to this, the Bengal Emergency Powers Ordinance had been issued in November 1931 for arming the Bengal Government with powers similar to those enjoyed by martial law authorities, for the suppression of the terrorist movement. This Ordinance was renewed on May 29th, 1932. Further powers were given to the Bengal Government on July 20th by the Government of India through the Bengal Emergency Powers (Second Amendment) Ordinance 1932. On September 1st, the Bengal Criminal Law Amendment Act 1932 was passed by the Bengal Legislative Council which gave increased powers to the Executive, the most important provision being that attempt at murder was made punishable with death sentence. Another Act was passed on September 6th, called the Bengal Suppression of Terrorist Outrages Act 1932, which empowered the Executive to seize buildings, to order citizens on pain of punishment to assist them in the suppression of terrorism, to impose collective fines on villagers, etc. The legislation passed in the Bengal Legislative Council armed the Government with permanent powers—so that in future, emergency ordinances would not be necessary. During the year, terrorist outrages took place from time to time, the most important of them being the murder of Mr. Douglas, the District Magistrate of

Midnapore and Mr. Ellison, Additional Superintendent of Police, Comilla. On the side of the Government the severest measures were taken. Troops were quartered in many districts where trouble had taken place or was apprehended and heavy collective fines were imposed in Chittagong, Midnapore and Twentyfour Parganas districts. Moreover, the abandoned prison for revolutionary prisoners in the Andaman Islands in the Bay of Bengal was reopened in spite of public protest and political prisoners were transported there.

During the year, two important Labour Conferences were held. The first session of the Indian Trades Union Federation (former Right Wing of the Trade Union Congress) was held at Madras on July 15th, with Mr. V. V. Giri in the chair. Among the resolutions passed was one relating to the position of labour in the future Indian Constitution. The All-India Trade Union Congress met on September 12th at Madras, with Mr. J. N. Mitra as President. The Trade Union Congress condemned the Communal Award and the Ottawa Pact as harmful to the best interests of the workers. It also passed a resolution saying that in view of the sporadic strikes at Matunga (near Bombay), Kharagpur (seventy miles from Calcutta), Lillooah (near Calcutta), Lucknow (in the United Provinces) and other places, it was clear that the workers in all the railways were resolved to declare a general strike and that the responsibility for postponing it indefinitely lay upon leaders like Mr. Jamnadas Mehta, Mr. V. V. Giri and Mr. S. C. Joshi (Right Wing leaders), who were guiding the policy of the Railwaymen's Federation. Attempts were made during the year to bring about unity between the Trades Union Federation and the Trade Union Congress, but they proved abortive. Though a ballot of the railway workers in May resulted in a vote for a general strike, the strike was not launched. There were sporadic strikes, however, in many centres and in October there was a strike at the Perambur railway workshop, near Madras, which dragged on for some months.

The communal situation in India was, on the whole,

fairly satisfactory—the only exception being Bombay, where Hindu-Moslem riots broke out in May. In some of the Indian States, however, there was trouble. The year before, there was trouble in Kashmir, where the peasants (who are predominantly Moslems) rose in revolt against the Hindu Maharajah. Though the grievances were mainly economic, a communal colouring was given to the movement by Moslem sympathisers in British India and also by the peasants themselves, who in some cases attacked their Hindu fellow-subjects. However, with the help of troops from British India, the revolt was suppressed, but as a price for the assistance rendered him, the Maharajah had to submit to the terms of the British Government in the matter of appointing British officers. To appease his subjects, the Maharajah undertook to make concessions in land revenue, to extend primary education, to give a share of State-appointments to all communities and to introduce a measure of constitutional reforms, including a Legislative Assembly. The first elections to the Kashmir Legislative Assembly took place in September 1934. In May 1932, trouble broke out in Alwar State, similar to that in Kashmir, the only difference being that the trouble was more communal and less economic than in Kashmir. To put down the rebellious Moslem subjects, troops from British India had to be called in. The assistance was welcomed by the Maharajah but when the British Government sought to impose their conditions,[1] the Maharajah refused to submit. The dispute between the Maharajah and the British Government went on for some time, but ultimately the former was ordered to leave his State. That order holds good today.

One of the surprises of the year was the result of the elections held in Burma in November 1932, to decide whether Burma was in favour of separation from India. The year before, Burma had been in the throes of a peasant rebellion, a serious disturbance, the like of which India had not seen since 1857. The rebellion continued for more than

---

[1] One of the conditions was that the Maharajah should submit to a Control Commission. The trouble of May 1932 subsided by September. But agrarian unrest of a violent type broke out in January 1933. In May 1933, the Maharajah was ordered to leave his State.

a year. In 1932, the situation gradually became quiet and orders were issued for a General Election. On the ground that the electoral rolls had been prepared in 1931, when many of the districts were in a state of revolt and the Anti-Separationist Party had no interest in an election, the Anti-Separationist leaders asked for fresh electoral rolls. The Government turned down the request and the elections were held on the basis of the old rolls. Nevertheless, the Anti-Separationists came out with a clear majority. When the newly-elected Council met in December, after a lengthy debate, the following resolution was carried without a division :

1. This Council opposes the separation of Burma from India on the basis of the Constitution for a separated Burma as outlined in the statement of the Prime Minister at the Burma Round Table Conference on January 12th, 1932.
2. This Council emphatically opposes the unconditional and permanent federation of Burma with India.
3. This Council will continue to oppose the separation of Burma from India until Burma is granted a Constitution on certain terms (as defined in the amendment).

    In the alternative, the Council proposes that Burma shall enter the Indian Federation on certain terms and conditions including the right of secession.
4. The Council urges that a conference be called at an early date for the purpose of determining the future Constitution of Burma as a separate unit on the basis defined or as a unit in the Indian Federation according to the terms defined with right to secede. (Clauses three and four were the amendments incorporated in the resolution.)

The Government, however, interpreted this resolution as a vote not given for unqualified federation with India,

## THE FIGHT RESUMED (1932) 285

and they maintained that conditional federation, i.e., federation with the right to secede, was not possible. The present policy of the Government is to separate Burma from India, and in accordance with that policy, Burma was not invited to send members to the third session of the Round Table Conference in November-December 1932.

Towards the end of November a very important matter came up for consideration before the Indian Legislative Assembly—the Ottawa Agreement. This Agreement had been entered into by the nominees of the Government of India who had attended the Imperial Economic Conference at Ottawa, in Canada, in August 1932. The purpose of the Agreement was to force on India a scheme of Empire preference whereby India was to give to Great Britain preferences covering no less than twenty-six per cent of her impoports. There was considerable agitation in the country against the ratification of the Ottawa Agreement. In the absence of the Nationalist members in the Assembly, it was, however, impossible to throw out the Agreement. The Agreement was referred to a Select Committee and the majority report moved by Sir H. S. Gour was adopted by the Assembly. The Agreement was ratified for a period of three years at the end of which the matter would come up again before the Assembly for consideration. It was further provided that the Government should prepare an annual report reviewing the effect on India's export and import trade of the preferences and that the report should be examined by a Committee of fifteen members appointed by the Assembly. The new Ottawa duties came into operation on January 16th, 1933.

In this connection it should be noted that since England went off the Gold Standard on September 21st, 1931, the total value of gold exported from Bombay up to December 31st, 1932, amounted to Rs. 105,27,60,190 (Rs. 13½ = £1 approximately) or about 1,053 million rupees. Repeated appeals were made to the Government by Chambers of Commerce, businessmen and public leaders to stop this flow of gold from the country, but to no avail. The Maharashtra Chamber of Commerce, Bombay, for instance, wrote to the

Government of India towards the end of October that following the example of the Bank of England the Government of India should buy up gold. According to the Chamber, since India had a gold bullion reserve of only Rs. 112.3 millions against a note circulation of Rs. 1,752.6 millions, the Government would be well advised to buy up more gold.[1]

There was another important matter which came up before the Assembly in September—the Criminal Law Amendment Bill 1932. The purpose of this Bill was to place on the Statute Book the Ordinance which had been promulgated in January by the Viceroy and had been renewed in June as Special Powers Ordinance 1932. As the Ordinance was to lapse in December, it had either to be renewed again or permanently placed on the Statute Book. In connection with this Bill, as in connection with the Ottawa Agreement, the absence of the Nationalist members, who had resigned in 1930, was keenly felt. The Bill was passed into Law in November.

In August a delegation of the India League of London, consisting of Miss Wilkinson, ex-M.P., Miss Monica Whately, Mr. Leonard Matters and Mr. Krishna Menon (Secretary), arrived in India to study the political situation in the country. During their stay in India they did not make public speeches, nor did they give interviews to the Press. Only once, on the occasion of the fast of Mahatma Gandhi, were they moved to breaking their silence and they declared : 'The removal of Mahatma Gandhi means the disappearance of the greatest force working for moderation, peace and friendship towards Britain.'

Reviewing the year 1932 as a whole, one may say that it opened in the midst of excitement and enthusiasm. But as had happened before with Mahatma Gandhi's movement, it ended in an anti-climax. The 'epic fast' of the Mahatma was the turning-point and from that moment onwards, the

---

[1] The flow of gold from India has been going on unchecked ever since. According to a Press statement issued from Bombay on October 6th, 1934, the total value of gold exported from Bombay since England went off the Gold Standard amounts to Rs. 197,89,40,886—or about 1979 million rupees.

Government definitely got the better of the Congress. As the year came to a close, the thought that was uppermost in the minds of most Congressmen was how to push on the anti-untouchability campaign and resolutions were being passed from many a platform, at the instance of the Congress leaders, asking the Viceroy to accord sanction to the Temple Entry Bills in the Madras Legislative Council and the Indian Legislative Assembly. Civil disobedience indeed !

## CHAPTER XIV

## DEFEAT AND SURRENDER (1933-34)

With the dawn of the new year, Congressmen who were more politically-minded began to realise that the civil-disobedience movement was in danger of fizzling out. The Independence Day celebrations on January 26th, 1933, were therefore organised with much enthusiasm with a view to rousing the people again. The response everywhere was encouraging. In Calcutta alone, the police had to make 300 arrests besides using force to break up the demonstrations. In Badanganj in Arambagh Sub-division of Hooghly district in Bengal, the police resorted to shooting for dispersing the Congress procession. Following the Independence Day celebrations, Mrs. Gandhi was arrested at Borsad in Gujerat and sentenced to six months' imprisonment, on February 7th, for leading a procession of women. As soon as the White Paper embodying the Government proposals regarding the Indian Constitutional Reforms was announced on March 17th, the annual session of the Indian National Congress was convened in Calcutta with Pandit Madan Mohan Malaviya as the President-elect. The Congress session was at once banned like the Delhi session of 1932—nevertheless, delegates and leaders assembled in Calcutta from all parts of the country on April 11th, for the occasion. The important leaders who could be easily spotted out were all arrested, including Pandit Malaviya, Mrs. Motilal Nehru, Mr. M. S. Aney (Central Provinces), Dr. Alam (Punjab), Dr. Syed Mahmud (Bihar), all of them being members of the Congress Working Committee with the exception of Mrs. Nehru. Thereafter, Mrs. J. M. Sengupta proceeded to the appointed place at the head of 2,500 Congressmen for holding the meeting and under her presidentship the meeting was held. Resolutions were passed reaffirming (1) the goal of independence, (2) the efficacy of the method of civil disobedience for attaining the goal, and (3) the boycott of foreign cloth and of British goods of all kinds. The most important resolution was one emphatically condemning the White Paper proposals. Before the meeting ended, large contingents of police arrived on the scene, arrested Mrs. Sengupta and 250 others, including 40 ladies, and dispersed the meeting by force. The following extract from the speech of the President-elect, the venerable Pandit Malaviya, reflects the feeling of the country at the time:

> 'It is estimated that nearly 120,000 persons including several thousand women and quite a number of children have been arrested and imprisoned during the last fifteen months. It is an open secret that when the Government started repression, the official expectation was that they would crush the Congress in six weeks' time. Fifteen months have not enabled the Government to achieve that object. Twice fifteen months will not enable it to do so.'

This was not the review made by a young hot-head but by one of the oldest and most moderate leaders of the Congress. Consequently, the response made by the country to the Congress appeal in 1932 and 1933, in spite of lack of preparation, in spite of the sudden arrest of the organisers and financiers of the Party early in January 1932, and in spite of the diversion caused by the Mahatma's fast in September 1932 and the anti-untouchability campaign thereafter—can by no means be regarded as unsatisfactory. Nevertheless, the country was startled one fine morning in May to hear that the Mahatma had suspended the civil-disobedience campaign.

While in prison the Mahatma had decided to go on a three weeks' fast[1] as a penance, because his followers outside had not made sufficient progress with the anti-untouch-

---

[1] After the famous September fast, the Mahatma had fasted once again in December, but that fast had been a short one. The present fast was described by him as a 'heart-prayer for purification of myself and my associates for greater vigilance and watchfulness in connection with the Harijan cause'.

ability campaign. The object of the fast was to bring about a change of heart—not in the bureaucracy but in his countrymen—who were responsible for the sad plight of the untouchables. The Government had no objection to a fast of that kind and as a matter of fact, thanks to British news-agencies, the fast was given wide publicity in the European Press,[1] because it helped to advertise the internal differences of the Indian people. However, the Government considered it prudent to set him free. The day after his release he made the announcement referred to above.[2] At first the civil-disobedience campaign was suspended for six weeks, but the suspension was subsequently extended for six weeks more, i.e. till the end of July. The sudden suspension of the campaign without rhyme or reason, would under ordinary circumstances have produced a widespread revolt in the Congress organisation, but since he was in the middle of a fast which could end fatally, all judgment was suspended for the time being. While suspending the civil-disobedience campaign, the Mahatma made an appeal to the Government of India to withdraw the Ordinances and release the civil-disobedience prisoners. But, unfortunately, a settled Government preserves a continuity of policy and cannot alter its policy overnight as an individual can. The Government's reply was therefore a refusal. While responsible Congressmen in India were unwilling or afraid to speak out against the Mahatma after his surrender of May 1933, a manifesto was issued by late

---

[1] The writer was in Vienna when the news regarding the fast appeared in the Continental Press. After 14 months' incarceration when his health was in an alarming condition, Lt.-Col. Buckley, I.M.S., of Lucknow who had been treating him, recommended his transfer to Europe for treatment. Thereupon the Government of India permitted him to leave for Europe on his own financial responsibility. He was released at Bombay when he sailed and arrived in Vienna in March 1933.

[2] It is a matter for conjecture if the Government knew that the Mahatma would suspend the civil-disobedience campaign if he were set free. On May 8th, 1933, when the Mahatma started his fast the Government issued a communique stating that in view of the nature of the object of the fast and the attitude of mind which it disclosed, the Government had decided that the Mahatma should be set at liberty. After his release, the suspension of civil disobedience was ordered by the Acting President of the Congress, Mr. Aney, on the 'recommendation' of the Mahatma.

Mr. Vithalbhai J. Patel [1] and the writer from Vienna, condemning the Mahatma's decision. The manifesto stated that the decision virtually undid the work and the sacrifice of the last thirteen years. It signified a failure of the civil-disobedience campaign, as also of Mahatma Gandhi's leadership. It was, therefore, time to turn to a more radical policy and leadership. Owing to the preoccupation of the public over Mahatma Gandhi's health, the manifesto did not, however, produce the effect which it would otherwise have. Even friends thought that it was an outrageous act to criticise the Mahatma when his life was in jeopardy because of the fast.

In July, a Conference of important Congressmen, then out of prison, was held at Poona. It could be regarded as an unofficial meeting of the All-India Congress Committee. Two groups were represented at the Conference—one in favour of calling off the movement altogether and the other in favour of resuming it with full vigour. The former group had probably a majority and most of the members of this group were in favour of reviving the Swarajist policy of carrying the fight inside the Legislatures which had been abandoned at the Lahore Congress in December 1929. Nevertheless, at the end, the Conference decided to give in to the Mahatma. At his instance it was decided that the Mahatma should make a further attempt to see the Viceroy and come to an understanding with him. If this failed, the Congress should resume 'individual' civil disobedience, but that 'mass' civil disobedience should be given up altogether. The purpose of this was that the Congress should not organise any campaign on a mass scale but should leave it to individual to break any laws that they felt called upon to on their personal responsibility. Soon after the Poona Conference the Mahatma approached the Viceroy for an interview, but all that he got was a humiliating rebuff. He and some of his closest followers, thereupon, proceeded to start civil disobedience individually

---

[1] The late Mr. V. J. Patel had returned from the United States after three months' strenuous propaganda on behalf of India, which ultimately cost him his life. He, as well as the writer, were undergoing treatment in Vienna at the time.

and by August 1933 they found themselves in prison once again. This time even the Mahatma's incarceration did not create a great stir.

'Individual' civil disobedience was offered all over India by the loyal adherents of the Mahatma and a few hundred persons were thereby thrust back into prison. But it was a foregone conclusion that where mass civil disobedience had failed, individual civil disobedience would not produce any appreciable effect. On reaching prison, the Mahatma found that the facilities afforded him since September 1932, during his last incarceration, for conducting the anti-untouchability campaign from behind the prison walls—would not be given him this time.[1] He thereupon gave notice to the Government that if he did not get those facilities, he would feel called upon to resort to fasting. It is difficult for a layman to reconcile this attitude of the Mahatma with his lifelong principle that a Satyagrahi prisoner should voluntarily submit to jail discipline. However, the Government once again found themselves in an uncomfortable position. By that time they had realised that individual civil disobedience was going to fizzle out and consequently there would be no risk in setting the Mahatma at liberty. So once more the Mahatma found himself a free man. On coming out from prison, the Mahatma announced that since he had been sentenced to one year's imprisonment in August 1933, and since he had been released by the Government before the expiry of his term, he would consider himself as a prisoner till August 1934, and would not offer civil disobedience during that period.

Before offering civil disobedience, the Mahatma had issued a statement in July to the effect that there was too much secrecy in the affairs of the Congress and in the management of the civil-disobedience campaign, and this secrecy was largely responsible for the failure that had overtaken the Congress. In the Mahatma's opinion, the Congress organisations had become corrupt bodies. Soon

---

[1] The reason given by the Government was that on the former occasion he had been incarcerated without trial, whereas on this occasion he was convicted after trial.

after this, at the instance of the Mahatma, the Acting-President of the Congress, Mr. M. S. Aney, issued orders, dissolving all Congress organisations in the country. Confusion worse confounded! What were the people to do? Normal human reason could not follow the logic of the Mahatma and those who could be expected to speak out the plain truth, were not available. At this juncture, Pandit Jawaharlal Nehru was released from prison after serving his term of two years' imprisonment. All eyes turned on him. He was the one man who could influence the Mahatma —who could drag the Congress out of the mess into which it had fallen. Pandit Nehru had long talks with the Mahatma and following that, an interchange of letters. The correspondence was duly published, but on perusal it was found to be more doctrinaire than practical. What the public wanted to know urgently was not whether and wherein Pandit J. L. Nehru and Mahatma Gandhi agreed or disagreed fundamentally—but how the Congress could be restored to life and vigour. During his four months of comparative freedom, Pandit Nehru wrote and spoke freely and gave expression to his socialistic—or communistic—ideas, but the Congress did not show any signs of resuscitation. In an exceedingly interesting and able article under the caption 'Whiter India?' he pleaded for social and economic equality, for the ending of all special class-privileges and vested interests, but that did not help the Congress one jot or tittle. With a popularity only second to that of the Mahatma, with unbounded prestige among his countrymen, with a clear brain possessing the finest ideas, with an up-to-date knowledge of modern world movements—that he should be found wanting in the essential quality of leadership, namely the capacity to make decisions and face unpopularity if need be,[1] was a great disappointment. But there was no help for it. What had been expected of him had to be accomplished by lesser men.

After Pandit Nehru, Mr. K. F. Nariman, the Bombay

---

[1] This defect in Pandit J. L. Nehru was manifest on other occasions as well, when the Congress passing through a crisis—e.g., in the crisis of 1923-24 and subsequently in the crisis of 1928-29.

leader, was released and without delay he began to give public expression to his views [1] on the decision of the Poona Conference in July 1933. Referring to the Mahatma's decision to start civil disobedience in August 1933, because the Viceroy did not grant him an unconditional interview, he said, ' "Interview or Death" is the national slogan for the present.... The renewed fight in August last is not for Swaraj, nor even for political constitutional advance, but for the assertion of a supposed "national right" of an unconditional interview. If that right was conceded, even the modified individual fight would be called off and peace between Government and the people restored, though the Congress political goal is not satisfied.' Speaking of the Mahatma's condemnation of secrecy, he remarked: 'By what rule of modern warfare or sport are we bound to disclose our plans and schemes beforehand to the enemy? But I forget, it is a religious fight and not political; so neither the rules of sport nor the canons of modern warfare apply! Secrecy of one's plans and future actions is the very essence of all modern national movements and struggles.' On the decision to call off 'mass', but retain 'individual' civil disobedience, he stated: 'Does it need an Indian National Congress to tell an individual to break laws on his own responsibility and take the consequences?.... That eternal liberty to act as he likes and take the consequences is given to man since the days of Adam.' Then he dealt with the Mahatma's assertion that 'continuance by even one person (of civil disobedience) ensures revival into such an irrepressible mass movement as no amount of repression will suppress.' And Mr. Nariman asserted on the contrary: 'If this "one man" theory were true, India as well as Ireland should have been transformd after this most inspiring, unforgettable, blood-curdling, patriotic, heroic example (referring to the self-immolation of Terence MacSwiney and Jatin Das).... The whole misconception is again based on the same unsustainable theory and slippery

---

[1] For a full statement of his views one should refer to his book, *Whither Congress?* Bombay Book Depot, Girgaon, Bombay, November 1933. Mr. Nariman has been a member of the Congress Working Committee since January 1930.

foundation—the "change of heart" theory exploded above, that the Britisher would pine at the suffering and yield.' Criticising the decision to dissolve or suspend all Congress organisations, he maintained : 'None can dissolve the National Assemblies that have come into existence by popular vote.' Then finally he asked : 'How can we induce Gandhiji to rid himself of this almost incorrigible habit... this perpetual blundering, blending of religion and politics?' Mr. Nariman opined that the remedy lay in securing for Gandhiji, in place of the late Pandit Motilal Nehru, another political taskmaster—'a plain-speaking outspoken giant and not lip-sealed mummies who always shake their heads like spring dolls, perpendicularly or horizontally, according as the Mahatma pulls the strings straight or sideways.'

It was refreshing and heartening to find in the Working Committee at least one man who could think boldly and have the courage to call a spade a spade. But though Mr. Nariman was brilliant in his analysis, he was weak in action. His suggestion for summoning the All-India Congress Committee to end existing stalemate was not taken seriously by the General Secretary, Pandit Nehru, and when the latter was clapped in prison in January 1934, for making an alleged seditious speech in Calcutta, no silver lining was visible in the dark horizon. It was left to Dr. M. A. Ansari, the Moslem leader of Delhi, to tackle the situation. During his visit to England in 1933 he had been pained and humiliated by the arrogance of the Conservative politicians and their assertion that the Congress was down and out. That feeling was heightened on finding on his return to India that the Congress was in a state of suspended animation. After appealing to the Mahatma to bring the Congress back to life once again, he along with Dr. B. C. Roy of Calcutta, summoned a conference of Congressmen of their way of thinking at Delhi in March 1934. By that time, civil disobedience was as dead as a doornail, but the Congress could not function because of the Ordinances and the Ordinances would not be withdrawn by the Government till civil disobedience was unconditionally withdrawn. The only way out of the mess was for the Congress leaders to eat the humble pie, call off the civil-disobedience campaign and thereby secure the withdrawal or suspension of the Ordinances. The Delhi Conference prepared the ground for that by resolving to revive the All-India Swaraj Party to contest the elections to the Legislatures.[1] The next month a larger Conference was summoned to pursue the same topic, and Ranchi (in Bihar) was chosen as the venue, because the Mahatma would be there at the time. The Conference confirmed the decision arrived at Delhi to revive the All-India Swaraj Party and the prime-movers, Drs. Ansari and Roy, were able to secure the support of the Mahatma. The next month, in May, a meeting of the All-India Congress Committee was summoned at Patna after an interval of about three years. This meeting offered a surprise to the public in as much as Mahatma Gandhi himself sponsored the idea that Congressmen should enter the Legislatures. This decision had added importance in view of the fact that meanwhile the Government had decided to dissolve the Indian Legislative Assembly and hold a General Election in November. The All-India Congress Committee decided that instead of permitting the Swaraj Party to function, the Congress should itself undertake the responsibility and a Parliamentary Board was therefore set up for running the elections. The Committee further decided to call off the civil-disobedience campaign, the Mahatma, however, retaining the right to offer civil disobedience.[2] Once again the Government came to know in advance what the decision of the All-India Congress Committee would be and no obstacles were therefore placed in the way of the Committee meeting openly, though it was still an unlawful body. After the meeting, when the

---

[1] Before the Delhi Conference, another Conference, called the Democratic Swarajya Party Conference, had been held at Bombay at the instance of Mr. N. C. Kelkar of Poona and Mr. Jamnadas Mehta of Bombay for popularising the idea of fighting the next elections. This Conference had large support from all parts of Maharashtra.

[2] As early as April 7th, 1934, the Mahatma issued a statement advising all Congressmen to suspend civil disobedience as a means of obtaining Swaraj and asserting that in the existing circumstances, only one person, and that himself, should bear the responsibility of civil disobedience. This curious reservation was accepted by the All-India Congress Committee in May and the Bombay Congress in October 1934.

Government felt that the defeat and humiliation of the Congress was complete—they withdrew the ban on most of the Congress organisations in the country and allowed them to function.

The decision of the All-India Congress Committee to contest the coming elections did not pass unchallenged. There was a solid group opposed to it—but this time it was not the old 'No-Change' Party that was opposing, because the leader of that Party, the Mahatma, was himself the sponsor of the council-entry proposal—but the newly-formed Congress Socialist Party. While the All-India Congress Committee was deliberating, the oppositionists held an All-India Conference of their Party. This Party had strong support from the United Provinces and Bombay, besides a fair measure of support from all parts of India. From such information as is available, it appears that the Congress Socialist Party has offered a platform not only to those who are Socialists by conviction, but also to those who are dissatisfied with the Congress policy of council-entry. It is unfortunate that the opposition to council-entry came from the Socialist Party, because there is nothing anti-Socialist in fighting within the Legislatures, if such a policy is otherwise deemed expedient. But it may be that the Socialist Party, representing some of the radical forces in the Congress, instinctively felt called upon to oppose a party that had rallied all the moderate elements. And there is no doubt that those who have taken a leading part in the Swarajist revival of 1934, are of a different calibre from that militant group which formed the backbone of the Swaraj Party in 1923. It is interesting to note here that as in 1928, the erstwhile Swarajists and 'No-Changers' made common cause against the Independence-wallahs—so also in 1934, these two groups seem to have closed up their ranks against the common enemy. Though the Congress Socialist Party has, in some respects, been harking back to the ideas and shibboleths that were popular forty or fifty years ago, it does stand for a radical tendency in the Nationalist movement and the formation of such a party is a very hopeful feature of the times. The latest reports go to show that the organisation of the party is making headway in most of the provinces, and in the recent elections to the Bombay Congress Committee, the Socialists claimed to have captured half the seats.

In spite of the menace of the Socialists, the official bloc in the Congress have not been a happy family. At the meetings of the Working Committee held at Bombay and Benares, after the Patna meeting in May, differences appeared over the attitude that should be adopted towards the so-called 'Communal Award' of the British Government. Pandit M. M. Malaviya and Mr. M. S. Aney held that the Communal Award, like the White Paper, should be strongly condemned. The rest of the Working Committee under the influence of the Moslem members, maintained that the Congress should 'neither accept nor reject' Communal Award, though they admitted that the Award was thoroughly obnoxious. Why the Moslem leaders in the Congress have taken up this attitude, it is difficult to say—especially when one remembers that after the Karachi Congress, it was they, who by their firm attitude, prevented the Mahatma from yielding to the demand of the communalist Moslems for separate electorate. Whatever the reason may be, the fact remains that today they are holding a pistol at the Working Committee—and because of their insistence, the Committee has been forced to take up this ridiculous attitude of neither accepting nor rejecting the Award. The argument ordinarily urged in favour of not rejecting the Award is a twofold one. Firstly, the Congress should represent all parties in the country, including the communalist Moslems, and secondly, that until the parties arrive at an agreed solution, the present solution should stand. Both the arguments are fallacious. The Congress does not represent all the parties in the land—for instance, it does not represent the loyalists, whether Hindus or Moslems. Secondly, it is the rejection of a bad solution that will force us to arrive at a good solution. Like the White Paper, the Communal Award should be straightaway rejected—no matter whether an alternative solution is immediately available or not. Moreover, this 'all parties' idea is a false and dangerous idea. The party that is fighting for freedom is the party that is solely responsible for producing the Constitution. And so far as the communal question is concerned, the Congress solution is already there. Be that as it may, in the present circumstances one is reluctantly driven to the conclusion that the Nationalist Moslems have been gradually—may be unconsciously—coming into line with their communalist co-religionists.

All attempts at a compromise having failed, Pandit Malaviya and Mr. Aney resigned from the Congress Working Committee and the Parliamentary Board and proceeded to form a separate party—under the name of the Congress Nationalist Party—with the object of fighting the Communal Award and the White Paper. This Party held an All-India Conference in Calcutta on August 19th, under the Presidentship of Pandit M. M. Malaviya—the Chairman of the Reception Committee being Sir P. C. Roy, the well-known chemist and philanthropist. The Conference was a successful one and it was evident that public opinion in Bengal—especially of the Hindu community—was behind the Party. Bengal Hindus have been suffering from a just grievance because the Communal Award has allotted them only 80 seats out of 250 in the new Legislature, while Moslems have been given 119 seats.[1] To add to this, the Poona Agreement concluded at the time of the Mahatma's fast, has allotted 30 seats to the depressed classes, out of these 80 seats, as against the provision for 10 in the Communal Award, though the depressed classes issue hardly exists in Bengal. Bengal Hindus [2] have therefore been greatly offended by the decision of the Working Committee not to reject the Communal Award. It is difficult to say at this stage what will be the result of the elections. It may, however, be a safe forecast to say that the majority of the elected seats for Hindus will be captured by the official Con-

[1] Under the existing Constitution, Hindus have 60 per cent of the elected seats in the Bengal Legislative Council. This is in accordance with the Lucknow Pact of 1916—the agreement arrived at between the Indian National Congress and the All-India Moslem League.
[2] This is also the case with the Punjab Hindus. Many of the Hindu constituencies in Bengal and Punjab have, therefore, returned members of the Congress Nationalist Party to the Assembly.

gress Party. But though the Congress Nationalist Party will have a smaller number of seats, they will have the solid support of the Hindu community in their propaganda as also in their work in the Assembly. In non-communal matters, the two Congress groups will be found in the same lobby. So far as the Nationalist Moslems are concerned, they hope to capture a fair percentage of the seats.

The last meeting of the Congress Working Committee and of the Congress Parliamentary Board was held at Wardha (Central Province) on September 8th, 9th and 10th. An eleventh-hour attempt was made to bring about a compromise between the two Congress groups, but the effort failed. At this meeting it transpired that the Mahatma had been thinking seriously of retiring from active politics. It was first surmised that the split among the Congress leaders over the Communal Award had upset him seriously. But one of his trusted lieutenants, Mr. Rajagopalachariar of Madras, issued a statement on September 7th, saying : 'The cause of the rumour that Gandhiji is giving up leadership of the Congress is to be traced to the fact that Gandhiji has been thinking of introducing reforms in the Constitution of the Congress in order to make it more definitely purged of all forms of violence. .....If the Congress does not adopt his reforms, he may even be prepared after the ensuing Congress session to start an independent organisation to have a body of strictly non-violent workers.' About ten days later, the Mahatma himself issued a statement confirming the rumour that he had the intention of retiring, but saying that at the request of friends, he had postponed his decision until after the session of the Congress at Bombay. He referred to corruption in the ranks of the Congress and declared that he proposed to move the following three amendments to the constitution of the Congress :

1. Replacing the words 'legitimate and peaceful' by 'truthful and non-violent' means to achieve the aims of the Congress.
2. Replacing the four-anna (anna is one-sixteenth of

a rupee; Rs. 13½ = £ 1 approximately) franchise[1] by the delivery by every member of the Congress Depot of 8,000 feet of well-tested even yarn of not less than fifteen counts spun by himself.
3. No one to be entitled to vote in a Congress election unless he has been on the Congress register for six months and has been a habitual wearer of Khaddar only during the same period.

The Mahatma concluded by saying that he apprehended that his suggestion would not be acceptable to the majority, but there was room for compromise, and if they wanted him as leader, they would have to give due consideration to his proposals.

The annual session of the Indian National Congress is to be held at Bombay on October 26th, 27th, and 28th, 1934, and the elections to the Indian Legislative Assembly under the existing Constitution are due in November. The withdrawal of the Congress Party from the Assembly in January 1930, made it possible for the Government to get the Ottawa Agreement ratified by the Assembly for three years and to have the Ordinances for suppressing the civil-disobedience movement placed on the Statute Book. The presence of Congressmen in the Assembly once again will cause embarrassment to the Government, but the Government will then have no law-breaking campaign in the country to keep them preoccupied. So far as the ensuing Congress session is concerned, a lively fight is expected on two issues. Firstly, the Congress Nationalist Party will appeal to the All-India Congress Committee and to the plenary session of the Congress to reject the Communal Award. Secondly, the Congress Socialist Party will press for the adoption of a Socialist programme. Both these attempts are sure to be defeated. On both these questions the Mahatma will get the support of the majority of his erstwhile opponents— the Swarajists. If they were to oppose him to a man, then

---

[1] According to the present constitution of the Congress, every member has to pay a minimum annual subscription of four annas. The Mahatma's idea is to make spinning obligatory on the members instead of merely paying a subscription.

he would run the risk of being defeated on either of the above two issues. But by sponsoring their proposal of entering the Legislatures, the Mahatma has won the majority of them over to his side and has thereby ensured his position within the Congress. The present intention of the Mahatma to retire[1] from active politics and strengthen his own Satyagrahi organisation or in the alternative to alter the Congress constitution according to his own ideas, will not come as a surprise to those who know him well. It is reminiscent of his attitude after his release from prison in 1924 and at the Belgaum Congress that year, when he left the field to his opponents, allowing them to stew in their own juice. The ultimate challenge to his leadership will, however, arise from the side of the Congress Socialist Party but not from that of Congress Nationalist Party.[2]

During the period of 1933-34 while the Congress proceeded from step to step in the direction of surrender, the Government was able to strengthen its position in other directions as well. In January 1933, judgment was finally delivered in the long-drawn Meerut Conspiracy Case, and out of thirty-one accused, twenty-seven were sentenced to various terms of imprisonment. About this time the leader of the Chittagong revolutionaries, Mr. Surjya Sen, who had successfully evaded arrest for three years, was captured, and after a trial before a special tribunal, was hanged together with another comrade. In February and March, there was trouble with some of the independent frontier tribes. But with the assistance of the friendly Afghan Government of King Nadir Shah and with the help of aerial bombing, the Government were able to cope successfully with the menace. After the publication of the

---

[1] After the above was written, the Mahatma announced his retirement to the plenary session of the Congress which met in Bombay on October 26th, 1934. This so-called retirement has been referred to in Chapter Eighteen.

[2] A message from India dated the 1st October, 1934, said that a Conference of the Congress Socialist Party was recently held at Benares. It was decided not to assist in the election campaign of the Congress nor to accept office in any Congress organisation which did not carry out the economic policy of the Party. Both the official Cogress Party and the Congress Nationalist Party were condemned by the Socialist Party.

White Paper in March, the Assembly passed the following resolution moved by Sir Abdur Rahim, the leader of the opposition :

> 'Unless the proposals for constitutional reform are substantially amended in the direction of conceding greater responsibility and freedom of action to the people's representatives in the central and provincial spheres of government, it will not be possible to ensure peace, contentment and progress of the country.'

The Government, it is hardly necessary to add, had no need to feel embarrassed at this milk-and-water resolution.

There was some amount of public agitation over the ill-treatment of political prisoners. For instance, in the Nasik Jail on October 27th, 1932, Mr. Amritlal Morarji, a political prisoner who had been given bar-fetters, was taken to a cell, beaten by five jail-officials with batons and lifted up and dashed down till he became unconscious. There was intense indignation when the news saw the light of day, and Government had to order the prosecution of the jail-officials responsible for the incident. Likewise, in the Amraoti Jail in the Central Provinces, some political prisoners, had been severely assaulted on April 22nd, 1932. Agitation and inquiry went on for about a year. Ultimately, on March 1st, 1933, the Government issued a white-washing report which, however, admitted the use of physical force on the occasion and promised a modification of the rules applying to civil-disobedience prisoners.

Following the publication of the White Paper in March 1933, early in April, the British Parliament appointed a Joint Select Committee consisting of sixteen members from each House. There were debates in both Houses on the occasion. In the House of Commons, the Opposition was led by Mr. Winston Churchill and Sir Henry Page-Croft and in the Lords by Lord Lloyd and Lord Halsbury. The Committee, on April 12th, elected Lord Linlithgow as Chairman and approved of a list of 'assessors' from India who would sit with them, but would not be entitled to vote on any issue nor submit any report to Parliament. The sittings of the Joint Select Committee, with the collaboration of the Indian assessors, commenced on May 10th, and continued for an unusually long period. The Secretary of State for India took the unusual step of appearing as a witness with a view to acquainting the Committee and the Indian assessors with the intentions of the Government. His examination lasted several weeks and he answered about 16,000 questions. In view of the agitation against constitutional advance in India carried on by the diehards in England led by Mr. Winston Churchill since 1929, and especially since the publication of the White Paper, in March 1933, it is likely that the Joint Parliamentary Committee will further whittle down the provisions of the White Paper.[1] The report of the Committee is expected to be out in November 1934.

During the year 1933, the country suffered a serious loss through the death of her two worthiest sons, Mr. J. M. Sengupta, who had been the Mayor of Calcutta for five years, and had been a member of the Congress Working Committee since 1925, suddenly died of apoplexy on July 26th, while he was in internment in Ranchi under Regulation III of 1818. On October 22nd, Mr. Vithalbhai J. Patel, former President of the Indian Assembly, and one of the outstanding leaders of the Congress, died of heart trouble in a Swiss clinic near Geneva. In accordance with his last wishes his mortal remains were brought to Bombay for cremation, where they were received by a procession of 200,000 people. He left all his assets (more than Rs. 100,000) for national work.

Towards the end of 1933, the second Burma Round Table Conference was held in London. The first Conference had been held in November 1931, and the representatives from Burma were not therefore invited to the second and third sessions of the Indian Round Table Conference. As the composition of the first Burma Round

---

[1] Since the above was written, the Report of the Joint Parliamentary Committee has been published and the apprehensions of the writer have proved to be true.

Table Conference had been strongly criticised on the ground that the anti-separationists had been poorly represented, the Government had agreed to a General Election in Burma on the issue of separation from India. This election, held in November 1932, gave a majority to the anti-separationists, but taking advantage of the fact that the Burma Legislative Council did not vote for unconditional federation with India, the Government proceeded with their pet scheme of separation from India. The second Burma Round Table Conference was therefore called in 1933, and the anti-separationists, though in a majority in Burma, were given less seats than the separationists. It is now certain that Burma will be separated from India[1] and will be given a bi-cameral legislature for dealing with both 'provincial' and 'central' subjects.

In December, important conferences were held as usual. The Liberal Federation met at Madras with Mr. J. N. Basu in the chair and condemned the White Paper. The All-India Women Conference had a successful session in Calcutta and great enthusiasm was evinced by women representatives from all parts of India in the matter of educational and social reform as well as in the matter of representation in International Committees in Geneva. The Trade Union Congress met at Cawnpore and among the resolutions passed was one dealing with the grievances of the textile workers in Bombay Presidency and the necessity of a general strike of textile workers for enforcing their demands. Following this decision, in the early part of 1934, a strike of textile workers was declared in Bombay. There was enthusiastic response to the strike-call in Bombay and there were sympathetic strikes in other parts of the country as well. To break the strike, the bogey of communism was raised once again and on that pretext, a large number of influential labour leaders in Bombay were thrown into prison. Following Bombay, other provinces like Punjab also saw the spectre of Communism stalking over the land

[1] The Report of the Joint Parliamentary Committee published on November 22nd, 1934, has provided for the separation of Burma from India.

and the Kirti (Workers), Kisan (Peasant) Party of Punjab was therefore declared illegal as being a Communist body. While strengthening the grip over the radical wing of the Workers' movement, the Government also took further measures in Bengal to crush the terrorist campaign of the revolutionaries. While, the year before, mere attempt to murder had been made punishable with death, in 1934, possession of arms, explosives, etc. was similarly made punishable with death. The recent attempt to assassinate the Governor of Bengal, Sir John Anderson, which is reminiscent of a similar attempt made two years ago[1]—shows, however, that the terrorist campaign is unfortunately not dead as yet—though public opinion has been expressing itself more and more against it.

The favourable situation created for the British Government through the surrender of the Congress and the official policy of ruthless repression, was utilised for promoting the trade interests of Great Britain in India. Reference has already been made to the ratification of the Ottawa Agreement, whereby the principle of Empire Preference was forced on India, in spite of her opposition and to her detriment. During the period under consideration, two other measures were adopted in connection with the textile trade of India—the Indo-Japanese Agreement and the Indo-British Agreement. In spite of all the specious arguments urged in favour of the two Agreements, Indian public opinion regards the first agreement as a conspiracy between British and Japanese industrialists to exploit the Indian market and the second agreement as an unholy alliance between the British capitalists and a section of the Indian capitalists to get the most out of the poor Indian consumer. Till the Nationalist Party is once again installed inside the Legislatures, it will not be possible to undo the harm done to India by these two measures.

[1] In February 1932, a young woman graduate, Miss Bina Das, attempted to shoot the Governor of Bengal, Sir Stanley Jackson, at the convocation of the University of Calcutta. The Governor had a providential escape and Miss Das was sentenced to nine years' imprisonment.

The latest news is to the effect that some of the would-be assassins of Sir John Anderson have been sentenced to death.

The elections to the Indian Legislative Assembly are at present (November 1934) in progress. During 1935, public attention in India will be directed towards the tactics of the Congress Party in the Assembly. It is extremely unlikely that there will be any startling developments between now and the inauguration of the new constitutional reforms.

## CHAPTER XV

## THE WHITE PAPER AND THE COMMUNAL AWARD[1]

The proposals contained in the White Paper issued in March 1933, represented the tentative conclusions arrived at by the British Government after three sessions of the Round Table Conference. According to this scheme, India is no longer to be divided into British India ruled directly by the British Government, and the Indian States ruled by Indian Princes or Rulers or Maharajahs under the suzerainty of the British Crown. India is to be a Federation composed of the provinces of British India, eleven in number including Sindh and Orissa, and such of the Indian States as would voluntarily join the Federation. Those Rulers who signify their desire to join the Federation will have to execute a formal Instrument of Accession transferring to the British Crown for the purposes of the Federation their powers and jurisdiction in respect of those matters which they are willing to recognise as Federal matters. The powers and jurisdiction so transferred will be exercised by the appropriate Federal organs created by the new Constitution Act. The Federation will be brought into existence by the issue of a Proclamation by His Majesty, the King-Emperor, but the proclamation will not be issued until :

1. His Majesty has received intimation that the Rulers of States representing not less than half the aggregate population of the Indian States and entitled to not less than half the seats to be allotted to the

---

[1] This chapter gives only a rough idea of the provisions of the White Paper and the Communal Award. For further details which are uninteresting to the general reader, one should refer to *Proposals for Indian Constitutional Reform* 1933, printed and published by His Majesty's Stationery Office, Adastral House, Kingsway, London, W.C. 2. Price 2s. nett.

States in the Federal Upper Chamber have signified their desire to accede to the Federation; and
2. Both Houses of the British Parliament have presented an address to His Majesty praying that such a Proclamation may be issued. It is further provided that before the first Federal Ministry comes into being, a Federal Reserve Bank,[1] free from political influence, will have been set up by Indian legislation and be already successfully operating.

The White Paper also states that 'it is probable that it will be found convenient or even necessary that the new Provincial Government should be brought into being in advance of the changes in the Central Government and the entry of the States'. It is, therefore, clear that the inauguration of the Federation may be indefinitely postponed even after the new Constitution Act is passed by the British Parliament.

The idea of bringing in the Princes into the constitutional machinery is to provide a Conservative element in the Federal Legislature, which will counteract the radical forces in British India. With this object in view, while the representatives from British India in the Federal Legislature will be returned through a direct (or indirect) election[2] with the help of a popular franchise, however restricted, the representatives from the States will be nominated by the Indian Rulers. The subjects of the Indian States comprising about one-fourth of the total population of India[3] will have no representation whatsoever in the Federal Parliament. The support of the Indian Rulers (or their nominees) to the British Government in the working of the Federal Constitution will be secured because the

[1] The Reserve Bank Bill has been already passed by the Indian Legislative Assembly.

[2] The White Paper recommended direct election in the case of the Federal Assembly (Lower House) and indirect election in the case of Council of State (Upper House). The Joint Parliamentary Committee, however, have recommended indirect election in both cases.

[3] In the 1931 census, the total population of India including Burma is about 352 millions. British India excluding Burma has a population of about 257 millions. The total population of the Indian States is about 81 millions.

British Government in its turn undertakes not to interfere in the internal autocratic administration of the Indian States. Thus, if the Federation is ultimately set up according to the White Paper proposal, the Princes will retain their sovereignty over their internal affairs and will have a further hand in working the Federal machinery. There will be no provision in the new Constitution for a democratic or popular or constitutional government in the Indian States. Moreover, the Indian States will enjoy special concessions or exemptions in the matter of Federal taxation, and in the Federal Legislature they will have representation far in excess of their population. In spite of these baits thrown out by the British Government, many of the Indian Rulers are fighting shy of the constitutional innovation.

According to the White Paper, the offices of the Viceroy and the Governor-General will be separated, though the two offices will be held by the same person. The Governor-General will be the executive head of the Federation and will have the supreme command of the military, naval and air forces of India as well, while the Viceroy will be the representative of the British Crown and will exercise the powers of the Crown in relation to the Indian States and all other matters outside the scope of the Federal Constitution. The Governor-General will himself direct and control the administration of certain Reserved Departments —namely, Defence, External Affairs and Ecclesiastical Affairs. In this administration he will be assisted by not more than three Counsellors, who will be appointed by himself and will be (*ex-officio*) members of both the Legislatures, without the right to vote. For the purpose of aiding and advising the Governor-General in the exercise of other powers, there will be a Council of Ministers. The Ministers will be appointed by the Governor-General, will hold office during his pleasure and must be members of one or other Chamber of the Federal Legislature. The Counsellors will be responsible to the Governor-General alone, but the Ministers will be responsible to the Legislature, subject to such control as the Governor-General will exercise over their departments. In regard to administration, the Governor-General will make, in his discretion, any rules which he regards as requisite to regulate the disposal of Government business and the procedure to be observed in its conduct. He will also be empowered in his discretion to appoint a Financial Adviser to assist him in his special responsibility for financial matters. The salary of the Financial Adviser will be fixed by the Governor-General and will not be subject to the vote of the Legislature, nor will he be responsible to the Legislature.

Apart from his exclusive responsibility for the reserved departments, the Governor-General will be declared to have a 'special responsibility' in respect of the following matters :

(a) The prevention of any grave menace to the peace and tranquillity of India or any part thereof.
(b) The safeguarding of the financial stability and credit of the Federation.
(c) The safeguarding of the legitimate interests of minorities.
(d) The securing to the members of the public services of any rights provided for them by the Constitution Act and the safeguarding of their legitimate interests.
(e) The prevention to commercial discrimination.
(f) The protection of the rights of any Indian State.
(g) Any matter which affects the administration of any department under the direction and control of the Governor-General.

It will be for the Governor-General to determine in his discretion whether any of the 'special responsibilities' here described are involved by any given circumstances.

In the Instrument of Instructions which will be issued to the Governor-General by the King-Emperor, it will be provided that in the administration of the departments under the direction and control of the Governor-General on his own responsibility and of matters committed to his discretion—he will be under the control of the Secretary of State for India. Though in other matters the Governor-General should ordinarily be guided by the advice of his Ministers, he may not accept their advice if it is considered by him as inconsistent with the fulfilment of a special responsibility entrusted to him by law and in such case the Governor-General may take such action as he will judge requisite, subject to the directions of the Secretary of State for India. It will be clear that in such matters the responsibility of the Ministers to the Legislature is non-existent.

The Governor-General will have the power to make and promulgate Ordinances for a period of six months and renew them for a second period if at any time he is satisfied that it is necessary for the requirements of the reserved departments or any of his 'special responsibilities'. He will also have the power of making and promulgating Ordinances for the good government of British India or any part thereof, if at a time, when the Federal Legislature is not in session, his Ministers are satisfied that an emergency exists. Both kinds of Ordinances, while in operation, will have the force and effect of Acts of the Legislature. Further, in the event of a breakdown of the Constitution, the Governor-General will be empowered at his discretion, by Proclamation, to assume to himself all such powers vested by law in any federal authority as appear to him to be necessary for the purpose of securing that the Government of the Federation shall be carried on effectively.

The Federal Legislature will consist of two Chambers to be styled the Council of State (Upper House) and the House of Assembly (Lower House). Each Council of State will continue for seven years and each House of Assembly for five years, unless sooner dissolved. The Council of State will consist of no more than 260 members of whom 150 will be elected from British India, not more than 100 will be appointed by the Rulers of the Indian States and not more than ten will be nominated by the Governor-General in his discretion. Out of 150 British Indian seats, 136 will be filled by election by means of the single transferable vote by the members of the Provincial Legislatures, the bigger provinces being entitled to 18 seats and the smaller to 5 seats each. Out of the remaining 14, Europeans, Indian Christians and Anglo-Indians will be entitled to 7, 2 and 1 seats respectively—while Coorg, Ajmer, Delhi and Beluchistan will be entitled to one seat each. One-third of the British-Indian seats in the Council of State will be reserved for the Moslem community, though their population is approximately only one-fourth of the entire population of British India. The House of Assembly will consist of not more than 375 members of whom 250 will be elected from British India and not more than 125 [1] will be appointed by the Rulers of Indian States. The number earmarked for British India will be allocated to the several communities and interests as follows : Depressed Classes (Hindus), 19; Sikh, 6; Moslem, 82; Indian Christian, 8; Anglo-Indian, 4; European, 8; Women, 9; Commerce and Industry, 11 (of whom approximately 6 will be Europeans[2]); Landholders, 7; Labour, 10; General (Hindus and others), 105. The Depressed Classes seats will be filled up in the manner prescribed in the Poona Pact adopted after the fast of Mahatma Gandhi in September 1932. Bills will be introduced in either Chamber, but Money Bills and Votes of Supply will be initiated only in the Assembly. No Bill will become law until it has been agreed to by both Chambers and has been assented to by the Governor-General, or in the case of a Reserved Bill until His Majesty in Council has signified his assent. Any Act assented to by the Governor General will within twelve months be subject to disallowance by His Majesty in Council. The Governor-General will, however, have the power to enact at his discretion as a Governor-General's Act any Bill which is not passed by the Chambers within a specified date in spite of a message from the Governor-General that that Bill should become law by that date. A Governor-General's Act will have the same force and effect as an Act of the

---

[1] With a population less than one-fourth of India, the Indian States will have $33\frac{1}{3}$ per cent of the seats in the assembly and more than 38 per cent of the seats in the Council of State.

[2] The European population in India is 168,134 out of a population of about 352 millions. Nevertheless, they are to have 14 seats in the Assembly and 7 seats in the Council of State.

Legislature. The Governor-General will be further empowered in his discretion, in any case in which he considers that a Bill introduced or proposed for introduction or any clause thereof or any amendment to a Bill moved or proposed, would affect the discharge of his responsibility, to direct that the said Bill, Clause or Amendment shall not be further proceeded with. It will thus be seen that the Governor-General has been vested with extraordinarily wide powers in the matter of modifying any legislation under consideration, withholding legislation completely and enacting fresh legislation. Such powers he does not possess even today.

The White Paper further says: 'Apart from the Reserved Departments and the 'special responsibilities' of the Governor-General outside the sphere of those departments, there is a third category of matters in which the Governor-General will not be under any constitutional obligation to seek or having sought, to be guided by ministerial advice. For this purpose certain specified powers will be conferred by the Constitution on the Governor-General and will be expressed as being exercisable 'at his discretion'. In this category of 'discretionary powers'.... His Majesty's Government anticipate that the following matters will be included:

(a) The power to dissolve, prorogue and summon the Legislature.
(b) The power to assent to, or withhold assent from Bills or to reserve them for signification of His Majesty's pleasure.
(c) The grant of previous sanction to the introduction of certain classes of Legislative measures.
(d) The power to summon forthwith a joint session of the Legislature in cases of emergency where postponement till the expiration of the period to be prescribed by the Constitution Act might have serious consequences.

With regard to Legislative procedure the Governor-

General will be empowered to make rules :

(a) Regulating the procedure of and the conduct of business in the Chamber in relation to matters arising out of, or affecting, the Administration of the Reserved Departments or any other special responsibilities with which he is charged.

(b) Prohibiting, save with the prior consent of the Governor-General given at his discretion, the discussion of or the asking of questions on :
  1. Matters connected with any Indian State other than matters accepted by the Ruler of the State in his Instrument of Accession as being Federal subjects, or
  2. Any action of the Governor-General taken in his discretion in his relationship with a Governor.
  3. Any matter affecting relations between His Majesty or the Governor-General and any foreign Prince or State.

In the event of conflict between a rule so made by the Governor-General and any rule made by the Chamber, the former will prevail and the latter will, to the extent of the inconsistency, be void.

From the above it will be clear that in order to nullify the effect of 'responsibility of the executive to the Legislature', not only have numerous reservations been made in the matter of responsibility, but the powers of the Legislature have been severely curtailed. The net result is that the Federal Legislature will be more helpless than the Indian Legislature of today and the Governor-General of the future will be more powerful than the Governor-General of today.

The Governor-General will cause a statement of the estimated revenue and expenditure of the Federation, together with a statement of all proposals for the appropriation of those revenues, to be laid, in respect of every financial year, before both Chambers of the Legislature. Proposals for appropriation of revenues will not be submitted to the vote of either Chamber of the Legislature if they relate to heads of expenditure like Interests, Sinking Fund Charges, Expenditure fixed by the Constitution Act, etc., salary and allowances of the Governor-General, of Ministers, of Counsellors, of the Financial Adviser, etc., expenditure required for the Reserved Departments, etc., salaries and pensions of the Judges of the Federal or Supreme Court, etc., salaries and pensions payable to, or to the departments of, certain members of the Public Services, etc.[1] The statement of proposals for appropriation will specify those additional proposals whether votable or non-votable, which the Governor-General regards as necessary for the discharge of any of his special responsibilities. The proposals for the appropriation of revenues, other than proposals relating to heads of expenditure enumerated above and proposals made by the Governor-General in discharge of his responsibilities, will be submitted to the vote of the Assembly. The Council of State, by a motion duly passed, may require that any demand which is reduced or rejected by the Assembly shall be brought before a joint session of both Chambers for final determination. At the conclusion of the budget proceedings, the Governor-General will authenticate by his signature all appropriations, whether voted or non-votable. In the appropriation so authenticated, the Governor-General will be empowered to include any additional amounts which he regards as necessary for the discharge of any of his special responsibilities—provided that the total amount does not exceed that was originally laid before the Legislature under that head in the statement of proposals for appropriation. Thus if any grant is refused by the Legislature, the Governor-General will be empowered to restore it. The respective legislative fields of the Centre and of the provinces will be defined in terms of the subjects which will be scheduled in the Constitution Act. It is proposed further to include in the provincial list a general power to legis-

---

[1] In the light of legislative experience, the expectation or rather apprehension is that the non-votable items will cover about 80 per cent of the total expenditure.
The White Paper provides that the Governor-General will decide which item is non-votable as falling under one of these heads.

late on any matter of a purely local and private nature in the province. But in order to provide for the possibility that a subject which in its inception is of a purely local or private character may subsequently become of All-India interest, it is proposed to make that power subject to a right of the Governor-General in his discretion to sanction general legislation by the Federal Legislature on the same subject-matter.

With regard to the position of the Federal Ministers, the White Paper says that 'the number of ministers and the amounts of their respective salaries will be regulated by Act of the Federal Legislature'.[1] Nevertheless, there is a further provision that the salary and allowances of the Federal Ministers will not be submitted to the vote of either Chamber of the Federal Legislature.[2] (There are similar provisions with regard to the Provincial Ministers.)

With regard to the Federal Judiciary, the White Paper provides for a Federal Court and a Supreme Court. The Federal Court will have an original and an appellate jurisdiction and will deal with all disputes involving the interpretation of the Constitution Act or any rights or obligations arising thereunder. An appeal will lie to His Majesty in Council from a decision of the Federal Court in any matter involving the interpretation of the Constitution Act. There will also be a Supreme Court for India, which will be a Court of Appeal from High Courts in British India. An appeal from the Supreme Court to His Majesty in Council will be allowed in civil cases only by leave of the Supreme Court. In criminal cases no such appeal will be allowed. After the publication of the White Paper, while giving evidence before the Joint Parliamentary Committee, Sir Samuel Hoare stated that the idea of having a separate Supreme Court might be abandoned and provision might be made enabling the Legislature, if and when it was thought desirable, to extend the jurisdiction of the Federal Court—so as to make it the one final Court of Appeal, subject always to the right of appeal to His Majesty

---

[1] Paragraph 15 of the White Paper Proposals.
[2] Paragraph 49 of the Proposals.

in Council. According to the White Paper, the Chief Justice and the Judges of the Federal Court (as also of the Supreme Court if it comes into being) will be appointed by His Majesty and will hold office during good behaviour. Their salaries, pensions, etc., will be fixed by Order in Council and will not be subject to the vote of the Legislature.

After the commencement of the Constitution Act, the present Council of the Secretary of State for India will be dissolved. The Secretary of State will then appoint not less than three and not more than six persons who will form his Advisory Council. Persons appointed by the Secretary of State to any of the Services before the commencement of the Constitution Act will continue to enjoy all Service rights possessed by them at that date. After the commencement of the Constitution Act, the Secretary of State will continue to make appointments to the Indian Civil Service, the Indian Police and the Ecclesiastical Department and the conditions as to pay and allowances, pensions, discipline and conduct of such persons will be regulated by rules made by the Secretary of State. Every person appointed by the Secretary of State will continue to enjoy all service rights existing at the date of his appointment. 'At the expiration of five years from the commencement of the Constitution Act, a statutory inquiry will be held into the question of the future recruitment for those services except the Foreign Department and the Ecclesiastical Department. The decision on the results of this inquiry, with which the Governments in India concerned will be associated, will rest with His Majesty's Government and be subject to the approval of both Houses of Parliament.'[1]

Thus the important services will continue to be under the control of the Secretary of State for India in London in spite of the so-called responsibility granted to India. The Federal and Provincial Ministers will have as subordinates, officials over whose destiny they will have no control and against whom they will not be able to take any discipli-

---

[1] White Paper Proposals, para 189.

nary measures. As for the other services, the Federal and Provincial Governments respectively will appoint and determine the conditions of service of all persons in the Federal and Provincial services respectively. For conducting competitive examinations for appointments to the Federal and Provincial services respectively, there will be a Federal Public Service Commission and Provincial Public Service Commissions. The members of the Federal Public Service Commission will be appointed by the Secretary of State and of the Provincial Public Service Commission by the Governor. The emoluments of the members of all Public Service Commissions will not be subject to the vote of the Legislatures. Thus the Public Service Commissions will be quite independent of the popular will.

Some other provisions have been made to safeguard the interests of Britishers. The Indian Reserve Bank [1] already referred to, which is a condition precedent to the inauguration of the Federation, will manage currency and exchange according to the dictation of London. To administer the Indian railways with their vast resources, there will be a Statutory Railway Board which will be so composed, as 'to perform its duties on business principles and without being subject to political interference'. In the composition of the Railway Board, the people will have no voice whatsoever. Lastly, there is a very important provision meant to preserve intact the vested interests of the British Mercantile community. The Federal Legislature or the Provincial Legislature will have no power to make laws subjecting any British subject domiciled in (or company incorporated in) the United Kingdom to any disability or discrimination in the exercise of certain specified rights, for instance, the right to enter, travel and reside in any part of British India; to hold property of any kind, to carry

[1] An announcement has been made by the India Office, London, on 4th October, 1934, saying that the Indian Reserve Bank Bill will be constituted early in 1935. The Governor, Deputy-Governors and the Central Board of the Bank will of course be appointed by His Majesty's Government. As a matter of fact, some appointments have already been made. Sir Osborne Smith has been appointed Governor of the Bank; Mr. J. B. Taylor, first Deputy Governor and Sir Sikandar Hayat Khan (some time Acting Governor of the Punjab) second Deputy Governor.

on any trade or business in, or with the inhabitants of, British India and to appoint and employ at discretion agents and servants for any of the above purposes. Such restrictions on legislation do not exist even today. The Indian Legislative Assembly today, for instance, can enact laws giving Indians special advantages in the matter of business and trade though they could be subsequently voted by the Governor-General. It appears that the British Government want to prohibit altogether legislation like the Indian Coastal Shipping Bill, which sought to reserve the coastal trade of India for Indian Shipping Companies.

With regard to the 'fundamental rights' which Indian public opinion so strongly demanded, the White Paper says: 'His Majesty's Government see serious objections to giving statutory expression to any large range of declarations of this character, but they are satisfied that certain provisions of this kind such, for instance, as the respect due to personal liberty and rights of property and the eligibility of all for public office, regardless of differences of caste, religion, etc., can appropriately, and should, find a place in the Constitution Act., There is no mention in this connection of such elementary rights as freedom of speech, freedom of association, etc. nor is there any assurance given that the scanty rights to be conceded will be made altogether inviolable.[1]

According to the White Paper the powers of the Governor in relation to his ministers, to the Provincial Legislature and to the Provincial Administration will be an exact replica of those enjoyed by the Governor-General at the centre. Hence it is not necessary to repeat all those provisions. The only difference will be that in the Provinces there will be no 'reserved departments' managed by 'Counsellors', but corresponding to them there may be 'Excluded Areas' or 'Partially Excluded Areas' the administration of which will be beyond the control of the Legislatures. Most of the provinces will have only one Chamber—but in

---

[1] For instance, it is not clear that imprisonment without trial will be rendered impossible in India as has been done in Great Britain owing to the Habeas Corpus Act.

Bengal, the United Provinces and Bihar there wil be two Chambers. The term of the Lower House—the Legislative Assembly—will be five years, and that of the Upper House —Provincial Council—will be seven years. The Provincial Council will be constituted partly by nomination by the Governor and partly by direct election from constituencies for Moslem and for non-Moslem voters. In Bengal and Bihar a certain number will also be elected by the Provincial Assembly by the method of the single transferable vote. And in Bengal one member will be elected by qualified European voters. The constitution of the Provincial Legislative Assembly has been explained below.

The Franchise Scheme embodied in the White Paper is based on the Lothian Committee's Report, the Prime Minister's Communal Award and the Poona Pact. Talking generally, the present provincial franchise has been made the franchise for the Lower House of the Federal Legislature. The present ratio of women to male voters will remain unchanged. The existing franchise in all the provinces is essentially based on property. The White Paper proposes to supplement property qualification by an educational qualification common to men and women. There will be a differential franchise in the case of the Depressed Classes in order to enfranchise about 2 per cent of their population. The White Paper proposes to enfranchise as voters for the Federal Legislature between 2 and 3 per cent of the total population of British India, i.e. about 7 or 8 millions.

The franchise for the future provincial assemblies is based on property to men and women alike—and by a qualification for women in respect of property held by a husband. There will be a differential franchise for the Depressed Classes in order to enfranchise 10 per cent of their population. The ratio of women to men voters will be about one to seven as compared with approximately one to twenty-one at the present time. According to the White Paper, the Governor's provinces will have an average electorate of about 14 per cent of the total population or about 27 per cent of the adult population.

Election to the seats allotted to the Sikhs, Moslems, Indian Christian, Anglo-Indian and European constituencies in the Provincial and the Federal Legislatures, will be by voters voting in separate communal electorates. All qualified voters, who are not voters, in one of these constituencies, will be entitled to vote in a 'general' constituency. Seats will be reserved for the Depressed Classes out of the 'general seats' as indicated in the following table, and the manner of election will be as prescribed in the Poona Pact, namely on the basis of a common electorate embracing all sections of Hindus, subject to a primary election by voters of the Depressed Classes only. Women's seats in the Assembly will be filled by the members of the Provincial Legislature voting by means of the single transferable vote, but the manner of election in the case of seats in the Provincial Legislatures is under consideration. The seats allotted to Commerce and Industry and to Landholders will be filled by special constituencies. The seats allotted to Labour will be filled from non-communal constituencies —partly trade-union and partly special constituencies. The organisation of the Indian Christians and of women were emphatically opposed to separate communal electorate but their wishes have been ignored. In Bengal and Punjab a statutory majority has been virtually provided for the majority community—the Moslems, without giving the Hindu minority representation according to their population such as the Moslem minorities in all provinces have received.

The effect of the above provisions will be that the Provincial Assemblies will be constituted in the manner shown in the following table.

The whole object of the Communal Award embodied in the White Paper seems to be to divide India still further, so that the effect of the meagre constitutional reforms may be sufficiently neutralised. Attempt has been made to provide representation in such a manner that the points of difference among the Indian people, if any, will be given exaggerated expression in the Legislatures and not their points of agreement. The entire scheme is based on the pernicious principle of 'Divide and Rule'. In trying to divide the people, attempt has naturally been made to placate those elements—the Moslems, for instance—who according to the official estimate, are likely to be more pro-British than the others. During the nineteenth century and till the beginning of this century, similar reliance was placed by the Government on the landholders, and in those days the Government distrusted the Moslems more than the Hindus. Since the beginning of this century, the landholders have not proved themselves to be sufficiently loyal. For instance, in Bengal they took part in the anti-partition and 'Swadeshi' agitation in 1905 and after. Hence a new device had to be created for dividing the Indians. In 1906, therefore, at the instance of the Viceroy, Lord Minto, and by prearrangement, some Moslem leaders for the first time broached the proposal of separate electorate. This demand was at once given effect to, because the constitutional advance made in the Morley-Minto Reforms of 1909 had to be neutralised. Separate electorates for Moslems were continued in the Government of India Act 1919. The experience of the last fourteen yars has shown that in spite of separate electorates and in spite of an official bloc in the Legislatures, the Government could be defeated repeatedly. Therefore the British Government found it necessary to divide the Indian community still further so that the chances of a united opposition against the British Government in the future Legislatures would be considerably minimised. Hence the proposal to give separate electorates to Indian Christians, women, Depressed Classes, etc. in addition to Moslems, Europeans, Anglo-Indians and Sikhs. The principle of 'Division before concession' reminds one of a similar policy followed in Ireland, when Ulster was separated before the Constitution of the Irish Free State was conceded by the British Government. In the case of India, it is needless to say, that on a basis so sectarian and reactionary, no constitution can thrive.

The above brief description of the White Paper proposals make it quite clear that no transference of power from the foreign Government to the Indian people will take place. Much of the power will still be retained by the Secre-

| Province (Population in Millions shown in brackets) | General | Number of General Seats reserved for Depressed Classes | Representatives from Backward Areas | Sikh | Moham-medan |
|---|---|---|---|---|---|
| Madras (45.6) | 152 (including 6 women) | 30 | 1 | 0 | 29 (including 1 woman) |
| Bombay (18.0) | 119 (b) (including 5 women) | 15 | 1 | 0 | 30 (including 1 woman) |
| Bengal (50.1) | 80 (including 2 women) | 30 | 0 | 0 | 119 (including 2 women) |
| United Provinces (48.4) | 144 (including 4 women) | 20 | 0 | 0 | 66 (including 2 women) |
| Punjab (23.6) | 43 (including 1 woman) | 8 | 0 | 32 (including 1 woman) | 86 (including 2 women) |
| Bihar (32.4) | 89 (including 3 women) | 15 | 7 | 0 | 40 (including 1 woman) |
| Central Provinces [with Berar] (15.5) | 87 (including 3 women) | 20 | 1 | 0 | 14 |
| Assam (8.6) | 48 (d) (including 1 woman) | 7 | 9 | 0 | 34 |
| North-West Frontier Province (2.4) | 9 | 0 | 0 | 3 | 36 |
| Sind (3.9) | 19 (including 1 woman) | 0 | 0 | 0 | 34 (including 1 woman) |
| Orissa (6.7) | 49 (including 2 women) | 7 | 2 | 0 | 4 |

(a) The composition of the bodies through which election to these seats will be conducted, though in most cases either predominantly European or predominantly Indian, will not be statutorily fixed. It is, accordingly, not possible in each province to state with certainty how many Europeans and Indians respectively will be returned. It is, however, expected that, initially, the numbers will be approximately as follows: Madras, 4 Europeans, 2 Indians; Bombay, 4 Europeans, 3 Indians; Bengal, 14 Europeans, 5 Indians; United Provinces, 2 Europeans, 1 Indian; Punjab. 1 Indian; Bihar, 2 Europeans, 2 Indians; Central Provinces (with Berar), 1 European, 1 Indian; Assam, 8 Europeans, 3 Indians; Sind, 1 European, 1 Indian; Orissa, 1 Indian.

## THE WHITE PAPER AND THE COMMUNAL AWARD 325

| Indian Christian | Anglo-Indian | European | Commerce and Industry, Mining and Planting (Special) (a) | Landholders (Special) | University (Special) | Labour (Special) | Total |
|---|---|---|---|---|---|---|---|
| 9 including 1 woman) | 2 | 3 | 6 | 6 | 1 | 6 | 215 |
| 3 | 2 | 3 | 7 | 2 | 1 | 7 | 175 |
| 2 | 4 (including 1 woman) | 11 | 19 | 5 | 2 | 8 | 250 |
| 2 | 1 | 2 | 3 | 6 | 1 | 3 | 228 |
| 2 | 1 | 1 | 1 | 5 (c) | 1 | 3 | 175 |
| 1 | 1 | 2 | 4 | 4 | 1 | 3 | 152 |
| 0 | 1 | 1 | 2 | 3 | 1 | 2 | 112 |
| 1 | 0 | 1 | 11 | 0 | 0 | 4 | 108 |
| 0 | 0 | 0 | 0 | 2 | 0 | 0 | 50 |
| 0 | 0 | 2 | 2 | 2 | 0 | 1 | 60 |
| 1 | 0 | 0 | 1 | 2 | 0 | 1 | 60 |

(b) Seven of these seats will be reserved for Mahrattas.

(c) One of these seats is a Tumandar's seat. The four Landholders' seats will be filled from special constituencies with joint electorates. It is probable from the distribution of the electorate, that the members returned will be 1 Hindu, 1 Sikh and 2 Mohammedans.

(d) This woman's seat will be filled from a non-communal constituency at Shillong.

tary of State for India on behalf of the Crown. All matters within the personal jurisdiction of the Governor in the provinces and of the Governor-General at the centre will be under his (the Secretary of State's) control. He will continue to control the higher services, and all legislation enacted in India will be liable to his veto. Appointment of High Court and Federal Court Judges and of members of the Federal Public Services Commission will be made by him. In India, the Governor-General will be made more autocratic and powerful than he is today. Under some label or other, like 'reserved department' or 'special responsibility' or 'discretionary power', he will wield wider powers than he has even today. Even in matters ordinarily within the control or supervision of the Legislature, he will have ample scope for interference. 80 per cent of the total expenditure will be non-votable. Even the business of the Legislature will be controlled by him more stringently than it is today. Moreover, the composition of the Federal Legislatures will be much more reactionary than that of the Central Legislatures of today. In the provinces, the position will be no better, and the much proclaimed 'provincial autonomy' will be a sham. In these circumstances, nobody who is anybody in India will be found to bless the new Constitution.

CHAPTER XVI

## THE ROLE OF MAHATMA GANDHI IN INDIAN HISTORY

The role which a man plays in history depends partly on his physical and mental equipment, and partly on the environment and the needs of times in which he is born. There is something in Mahatma Gandhi, which appeals to the mass of the Indian people. Born in another country he might have been a complete misfit. What, for instance, would he have done in a country like Russia or Germany or Italy? His doctrine of non-violence would have led him to the cross or to the mental hospital. In India it is different. His simple life, his vegetarian diet, his goat's milk, his day of silence every week, his habit of squatting on the floor instead of sitting on a chair, his loin-cloth—in fact everything connected with him—has marked him out as one of the eccentric Mahatmas of old and has brought him nearer to his people. Wherever he may go, even the poorest of the poor feels that he is a product of the Indian soil—bone of his bone, flesh of his flesh. When the Mahatma speaks, he does so in a language that they comprehend, not in the language of Herbert Spencer and Edmund Burke, as for instance Sir Surendra Nath Banerji would have done, but in that of the *Bhagavad-Gita* and the *Ramayana*. When he talks to them about Swaraj, he does not dilate on the virtues of provincial autonomy or federation, he reminds them of the glories of *Ramarajya* (the kingdom of King Rama of old) and they understand. And when he talks of conquering through love and *ahimsa* (non-violence), they are reminded of Buddha and Mahavira and they accept him.

But the conformity of the Mahatma's physical and mental equipment to the traditions and temperament of the Indian people is but one factor accounting for the former's success. If he had been born in another epoch in Indian history, he might not have been able to distinguish himself so well. For instance, what would he have done at the time of the Revolution of 1857 when the people had arms, were able to fight and wanted a leader who could lead them in battle? The success of the Mahatma has been due to the failure of constitutionalism on the one side and armed revolution on the other. Since the eighties of the last century, the best political brains among the Indian people were engaged in a constitutional fight, in which the qualities most essential were skill in debate and eloquence in speech. In such an environment it is unlikely that the Mahatma would have attained much eminence. With the dawn of the present century people began to lose faith in constitutional methods. New weapons like Swadeshi (revival of national industry) and Boycott appeared, and simultaneously the revolutionary movement was born. As the years rolled by, the revolutionary movement began to gain ground (especially in Upper India) and during the Great War there was an attempt at a revolution. The failure of this attempt at a time when Britain had her hands full and the tragic events of 1919 convinced the Indian people that it was no use trying to resort to the method of physical force. The superior equipment of Britain would easily smash any such attempt and in its wake there would come indescribable misery and humiliation.

In 1920 India stood at the cross-roads. Constitutionalism was dead; armed revolution was sheer madness. But silent acquiescence was impossible. The country was groping for a new method and looking for a new leader. Then there sprang up India's man of destiny—Mahatma Gandhi —who had been bidding his time all these years and quietly preparing himself for the great task ahead of him. He knew himself—he knew his country's needs and he knew also that during the next phase of India's struggle, the crown of leadership would be on his head. No false sense of modesty troubled him—he spoke with a firm voice and the people obeyed.

The Indian National Congress of today is largely his creation. The Congress Constitution is his handiwork. From a talking body he has converted the Congress into a living and fighting organisation. It has its ramification in every town and village in India, and the entire nation has been trained to listen to one voice. Nobility of character and capacity to suffer have been made the essential tests of leadership, and the Congress is today the largest and the most representative political organisation in the country.

But how could he achieve so much within this short period? By his single-hearted devotion, his relentless will and his indefatigable labour. Moreover, the time was auspicious and his policy prudent. Though he appeared as a dynamic force, he was not too revolutionary for the majority of his countrymen. If he had been so, he would have frightened them, instead of inspiring them; repelled them, instead of drawing them. His policy was one of unification. He wanted to unite Hindu and Moslem; the high caste and the low caste; the capitalist and the labourer; the landlord and the peasant. By this humanitarian outlook and his freedom from hatred, he was able to rouse sympathy even in his enemy's camp.

But Swaraj is still a distant dream. Instead of one, the people have waited for fourteen long years. And they will have to wait many more. With such purity of character and with such an unprecedented following, why has the Mahatma failed to liberate India?

He has failed because the strength of a leader depends not on the largeness—but on the character—of one's following. With a much smaller following, other leaders have been able to liberate their country—while the Mahatma with a much larger following has not. He has failed, because while he has understood the character of his own people —he has not understood the character of his opponents. The logic of the Mahatma is not the logic which appeals to John Bull. He has failed, because his policy of putting all his cards on the table will not do. We have to render unto Caesar what is Caesar's—and in a political fight, the art of diplomacy cannot be dispensed with. He has failed, because he has not made use of the international weapon. If we desire to win our freedom through non-violence, diplomacy and international propaganda are essential. He has failed, because the false unity of interests that are inherently opposed is not a source of strength but a source of weakness in political warfare. The future of India rests exclusively with those radical and militant forces that will be able to undergo the sacrifice and suffering necessary for winning freedom. Last but not least, the Mahatma has failed, because he had to play a dual role in one person—the role of the leader of an enslaved people and that of a world-teacher, who has a new doctrine to preach. It is this duality which has made him at once the irreconcilable foe of the Englishman, according to Mr. Winston Churchill, and the best policeman of the Englishman according to Miss Ellen Wilkinson.

What of the future? What role will the Mahatma play in the days to come? Will he be able to emancipate his dear country? Several factors have to be considered. So far as his health and vitality are concerned, it is highly probable that he will be spared many years of active and useful public life and his determination to achieve something tangible in the direction of his country's freedom will keep up his spirits. So far as his popularity and reputation are concerned, they will endure till the end of his life—because unlike other political leaders, the Mahatma's popularity and reputation do not depend on his political leadership —but largely on his character. The question we have to consider, however, is whether the Mahatma will continue his political activities or whether he will voluntarily withdraw himself from active politics—of which there are indications at the present moment—and devote himself exclusively to social and humanitarian work. A prediction in the case of the Mahatma is a hazardous proposition. Nevertheless, one thing is certain. The Mahatma will not play second fiddle to anyone. As long as it will be possible for him to guide the political movement, he will be there—but if the composition or the mentality of the Congress changes, he may possibly retire from active politics. That retirement may be temporary or permanent. A temporary retirement is like a strategic retreat and is not of much significance because the hero will come back into the picture once again. We have had experience of the Mahatma's retirement from active politics once before—from 1924 to 1928. Whether there is a possibility of the Mahatma's permanent retirement depends to some extent at least, on the attitude of the British Government. If he is able to achieve something tangible for his country, then his position will be unassailable among his countrymen. Nothing succeeds like success, and the Mahatma's success will confirm public faith in his personality and in his weapon of non-violent non-co-operation. But if the British attitude continues to be as uncompromising as it is today, public faith in the Mahatma as a political leader and in the method of non-violent non-co-operation will be considerably shaken. In that event they will naturally turn to a more radical leadership and policy.

In spite of the unparalleled popularity and reputation which the Mahatma has among his countrymen and will continue to have regardless of his future political career, there is no doubt that the unique position of the Mahatma is due to his political leadership. The Mahatma himself distinguishes between his mass-popularity and his political following and he is never content with having merely the former. Whether he will be able to retain that political following in the years to come in the event of the British attitude being as unbending as it is today, will depend on his ability to evolve a more radical policy. Will he be able to give up the attempt to unite all the elements in the country and boldly identify himself with the more radical forces? In that case nobody can possibly supplant him. The hero of the present phase of the Indian struggle will then be the hero of the next phase as well. But what does the balance of probability indicate?

The Patna meeting of the All-India Congress Committee in May 1934, affords an interesting study in this connection. The Mahatma averted the Swarajist revolt by advocating council-entry himself. But the Swarajists of 1934, are not the dynamic Swarajists of 1922-23. Therefore, while he was able to win them over, he could not avoid alienating the Left Wingers, many of whom have now combined to form the Congress Socialist Party. This is the first time that a Socialist Party has been started openly within the Indian National Congress, and it is extremely probable that economic issues will henceforth be brought to the fore. With the clarification of economic issues, parties will be more scientifically organised within the Congress and also among the people in general.

The Congress Socialists appear at the moment to be under the influence of Fabian Socialism and some of their ideas and shibboleths were the fashion several decades ago. Nevertheless, the Congress Socialists do represent a radical force within the Congress and in the country. Many of those who could have helped them actively are not available at present. When their assistance will be forthcoming, the Party will be able to make more headway.

At the present moment another challenge to the Mahatma's policy has crystallised within the Congress in the Congress Nationalist Party led by Pandit Malaviya. The dispute has arisen over the Communal Award of the Prime Minister, Mr Ramsay Macdonald. The issue is, however, a comparatively minor one, because the official Congress Party and the Congress Nationalist Party are agreed in the total rejection of the White Paper of which the Communal Award is an integral part. Only the official Congress Party is foolishly afraid of openly condemning the Communal Award. Since the Congress Nationalist Party does not represent a more radical force in the country, the ultimate challenge to the Mahatma's leadership cannot come from that direction.

One definite prediction can be made at this stage—namely, that the future parties within the Congress will be based on economic issues. It is not improbable that in the event of the Left Wingers capturing the Congress machinery, there will be a further secession from the Right and the setting up of a new organisation of the Right Wingers like the Indian Liberal Federation of today. It will of course take some years to clarify the economic issues in the public mind—so that parties may be organised on the basis of a clear programme and ideology. Till the issues are clarified, Mahatma Gandhi's political supremacy will remain unchallenged, even if there is a temporary retirement as in 1924. But once the clarification takes place, his political following will be greatly affected. As has been already indicated, the Mahatma has endeavoured in the past to hold together all the warring elements—landlord and peasant, capitalist and labour, rich and poor. That has been the secret of his success, as surely as it will be the ultimate cause of his failure. If all the warring elements resolve to carry on the struggle for political freedom, the internal social struggle will be postponed for a long time and men holding the position of the Mahatma will continue to dominate the public life of the country. But that will not be the case. The vested interests, the 'haves', will in future fight shy of the 'have-nots' in the political fight and will gradually incline towards the British Government. The logic of history will, therefore, follow its inevitable course. The political struggle and the social struggle will have to be conducted simultaneously. The Party that will win political freedom for India will be also the Party that will win social and economic freedom for the masses. Mahatma Gandhi has rendered and will continue to render phenomenal service to his country. But India's salvation will not be achieved under his leadership.

CHAPTER XVII

## THE BENGAL SITUATION

In dealing with the events between 1920 and 1934 it has not been possible to do justice to all aspects of the Indian struggle. On analysing, we find several streams of activity. There is the main stream—the political movement, which is under the leadership of the Indian National Congress. Then there is a subsidiary stream—the workers' movement under the leadership of the All-India Trade Union Congress. There is also an independent movement of the peasantry in the different provinces, which has not yet emerged as a centralised all-India movement. Besides other subsidiary movements like the women's movement, the youth movement and the students' movement, there is one other movement quite independent of the Congress, which has been a serious problem to the Government. This is the revolutionary movement. This movement has had its ramifications all over India, more or less, but one could say that on the whole it has found greater support in Upper India and that comparatively speaking, Bengal is the stronghold of this movement. Up till now no serious attempt has ever been made to understand the psychology behind the movement. An important officer of the Government, Lieut.-Col. Berkeley-Hill, I.M.S., a well-known psychiatrist, who has been for years in charge of a mental hospital in India, once suggested to the Government that they should attempt a systematic psychological study of the problem, but his advice was not taken. In the present circumstances of the country it is extremely risky for an honest Indian to volunteer an explanation. He would at once be accused of sympathy with the movement and would be liable to be put in prison without trial. Therefore, when Indians do attempt to throw light on this problem, they usually make silly statements with the sole object of pleasing the rulers. For instance, it is customary for people to say that the revolutionary movement is the result of unemployment among middle-class youths.

At the outset it should be pointed out that the revolutionary movement is not an anarchist movement, nor is it merely a terrorist movement. The revolutionaries do not aim at creating anarchy or chaos. While it is a fact that they do occasionally resort to terrorism, their ultimate object is not terrorism but revolution and the purpose of the revolution is to install a National Government. Though the earliest revolutionaries studied something about revolutionary methods in other countries, it would not be correct to say that the inspiration came from abroad. The movement was born out of a conviction that to a Western people physical force alone makes an appeal. It is not generally realised by Britishers, that it is they who have been primarily responsible for teaching the Indian people the efficacy of physical force. Two or three dcades ago (and even till today in some cases) the average Britisher in India, especially when he was a member of the army, or of the police, was so haughty in his general behaviour towards Indians, that no Indian with a grain of self-respect could help feeling the humiliation of being under a foreign government. In the street, in the railways, in the tram-cars, in public places and in public functions, in fact everywhere, the Britisher expected the Indian to make way for him, and if he refused to do so, the Indian would be assaulted. In such cases of friction, the forces of the Government were always on the side of the Britishers. Cases frequently happened in which Indians of the highest position and rank —even Judges of the High Court—would be insulted in this way. Even during the Great War, when India was fighting on the side of England, such cases of friction between Indians and Britishers would constantly occur in the tram-cars in Calcutta.[1] No legal or constitutional remedy could be found for such insults, for neither the police nor the subordinate Law Courts would venture to do justice. Then the time came when Indians began to hit back, and when

---

[1] The writer has had personal experience of many such cases.

they did so the effect was immediate and remarkable. Ever since then, in proportion as they have been able to hit back, Indians have been able to move about in their own country without losing their self-respect. Even in the colleges in Calcutta, British members of the staff would often be guilty of insulting behaviour towards Indian students and the fact that today such cases are not frequent, is because Indian students also made use of physical force in upholding their self-respect.

This then is the psychology behind the revolutionary movement; but a further explanation is necessary to show why Bengal has, comparatively speaking, become its stronghold. The trouble began with Macaulay. When he was out in India as a member of the Government, Macaulay wrote a scathing denunciation of the Bengalees and called them a race of cowards. That calumny went deep into the hearts of the Bengalee people. Simultaneously the Government took the step of excluding the Bengalees from the army on the ground that they were not sufficiently warlike or brave. The climax came when the Grand Moghul, Lord Curzon of Kedleston, attempted to crush the Bengalees by partitioning their province. The people at first retorted with the help of Swadeshi and boycott. But when brute force was used—as at Barisal in 1906—to break up peaceful processions and meetings, the people felt that peaceful methods would not suffice. In sheer despair, young men took to the bomb and the revolver. The effect was immediate. The behaviour of the Britisher began to improve. The impression gained ground that for the first time the Bengalee was being respected by the Britisher. Many of the revolutionaries were hanged but they were able to demonstrate that the race to which they belonged was not a race of cowards. They were, therfeore, regarded as martyrs in many a Bengalee home and they had the silent homage of the Bengalee race.

On this soil and in this manner has grown up the revolutionary movement in Bengal. What is the remedy for it? Two courses are open to the Government—firstly, to demonstrate to the people that for winning political freedom it is not ncessary to resort to revolutionary methods and secondly, to give individual revolutionaries a chance of serving their country along peaceful and constructive lines. With regard to the first, the short-sighted policy of the Government has served to strengthen the arguments of the revolutionaries. The reforms introduced at the end of the Great War were so meagre as to cause widespread discontent. The revolutionary who came out of prison at the end of the war after years of confinement found that the promised liberty was an empty dream and there was no opening for serving his country along peaceful and constructive lines. Nevertheless, in response to the appeal made by Mahatma Gandhi and Deshabandhu C. R. Das, they promised to eschew the path of violence and give a trial to the new method of non-violence and non-co-operation, and it must be admitted that the vast majority did keep their promise. But what did the Government do? On the plea that some stray acts of violence had been committed in a corner of a great province, the Government rounded up a large number of men from all over the province in 1923, and again in 1924, and kept them in prison for a number of years without trial. The public feeling at the time was that there were over-zealous officers in the Intelligence Branch of the Bengal Police, who in order to justify their existence and the existence of their department, imagined more than they actually saw. And it was even believed that *agents provocateur* were employed for the purpose of entrapping innocent young men. It will not do to ignore such complaints with an official sneer, for if one really desires to go to the root of the problem, he should investigate all such complaints with an open mind. After some years, that is in 1927 and 1928, the Government again began to release the *detenus*. But as in 1919-20, so also in 1927-28, a real amnesty did not take place. Both before and after his release, every *detenu* was harassed so much by the police that the release instead of producing a sense of relief, left bitterness in his mind. If the releases had been ordered as a stroke of generous-hearted statesmanship, the effect would have been quite different.

The 1930-34 phase of the revolutionary movement in Bengal could have been possibly avoided if some special circumstances had not cropped up. Firstly, the attitude of Mahatma Gandhi at the Calcutta Congress had a very unfavourable effect on the minds of the youths. It gave them the impression that the Mahatma was a spent force and that a mass movement under the leadership of the Congress was highly improbable. Owing to this feeling a section of the youths began to prepare for independent action on their own behalf on revolutionary lines. Thus it was that the Chittagong Armoury Raid took place. This activity was, however, restricted in a very small area and when the Mahatma launched his movement early in 1930, the youths all over the province were drawn towards it. For the subsequent development of the revolutionary movement in Bengal, and for the repeated acts of terrorism, the Government themselves were to blame more than anyone else. Whether in Midnapore or in Dacca or in Tipperah district, in each case atrocities committed by the agents of the Government and the failure of the public to secure any redress by constitutional means were responsible for provoking people to acts of terrorism as a retaliation. Even the subsequent acts of terrorism in Chittagong district should be attributed not to a desire to work up a revolution in the country but to a desire to retaliate against what the revolutionaries regarded as acts of official terrorism.

The question arises here—Is it possible in the circumstances to come to an understanding with the revolutionaries? Yes, it is, provided the approach is made in the right way and the intentions are really sincere. A broad mind is required for an understanding of the problem, and courage is needed for solving it. A direct negotiation with the Party is indispensable. This necessity would not have arisen if Mahatma Gandhi or any other public leader had volunteered to be their spokesman. Since that is not possible, direct negotiation is the only alternative.

It is generally urged by police-officers that the revolutionaries are out for the severance of the British connection and that they are altogether irreconcilable. There is no doubt that the revolutionaries stand for independence; but so also does the Indian National Congress. If an understanding could be attempted with the Congress, it could be equally done with the former. In 1931, the then Governor of Bengal, Sir Stanley Jackson, thought it desirable to make the attempt, and he used the late Mr. J. M. Sengupta as an intermediary. The result was not altogether hopeless. That the negotiations then proved to be abortive was due entirely to the fact that the Government did not comply with the request of the state prisoners in Buxa Detention Camp, that the negotiations should be conducted directly with them and not through any police-officer.

There are two conditions essential to the success of an attempt of this sort. Firstly, the Governor should really be able to demonstrate by their own liberal policy that it is possible for the Indians to win their political rights without any resort to violence. If their policy, however, be to resist for all time the Indian demand for freedom, then no understanding will ever be possible. Secondly, the Government must see to it that those who are to give up revolutionary methods are given other opportunities for serving their country along peaceful and constructive lines. Merely to find some employment for them will not be enough. It is foolish to suggest, as many have done in order to please the Government, that middle-class unemployment is the cause of the revolutionary movement. If that had been the case, well-to-do people would never have been drawn into the movement. But while it is true that middle-class unemployment is not the cause of the revolutionary movement, it is, of course, true that if opportunities for public service had been open to young men in Bengal, then the attempts of the revolutionaries to obtain recruits would have failed. The present temper and policy of the Government whereby every young man is regarded as a potential revolutionary and treated as such, and the present conditions in the province, whereunder it is quite hopeless to win Swaraj by working along constructive lines, are among the most fruitful causes of the revolutionary movement.

Revolutionary methods are, in their ultimate analysis, an expression of utter despair. If this despair is once removed, an understanding with the revolutionaries is certainly possible. That will not mean that they will cease to be patriots or that they will give up serving their country. It will only mean that they will direct their activities along other channels.

Whether an understanding could be reached in the near future depends largely on the personality of the present Governor of Bengal, Sir John Anderson. Before he went out of India, he made statements to the effect that he was going out not merely to suppress the revolutionary movement but with a view to understanding the deeper causes of it in order to effect a reconciliation. Unfortunately, since his arrival in Bengal, he has hardly done anything towards a genuine reconciliation. Nor has he given any proof of his desire to understand the deeper causes of the movement, though in the meantime he has done everything that a zealous police-officer could hope to do. Sir John Anderson has the reputation of being a strong man and that reputation is not without foundation. Only a strong man can tackle a problem of this sort which has baffled so many people. The diehards in the Indian Civil Service and in the Indian Police Service are not the people who would welcome an understanding with any party in the country—much less with the revolutionary party. Therefore, it is not unfortunate that the Governor of Bengal is a strong man. It is only to be hoped that he will show his strength of mind and firmness of resolve to better purpose than in the past during the remaining years of his office.

CHAPTER XVIII

## EPILOGUE 1934

Since the above was written, three events deserving of notice have taken place. The plenary session of the Congress met in Bombay on October 26th, 1934. The elections to the Indian Legislative Assembly, in which the Congress has been participating, began in November. And the Report of the Joint Parliamentary Committee on Indian Constitutional Reforms was published on November 2nd, 1934.

The two important resolutions passed by the Bombay Congress refer to (1) a change of the Congress Constitution and (2) Constitution of an All-India Village Industries Association. The second resolution connotes an extension of the existing Khadi (spinning and weaving) programme of the Congress and indicates that the Congress desires to emphasise non-political work. The first resolution has two principal parts : (1) Reduction in the numerical strength of the Congress delegates and of the All-India Congress Committee and (2) provision of a rule that one must habitually wear Khadi for six months in order to be elected a member of a Congress Executive. Both the above resolutions may be regarded as the Mahatma's handiwork.

According to the Congress Constitution in vogue for thirteen years, the number of delegates to be elected to a Plenary Session of the Congress was 6000, while the strength of the All-India Congress Committee was about 350. At the Lahore Congress in December 1929, an attempt was made by Mahatma Gandhi, Pandit Nehru and others to reduce the stand of the former to 1000 and of the latter to 100. But the attempt was defeated. The Bombay Congress has now reduced the former to 2000 and the latter to 155. The significance of this move is very great. When in 1920, the Mahatma seized the Congress machinery and turned out the older leaders, the forces of democracy were on his side and the Nagpur Congress of 1920 was attended by no less than 14,000 delegates. Today, the Mahatma is afraid of the forces of democracy which he has helped to stir up, hence his attempt to reduce the stand not only of the Congress delegates, but also of the All-India and Provincial Congress Committees. Verily, the Mahatma has ceased to be a dynamic force. May be, it is the effect of age.

But why did the Congress swallow the constitutional amendment? The reason is not far to seek. In May 1933, the Mahatma was able to suspend the civil-disobedience movement under cover of this three weeks' fast. In November 1934, he was able to alter the constitution under cover of his retirement from the Congress. On both occasions, so great was the sympathy roused for the Mahatma that emotional and unthinking people accepted everything that the Mahatma proposed, if only that would please him.

The question here arises: 'Has the Mahatma retired? If so, why?' He has retired in the sense that his name does not appear in the list of members of the Supreme Executive of the Congress. But the executive—the Working Committee—has been backed by his blind supporters. The present Working Committee is more submissive to the Mahatma than even the Working Committee of last year, of which the Mahatma was himself a member. Among the personnel of the present Working Committee, the Swarajists or Parliamentarians are conspicuous by their absence. Even Mr. M. S. Aney who dared to differ from the Mahatma on the question of Communal Award, is not there, despite his loyalty and submissiveness in the past. And poor Mr. Nariman who ventured to think independently has been virtually kicked out of the Committee. In 1924, the Mahatma had really retired from Congress politics together with his Party, as the Congress machinery had been seized by his opponents, the Swarajists. Today, the person of the Mahatma may not be in the Committee—but his Party is there, stronger than ever. Moreover, he has a direct control over the most important department of future Congress activity—the Village Industries Association. The so-called retirement of the Mahatma will not, accordingly, diminish his hold over the

Congress machinery in any way—but will enable him to disown all responsibility for the failures of the official Congress Party during the next few years. His retirement, therefore, is only one of his strategic retreats to which he is in the habit of resorting whenever there is a political slump in the country.

With regard to the elections to the Indian Legislative Assembly the latest report (dated November 24th, 1934) goes to show that the official Congress Party has captured 43 seats, the Congress Nationalist Party 8 seats and others approximately 46. Among the 46 non-descripts, at least 10 are expected to be close upon sixty in a house of approximately 145 members.

The Report of the Joint Parliamentary Committee on Indian Constitutional Reforms contains no surprise for one who is familiar with the contents of the White Paper. The Report is approved by a large majority of 31 members of the Committee. The labour members of the Committee have submitted an alternative scheme which is more liberal than the majority report. On the other hand, Lord Salisbury and four other members have submitted another report, and the report concedes only provincial autonomy and opposes responsible Government at the centre. The majority report has whittled down still further the already inadequate proposals of the White Paper with a view to placating the diehard opposition in Parliament. In view of the whittling down, it is widely believed that when the Government of India Bill is introduced on the basis of the report of the Joint Committee, it will have the support of an overwhelming majority in the House of Commons.

The following are some of the important points on which the Joint Committee modify the White Paper proposals :

1. Additional provisions are recommended in relation to 'Law and Order' as follows :

    (i) The consent of the Governor, given in his discretion, should be required to any legislation affecting Police Acts and to any rules made thereunder affecting the organisation or discipline of the Police.

(ii) Records of the Intelligence Department relating to terrorism should not be disclosed outside the Police force except to such public officers as the Governor may direct.

(iii) For the purpose of combating terrorism, the Governor should have the power to take under his own control any branch of Government which it is necessary to use for that purpose.

2. Ministers and Secretaries to Government would be required to bring to the notice of the Governor anything that is likely to involve his 'special responsibilities'.
3. Upper Chambers should be established in Madras and Bombay as well as in Bengal, United Provinces and Bihar.
4. Election to the Federal Lower House should be indirect, by the members of the Provincial Lower Houses, instead of direct by voters in territorial constituencies.
5. If less than 90 per cent of the State adhere to the Federation, additional States representatives should be appointed to the Federal Legislature to the extent of half the difference between the seats to which the Federating States would ordinarily be entitled and the full State's representation if all the States acceded.
6. The High Courts should have control over the promotions and postings of subordinate Judges, and the Governor should have the final word in the appointment of District Judges.
7. The Governor-General should have a special responsibility to prevent the imposition of penal tariffs on goods imported from the United Kingdom.
8. The Legislatures in India should, after ten years, have the Constitutional right to present Addresses,

for the consideration of His Majesty's Government and Parliament, recommending amendment of the Constitution on certain specified matters such as composition of the Legislatures and franchise.
9. The separation of Burma from India should be accompanied by a Trade Agreement between the two countries binding for a specified time.

As far as it can be ascertained, public opinion in India is exceedingly hostile to the Joint Committee's Report. Nevetheless, the Bill, based on the Report, is expected to be put through the British Parliament before the end of 1935.

## CHAPTER XIX

## A GLIMPSE OF THE FUTURE

As the life of the present British House of Commons will come to an end in 1936, the Constitution Bill for India will certainly be put through Parliament before the next General Election. There is at present a keen controversy going on in England between the supporters of the White Paper and the Conservative diehards led by Mr. Winston Churchill. For India, the controversy has no interest whatsoever. As we have already seen, the White Paper contains precious little, and few people in India will be sorry if the scheme is whittled down further, as seems likely, or suffers complete shipwreck. What really interests India in connection with the White Paper is the fact that it leaves no room for co-operation for those who may feel tired of the prolonged struggle and would like to settle down to some useful, constructive work. The policy of the Government, therefore, will help to keep up the present opposition.

The Government hope to stifle or ignore the Nationalist opposition in the country with the help of the minorities—the Moslems, the Depressed Classes, the Indian Christians and the Anglo-Indians. But will they succeed? It is probable that for a time a large section of the different minority communities in India will be under official influence. This will be their return for the concessions made to them in the Communal Award. But this position cannot last long. The Communal Award has at best given these Communities better representation in the Legislatures under the new Constitution. But the new Constitution will give no power to the Indian people as a whole or to any section of them. It will not, therefore, take the representatives of the different communities in the Legislatures long to realise that though the Government gave them seats, they did not give them power. Seats in the Legislatures are only meant for a few. These few can retain their hold over the general public, only if they can do something for the betterment of the entire community. That will not be possible, since no power will be actually transferred to the people. When the different communities realise that their representatives are not able to do anything for them, they will cease taking any interest in the Legislatures and popular discontent against the Constitution will begin to grow. This discontent will be further augmented by the economic crisis in India—and even if an improvement takes place in Great Britain or in any other country, it will not have any repercussions in India. The Indian economic crisis is only partly an effect of the world crisis. It is also an independent phenomenon, being due to a large extent to exploitation of India's resources and of the Indian market by foreign, and especially British, industries and also to her inability to modernise her industrial system, in order to cope with foreign competition. An improvement in the Indian economic situation will necessitate, therefore, not only an improvement in the world economic situation, but also a modernisation of India's industrial system.

There are other reasons why the help of the Indian minority communities will not be of much avail to Great Britain. Firstly, among the Moslems there is a large and influential section who are Nationalists and who are as anti-Government as the Nationalist Hindus. Their influence is not likely to suffer eclipse, but will probably increase in the days to come. Secondly, among the Depressed Classes, the majority even today are supporters of the Congress. The Congress propaganda to abolish untouchability altogether will certainly bring more members of the Depressed Classes into the fold of the Congress. Thirdly, the Indian Christian community can no longer be labelled as pro-Government. In their annual conferences they have repeatedly condemned separate electorate and advocated joint electorate. In recent years there has been a remarkable change of feeling among the younger generation of Indian Christians. On the religious side they have begun to resent the domination of European Christian and they demand a national church for themselves. On the political side, the younger generation of Indian Christians is becoming rapidly pro-Congress. In 1930, when the writer was in prison in the Alipore Central Jail in Calcutta, among his fellow-prisoners there was a fine set of young Indian Christians who had joined the civil-disobedience movement, and they were typical of the awakening in their community. Fourthly, so far as the Anglo-Indians are concerned, a distinct change is visible. Till recently they were the loyal supporters of the Government and the henchmen of the British. They looked upon England as their spiritual home and themselves as British in everything except in the pigment of their skin. The Government, too, gave them special facilities and privileges—not granted to Indians. But things are changing now. Anglo-Indians have been made statutory natives of India under the law of the land. The leader of the community, Lieut.-Col. Sir H. Gidney, addressed an appeal to his community the other day asking them to look upon India as their home and to feel proud of India. Feeling is steadily growing in the community that they should no longer try to hobnob with Britishers, but should throw in their lot with children of the soil. Fifthly, so far as the non-official Britishers are concerned, they can hardly do anything more for the Government in suppressing the Nationalist movement. There has long been close co-operation between the Government and the non-official British community in this matter—but in spite of that, the Nationalist movement has been making headway. In the days to come, the influence of the non-official British community is likely to diminish rather than increase. In Bombay, for instance, business supremacy has already passed into the hands of the Indians. In 1932, the British firms in Bombay had to pass a resolution, expressing sympathy with the Nationalist movement in order to save themselves from a crushing and effective boycott. The Ottawa Pact and the Indo-British Textile Agreement represent the last attempt of the non-official British community to maintain the *status quo*—but how long can they stem the rising tide of Nationalism ?

Thus, according to human calculation, it appears certain that the Government will be able to permanently weaken the nationalist forces in India by placating the minorities. No popular upheaval is, however, possible till the promulgation of the new reforms. Thereafter it will take a few years—probably two or three—for the people to be completely disillusioned. Then there will be the beginning of another mass upheaval. What exact form this upheaval will take, it is difficult to determine at this stage.

During the next few years the inner conditions of the Congress will be somewhat unsettled, that is to say, no party will be sufficiently strong to be able to suppress the others. The Socialist Party in the form it has assumed today—cannot make much headway. The composition of the Party is not homogeneous and some of its ideas are out-of-date. But the instinct that has urged the formation of the Party is right. Out of this Left-Wing revolt there will ultimately emerge a new full-fledged party with a clear ideology, programme and plan of action. It is not possible at this stage to visualise the details of this Party's programme and plan of action—but one may attempt to give the bare outlines:

1. The Party will stand for the interests of the masses, that is, of the peasants, workers, etc., and not for the vested interests, that is, the landlords, capitalists and money-lending classes.
2. It will stand for the complete political and economic liberation of the Indian people.
3. It will stand for a Federal Government for India as the ultimate goal, but will believe in a strong Central Government with dictatorial powers for some years to come, in order to put India on her feet.
4. It will believe in a sound system of state-planning for the re-organisation of the agricultural and industrial life of the country.
5. It will seek to build up a new social structure on

the basis of the village communities of the past, that were ruled by the village 'Panch' and will strive to break down the existing social barriers like caste.

6. It will seek to establish a new monetary and credit system in the light of the theories and the experiments that have been and are current in the modern world.
7. It will seek to abolish landlordism and introduce a uniform land-tenure system for the whole of India.
8. It will not stand for a democracy in the Mid-Victorian sense of the term, but will believe in government by a strong party bound together by military discipline, as the only means of holding India together and preventing a chaos, when Indians are free and are thrown entirely on their own resources.
9. It will not restrict itself to a campaign inside India but will resort to international propaganda [1] also, in order to strengthen India's case for liberty, and will attempt to utilise the existing international organisations.
10. It will endeavour to unite all the radical organisations under a national executive so that whenever any action is taken, there will be simultaneous activity on many fronts.

A question which is on everybody's lips in Europe is: 'What is the future of Communism in India?' In this connection it is worthwhile quoting the expressed opinion of Pandit Jawaharlal Nehru,[2] whose popularity in India today

---

[1] In 1920, when Mahatma Gandhi took charge of the Congress, he abolished the Congress Committee in London and its paper *India* which represented the only organ for propaganda for India outside her shores. Recently a change seems to have come over him. In January 1932, just before his arrest, the Congress Working Committee, at his instance, issued an appeal to the nations of the world for sympathy for India in her struggle for liberty.

[2] It should be made perfectly clear that this is Pandit Nehru's personal opinion and not the opinion of the Indian National Congress. Nor does his popularity imply that his views find acceptance among the rank and file of the Congress—just as Mahatma Gandhi's unprecedented popularity does not imply that his followers wear loin-cloth or drink goat's milk.

A GLIMPSE OF THE FUTURE 351

is, according to the writer, second only to that of Mahatma Gandhi. In a Press statement issued on December 18th, 1933, he said : 'I do believe that fundamentally the choice before the world today is one between some form of Communism and some form of Fascism, and I am all for the former, that is Communism. I dislike Fascism intensely and indeed I do not think it is anything more than a crude and brutal effort of the present capitalist order to preserve itself at any cost. There is no middle road between Fascism and Communism. One has to choose between the two and I choose the Communist ideal. In regard to the methods and approach to this ideal, I may not agree with everything that the orthodox Communists have done. I think that these methods will have to adapt themselves to changing conditions and may vary in different countries. But I do think that the basic ideology of Communism and its scientific interpretation of history is sound.'

The view expressed here is, according to the writer, fundamentally wrong. Unless we are at the end of the process of evolution or unless we deny evolution altogether, there is no reason to hold that our choice is restricted to two alternatives. Whether one believes in the Hegelian or in the Bergsonian or any other theory of evolution—in no case need we think that creation is at an end. Considering everything, one is inclined to hold that the next phase in world-history will produce a synthesis between Communism and Fascism. And will it be a surprise if that synthesis is produced in India? The view has been expressed in the Introduction that in spite of India's geographical isolation, the Indian awakening is organically connected with the march of progress in other parts of the world and facts and figures have been mentioned to substantiate that view. Consequently, there need to be no surprise if an experiment, of importance to the whole world, is made in India—especially when we have seen with our own eyes that another experiment (that of Mahatma Gandhi) made in India has roused profound interest all over the world.

In spite of the antithesis between Communism and Fascism, there are certain traits common to both. Both

Communism and Fascism believe in the supremacy of the State over the individual. Both denounce parliamentary democracy. Both believe in party rule. Both believe in the dictatorship of the party and in the ruthless suppression of all dissenting minorities. Both believe in a planned industrial reorganisation of the country. These common traits will form the basis of the new synthesis. That synthesis is called by the writer 'Samyavada'—an Indian word, which means literally 'the doctrine of synthesis or equality'. It will be India's task to work out this synthesis.

There are several reasons why Communism will not be adopted in India. Firstly, Communism today has no sympathy with Nationalism in any form and the Indian movement is a Nationalist movement—a movement for the national liberation of the Indian people. (Lenin's thesis on the relation between Communism and Nationalism seems to have been given the go-by since the failure of the last Chinese Revolution.) Secondly, Russia is now on her defensive and has little interest in provoking a world revolution, though the Communist International may still endeavour to keep up appearances. The recent pacts between Russia and other capitalist countries and the written or unwritten conditions inherent in such pacts, as also her membership of the League of Nations, have seriously compromised the position of Russia as a revolutionary power. Moreover, Russia is too preoccupied in her internal industrial reorganisation and in her preparations for meeting the Japanese menace on her eastern flank and is too anxious to maintain friendly relations with the Great Powers, to show any active interest in countries like India. Thirdly, while many of the economic ideas of Communism would make a strong appeal to Indians, there are other ideas which will have a contrary effect. Owing to the close association between the Church and the State in Russian history and to the existence of an organised Church, Communism in Russia has grown to be anti-religious and atheistic. In India, on the contrary, there being no organised Church among the Indians and there being no association between the Church and the State, there is no feeling against religion as such.[1] Fourthly, the materialistic interpretation of history which seems to be a cardinal point in Communist theory will not find unqualified acceptance in India, even among those who would be disposed to accept the economic contents of Communism. Fifthly, while Communist theory has made certain remarkable contributions in the domain of economics (for instance the idea of state-planning), it is weak in other aspects. For instance, so far as the monetary problem is concerned, Communism has made no new contribution, but has merely followed traditional economics. Recent experiences, however, indicate that the monetary problem of the world is still far from being satisfactorily solved.

While, therefore, it would be safe to predict that India will not become a new edition of Soviet Russia, one may say with equal strength that all the modern socio-political movements and experiments in Europe and in America will have considerable influence on India's development. Of late, India has been taking and in future will continue to take, more and more interest in what goes on in the outside world.

To come back to the Congress. The present controversy between Mahatma Gandhi and Pandit Madan Mohan Malaviya is of passing interest as the issue is a very minor one. Neither the Congress Nationalist Party nor the official Congress Parliamentary Party has a role to play in future, because both of them are heterogeneous parties without any clear ideology or programme. It only remains to consider the future of Gandhism in India. It has been urged sometimes that Gandhism is an alternative to Communism. This idea is, in the opinion of the writer, erroneous. Mahatma Gandhi has given the country (and may be, the world) a new method—the method of passive-resistance or Satyagraha or non-violent non-co-operation. He has not given his country or humanity a new programme of social reconstruction as Communism has—and the alternative to Communism can be only another theory of social recon-

[1] Further, in India a national awakening is in most cases heralded by a religious reformation and a cultural renaissance.

struction. No doubt, the Mahatma has condemned the 'machine civilisation' of the modern world and has eulogised the good old days when men were content with their cottage industries and their wants were few. But that is a personal belief or idiosyncrasy. Whenever he has expounded the contents of Swaraj, he has spoken in the language of Mid-Victorian Parliamentary Democracy and of traditional capitalist economics. The 'Eleven Points' which he enunciated in 1930 as connoting his 'substance of independence', will be unreservedly accepted by any Indian industrial magnate. One could, therefore, say that the Mahatma does not intend pulling down the modern industrial structure if he were to get political mastery over his country, nor does he desire to completely industrialise the country. His programme is one of reform—he is fundamentally a reformist and not a revolutionary. He would leave the existing social and economic structure much as it is today (he would not even abolish the army altogether) and would content himself with removing the glaring injustices and inequalities against which his moral sense revolts. There are millions of his countrymen who accept his method owing to the pressure of circumstances, but not his programme of reconstruction, and who would like to build up quite a different India if they had the power. As has been already indicated, the future of India ultimately lies with a party with a clear ideology, programme and plan of action—a party that will not only fight for and win freedom, but will put into effect the entire programme of post-war reconstruction—a party that will break the isolation that has been India's curse and bring her into the comity of nations—firm in the belief that the fate of India is indissolubly linked up with the fate of humanity.

CHAPTER XX

# INDIA SINCE 1857—A BIRD'S EYE VIEW [1]

Though the British conquest of India began in 1757 with the Battle of Plassey and the overthrow of the then independent King of Bengal, Nawab Sirajudowla, it was only by slow and gradual stages that the British occupation of India made progress. For instance, after the Battle of Plassey, only the financial administration of Bengal passed into the hands of the British—the political administration remaining in the hands of Nawab Mir Jaffar, the man who had betrayed Nawab Sirajudowla at the last moment and gone over to the British. It was only by stages that the British could take over the entire administration of Bengal. Likewise it was only by slow and gradual stages that the British rule could be extended over other parts of India. While this process of gradual annexation was going on, the British still formally recognised the suzerainty of the Emperor at Delhi. It should be noted that in the occupation of India, the British used not only arms—but more than arms, the weapons of bribery, treachery and every form of corruption. For instance, the founder of the British Empire in India, Robert Clive, who was later made a Lord, has been proved by historians to have been guilty of forgery. Likewise Warren Hastings, a Governor-General of India, was accused before the British Parliament by Edmund Burke, a member of the House of Commons, as being guilty of "high crimes and misdemeanours".

The greatest folly and mistake of our predecessors was their inability to realise at the very beginning, the real character and role of the Britishers who came to India. They probably thought that like the innumerable tribes that had wandered to India in the past and had made India

---

[1] The preceding pages were written in English in the original in 1934 and deal with the period up to 1934. The following pages were written in 1943 and bring the book up to date—Writer.

their home, the British were just another such tribe. It was much later that they realised that the British had come to conquer and plunder and not to settle down in India. As soon as this was generally understood all over the country, a mighty revolution broke out in 1857, which has been incorrectly called by English historians "the Sepoy Mutiny", but which is regarded by the Indian people as the First War of Independence. In the Great Revolution of 1857, the British were on the point of being thrown out of the country—but partly through superior strategy and partly through luck—they won at the end. Then there followed a reign of terror, the parallel of which it is difficult to find in history. Wholesale massacres took place in the course of which innocent men were bound hand and foot and were blown up from the mouths of cannon.

After the Revolution of 1857, the British realised that by sheer brutal force, they could not hold India long. They, therefore, proceeded to disarm the country. And the second greatest folly and mistake that our predecessors committed was to submit to disarmament. If they had not given up their arms so easily, probably the history of India since 1857 would have been different from what it has been. Having once disarmed the country completely, it has been possible for the British to hold India with the help of a small but efficient modern army.

Along with disarmament, the newly established British Government, now controlled directly from London, commenced its policy of "divide and rule". This policy has been the fundamental basis of British rule from 1858 till today. After 1857, for nearly forty years, the policy was to keep India divided, by putting three-fourths of the people directly under British control and the remaining one-fourth under the Indian Princes. Simultaneously, the British Government showed a great deal of partiality for the big landlords in British India. It is interesting to note, in this connection, the attitude of the British Government towards the Indian Princes since 1857. Up to 1857, the policy of the British was to get rid of the Princes, wherever possible, and take over the direct administration of their states. In

the Revolution of 1857, though a number of Indian rulers
—e.g. the famous and heroic Rani (Queen) of Jhansi—
fought against the British, many remained neutral or
actively sided with them. Among the latter was the Maharaja of Nepal. It then occurred to the British for the first
time that it would perhaps be advisable not to disturb the
existing Princes, but to make a treaty of alliance and friendship with them, so that in the event of there being trouble
for the British, the Princes would come to their aid. The
present British policy of partiality towards the Indian
Princes goes back, therefore, to the year 1857. By the
beginning of the present century the British realised, however, that they could no longer dominate India by simply
playing the princes and the big landlords against the people.
Then they discovered the Muslim problem in the year 1906,
when Lord Minto [1] was the Viceroy. Prior to this, there
was no such problem in India. In the great Revolution of
1857, Hindus and Muslims had fought side by side against
the British and it was under the flag of Bahadur Shah, a
Muslim, that India's First War of Independence had been
fought.

During the last World War, when the British found
that further political concessions would have to be made
to the Indian people, they realised that it was not enough
to try and divide the Muslims from the rest of the population and they then set about trying to divide the Hindus
themselves. In this way, they discovered the caste problem in 1918 and suddenly became the champions and
liberators of the so-called depressed classes. Till the year
1937, Britain had hoped to keep India divided by posing
as the champions of the Princes, the Muslims, and the so-called depressed classes. In the general election held
under the new constitution of 1935—they found, however, to their great surprise, that all their tricks and
bluffs had failed and that a strong nationalist feeling permeated the whole nation and every section of it. Conse-

[1] Lord Morley, who was the Secretary of State for India in the British Cabinet when Lord Minto was the Viceroy of India, stated that Lord Minto "had started the Moslem Hare" in 1906.

quently, British policy has now fallen back on its last hope. If the Indian people cannot be divided, then the country —India—has to be divided geographically and politically. This is the plan, called Pakistan, which emanated from the fertile brain of a Britisher and which has precedents in other parts of the British Empire. For instance, Ceylon which belonged geographically and culturally to India, was separated from India long ago. Immediately after the last war, Ireland which was always a unified state, was divided into Ulster and the Irish Free State. After the new constitution of 1935, Burma was separated from India. And if the present war had not intervened, Palestine would already have been divided into a Jewish State, an Arab State, and a British corridor running between the two. Having themselves invented Pakistan—or the plan for dividing India—the British have been doing a colossal, but skilful, propaganda in support of it. Though the vast majority of the Indian Muslims want a free and independent India —though the President of the Indian National Congress is Moulana Abul Kalam Azad, a Muslim—and though only a minority of the Indian Muslims supports the idea of Pakistan—British propaganda throughout the world gives the impression that the Indian Muslims are not behind the national struggle for liberty and want India to be divided up. The British themselves know that what they propagate is quite false—but they, nevertheless, hope that by repeating a falsehood, again and again, they will be able to make the world believe it. When Pakistan was originally invented, the idea was to divide India into a so-called Hindu India and a so-called Muslim India, however fantastic the plan might have been. Since then the fertile brains of the Britishers have developed the plan still further and if they could have their own way, they would now divide India not into two states, but into five or six. For instance, British politicians say that if the Indian Princes want to secede from the rest of India, they should have a separate state called Rajasthan. If the Sikhs want to secede, they should also have a separate state called Khalsaistan. And these cunning Britishers are showing special solicitude for the

Pathans—that section of the Indian Muslims living in the North-West of India—and they are urging that there should be a separate state in the North-West of India called Pathanistan. Pathanistan seems to be the hot favourite of British politicians at the present moment. They hope that through this plan of Pathanistan they would win over some of the most troublesome people in India—namely, the people of the North-West Frontier Province of India and the independent tribes living between India and Afghanistan—and at the same time, get the sympathy of the Afghan people.

Pakistan is, of course, a fantastic plan and an unpractical proposition—for more reasons than one. India is geographically, historically, culturally, politically and economically an indivisible unit. Secondly, in most parts of India, Hindus and Muslims are so mixed up that it is not possible to separate them. Thirdly, if Muslim states were forcibly set up, new minority problems would be created in these states which would present new difficulties. Fourthly, unless Hindus and Muslims join hands and fight the British, they cannot liberate themselves and their unity is possible only on the basis of a free and undivided India. An independent Pakistan is an impossibility and Pakistan, therefore, means in practice, dividing India in order to ensure British domination for all. It is noteworthy that in his latest utterances, Mr. Jinnah, the President of the Muslim League, and a champion of Pakistan, has acknowledged that the creation and maintenance of Pakistan is possible only with the help of the British.

Now to resume our story. The struggle that is now going on in India is, in reality, a continuation of the Great Revolution of 1857. In the last four decades of the nineteenth century, the Indian movement expressed itself in agitation in the press and on the platform. This movement was crystallised into one organisation when the Indian National Congress was inaugurated in 1885. The beginning of this century saw a new awakening in India and along with it, new methods of struggle were devised. Thus, during the first two decades, we see the economic boycott of British goods, on the one side, and revolutionary terrorism on the other. The Indian revolutionaries made a desperate attempt to overthrow British rule with the help of arms during the last war—at a time when Germany, Austria-Hungary and Turkey were fighting our enemy—but they, the Indian revolutionaries, were crushed. After the war, India needed a new weapon of struggle—and at this psychological moment, Mahatma Gandhi came forward with his method of Satyagraha or passive resistance or civiil disobedience.

During the last twenty-two years, the Congress under the Mahatma's leadership has built up a powerful organisation all over the country—including the states of the Princes. It has awakened political life in the remotest villages and among all sections of the people. Most important of all is the fact that the masses of India have learnt how to strike at the powerful enemy even without arms, and the Congress, under Gandhi's leadership, has demonstrated that it is possible to paralyse the administration through the weapon of passive resistance. In short, India has now a disciplined political organisation reaching the remotest villages with which a national struggle can be conducted and with the help of which—a new, independent state can be, later on, built up.

The younger generation in India has, however, learnt from the last twenty years' experience that while passive resistance can hold up or paralyse a foreign administration—it cannot overthrow or expel it, without the use of physical force. Impelled by this experience, the people today are spontaneously passing on from passive to active resistance. And that is why you read and hear today of the unarmed Indian people destroying railway, telegraph and telephone communications—setting fire to police stations, post-office, and Government buildings, and using force in many other ways in order to overthrow the British yoke. The last stage will come when active resistance will develop into an armed revolution. Then will come the end of British rule in India.

CHAPTER XXI

## FROM JANUARY, 1935 TILL SEPTEMBER, 1939

At the end of November, 1934, immediately after finishing the original book in English, the writer flew to India, on receipt of a cablegram from his mother saying that his father was on his death-bed. He arrived in Calcutta one day late. At the aerodrome he was received by a strong posse of police who put him under arrest. In his house, which was then in a state of mourning, he was interned for six weeks, until he left for Europe to resume his medical treatment.

During his stay in India, the writer found that the main topic of discussion was the recent elections to the Indian Legislative Assembly, India's Parliament. Contrary to the expectations of the Viceroy, Lord Willingdon, the Congress Party had remarkable success at the polls. It was clear that despite the repressive measures employed by Lord Willingdon's Government against the Congress Party from 1932 onwards, the vast majority of the people stood behind the Indian National Congress. It should be noted here that, unlike 1923-24, the parliamentary activity of the Congress was this time conducted by the Gandhi Wing.

The President of the Congress for the next twelve months in 1935 was Mr. Rajendra Prasad, an orthodox follower of Mahatma Gandhi, who was expected to adhere to the Gandhian line strictly.

The most important political event during 1935, was the passing of a new constitution for India by the British Parliament, called the Government of India Act, 1935. This constitution was brought into operation two years later— in 1937—when the first elections were held. It is theoretically still in force, though actually suspended since the outbreak of the present war, in September 1939. The new constitution was unanimously rejected by Indian public opinion and, in particular, by the Congress,—because it was a scheme, not for self-government, but for maintaining British rule in the new political conditions, through the help of the Indian Princes and sectarian, reactionary and pro-British organisations.

The provisions of the 1935 Constitution consisted of two parts, the Federal and Provincial. The proposed "Federation" was a new departure in that it provided for an all-India Central Government uniting both "British India" and the "Indian States". The federal chamber was to consist of two houses, in which the princes were to nominate two-fifths and one-third of the members respectively. Elaborate weighting governed the choice of elected members. Seats were allocated to prescribed groups, Moslems, Sikhs, Scheduled-Castes, Women, Anglo-Indians, Labour etc. In the Upper House, only 75 out of 260 seats were open to general election; in the Lower House, only 86 out of 375. In the Upper House the electorate was restricted to about 0.05 of the population of British India; in the Lower, it was about one-ninth. The powers of these legislatures were extremely limited. Defence and foreign policy were reserved for the Viceroy; financial policy and control of bureaucracy and police was also excluded from the competence of the Assemblies. No legislation could be passed on certain prescribed topics. The Viceroy had wide discretionary powers including the right to veto any legislation, dismiss Ministers, pass legislation rejected by the legislatures, dissolve the legislatures and suspend the constitution.

The provincial section of the constitution, applicable only to the eleven provinces of British India, was somewhat less narrow. There were no appointees of the Princes. The legislatures were wholly elected, though the franchise for the Upper House was restricted. There were no reserved topics except that the Secret Police was under the control of the Governor, who also had full emergency powers, if he thought the "tranquillity of the province is endangered". The provinces thus offered some limited possibilities for popular government. The seats on the Assemblies were allocated to communal groups as at the centre, but 657 "general seats" were left open out of the 1585 in the eleven provinces. It was therefore possible for the National Congress while opposing the constitution, to participate in the first provincial elections in 1937, in which it won majorities in seven (later eight) out of eleven provinces.

As already anticipated at the end of Chapter XIV of "The Indian Struggle 1920-34" nothing sensational happened in India during the years 1935 and 1936. The parliamentary wing of the Congress continued its activity and began slowly to gain influence. On the other hand, the Congress Socialist Party began to rally the younger generation and also the more radical elements inside the Congress and among the Indian people in general. For the time being, both Satyagraha or Civil Disobedience and revolutionary terrorism had lost their charm and in the vacuum created thereby, the Congress Socialist Party naturally made headway. The Communist Party of India, a small group which had been declared illegal by the British Government, instructed its members to join the Congress Socialist Party and thereby use the public platform of the Congress Socialist Party, in order to push forward its own organisation and objective. It did succeed in extending its influence among a section of the students and factory workers. Later on, the Communist Party took the name of "National Front", in order to function publicly.

The Congress Socialist Party had the historic opportunity to throw up an alternative leadership, in place of the Gandhian leadership which had monopolised the political field since 1920. This development would have been easier, if Pandit Jawaharlal Nehru, who gave his moral support to that party, had openly joined it and accepted its leadership. But he did not do so.

In the autumn of 1935, Pandit Nehru was suddenly released from prison in order to enable him to join his wife who was on her death-bed in Europe. He spent most of his time in Badenweiler in Germany, visiting London and Paris from time to time. During this visit to Europe, which terminated in March, 1936, he made contacts in London and in Paris which were to influence his future policy. He did not visit such countries as Russia or Ireland which were then regarded as anti-British, though during his previous tour in Europe, he had gone to Moscow. In countries like Italy and Germany, he carefully avoided making any contacts, either because of his dislike of Fascism and National Socialism, or because he did not want to offend his friends in England and France. During his stay in Europe, he published his Autobiography which made him tremendously popular with the liberal section of the English public.

In 1936, Nehru was elected President of the Indian National Congress and he presided over its annual session held at Lucknow in April. He was re-elected President at the end of the year and he presided over the next annual session held at Faizpur in Bombay Presidency. In the Presidential election, Nehru had the full support of the Gandhian Wing of the Congress on both occasions. As President, he held a middle position between the Gandhian Wing and the Congress Socialist Party—causing no annoyance to either, but giving a certain measure of moral support to the latter.

Betwen 1933 and 1936, the writer toured practically the whole of Europe outside Russia and studied at first hand the conditions of post-Versailles Europe. He was several times in Italy and in Germany, and in Rome he was received by Signor Mussolini on several occasions. He studied, on the one hand, the growth of the new forces that were ultimately to challenge the old order that had been set up by the Treaty of Versailles—and on the other, he studied the League of Nations which symbolised that old order. He was specially interested in the changes that had been brought about by the Treaty of Versailles and, for that purpose, he made it a point to visit Austria-Hungary, Czechoslovakia, Poland and the Balkans. Through travel and study, he was able, not only to understand the situation in Europe at the time, but also to have a glimpse of coming events. In many countries in Europe, he was able to rouse interest in India and to help in founding organisations for developing contact with India. The tour concluded with a visit to Ireland, where he met President de Valera and other Ministers of his Government, as well as the leaders of the republican movement.

The writer spent a part of his time in Geneva in 1933 and 1934 with a view to studying the organisation of the League of Nations and exploring the possibility of utilising the League for advancing the cause of India's freedom. This was also the aim of the veteran nationalist leader, Mr. V. J. Patel, ex-President of the Indian Legislative Assembly, who had come to Geneva for that purpose. Unfortunately, Mr. Patel [1] was taken ill immediately after his arrival and he died in a Swiss Sanatorium in October, 1933. After his death, the writer was left alone but he continued his work in Geneva for some time. During this period, he worked in collaboration with the International Committee on India which had its headquarters in Geneva and he helped in the publication of a monthly bulletin on India. This bulletin was published in three languages—French, German, and English—and was sent all over the world to people interested in India. Towards the end of his stay in Geneva, the writer realised that the machinery of the League of Nations was controlled fully by Britain and France and that it was impossible to utilise the League for India's liberty, though India was an original member of that body. Thereupon, he started an agitation to the effect that India was wasting her money by remaining a member of the League and that she should resign from that body as soon as possible. This agitation found wide support among the Indian public.

During his stay in Europe, the writer was everywhere watched and followed by the agents of the British Government who tried their best to prevent his making contacts with different governments and with important personalities in different countries. In Fascist or pro-Fascist countries, the British agents tried to paint him as a Communist. In Socialist or democratic countries, on the other

---

[1] Mr. Patel was one of the few Indian leaders interested in foreign propaganda. He was responsible for founding the Indo-Irish League in Dublin.

hand, they tried to describe him as a Fascist. In spite of these obstacles, however, he was able to do useful propaganda for Indin and rouse sympathy for the Indian freedom movement in several countries in Europe. In some of these countries, organisations were started for developing cultural and economic contact with India.

In April, 1946, the writer returned to Bombay with the intention of attending the Lucknow session of the Congress. He had been warned in writing by the British Government through the British Consul in Vienna that he would be arrested if he returned to India, but in a spirited reply, he had rejected that warning, challenging the Government to do its worst. He was taken to prison at Bombay, the moment he set foot on Indian soil.

In the autumn of 1936, Mr M. N. Roy, formerly of the Communist International, was released from prison after serving a term of six years in connection with Bolshevist Conspiracy Case at Cawnpore. Because of his revolutionary past and his international experience, Mr. M. N. Roy was a popular and attractive figure, with a halo round his name. Youngmen flocked to him and very soon a new group, called the Roy group, came into public limelight.

The New Constitution for India which brought about the separation of Burma from India had been passed by the British Parliament in 1935. This gave the Indian people a certain measure of autonomy in the Provinces. Provincial elections under the new Constitution were to be held in the winter of 1936-37. The Parliamentary Wing of the Congress (which was now synonymous with the Gandhian Wing) began to prepare for these elections and also for the acceptance of ministerial office, thereafter, in the provinces. The Congress Socialist Party had originally opposed participation in these elections—an attitude which was reminiscent of the attitude of the orthodox Gandhiite "no-change party" in 1922-23. Later on, the C. S. Party modified its attitude and supported the idea of contesting the elections, but strongly opposed the idea of accepting ministerial offie. The C. S. P. did not have a clear revolutionary perspective and this was probably due to the fact that in the ranks of that Party, there were dissillusioned ex-Gandhiites who were, however, still under the influence of Gandhian concepts—while there were others in the Party who were under the influence of Nehru's sentimental politics.

In 1936-37, the C. S. Party sponsored an "Anti-Ministry" movement with the objective of opposing the acceptance of ministerial office by Congressmen. Among those who supported this move, but were not members of the C.S.P., were Sardar Sardul Singh Cavesheer of Punjab[1], Rafii Ahmed Kidwai[2], of the United Provinces, Mrs. V. L. Pandit[3] and Sarat Chandra Bose[4] (brother of the writer). Pandit Nehru gave his moral support to the movement.

In spite of all the checks and safeguards provided in the New Constitution for preventing the Nationalists from getting a majority, the Congress Party emerged from the provincial parliamentary elections with a practical majority in seven out of eleven provinces in British India. At that time, the anti-ministry movement was going strong—but the Parliamentarian (or Gandhian) leaders of the Congress handled the situation with such consummate skill, that in July, 1937, they successfully torpedoed the anti-ministry movement and got the All India Congress Committee to decide in favour of taking Cabinet office in the provinces.

The writer was released from internment from a Calcutta hospital in March, 1937, after the parliamentary elections were over. Within the next few months, the majority of political prisoners were gradually set at liberty, with the exception of those in Bengal and in the Andaman Islands. The political prisoners in Bengal numbered several thousands, the majority of whom had been imprisoned or interned without any trial whatsoever. There were also a few hundred political prisoners in the Andaman Islands

---

[1] Cavesheer later became the Vice-President of the All-India Forward Bloc.
[2] Kidwai later became the Home Minister of the Congress Cabinet in U.P.
[3] Mrs. Pandit also became a Minister in U. P.
[4] Bose became later the leader of the Congress Party in the Bengal Legislature.

—the penal settlement in the Bay of Bengal, who had been sentenced to long terms of imprisonment and they were mostly from Bengal, Punjab and the United Provinces. In July, 1937, the Congress Party took Cabinet-office in seven out of eleven provinces, and in these provinces, practically all the political prisoners were released. Soon after this, the political prisoners in the Andaman Islands went on hunger-strike, demanding their release, whereupon they were brought over to prisons in the mainland.

The seven provinces which had a Congress Cabinet were—Frontier Province, United Provinces, Bihar, Bombay Presidency, Central Provinces, Madras Presidency and Orissa. Assam had a Congress Cabinet in September, 1938, after the first Cabinet was thrown out. Sindh[1] has had a Cabinet supported by the Congress Party, without participating in it. In Bengal[2], since December, 1941, there has been a new Cabinet with the Congress Party participating in it. Only in Punjab, has the Ministry of Sir Sikandar Hyat Khan been always in opposition to the Congress Party.

After the Congress Party took office in seven provinces—the administration there became distinctly nationalist in character and the prestige of the Congress went up by leaps and bounds. People in general had the feeling that the Congress was the coming power. But apart from this, there was no remarkable change. Power still remained in the hands of the Provincial Governor and of the permanent officials of the Indian Civil Srvice, the majority of whom were British, and the Congress Party could not therefore undertake far-reaching reforms in the administration. After some time, it could be noticed that a large section of Congressmen was gradually being infected with the parliamentary or constitutionalist mentality and was

---

[1] The pro-Congress Premier of Sindh, Mr. Allah Buksh, resigned his post in October, 1942, as a protest against the repressive policv of the British Government in India and also gave up the title of "Khan Bahadur" which he had received from the British Government.

[2] It is reported that the Ministers belonging to the Congress Party were unconstitutionally removed from the Cabinet by the British Governor of the province a few months ago, on the ground that they were secretly in league with the "Forward Bloc".

losing its revolutionary fervour.

The emergence of the Congress Socialist Party in 1934 was a sure indication of the resurgence of the radical or left-wing forces in the country. This was accompanied by a phenomenal awakening among the peasantry and the students, and to some extent, among the workers. For the first time, there emerged a centralised All India Peasants' Organisation, called the All India Kisan Sabha, the most prominent leader of which was Swami Sahajananda Saraswati. The students' movement also, which had gone through many ups and downs in the past, was centralised under the leadership of the All India Students' Federation[1]. The All India Trade Union Congress, which had experienced two successive splits—in 1929 at Nagpur and again in 1931 in Calcutta—was once again unified under a joint leadership representing all shades of opinion, both Right and Left. In the literary world, too, there was an attempt to organise the progressive writers.

Pandit Nehru's Presidentship for two terms was marked by energy and initiative at the top and gave a fillip to the radical forces in the Congress, while, at his instance a number of socialists were employed as permanent Congress officials. But Pandit Nehru could have achieved much more. The years 1936-37 represented the high water mark of his popularity and in a certain sense, his position was then stronger than that of Mahatma Gandhi, because he had the support of the entire Left, which Gandhi had not. But the Mahatma's position was organisationally very strong, for he had built up a party of his own, the Gandhi Wing, within the Congress Party, and with the help of the former he could dominate the latter. Nehru, on the other hand, inspite of his tremendous popularity, did not have a party of his own. There were two courses open to him, if he wanted to live in history—either to accept the tenets of Gandhism and join the Gandhi Wing within the Congress Party, or to build up his own party in opposition to the Gandhi Wing.

---

[1] A split in the All-India Student's Federation occurred at Nagpur, in December, 1940. The Communist group in the Federation seceded and set up a separate organisation. The main body of students now follows the political lead of the Forward Bloc.

He could not do the former, because though he was personally loyal to the Mahatma, he did not accept all the tenets of Gandhism. On the other hand, he did not build up his own party, because that could have given offence to the Gandhi Wing, and he has never in his own life had the courage to do anything in opposition to the Mahatma. Thus, Nehru began to drift along, trying to please both the Right and the Left—without joining either the Gandhi Wing or any other radical party—and thus remaining in effect, a lone figure within the Congress Party. That is his position today—in December, 1942. After 1937, he moved closer to Gandhi, till in 1939, he almost became a member of the Gandhi Wing. For this, he was rewarded by the Mahatma, when the latter announced in January, 1942, that he was appointing Nehru as his successor. If Nehru had given unquestioning obedience to Gandhi, he would have remained in that position. But over the visit of Sir Stafford Cripps to India and the problem of the future relations between India and Britain, Nehru advocated a policy of compromise and collaboration, which was repudiated by the Mahatma and his party. As a result of his difference of opinion, Nehru now stands virtually alone and it is highly probable that after this experience, the Gandhi Wing will not easily accept Nehru as leader in succession to the Mahatma.

In December, 1937, the writer paid another visit to his favourite health-resort, Badgastein, in Austria, and from there he visited England. While in England, in January, 1938, he received news that he had been unanimously elected President of the Congress. During the course of this visit, he met members of the British Cabinet, like Lord Halifax and Lord Zetland, as well as prominent members of the Labour and Liberal Parties who then professed sympathy for India, e.g. Mr. Attlee, Mr. Arthur Greenwood, Mr. Mr. Bevin, Sir Stafford Cripps, Mr. Harold Laski, Lord Allen, etc.

As Congress President, the writer did his best to stiffen the opposition of the Congress Party to any compromise with Britain and this caused annoyance in Gandhian circles who were then looking forward to an understanding with the British Government. Later in the year 1938, he launched the National Planning Committee for drawing up a comprehensive plan of industrialisation and of national development. This caused further annoyance to Mahatma Gandhi who was opposed to industrialisation. After the Munich Pact, in September, 1938, the writer began an open propaganda throughout India in order to prepare the Indian people for a national struggle, which should synchronise with the coming war in Europe. This move, though popular among the people in general, was resented by the Gandhiites who did not want to be disturbed in their ministerial and parliamentary work and who were at that time opposed to any national struggle.

The breach between the writer and the Gandhi Wing was now wide, though not visible to the public. At the Presidential election in January, 1939, he was therefore vigorously opposed by the Gandhi Wing as well as by Pandit Nehru. Nevertheless, he was victorious with a comfortable majority. This was the first time since 1923-24 that the Mahatma suffered a public defeat and in his weekly paper, *Harijan*, he openly acknowledged the defeat. The election had served to show the wide and influential following that the writer had, throughout the country, in open opposition to both Gandhi and Nehru.

In March, 1939, at the annual session of the Congress, the writer who presided made a clear proposal that the Indian National Congress should immediately send an ultimatum to the British Government demanding Independence within six months and should simultaneously prepare for a national struggle. This proposal was opposed by the Gandhi Wing and by Nehru and was thrown out. Thus a situation arose in which though the writer was the President of the Congress, his lead was not accepted by that body. Moreover, it was seen that on every conceivable occasion, the Gandhi Wing was opposing the President with a view to making it impossible for him to function. A complete deadlock within the Congress was the result. There were two ways of removing this deadlock—either the Gandhi Wing should give up its obstructionist policy, or the President should submit to the Gandhi Wing. With a view to finding a possible compromise, direct negotiations between Mahatma Gandhi and the writer took place, but they proved to be abortive. Under the constitution of the Congress, the President was entitled to appoint the Executive (Working Committee) for the coming year, but it was clear that the Gandhi Wing would continue to obstruct, if the Executive was not appointed according to its choice. And the position of the Gandhi Wing within the Congress was such that determined obstruction on its part would render it virtually impossible for the President to function in an independent manner.

The Gandhi Wing was determined neither to accept the lead of the writer, nor to allow him to control the machinery of the Congress, and it would tolerate him only as a puppet President. The Gandhi Wing had, moreover, this tactical advantage that it was the organised party within the Congress, acting under a centralised leadership. The Left Wing or radical elements in the Congress who were responsible for the writer's re-election as President in January, 1939, were numerically in a majority—but they were at a disadvantage, because they were not organised under one leadership, as the Gandhi Wing was. There was till then, no party or group commanding the confidence of the entire Left Wing. Though at that time the Congress Socialist Party was the most important party in the Left Wing, its influence was limited. Moreover, when the fight between the Gandhi Wing and the writer began, even the Congress Socialist Party began to vacillate. Thus, in the absence of an organised and disciplined Left Wing, it was impossible for the writer to fight the Gandhi Wing. Consequently, India's primary political need in 1939 was an organised and disciplined Left Wing Party in the Congress.

The negotiations between Mahatma Gandhi and the writer revealed that on the one side, the Gandhi Wing would not follow the lead of the writer and that, on the other, the writer would not agree to be a puppet President. There was, consequently, no other alternative but to resign the Presidentship. This the writer did on the 29th April, 1939, and he immediately proceeded to form a radical and progressive party within the Congress, with a view to rallying the entire Left Wing under one banner. This Party was called the Forward Bloc. The first President of the Bloc was the writer and the Vice-President (now acting President) was Sardar Sardul Singh Cavesheer of Punjab.

Long before 1939, the writer had been convinced that an international crisis in the form of a war would break out in the near future and that India should make the fullest use of that crisis in order to win her freedom. Since the Munich Pact—that is, since September, 1938—he had been trying to bring the Indian public round to this point of view and he had been endeavouring to induce the Congress to shape its own policy in conformity with the march of events abroad. In this task, he had been obstructed by the Gandhi Wing at every step—because the latter had no comprehension of coming international developments and was looking forward eagerly to a compromise with Britain without the necessity of a national struggle. Nevertheless, the writer knew that within the Congress and among the people in general, he had a very large measure of support and that all that he needed was an organised and disciplined Party behind him.

In organising the Forward Bloc, the writer had two expectations. Firstly, in the event of a future conflict with the Gandhi Wing, he would be able to fight more effectively; and further, he could hope to win the entire Congress over to his point of view one day. Secondly, even if he failed to win over the entire Congress to his point of view, he could, in any major crisis, act on his own, even if the Gandhi Wing failed to rise to the occasion. Future developments fulfilled the expectations of the founder of the Forward Bloc to a remarkable degree.

As soon as the Forward Bloc was launched, the full wrath of the Gandhi Wing fell on it. Since the death of Deshabandhu C. R. Das in 1925, this was the first serious challenge to Gandhi's leadership and could not be tolerated by him or by his followers. While facing the frowns of the Gandhi Wing, the Forward Bloc had simultaneously to put up with persecution and harassment at the hands of the

British Government, because for the latter, the Forward Bloc was politically much more dangerous than the Gandhi Wing was.

The birth of the Forward Bloc sharpened the internal conflict within the Congress and it was not possible for anybody to avoid taking sides any longer. In this internal crisis the man who was inconvenienced most was Pandit Jawaharlal Nehru. Up till now, he had, with great skill and ingenuity, been able to ride two horses at the same time and had thereby been able to secure the support of the Gandhi Wing, while being a friend or patron of the Left. Challenged by the Forward Bloc, he had to make his choice and he began to move towards the Right—the Gandhi Wing. And as the relations between the Gandhi Wing and the Forward Bloc became strained, Nehru rallied more and more to the support of the Mahatma.

The best thing for India would have been for the entire Congress led by the Gandhi Wing to take up the policy advocated by the Forward Bloc. This would have obviated a loss of energy and time caused by internal conflict and would have enhanced the fighting strength of the Congress, *vis-a-vis* the British Government. But human nature acts under its own laws. Since September, 1938, Mahatma Gandhi had consistently urged that a national struggle was out of the question in the near future, while others, like the writer, who were not less patriotic than him, were equally convinced that the country was internally more ripe for a revolution than ever before and that the coming international crisis would give India an opportunity for achieving her emancipation, which is rare in human history. When all other attempts to influence Gandhi failed, the only way left was to organise the Forward Bloc and proceed to win over the mass of the people and thereby put indirect pressure on the Mahatma. This method ultimately proved to be effective. As a matter of fact, if this had not been done, Gandhi would not have altered his original attitude and would have still remained where he stood on the outbreak of the war in September, 1939.

The writer still remembers clearly the long and interesting discussion which he had with Nehru in Calcutta, in April, 1939, when he announced his desire to resign the Presidentship of the Congress and organise a new party. Nehru argued that such a step would create a split within the Congress and would thereby weaken the national organisation at a critical moment. The writer urged, on the contrary, that one should distinguish between the unity which led to more effective action and the unity which resulted in inaction. Unity could be preserved superficially in the Congress only by surrendering to the Gandhi Wing—but since the Gandhi Wing was opposed to the idea of a national struggle, such unity if maintained, would serve to stultify all dynamic activity on the part of the Congress in future. If, on the contrary, a party with a dynamic programme was organised within the Congress now, that party might one day move the Gandhi Wing and the entire Congress to militant action. Moreover, more critical times were ahead and a war was bound to break out in the near future. If one wanted to act in such an international crisis, then there should be a party ready to seize that opportunity. If the Gandhi Wing was unwilling to play that role, another party should be formed at once—when there was still time to organise such party. If that task was neglected or postponed, it could not be done later, when the international crisis actually overtook India. And without a well-organised party ready to utilise the coming international crisis for winning fredom, India would once again repeat her mistake of 1914.

This discussion did not, however, convince Nehru and he continued to support the Gandhi Wing. But the more he did so, the more was he isolated from the Left Wing.

It was in September, 1938, that the writer for the first time realised that in the event of an international crisis, Gandhi would not seize the opportunity for attacking the British Government. It was then that he also realised for the first time that Gandhi regarded a struggle with Britain in the near future as outside the domain of possibility (This estimate of the Indian situation was, however, a purely subjective one—due probably to Gandhi's old age.

In September, 1938, at the time of the Munich crisis, the writer was the President of the Congress and he naturally presided over the meetings of the Congress Working Committee which met in order to decide what steps should be taken if a war actually broke out in Europe at that time. These meetings were in the nature of a rehearsal of the meetings held one year later, in September, 1939, when war actually broke out, and they afforded a clear insight into the mentality of Mahatma Gandhi and other important leaders of the Congress.

When in September, 1938, it appeared to the intelligent observer that Mahatma Gandhi, for some reason or other, had lost dynamism and initiative, the following possibilities for developing an alternative leadership existed in India:

(1) *Through Pandit Nehru.*

As we have already remarked above, Pandit Nehru deliberately neglected this opportunity, largely because of his internal weakness, lack of self-confidence, and lack of revolutionary perspective.

(2) *Through M. N. Roy.*

M. N. Roy did form a party and did talk of alternative leadership. But there was some defect in his character, owing to which, within a short time, he made more enemies than friends. Nevertheless, he still had a future—but with the outbreak of the present war, he began to advocate unconditional co-operation with the British Government, and that brought about his political doom.

(3) *Through the Congress Socialist Party.*

Between 1934 and 1938, this party had the best chance of developing as the future national party of India, but it failed. This was anticipated by the writer in Chapter XVIII of "The Indian Struggle 1920-34". The C. S. Party lacked a clear revolutionary perspective from the outset. It began to function more as a parliamentary opposition within the Congress than as the spearhead of a revolutionary movement. After September, 1939, the leaders of this party were won over by Gandhi and Nehru and that blasted the future of the Party.

(4) *Through the Communist Party.*
When the Congress Socialist Party failed to rise to the occasion, there was an opportunity for the Communist Party—then functioning under the name "National Front" —to come to the forefront. But the Communist Party, besides being numerically small, lacked a proper national perspective and could not develop as the organ of national struggle. Not having its roots in the soil, this party very often erred in estimating a particular situation or crisis and consequently adopted a wrong policy.

Throughout 1938, the writer repeatedly advised the Congress Socialist Party to broaden its platform and form a Left Bloc, for rallying all the radical and progressive elements in the Congress. This the Party did not do. The mistake of the C. S. Party was that it talked too much about Socialism, which was after all a thing of the future. India's immediate requirements were an uncompromising struggle with British Imperialism and methods of struggle more effective than what Mahatma Gandhi had produced. Gandhism had been found wanting, because it was wedded to non-violence and therefore contemplated a compromise with Britain for the solution of the Indian problem. Moreover, it lacked a proper understanding of international affairs and of the importance of an international crisis for achieving India's liberation. A party was needed which could remedy these defects and bring about the complete liberation of India.

The immediate objective of the Forward Bloc was an uncompromising struggle with British Imperialism for winning India's independence. To this end, all possible means should be employed and the Indian people should not be hampered by any philosophical notions like Gandhian non-violence, or any sentimentalism like Nehru's anti-Axis foreign policy. The Bloc stood for a realistic foreign policy and a post-war order in India on a Socialist basis.

The Forward Bloc sprang into existence in response to an historical necessity. That is why from the very beginning, it had a tremendous mass appeal—and its popularity began to increase by leaps and bounds. In fact, some months later, the Mahatma remarked that the writer's popularity had increased after he resigned the Congress Presidentship.

When war broke out in Europe, in September, 1939, the people who had been sceptics before, appreciated the writer's political foresight in having advocated a six month's ultimatum to the British Government in March of that year, at the annual session of the Congress at Tripuri. This further enhanced the Bloc's popularity.

CHAPTER XXII

## FROM SEPTEMBER, 1939 TILL AUGUST, 1942

The propaganda offensive of the Forward Bloc was in full swing from May, 1939, onwards. In July of that year, the Gandhi Wing reacted by trying to curb this activity. On some pretext or other, "disciplinary action" was taken against some members of the Bloc by the Congress Working Committee. But this only served to strengthen the morale of the Bloc members and to increase their popularity among the masses.

On September 3, 1939, the writer was addressing a mammoth meeting on the sea-beach in Madras where about two hundred thousand people were present—the biggest meeting he has ever addressed—when somebody from the audience put an evening paper into his hand. He looked and read that Britain was at war with Germany. Immediately, the speaker switched over to the subject of the war. The much expected crisis had at last come. This was India's golden opportunity.

On the same day that Britain declared war on Germany, the Viceroy declared India a belligerent and issued an ordinance containing the most stringent powers for the suppression of internal disorder. On September 11th, he announced that the inauguration of the federal constitution under the Act of 1935 was postponed for the duration of the war.

On September 6th, Mahatma Gandhi, after meeting the Viceroy, Lord Linlithgow, issued a press statement saying that in spite of the differences between India and Britain on the question on Indian independence, India should co-operate with Britain in her hour of danger. This statement came as a bomb-shell to the Indian people, who since 1927, had been taught by the Congress leaders to regard the next war as a unique opportunity for winning freedom. Following the above statement of Gandhi, many leaders belonging to the Gandhi Wing began to make public declarations to the effect that though they demanded freedom for India, they wanted Britain to win the war. As this sort of propaganda was likely to have a very unfortunate effect on Indian public opinion, the Forward Bloc, which was by now an All-India organisation, commenced counter-propaganda on a large scale. As against the Gandhi Wing, the Forward Bloc took the line that the Congress had since 1927 repeatedly declared that India should not co-operate in Britain's war and that the Congress should now put that policy into practice. The members of the Forward Bloc also declared openly that they did not want Britain to win the war because only after the defeat and break-up of the British Empire could India hope to be free.

Apart from the general propaganda carried on by the Forward Bloc, the writer made a lecture tour throughout the country, in the course of which he must have addressed about a thousand meetings in the course of ten months. That the British Government should permit such anti-British and anti-war propaganda came as a surprise to many, including the writer. The fact, however, was that the British Government was afraid that if drastic measures were taken against the Forward Bloc, it would provoke the Congress and the public in general to launch a campaign of passive resistance against the British Government. Because of sheer nervousness on the part of the British Government, the Forward Bloc was able to continue its anti-British and anti-war propaganda, though in the course of this propaganda, many members were thrown into prison.

The propaganda of the Forward Bloc found an enthusiastic echo all over India. Mahatma Gandhi and his followers thereupon realised that the policy of co-operation with Britain would not find any support among the public and would surely lead to the loss of their influence and popularity. Consequently, they began to alter their attitude gradually.

More strange even than Gandhi's attitude was the attitude of Nehru. From 1927 to 1938, he had figured prominently in all the anti-war resolutions of the Congress. Consequently, when the war broke out, people naturally expected him to take the lead in an anti-war policy. According to the previous resolutions of the Congress, the party should have immediately non-co-operated with Britain's war-effort in September, 1939, and if after that, the Government had exploited India for the war—the Congress party should have actively resisted the British Government. Not only did Nehru not adopt this policy, but he used all his influence in order to prevent the Congress from embarrassing the British Government while the war was on.

The Executive (Working Committee) of the Congress met on September 8th, at Wardha to decide what attitude the Congress should take up towards the war. The writer, who was not a member then, was especially invited to the meeting and he gave expression to the view of the Forward Bloc that the struggle for freedom should begin at once. He added that in case the Congress Executive did not take the necessary steps in this connection, the Forward Bloc would consider itself free to act as it thought fit in the best interest of the country.

This uncompromising attitude had its effect and the Gandhi Wing gave up altogether the idea of co-operation with the British Government. Then there followed prolonged discussions and ultimately on September 14th, the Working Committee passed a lengthy resolution asking the British Government to declare its war aims. The resolution, further, declared that if India were granted freedom, then "a free and democratic India will gladly associate herself with other free nations for mutual defence against aggression and for economic co-operation."

This resolution was, in substance, an offer of co-operation in Britain's war-effort under certain conditions.

On October 17th, the Viceroy replied to this resolution of the Congress with a statement which was published in London as a White Paper. The Viceroy's offer was a proposal to establish a "Consultative Group", including Indian representatives, which would advise the Viceroy on questions pertaining to the war. He also reaffirmed the pledge of Dominion Status at some future date, which had been first made ten years ago by the then Viceroy, Lord Halifax (Irwin).

Apart from this reply of the British Government, what infuriated the Indian people most was that while the Allied powers were talking of fighting for "freedom and democracy", in India the Constitution of 1935 was suspended, all powers were concentrated in the hands of Viceroy, and in many parts of India severe restrictions on personal liberty were imposed—e.g. prohibition of all public meetings and demonstrations, imprisonment without trial, etc.

The writer is definitely of the opinion that if the Congress as a whole had taken up a bold and unequivocal attitude of determined opposition to the war from the very outset—Britain's war-production in India would have been seriously affected and it would not have been easy for the British Government to send Indian troops on active service to different theatres of war, far away from India. Consequently, in his view, by postponing a final decision on the war-issue —Gandhi, Nehru and their followers helped the British Government indirectly. It is but natural that when the Congress did not give a clear lead to the country, the propaganda carried on by the agents of British Imperialism in India should partially succeed in winning the co-operation of certain sections of the Indian people.

On October 29th, the Congress Working Committee replied the Viceroy's pronouncement of October 17th with a resolution which contained a threat of civil disobedience (or passive resistance). Along with this, the Committee ordered the Congress Ministers in eight provinces to lay down office. Since the Viceroy was issuing orders to the Provincial Governments to carry out the war-policy of the British Government, the Congress Ministers had either to co-operate in the war-effort or to resign office.

It was generally expected that after the Congress Ministers resigned office, the campaign of passive resistance would begin. But this expectation was not fulfilled. Many people are of opinion that British intrigue was responsible for this. The British Government sent out to India some

British Liberals and Democrats in order to influence Congress leaders. For instance, in October, 1939, the well-known writer, Mr. Edward Thompson, visited India and he was followed by Sir Stafford Cripps who came in December.

Besides carrying on a continuous propaganda against co-operation in the war and in favour of commencing a national struggle for independence, the Forward Bloc organised periodic demonstrations for focussing public attention on these issue. For instance, in October, 1939, an Anti-Imperialist Conference was held at Nagpur which was a great success. And at the end of six months, the Bloc's propaganda culminated in a huge demonstration at Ramgarh in March, 1940, where the annual session of the Congress was being held at the time. The demonstration was called the All-India Anti-Compromise Conference. It was convened by the Forward Bloc and the Kisan Sabhh (Peasants' Organisation) and it was a greater success than the Congress meeting at Ramgarh which was presided over by Moulana Abul Kalam Azad.

The Congress did not decide anything at Ramgarh about its war policy. For six months its policy had been non-committal, with the result that the British Government had been going on exploiting India for war purposes. The Anti-compromise Conference at Ramgarh, led by the writer and Swami Sahajananda Saraswati, the peasant leader, decided, therefore to immediately launch a fight over the issue of the war and of India's demand for independence. During the National Week in April (April 6th to April 13th), 1940— the Forward Bloc commenced, all over the country, its campaign of civil disobedience. Prominent members of the Bloc were gradually put in prison. In Bengal too, where the writer was living at the time, the campaign flared up and early in July, the writer along with hundreds of his co-workers were put in prison.

A few days before he was thrown into prison, that is, in June, 1940, the writer had his last long talk with Mahatma Gandhi and his principal lieutenants. India had received the news of the final collapse of France. The German troops had made a triumphal entry into Paris. British morale, in England and in India, had sunk low. A British Minister had found it necessary to rebuke the British public for going about "with long faces as if they were at a funeral". In India, the civil disobedience campaign started by the Forward Bloc was going on and many of the Bloc leaders were already in prison. The writer, therefore, made a passionate appeal to the Mahatma to come forward and launch his campaign of passive resistance—since it was now clear that the British Empire would be overthrown and it was high time for India to play her part in the war. But the Mahatma was still non-committal and he repeated that, in his view, the country was not prepared for a fight and any attempt to precipitate it, would do more harm than good to India. However, at the end of a long and hearty talk, he told the writer that if his (the writer's) efforts to win freedom for India succeeded—then his (Gandhi's) telegram of congratulation would be the first that the writer would receive.

On this occasion, the writer had also long talks with the leaders of some other organisations—e.g. with Mr. Jinnah, the President of the Muslim League and Mr. Sarvarkar, the President of the Hindu Mahasabha. Mr. Jinnah was then thinking only of how to realise his plan of Pakistan (division of India) with the help of the British. The idea of putting up a joint fight with the Congress, for Indian independence, did not appeal to him at all though the writer suggested that in the event of such a united struggle taking place, Mr. Jinnah would be the first Prime Minister of Free India. Mr. Savarkar seemed to be oblivious of the international situation and was only thinking how Hindus could secure military training by entering Britain's army in India. From these interviews, the writer was forced to the conclusion that nothing could be expected from either the Muslim League or the Hindu Mahasabha.

On May 20th, 1940, Pandit Nehru made an astounding statement in which he said, "Launching a civil disobedience campaign at a time when Britain is engaged in a life and

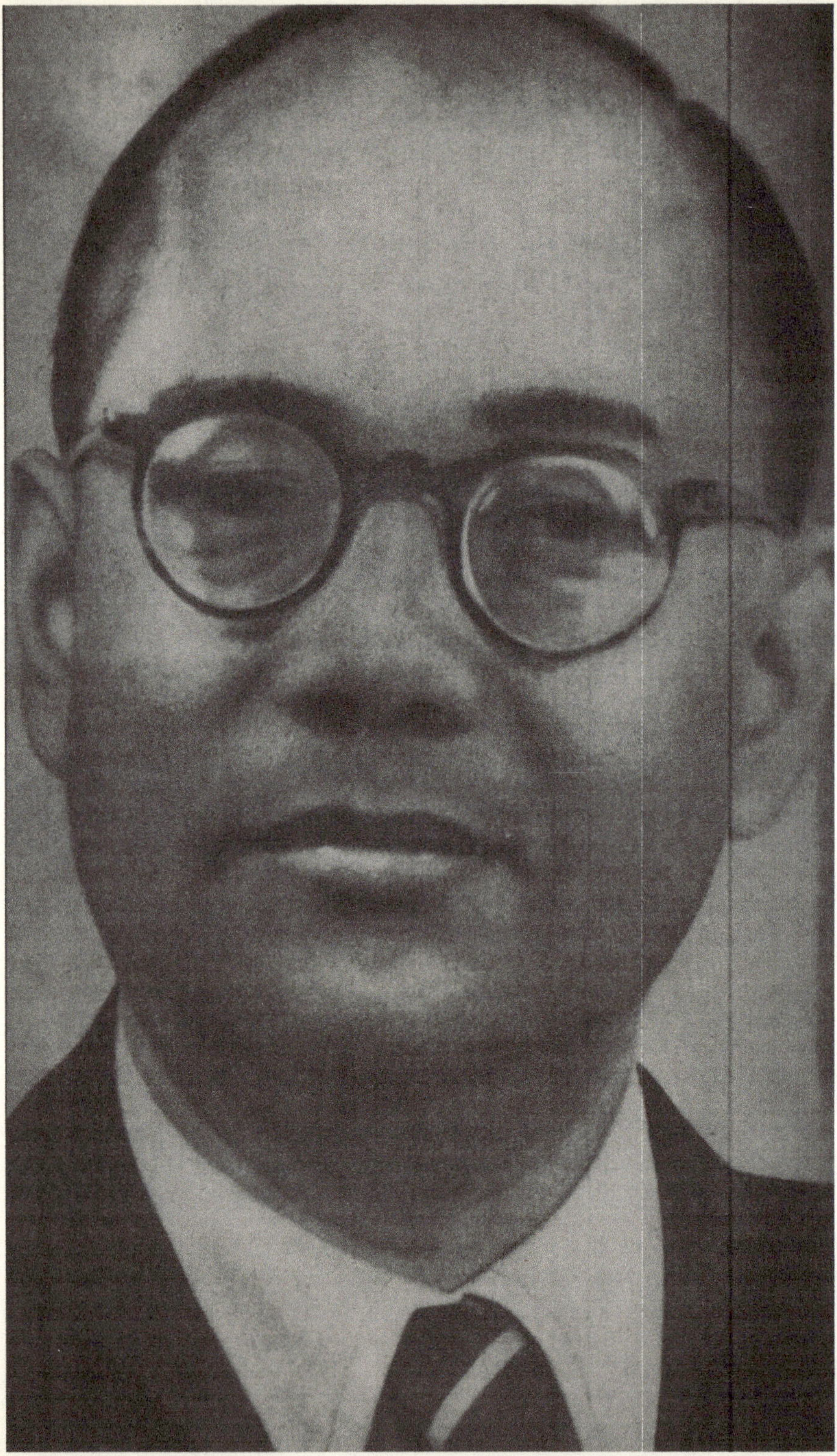

death struggle would be an act derogatory to India's honour." Similarly, the Mahatma said, "We do not seek our indpendence out of Britain's ruin. That is not the way of non-violence." It was clear that the Gandhi wing was doing everything possible in order to arrive at a compromise with Britain.

On July 27th, the All-India Congress Committee in a meeting at Poona which the Mahatma did not attend, made an offer of co-operation with Britain in the war, provided the demand of the Congress for independence was conceded. At this time, the Mahatma retired from the leadership of the Congress, because it was difficult for him to support the war-effort owing to his faith in non-violence.

The Viceroy's reply to the Congress resolution came on August 8th, when he made an offer to include a number of representative Indians in his Executive Council, as well as on nis Consultative Council. But that was not independence or anything approaching it.

In the meantime, after the writer's incarceration in July, 1940, the campaign of the Forward Bloc continued with increasing vigour. This campaign stirred the rank and file of the Gandhi Wing. In spite of orders from above that no followers of the Gandhi Wing shoud commence passive resistance, the rank and file, and especially the volunteers, took up the campaign in some provinces. This produced a great commotion among the Gandhian leaders. Some of them began to press the Mahatma to launch the fight—otherwise they would lose all influence and prestige in the country. Others began gradually to join the fight without waiting for his orders. Ultimately, Gandhi's hands were forced. On September 15th, the Congress withdrew its offer of co-operation and invited the Mahatma to resume the leadership of the Congress. In October, 1980, the Mahatma declared that he had decided to commence resistance to the British Government's war-efforts—but not on a mass scale. In November, 1940, Gandhi's campaign began and within a short time, all the Congress Ministers in eight provinces who participated in the movement were taken to prison, along with hundreds of influential leaders.

The campaign in 1940-41 was not conducted by the Mahatma with that enthusiasm and vehemence which one had seen in 1921 and again in 1930-32—though objectively the country was more ripe for a revolution than before. Evidently, Gandhi still wanted to keep the door open for a compromise—which would not be possible if too much bitterness against the British was roused in the course of the campaign. Nevertheless, the Forward Bloc was jubilant that Gandhi's hands had been forced. Now that both wings of the Congress—the Gandhi Wing and the Forward Bloc—were definitely committed to an anti-British and anti-war policy, it was time to consider bigger plans for achieving the independence of India.

The writer was then confined in prison without any trial. Long study and deliberation had convinced him about three things. Firstly, Britain would lose the war and the British Empire would break up. Secondly, in spite of being in a precarious position, the British would not hand over power to the Indian pepole and the latter would have to fight for their freedom. Thirdly, India would win her independence if she played her part in the war against Britain and collaborated with those powers that were fighting Britain. The conclusion he drew for himself was that India should actively enter the field of international politics.

He had already been in British custody eleven times, but he now felt that it would be a gross political blunder to remain inactive in prison, when history was being made elsewhere. He then explored the possibility of being released in a legal manner, but found that there was none, because the British Government was determined to keep him locked up, so long as the war lasted. Thereupon, he sent an ultimatum to the Government pointing out that there was no moral or legal justification for detaining him in jail and that if he was not released forthwith, he would fast unto death. He was determined to get out of prison, whether dead or alive.

The Government laughed at the ultimatum and did not reply. At the last moment, the Home Minister requested his brother, Sarat Chandra Bose, Leader of the Congress

Party in the Provincial Parliament, to inform the writer that it was a mad project and that Government could do nothing. Late at night, he was visited in his prison-cell by his brother who conveyed the Minister's message to him and informed him, further, that the attitude of the Government was very hostile. The next morning the fast began as already announced. Seven days later, the authorities suddenly got frightened, lest the writer should die in prison. A secret conference of high officials was hurriedly held and it was decided to release him, with the intention of re-arresting him after a month or so, when his health improved.

After his release, the writer was at home for about forty days and did not leave his bed-room. During this period, he surveyed the whole war-situation and came to the conclusion that Indian freedom-fighters should have first-hand information as to what was happening abroad and should join the fight against Britain and thereby contribute to the break-up of the British Empire. After considering the different means whereby this could be done, he found no other alternative but to travel abroad himself. Towards the end of January, 1941, he quietly left his home one night at a late hour. Though he was always closely watched by the Secret Police, he managed to dodge them and after an adventurous journey, managed to cross the Indian frontier. It was the biggest political sensation that had happened in India for a long time.

During the year 1941, the Civil Disobedience Movement continued—but without much enthusiasm on the part of Gandhi and his followers. The Mahatma had calculated that by following a mild policy, he would ultimately open the door towards a compromise—but in this, he was disappointed. His goodness was mistaken for weakness and the British Government went on exploiting India for war-purposes to the best of its ability. The Government also exploited to the fullest extent such agents, as the erstwhile Communist leader, M. N. Roy, who were prepared to sell themselves to Britain.

Ultimately, the British Government woke up from its

self-complacency when in November, 1941, war-clouds appeared in the Far Eastern horizon. Early in December, the Congress leaders belonging to the Gandhi Wing were suddenly set free. But simultaneously, leaders belonging to the Left Wing were clapped in prison. For instance, when the war in the Far East broke out, Sarat Chandra Bose, the brother of the writer, was sent to prison without any trial. This was followed, some time later, by the incarceration of Sardar Sardul Singh Cavesheer, the Acting President of the Forward Bloc. The Government probably thought that by this dual policy of arresting the Leftists and releasing the Gandhiites, it would come to a settlement with the Congress.

The desire of the British Government for a compromise with the Congress was reciprocated by the Gandhi Wing. The Congress Working Committee, meeting at Wardha on the 16th January, 1942, passed a resolution offering co-operation in the war-effort once again. Soon after—that is, in February, 1942 at the instance of the British Government, Marshal Chiang Kai Shek visited India with a view to inducing the Congress leaders to come to an understanding with the British Government. A month later—in March, 1942,—an American Technical Mission, some American diplomats and journalists and several American military units arrived in India. In April, the British Commander-in-Chief in India was forced to seek the help of Marshal Chiang Kai Shek and bring Chinese troops to Burma.

The fall of Singapore on February 15, 1942, after one week's fighting, caused consternation in Britain and in America. When the Japanese forces after fighting the Malayan campaign advanced into Burma, the British Prime Minister was forced to turn over a new leaf and on March 11, made a conciliatory speech announcing the visit of Sir Stafford Cripps to India on behalf of the War Cabinet.

Sir Stafford Cripps arrived in India in March, 1942, under auspicious circumstances. In view of the rapid and brilliant success of the Japanese forces, the British Government was in a chastened mood and Cripps was regarded by the general public as the right man for the job. But his efforts, nevertheless, failed, because all that he had brought with him, was a promise of Dominion Status after the war ended. Coupled with this promise, was the threat that India would probably be divided, when the war was over. On April 10, the Congress Working Committee rejected the Cripps proposals on the ground that they in no way met India's demand for freedom. Sir Stafford Cripps made his farewell broadcast to the Indian people on the 11th April and then left India a disappointed man.

Following the departure of Cripps from India, the Congress working Committee met at Allahabad on April 27th and the following days. On May 1, a resolution was passed rejecting the Cripps proposals and at the same time resolving to offer non-violent non-co-operation, if any foreign army entered India. In the absence of a compromise with Britain, there was no question of actively fighting on the side of Britain, against the Japanese or any other army.

Mahatma Gandhi did not attend this meeting, but he sent a draft resolution to the Committee which was strongly criticised by Nehru and some other members. "The whole background of the draft", declared Nehru, "is one which will inevitably make the whole world think we are passively linking up with the axis powers." Then Nehru made another draft which was at first rejected—but later on, owing to the passionate appeal of the Congress President, Moulana Abul Kalam Azad, it was adopted unanimously. The Congress President, in supporting Nehru's draft said that there was no difference in meaning between the original draft of the Mahatma and the subsequent draft of Nehru and the difference was only one of approach.

In his original draft resolution, the Mahatma had *inter alia* said :

"Britain is incapable of defending India.... The Indian Army is a segregated body, unrepresentative of the Indian people, who can in no sense regard it as their own....Japan's quarrel is not with India. She is warring against the British Empire. If India were freed, her first step would probably be to negotiate with Japan. The Congress is of opinion that if the British withdrew from India, India would be able to defend herself in the event of the Japanese or any other aggressors attacking India."

In the same draft resolution, the Committee assured the Japanese Government and people that India bore no enmity towards Japan, etc. Nehru's draft which was finally accepted by the Congress Working Committee contained no reference to Japan or to Britain's incapacity to defend India.

There was, however, nothing objectionable in the above draft resolution and its contents were in full accord with the policy consistently propagated by the Forward Bloc.

The much criticised draft resolution showed that Gandhi was not an ideological fanatic like Nehru and was much more of a realist than the latter. The outstanding feature of the Congress meeting was the departure from the Congress movement of Rajagopalachari, the leading protagonist of a compromise with Britain.

After the failure of Cripps' mission, people gradually thought that was the end of all talk of a compromise between India and Britain and that co-operation between the two was, therefore, impossible. Nevertheless, Pandit Nehru began a propaganda to the effect that even without a compromise, India should fight with Britain against Fascism. But this point of view was not accepted either by the Mahatma, or by the Gandhi Wing or by the general public. Ultimately Nehru had to climb down and come round to the Mahatma's point of view.

Although the majority of the Congress was gradually coming round to the conclusion that, in view of the intransigence of the British War Cabinet, an open conflict with Britain was inevitable, the idea of a possible compromise with Britain was not altogether dead.

But as nothing more was to be expected from the British Government beyond the mess of pottage offered by Sir

Stafford Cripps and unanimously rejected by the Congress, there was no other alternative for the Congress than to give practical expression to the Congress' demand for immediate independence. The Indian public opinion was also getting restless and it was no more possible to continue the policy of drift. As the Congress itself registered in its resolution of July 14th, there was a "rapid and widespread increase of ill-will against Britain and a growing satisfaction at the success of Japanese arms". Something positive had to be done.

After two months of relative passivity the Congress Working Committee finally met in Wardha on July 6th, 1942, and after 9 days' deliberations passed the famous "Quit India" resolution on July 14, declaring that "Britain's rule in India must end immediately". In case this "appeal" went unheeded, the resolution further said, the Congress would then reluctantly be compelled to utilise, under the inevitable leadership of Gandhi, "all the non-violent strength it has gathered since 1920, when it adopted non-violence as part of its policy for the vindication of its political rights and liberty". There is no doubt that the Congress resolution came nearest in expressing the wish of the vast majority of the Indian people. It also brought the Congress fundamentally near the stand always taken by the writer, namely, that the destruction of British power in India was the *sine qua non* for the solution of all India's problems, and that the Indian people would have to fight for the achievement of this goal.

Although the resolution passed by the Congress at Wardha was interpreted by Gandhi as "open rebellion", it did not entirely bridge the gulf that separated the Congress leadership as a whole from the policy of immediate, uncompromising and all-out fight against the British rule in India advocated by the writer. Expressions in the resolution itself, such as, that the Congress has no desire whatever "to embarrass Great Britain or the Allied Powers in their prosecution of the war", or "jeopardize the defensive capacity of the Allied Powers", or that the Congress would be agreeable to the stationing of the armed forces of the allies in India for defensive purposes if India was free, clearly show that the idea of the desirability of an understanding with Britain and the possibility for realising this desired understanding was still in the minds of some Congress leaders. They also show much shifting of ground by the Congress from the position taken by Gandhi in his draft resolution submitted to the Congress Working Committee on May 27th. This draft resolution, we may recall, declared *inter alia* that Japan's quarrel was not with India; she was warring against the British Empire; India's participation in the war had not been with the consent of the Indian people; and that if India were freed, her first step would probably be to negotiate with Japan. In fact, the illusions cherished by a few Congress leaders made them go so far as to hope that the United Nations and specially America might intervene in the Indian question in favour of India's national demand.

However, these people constituted a very tiny minority. Even Nehru who most ardently wished an understanding with Britain answered in the negative when asked by foreign correspondents after the Wardha meeting "if an American guarantee of the British promise to give India complete independence after the war would meet the case". What Congress was interested in, said Nehru, was "independence here and now". No doubt this was also the mood of the country.

The passing of the "Quit India" resolution by the Congress cleared the political atmosphere of the country vitiated by Cripps negotiations. By declaring that the Congress would launch civil disobedience movement, it forestalled all possible weakening through mutual dissension of the national will for independence, which it was the intention of the British Government to undermine by sending Sir Stafford Cripps to India.

The Congress Working Committee decided to meet early in August to discuss once again the Wardha resolution before submitting it for final ratification to the All-India Congress Committee scheduled to meet in Bombay on August 7. The political fever in the country rose as

August approached. British correspondents in India complained in their despatches that Congress leaders were "stumping the country" calling the people to revolt. In any case, moderates and liberals through their frantic activities to persuade the Congress not to begin direct action before a new *modus vivendi* could be found to end the deadlock, indicated that the Congress decision effectively pointed to a vevolutionary development of the political tension prevailing in the country.

The final draft resolution passed by the Congress Working Committee on August 4th, on which the All-India Congress Committee were to begin deliberations on August 7th, displayed what the correspondent of the *Manchester Guardian* called "a more constructive approach" than the Wardha resolution of mid-July. The assurance that Free India will "throw all her great resources" into the struggle on Britain's side indicated that in Congress view a free India would nver contemplate a separate peace. Thus it is clear that before finally launching its decisive struggle to achieve India's freedom, the Congress went still farther in holding out the olive branch to the British Government.

On August 8th, the All-India Congress Committee adopted by overwhelming majority the Working Committee's resolution. Only a negligible minority consisting of Communists and some followers of Rajagopalachari voted against it. After the announcement of the result, Mahatma Gandhi, in a stirring ninety minute speech, gave expression to his determination to fight to the finish even if he stood alone against the whole world.

While all this was taking place, the British authorities were not sitting idle. Preparations were in full swing to strike at the Congress first and hard. But in keeping with the practice of the British Imperialists to give an air of constitutional legality to all their repressive and illegal acts against the Indian people, the Indian Government published a lengthy justificatory statement immediately following the ratification of the "Quit India" resolution by the All-India Congress Committee. This statement, referring to the Congress demand for the immediate withdrawal of British power from India, and the decision to start "a mass struggle on non-violent lines on the widest possible scale", declared that the Government "had been aware, too, for some days past of the dangerous preparations by the Congress party for unlawful, and in some cases violent, activities directed, among other things, to interruption of communications and public utility services, the organisation of strikes, tampering with the loyalty of Government servants, and interference with defence measures, including recruitment". In the view of the Government of India, so went on the statement,—a masterpiece of British hypocrisy —the acceptane of the Congress demand would mean not only the betrayal of "their responsibilities to the people of India" but must also "mean betrayal of the allies, whether in or outside India, the betrayal in particular of Russia and China, the betrayal of those ideals to which so much support has been given and is being given today from the true heart and mind of India..." The fact was however that the British Government, in preparing for the brutal suppression of the national will to freedom of the Indian people, was acting in total and cynical disregard of the principles of freedom so pompously enunciated in the Atlantic Charter by Churchill and the President of the United States.

The All-India Congress Committee concluded its session on Saturday night. In the early hours of the morning of Sunday, August 9th, the Indian Government struck. As Bombay's British Commissioner of Police came to arrest Mahatma Gandhi, he very typically asked for half an hour's grace to finish his morning prayers. Gandhi's last message was: we get our freedom or we die.

At the same time, the police were busy rounding up all the Congress leaders assembled in Bombay and elsewhere. In the course of a few hours, the entire Congress movement with its ramifications spread over the length and breadth of the country had become underground. The Churchill Amery and Company had dropped their hypocritical mask as champions of liberty and democracy. The horrible face of a soulless alien despotism had revealed itself to the Indian people in all its nakedness. A new chapter in the history of India's struggle for freedom had begun.

## Appendix

### "THE INDIAN STRUGGLE : QUESTIONS ANSWERED" [1]

*Question*: National Government spokesmen here claim that the new Constitution in India is a great success, and that the acceptance of office by the Congress is proof of this. What is the opinion of the National Congress on this view?

*Answer*: The acceptane of office is no proof that the Congress is going to work the Constitution for all time. The Congress Party has gone into office with considerable misgiving.

Its object in doing so is two-fold : firstly, to consolidate its own position; and secondly, to demonstrate that within the conditions of the present Constitution it is not possible to achieve anything really big or substantial. If contrary to its apprehension something substantial is achieved, then that will strengthen the political organisation of the people in their struggle for freedom.

*Question*: Is there any likelihood of the Congress accepting the Federal part of the Constitution?

*Answer*: There is no possibility of the Congress changing its mind and agreeing to work the Federal part of the Constitution, as it did in the case of the Provinces. There is no analogy between the Provincial part and the Federal part of the Constiution.

*Question*: What in your view is the next stage of the national struggle? Is it true that there is rapid development of peasant unrest and of the strike movement?

*Answer*: The next stage of the national struggle will be a further growth of mass consciousness at an increasing tempo. The problem for the Congress will be to mobilise this strength and direct it along the right lines.

---

[1] Report of an interview with R. Palme Dutt, published in the *Daily Worker*, London, January 24, 1938.

In other words, the problem will be to build up the Party organisation on a broad anti-imperialist front. If we can do that, we shall be prepared to face with hope and courage any crisis that the future may have in store for us. Peasant unrest and labour strikes are an expression of the further growth of mass consciousness since the Congress Party took office.

*Question*: Are you in favour of broadening further the mass basis of the National Congress as an all-inclusive national front by this collective affiliation of labour and peasant organisations?

*Answer*: Yes, definitely.

*Question*: What policy would you like to see the British Labour Party or a future Labour Government adopt in relation to India?

*Answer*: We would like the British Labour Party to stand for the Congress objective in its entirety.

*Question*: Many questions have been asked about the references to Fascism in the closing part of your book *The Indian Struggle*. Would you care to make any comment on your view of Fascism?

Many questions have also been asked about your criticisms of Communism in the same section. Would you care to make any comment on this?

*Answer*: My political ideas have developed further since I wrote my book three years ago.

What I really meant was that we in India wanted our national freedom, and having won it, we wanted to move in the direction of Socialism. This is what I meant when I referred to 'a synthesis between Communism and Fascism'. Perhaps the expression I used was not a happy one. But I should like to point out that when I was writing the book, Fascism had not started on its imperialist expedition, and it appeared to me merely an aggressive form of nationalism.

I should point out also that Communism as it appeared to be demonstrated by many of those who were supposed to stand for it in India seemed to me anti-national, and this impression was further strengthened in view of the hostile attitude which several among them exhibited towards the Indian National Congress. It is clear, however, that the position today has fundamentally altered.

I should add that I have always understood and am quite satisfied that Communism, as it has been expressed in the writings of Marx and Lenin and in the official statements of policy of the Communist International, gives full support to the struggle for national independence and recognises this as an integral part of its world outlook.

My personal view today is that the Indian National Congress should be organised on the broadest anti-imperialist front, and should have the two-fold objective of winning political freedom and the establishment of a socialist regime.

# INDEX

Abhayankar, 33, 53
Abolition of the Excise Duty, 133
Abolition of the Khalifate, 134
Achariar, Vijayaraghav, 278
Adi or Original Brahmo Samaj, 21
Advocate General of Madras, 92
Afghan Government, 302
Afghanistan, 5, 18, 73, 220, 359
Africa, 100, 111
Afridi Tribes, 209
Agarkar, G.G., 24
'Agent' of the Indian Government, 140
Agnostic, 22
Ahimsa (non-violence), 126, 327
Ahmedabad, 56, 75, 129, 201, 268
Ahmedabad Congress, 75, 76, 82
Aiyer, Sivaswami, 108
Ajmer, 269, 313
Akali Movement in the Punjab, 68, 73, 100, 111
Akalis, 69
Akali Sikhs, 85
Akbar, 7
Alam, Mohammed, 30, 32, 224, 288
Alam, Emperor Shah, 11
Alderman of the Calcutta Municipality, 271
Alexander the Great, 5
Ali, Mr., Asaf, 32
Ali Brothers, 44, 45, 54, 63, 67, 68, 74, 96, 102, 138, 160
Aligarh, 132
Ali, Moulana Mohammed, 43, 54, 62, 63, 66, 67, 96, 102, 132, 220
Ali, Moulana Shaukat, 33, 44, 54, 67, 134, 278
Alipore, 142
Alipore, Central Jail, 86-88, 205, 222, 348
Allahabad, 12, 30-32, 53, 94, 165, 213, 221, 263 267, 278, 389
All-Bengal Conference of Students, 170
Allen, Lord, 370
Allied Powers, 16, 28
Allied Troops, 43
All-India All Parties Conference, 161
All-India Anti-Compromise Conference, 383
All-India Anti-Untouchability League, 276
All-India Communist Conspiracy Case, 183
All-India Congress Committee, 30, 48, 87, 92, 94, 95, 102, 174, 186, 187, 189, 194, 227, 291, 295-297, 301, 331, 341, 342, 367, 385, 392-394
All-India Congress of Students, 37, 182
All-India Congress Socialist Party, 32
All-India Conspiracy Case, 177
All-India Federal basis, 249
All-India Hartal, 163
All-India Khilafat Committee, 33, 44-46, 115
All-India Kisan Sabha, 369
All-India Liberal Federation, 27, 32, 42
All-India Moslem Conference, 33
All-India Moslem League, 27, 33, 115, 160, 168, 299
All-India Naujawan Bharat Sabha (All-India Youth Congress), 178, 230
All-India Peasants' Organisation, 360
All-India Prisoners' Day, 267
All-India Services, 99
All-India Spinners' Association, 113, 137, 193
All-India Swadeshi Day, 267
All-India Swaraj Party, 296
All-India Students' Federation, 369
All-India Trade Union Congress, 35, 91, 160, 171, 185, 257, 282, 334, 369
All-India Trade Union Federation, 184
All-India Women's Conference, 38, 305
Anti-Ministry movement, 367
All-Parties Conference, 165, 169, 170, 173
All-Parties Convention, 165 171, 172
All-White Commission, 160, 161
Almora, 155
Almora Jail, 154
Amanulla, King, 220
Ambedkar, 34, 245, 263, 274, 275
Ambulance Service, 205
America, 22, 255, 353, 388
American Military Units, 388
American Technical Mission, 388
Amraoti Jail, 303
Amritlal, Ranchoddas, 268
Amritsar, 28, 39, 40, 44, 49, 101
Amritsar Congress, 28, 39, 40, 42, 45, 46, 52, 128
Amritsar massacre, 83, 267

Amritsar Session, 41
Amsterdam, 160
Anarchist movement, 335
Anatolia, 103
Andaman Islands, 209, 282, 367, 368
Anderson, John, 306, 340
Andhra, 37, 48, 81
Andrews, C. F., 251
Aney, M.S., 32, 165, 288, 290, 293, 298, 299, 342
Anglican Metropolitan of India, 114
Anglo-Indians, 33, 201, 313, 323, 325, 346, 348
Anglo-Indian papers of Calcutta, 118
Ansari, M. A., 32, 54, 90, 102, 160, 190, 233, 238, 295
Apte, V. S., 24
Arab State, 358
Arambagh, 288
Areas Reservation Bill, 140
Armoury Raid, 209, 259
Arms Act Satyagraha, 138
Army Staff, 139
Arthashastra of Kautilya, 9
Aryan Conquest, 4, 8
Aryan Influence, 4
Aryan kingdoms, 9
Arya Religion, 23
Aryas, 23
Arya Samaj, 22, 23, 25
Arya Samajist procession, 135
Ashrama, 3, 57, 76, 199, 200
Ashrama of Sri Aurobindo Ghosh, 117
Asia, 6, 43
Asiatic Law Amendment Ordinance, 44
Asia Minor, 43
Asoka, 5, 6
Assam, 61, 324, 368
Assam-Bengal Railway Strike, 61
Assembly, 8, 84, 108, 117, 124, 137, 194
Assembly at Delhi, 177
Aswamedha, 5
Attlee, 370
Attlee, Major, 158
Aurangjeb, 7
Austria, 370
Austria-Hungary, 360, 364
Autonomous Village Institutions, 8
Avatar, 125, 126
Awari, 138
Azad Maidan, 257
Azad, Moulana Abul Kalam, 33, 54, 74, 75, 95, 258, 383, 389

Baba Taraknath, 111
Back Bay Reclamation Scheme, 172
Badanganj, 288
Badenweiler, 363
Badgastein, 370

Badrinath, 2
Bakhale, R. R., 35
Bakshi, S. R., 205
Baldwin, 103, 220
Balilla, 255
Balkans, 364
Baluchistan, 5, 313
'Banglar Katha', 93
Bank of England, 285
Banerjee, Professor N. C., 205
Banerjee, Shib Nath, 35
Banerjee, Surendranath, 26, 31, 40, 42, 104, 327
Bardoli, 80-82, 86, 87, 163, 168, 169
Bari, Abdul, 190
Barisal, 89, 336
Baroda, 205
Basu, J. N., 32, 153, 305
Battle of Plassey, 355
Bay or Bengal, 209, 282, 368
Belgaum, 120
Belgaum Congress, 120, 302
Bellari Jail, 369
Benn, Capt. Wedgwood, 183, 219, 251
Benaras, 32, 57, 298, 302
Bihar, 11, 53, 54, 57, 136 207, 216, 288, 296, 321, 324, 344, 368
Birkenhead, Lord, 118, 122, 139, 159, 161, 165, 192
Black and Tan methods, 260
Blackett, Basil 85, 99, 139, 140
Blavatsky, Madame, 24
Board of Control, 11
Boer War, 29
Boers, 25
Bolshevist Conspiracy Case, 366
Bombay, 11, 26, 27, 30-32, 36, 37, 42, 56-58, 60, 64, 69, 85, 98, 128, 134, 169, 204, 205, 207, 210, 216, 220, 257, 258, 263, 271, 274, 282, 285, 293, 296-298 300-302, 304, 324, 344, 366, 392, 394
Bombay Book Depot., 294
Bombay Congress, 296, 341
Bombay Congress Committee, 257, 298
Bombay Group, 98
Bombay Legislative Council, 171
Bombay Presidency, 21, 53, 56, 80, 93, 120, 136, 210, 272, 305, 364, 368
Bombay Presidency Youth League, 168
Bombay Presidency Youth Conference in Ahmedabad, 182
Bombay Textile Strike, 171
Borsad, 288
Bose, Sarat Chandra, 271, 367, 386, 388
Bose, Sunil C., 154

## INDEX

Boycott of British goods, 25
Boycott of foreign cloth, 289
Brahman Sabha, 112
Brahmanical Hinduism, 6
Brahmo Samaj, 21-23
Brahmo Samaj Movement, 20
Brailsford, H. N., 203, 262
Bright, John, 12
Britain, 20, 42, 242, 276, 286, 328, 365, 370, 373, 375, 379, 380, 385, 388-390
British, 9, 10, 19, 25, 65, 84, 124, 127, 196, 211, 215, 216, 246, 247, 336
British Branch of the Indian National Congress, 49
British Cabinet, 12, 42, 43, 64, 107, 122, 200, 201, 370
British cloth, 55
British Commercial Houses, 19
British Commonwealth of Nations, 221
British connection with India, 83
British corridor, 358
British Consul, 366
British Court of Law, 86
British Crown, 12, 308, 310
British Domination, 3
British Empire, 15, 26, 29, 100
British Goods, 26, 202, 220, 289
British Government, 16, 17, 27, 34, 39, 43, 45, 57, 59, 84, 191, 192, 195, 197, 200, 210, 212, 217, 218, 226, 230, 239, 241, 244, 254, 264, 272, 273, 275, 283, 298, 306, 308-310, 320, 323, 331, 333, 356, 368, 371, 374-376, 378, 380-383, 385-390, 392-394
British Historians, 1, 7, 8
British House of Commons, 189, 346
British India, 16, 84, 216, 217, 230, 241, 245, 273, 280, 283, 309, 312, 313, 317, 319, 321, 362
British Indian History, 25
British Indian Provinces, 188
British Labour Circle, 183
British Labour Party, 398
British Landlords, 50
British Law Courts, 50, 54, 71
British Manufactures, 196
British Mercantile Community, 66
British Missionaries, 19
British Model, 20
British News-agencies, 290
British Parliament, 11, 13, 17, 49, 107, 120, 131, 158, 159, 178, 230, 303, 308, 345, 366
British Parties 241
British People, 3, 39
British Politician, 42
British Power, 19

British Press, 34
British Prime Minister, 42, 272
British Raj, 210
British Rule, 1, 3, 8-10, 15, 19, 23, 27
British Textile Industry, 133, 160
British Trade Union Congress, 35
British War Cabinet, 390
Britishers, 20, 50, 99, 106, 114, 251, 252, 261
Broomfield, 39, 84
Brown, 147, 148
Buckley, Lt. Col., 290
Buckingham Palace, 241
Buddha, 126, 327
Buddhism, 6, 149
Buddhistic Period, 6, 8
Budget, 13
Buksh, Allah, 368
Bull, John, 253, 254
Bulsar, 208
Burke, Edmund 327, 255
Burma, 46, 144-151, 154, 168, 215, 216, 283-285, 305, 309, 345, 388
Burma Committee, 217
Burma Government, 146
Burma Legislature, 150
Burma Legislative Council, 150, 305
Burma politics, 149
Burman Political Prisoners, 149
Burmese Language, 145
Burmese prisons, 146
Burmese war, Second, 144
Burmese Woman, 145
Burnham, Viscount, 158
Buxa Detention Camp, 235, 339
'Buy Indian' League, 267

Cabinet, 43, 59, 99
Cabinet of the Congress, 95
Cabinet in England, 83, 118
Cadogan, Edward, 158
Caesar, 329
Calcutta, 15, 27, 31-33, 35, 37, 38, 46, 57, 59, 60, 65, 69, 70, 73-75, 86, 91, 93, 94, 98, 111, 119, 201, 202, 214, 257-260, 282, 288, 295, 299, 305, 335, 336, 348, 361, 369, 375
Calcutta Bar, 53, 60, 73
Calcutta Congress, 46, 47, 49, 51, 87, 125, 175, 176, 180, 338
Calcutta Constituency, 153
Calcutta Corporation, 118, 119
Calcutta Municipal Act, 104
Calcutta Municipal Corporation, 104, 137, 141, 261
Calcutta Municipal Gazette, 106
Calcutta Municipality, 105, 117, 214
Cambridge, 59, 162, 250
Campbell, Miss Mary, 203

# INDEX

Abhayankar, 33, 53
Abolition of the Excise Duty, 133
Abolition of the Khalifate, 134
Achariar, Vijayaraghav, 278
Adi or Original Brahmo Samaj, 21
Advocate General of Madras, 92
Afghan Government, 302
Afghanistan, 5, 18, 73, 220, 359
Africa, 100, 111
Afridi Tribes, 209
Agarkar, G.G., 24
'Agent' of the Indian Government, 140
Agnostic, 22
Ahimsa (non-violence), 126, 327
Ahmedabad, 56, 75, 129, 201, 268
Ahmedabad Congress, 75, 76, 82
Aiyer, Sivaswami, 108
Ajmer, 269, 313
Akali Movement in the Punjab, 68, 73, 100, 111
Akalis, 69
Akali Sikhs, 85
Akbar, 7
Alam, Mohammed, 30, 32, 224, 288
Alam, Emperor Shah, 11
Alderman of the Calcutta Municipality, 271
Alexander the Great, 5
Ali, Mr., Asaf, 32
Ali Brothers, 44, 45, 54, 63, 67, 68, 74, 96, 102, 138, 160
Aligarh, 132
Ali, Moulana Mohammed, 43, 54, 62, 63, 66, 67, 96, 102, 132, 220
Ali, Moulana Shaukat, 33, 44, 54, 67, 134, 278
Alipore, 142
Alipore, Central Jail, 86-88, 205, 222, 348
Allahabad, 12, 30-32, 53, 94, 165, 213, 221, 263 267, 278, 389
All-Bengal Conference of Students, 170
Allen, Lord, 370
Allied Powers, 16, 28
Allied Troops, 43
All-India All Parties Conference, 161
All-India Anti-Compromise Conference, 383
All-India Anti-Untouchability League, 276
All-India Communist Conspiracy Case, 183
All-India Congress Committee, 30, 48, 87, 92, 94, 95, 102, 174, 186, 187, 189, 194, 227, 291, 295-297, 301, 331, 341, 342, 367, 385, 392-394
All-India Congress of Students, 37, 182
All-India Congress Socialist Party, 32
All-India Conspiracy Case, 177
All-India Federal basis, 249
All-India Hartal, 163
All-India Khilafat Committee, 33, 44-46, 115
All-India Kisan Sabha, 369
All-India Liberal Federation, 27, 32, 42
All-India Moslem Conference, 33
All-India Moslem League, 27, 33, 115, 160, 168, 299
All-India Naujawan Bharat Sabha (All-India Youth Congress), 178, 230
All-India Peasants' Organisation, 360
All-India Prisoners' Day, 267
All-India Services, 99
All-India Spinners' Association, 113, 137, 193
All-India Swadeshi Day, 267
All-India Swaraj Party, 296
All-India Students' Federation, 369
All-India Trade Union Congress, 35, 91, 160, 171, 185, 257, 282, 334, 369
All-India Trade Union Federation, 184
All-India Women's Conference, 38, 305
Anti-Ministry movement, 367
All-Parties Conference, 165, 169, 170, 173
All-Parties Convention, 165 171, 172
All-White Commission, 160, 161
Almora, 155
Almora Jail, 154
Amanulla, King, 220
Ambedkar, 34, 245, 263, 274, 275
Ambulance Service, 205
America, 22, 255, 353, 388
American Military Units, 388
American Technical Mission, 388
Amraoti Jail, 303
Amritlal, Ranchoddas, 268
Amritsar, 28, 39, 40, 44, 49, 101
Amritsar Congress, 28, 39, 40, 42, 45, 46, 52, 128
Amritsar massacre, 83, 267

# INDEX 405

297-300, 302, 304, 306, 307, 329, 330, 332, 334, 341, 347, 362, 372-376, 380, 381, 383, 385, 386, 388, 393, 394
Congress Cabinet, 32, 67, 368
Congress Camp, 114
Congress Committee, 263, 350
Congress Committees in India, 37
Congress Constitution, 48, 192, 328, 341
Congress Delegation, 252
Congress Dictator, 70
Congress Enquiry Committee, 28, 41
Congress Executive, 341
Congress-League Scheme, 167, 168
Congress Left Wing, 15, 169, 171, 187, 188
Congressmen, 77, 126, 193, 287, 288
Congress Nationalist Party, 299-302 332, 343, 353
Congress Parliamentary Board, 300
Congress Parliamentary Party, 353
Congress Party, 135, 136, 138, 185, 186, 198, 210, 301, 343, 361, 367-370, 381, 398
Congress President, 267
Congress Socialist Party, 297, 301, 302, 332, 363, 364, 366, 367, 369, 372, 371, 377
Congress Working Committee 67, 69, 81, 89, 132, 163, 172, 186, 263, 267, 270, 288, 294, 299, 300, 304, 350, 379, 383, 389-393
Congress of Youths, 37
Conservatives, 84, 85, 103, 159, 253, 269
Conservative Cabinet, 122, 251
Conservative Party, 118, 158, 183, 239
Conservative Secretary of State, 118
Conspiracy Cases, 240
Constantinople, 43, 103
Constitution, 17, 27-29, 47, 49, 64, 85, 130, 264
Constitution Act, 320
Constitution of an All-India Village Industries Association, 341
Constitution Bill for India, 346
Constitution of India, 107
Constitution for Ireland, 191
Constitutional Reforms, 41
Constructive programme, 81
Consultative Committee, 279, 280
Consultative Council, 325
Consultative Group, 381
Continent, Mahatma Gandhi's tour on, 255-256
Continental Press, 280
Control Commission, 283
'Co-operator', Mr. Gandhi, 41
Coorg, 313

Corporation, 106
Cotton Tariff Bill, 209
Council-entry, 113
Council-entry proposal, 90
Council Hall, 121
Council of Secretary of State for India, 72
Council of States, 16, 309, 312, 313, 316
Court of Directors, 12
Credential Committee of the Trade Union Congress, 258
Criminal Law Amendment Bill, 1932., 286
Cripps, Stafford, 370, 383, 388-392
Crown, 12, 16, 40, 41, 202, 205
Crown Colony of Kenya, 110, 111
Curzon, Lord, 13, 15, 25, 50, 196, 336
Czechoslovakia, 29, 364

Dacca, 57, 259-261, 272, 338
Daily Herald, 211
Daily Worker, 397
Dange, 39, 98
'Danger' allowance, 148
Darjeeling, 122
Das, C. R. (Deshabandhu), 31, 39, 46, 47, 53, 54, 56, 59, 60, 66, 70, 72-78, 82, 83, 85-87, 89-94, 96, 97, 102-105, 111-113, 119-124, 127-129, 133, 136, 137, 164, 182, 188, 337, 373
Das, Mrs. C. R. (Basanti Devi), 60, 71 72, 88
Das Bina, 306
Das, Jatindra Nath, 178-181, 192, 227, 294
Das, Seth Govindh, 31
Das, young, 71
Daudi, Shafi, 33
Daulatram, Jairamdas, 33
Day, Mr., 112
Deccan Education Society, 24
Declaration of 1917, 189
Delhi, 8, 11, 15, 32, 45, 54, 75, 95, 114, 201, 203, 207, 221, 243, 251, 253, 254, 267, 288, 296, 313, 315
Delhi Congress, 95, 96, 116, 267, 268
Delhi Conference, 296
Delhi formula, 176
Delhi Pact, 222, 226, 231, 236, 237, 257-261, 265, 269
Delhi Truce, 271
Democratic Swarajya Party Conference, 296
Deoli Detention Camp, 269
Depressed Classes, 346, 347
Deputy Commissioner of Police, Calcutta, 141

Deputy Leader of the Congress Party, 138
Deputy Leader of the Party (Swaraj), 131, 133
Deputy Mayor, 104
Desai, Bhulabhai, 71
Devi, Basanti, 60
Devi, Suniti, 71
Devi, Urmila, 71
Dewani of Bengal, 11
Dey, Dr. B. N., 106
Dharma Shastras, 9
Dharsana Salt Depot., 208
Diamond Harbour, 155
Diarchy, 109
Diarchy in the Central Government, 76
Dictator, 82, 83, 87
Dictator of the Congress, 51
Dictator's Decree, 81
Dictator of Italy, 255
Dictator for the Province, 76
Dictator for the whole country, 76
Director of Public Health, 106
District Congress Committee, 30, 48
'Divide and Rule', 181, 322
Division before concession, 323
Dominion of India, 384
Dominions, 29, 100
Dominion Constitution for India, 190
Dominion form of Government 174
Dominion Home Rule, 158, 175, 176, 192
Dominion Status, 76, 94, 121, 131, 161, 166, 189, 190, 192, 201, 229, 232, 242, 251
Dominion Status to India, 176
Douglas, 281
Drainage Engineer of the Municipality, 106
Dual policy of segregation and repatriation, 140
Dublin, 365
Duke of Connaught, 62
Dutch, 9, 18
Dutta, Batukeshwar., 177
Dutta, R. Palme, 397
Dutta, Bhupendra Kumar, 148, 149
Durga Pujah, 152
Dyer, General, 28, 41

East, 18
East Bengal, 61, 209, 259
East India Company, 10-12, 158
East Indian Railway, 171, 185
Education Department, 105
Education, Minister of the office of, 64
Egypt, 201
Ellison, 281
Emigration of Indians, 140

Empire, 47
England, 10, 17, 28, 29, 41, 57, 59, 85, 99, 101, 103, 124, 241, 250, 251, 253, 255, 256, 269, 270, 276, 285, 286, 295 304, 335, 364, 370, 384
English, 1, 18-20, 23
English language, 77
'Englishman', 69, 118
Epic fast, 275, 286
Epic Literature, 4
Epic Periods, 5
Europe, 1, 6, 18, 20, 43, 50, 64, 125, 241, 252, 276, 290, 353, 361, 363-365, 376, 378
Europeans, 18, 19, 313, 323, 325,
European Christians, 347
European Community, 247
European Powers, 9
European Press, 240
European Prisoners, 181
European Races, 18
European Ward, 181
European Writers, 2
Excise Duty, 133
Executive Council of the Governor General, 16
Executive Council of the Viceroy, 64
Executive Council of the Governor of Bengal, 61
Extremists, 15, 24, 26, 27, 32, 46, 49, 50, 176

Fabian Socialism, 332
Faizpur, 364
Faridpur, 89, 121
Faridpur Conference, 122
Far East, 151
Far Eastern horizon, 388
Fascism, 351, 352, 364
Fascist authorities, 255
Fascist boys (the Balilla), 255
Federal Assembly, 309
Federal Constitution, 309, 310
Federal Court, 246, 317, 318, 326
Federal Government for India, 349
Federal Law, 246
Federal Legislature, 280, 309, 310, 312, 315, 316, 319, 321, 322, 326, 344
Federal Lower House, 344
Federal Ministry, 280
Federal Parliament, 309
Federal Public Service Commission, 319, 326
Federal Structure Committee, 216, 242, 245, 246
Federating States, 344
Federation, 218, 221, 223, 230, 309, 310, 312, 319

INDEX 407

Finance Bill, 107
Finance Department, 146
Finance Member, 85, 99
Findlay, Major, 148, 152, 154
First War of Independence, 12, 356
Flowerdew, Major, 154
'Forward', 89, 97, 119, 152, 153, 185, 186
Forward Block, 368, 369, 373, 374, 377, 379, 380, 383, 385, 386, 388
'Fourteen Points', 172
Fox, Col. Lane, 158
France, 364, 365, 383
Francise, 216
French, 9, 10, 18
French Pondicherry, 31
Friend of the Country, 53
Frontier Gandhi, 31, 204, 262
Frontier Ordinance, 264
Frontier Province, 31, 206, 220, 250, 262, 269, 271, 272, 368
'Fundamental rights resolution', 229


Ganas, 7
Ganapati Festival, 24
Gandhi, (Mahatma) M. K., 16, 27, 28, 30-32, 36, 37, 39-41, 44-67, 70, 74-78, 80-83, 86, 87, 89, 91, 92, 95, 96, 105, 107, 113, 114, 119, 120, 123, 125-128, 132, 136-138, 157, 161-165, 168, 169, 172, 174-177, 180, 186-188, 190-193, 195, 197-202, 206-208, 210-213, 220-233, 235-247, 249-257, 262, 263, 265, 268-270, 272-278, 286, 289-293, 295, 296, 298, 300, 301, 313, 327, 328, 333, 337, 338, 341, 342, 350, 351, 353, 354, 360, 361, 369-372, 374, 376, 377, 379, 380, 383, 385-387, 389, 394
Gandhi, Mrs., 288
Gandhi caps, 210
Gandhi-Das Pact, 113
Gandhi-Irwin Pact, 222, 225, 228-230, 251
Gandhiite 'no-change party', 366
Gandhism, 92, 94, 98, 125
Gandhist, 95, 98
Gandhi Wing, 366, 369-375, 380, 381, 385, 388
Gandhian Wing of the Congress, 364
Garhwali, 206
Garhwali soldiers, 231
Gauhati Congress in 1926, 138
Gaya, 91-93, 95
Gaya Congress, 83, 90, 93, 94, 127
G. C. B. A., 151
'General', 138
General Council of Burmese Association, 151

General Education, 85, 99, 118, 251, 254, 269, 283, 296, 305
General Election of 1926, 136
General Election in England, 158
General Strike, 282
General Strike of Textile Workers, 305
Geneva, 255, 304, 305, 365
German troops, 383
Germany, 124, 126, 327, 360, 363, 364, 379
George V, King, 15
George, Mr., 203
George, Mr. Lloyd, 42, 84, 110, 191, 253
Ghosh, Sri Aurobindo, 15, 26, 31, 50, 172
Ghosh, Dr. P. C., 95
Ghoshal, Mr., 234
Gidney, Lieut-col. Sir H., 248
Girgaon, 294
Giri, V. V., 35, 258, 282
Girni-Kamgar Union of Bombay, 258
G. O. C. (Chief Officer), 180
Gokhale, Mr G. K., 24, 26, 31, 101
Golden Age, 6
Gold Standard, 285, 286
Gopinath Saha resolution, 229
Goswami, T. C., 152
Government, 20, 27, 34, 47, 50, 51, 55, 58, 59, 63, 64, 68, 69, 72-75, 80, 82, 87, 89, 91, 96
Government of Bengal, 70, 90
Government of India, 12, 28, 40-43, 62, 83-85, 99, 111, 145, 154, 266, 270
Government of India Act, 361
Government of India Act 1858, 12
Government of India Act 1919, 16, 17, 28, 34, 39, 45, 88, 107, 323
Government of India Bill, 273, 343
Government in Ireland, 154
Government in the Legislature, 131
Government proclamation, 86
Government of South Africa, 140
Governor of Bengal, 119, 124
Governor's Cabinet, 16
Governor's Executive Council, 16, 90, 130
Governor-General (of India), 11, 120, 124, 249
Governor-General in Council, 12
Governor-General's Legislative Council, 13
Gour, Sir H. S., 100, 101, 285
Govindanand, Swami, 31
Grama or Village, 4
Grand Moghul, 336
Great Britain, 1, 29, 43, 73, 149, 212, 220, 306, 347
Great Revolution of 1857, 356, 359

Great War, 15, 26, 29, 42, 51, 65, 67, 328, 337
Greeks, 103
Greenwood, Mr. Arthur,, 370
Gujerat, 32, 36, 80, 202, 204, 208, 220, 234, 271, 288
Guptas, 8
Gupta, Dinesh Chandra, 261
Gupta Emperors, 6
Gupta Empire, 6
Gupta Period, 6
Gurkhas, 23, 206
Guru, 125
Gurudwara (Sikh Shrines), 68
Guruvayur, 277, 278

Habeas Corpus Act, 320
Habibullah, Sir Mohammed, 140
Haig, H. G., 272
Hailey, Malcolm, 107
Halifax, Lord, 101, 370, 382
Halsbury, Lord, 303
Handloom Industry, Indian, 55
Harappa, 4
Hardinge, Lord, 15
Harijan, 277, 289, 371
Haripur Jail, 269
Harsha, 8
Hartal (boycott), 69
Hartog, Sir Philip, 211
Hartshorn, Vernon, 159
Hastings, Warren, 11, 355
Health Association, 105
Hertzog, General, 140
High Court, 326, 335
High Court in Burma, 147
High Court of Calcutta, 112
Hijli, 261
Hijli Detention Camp, 260
'Himalayan blunders', 78
Himalayas, 2
Hindi, 77
Hindu(s), 2, 3, 7, 23, 33, 45, 49, 69, 101, 102, 112, 125, 134, 135, 167, 238, 245, 272-274, 278, 279, 298, 300, 313, 325, 329, 359
*Hindu* (paper), 93
Hindu Congressmen, 131
Hindu electorate, 135
Hindu, Fashion, 22
Hinduism, 20, 24
Hindu India, 358
Hindu Maharajah, 283
Hindu Mahasabha, 32, 33, 101, 102, 131-135, 165, 172, 274, 275, 384
Hindu-Moslem differences, 131
Hindu-Moslem dissension, 114
Hindu-Moslem interests, 168
Hindu-Moslem Pact, 102
Hindu-Moslem question, 102
Hindu-Moslem relations, 128, 129

Hindu-Moslem riot, 101, 138, 259, 271, 282
Hindu-Moslem riots in Calcutta, 135
Hindu-Moslem Settlement, 279
Hindu-Moslem-Sikh representation, 165, 167
Hindu-Moslem strife, 134
Hindu-Moslem tension in the Punjab, 133
Hindu-Moslem Unity, 69, 160
Hindu Polity, 5
Hindu Religion, 2, 21, 22
Hindu Scriptures, 23
Hindu Society, 21, 125
Hindustani, 77
Hindu temple, 134
Hingston, Major, 155
His Majesty, 308, 309, 313
His Majesty's Government, 15, 16, 188, 270, 273, 274, 279, 314, 315, 317-320, 345,
Hitler, Fuehrer., 124, 126, 254
Hoare, Samuel, 251, 272, 273, 279-281, 317
Holy Places of Islam, 43
Home Government, 10
Home Member, 147
Home Member of the Bengal Government, 89
Home Rule, 24, 58, 158
Home Rule for India, 25, 27, 120, 134
Hooghly, 288
House of Assembly, 312, 313
House of Commons, 12, 134, 303, 343, 355
House of Lords, 41, 110, 159, 161
'hpongyis', 149, 150
H. R. H., 218
Hunter Committee, 41
Hussain, Mian Fazil, 101, 132

Imam, Sir Ali, 132, 165
Imam, Mr. Hassan, 27
Imperial Legislative Council, 40, 41
Inchcape, Committee, 99
Inchcape, Lord, 99
Indemnity Act, 41
Independence, 121
Independence Day (26th January 1931), 234
Independence Day celebrations (26th January, 1933), 288
Independence League, 169, 170, 188
Independence Movement, 170
Indpendence Party, 133
'Independence-wallah', 176, 192
India, 1-20, 22-25, 28-30, 33-37, 39-44, 49-52, 54, 55, 57, 62, 63, 65, 69, 77, 80, 84, 85, 88-90, 94-96, 99, 101, 111, 126, 196, 201, 204,

# INDEX

241, 245, 246, 248, 253, 254, 256, 257, 276-278, 280, 282, 284, 286, 290-292, 295, 297, 302, 303, 305-308, 312, 317, 326, 327, 329, 333, 335, 347, 350, 352, 353, 355, 356, 358-361, 370, 371, 374, 379, 380, 382-384, 387-390, 392-394
India League Deputation, 219
India League of London, 286
India Office, 111, 118, 119, 251, 319
Indian, 18-20, 246, 253
Indian Administration, 84
Indian Army, 139
Indian Assembly, 304
Indian Chief Engineer, 106
Indian Christians, 33, 313, 322, 323, 325, 346-348
Indian Civil Service, 57, 59, 110, 318, 340
Indian Coastal Shipping Bill, 320
Indian Constitution, 282
Indian Constitutional Reforms, 288, 341, 343
Idian Council Act, 13
Indian Council Act of 1861, 29
Indian Council Act of 1892, 13, 14, 29
Indian Council Act of 1909, 14, 29
Indian Federation, 284
Indian Graduate of Cambridge, 105
Indian Handloom Industry, 55
Indian Historians, 7
Indian History, 1, 4, 6
Indian Jails, 89
Indian Jail Committee (1919-21), 152
Indian Labour Circles, 184
Indian Labour Movement, 184
Indian Legislative Assembly, 16, 40, 63, 88, 99, 100, 111, 130, 136, 152, 153, 163, 209, 211, 220, 272, 278, 280, 285, 287, 296, 301, 307, 309, 320, 341, 343, 361
Indian Legislature, 107, 217, 315
Indian Liberals, 63, 160, 252
Indian Liberal Federation, 332
Indian Liberal leaders, 85
Indian Liberal members, 250
Indian Literature, 8
Indian Mohammedans, 42
Indian Moslems, 28, 43, 54, 101
Indian Muslims, 358, 359
Indian National Congress, 13, 15, 24, 26, 27, 29, 30, 32, 34-39, 41, 42, 45-47, 51, 62, 67, 68, 76, 78, 91, 101, 115, 121, 131, 132, 150, 158, 160, 161, 167, 171, 173, 195, 230, 288, 294, 299, 301, 328, 332, 334, 339, 350, 358-361, 399
Indian National Congress, Allahabad, 1928, 165
Indian National Congress, British Branch of the, 49
Indian Nationalist, 12, 133, 158
Indian Nationalist Movement, 49
Indian Parliament, 361
Indian People, 3, 24, 52, 55
Indian Police, 318
Indian Police Service, 340
Indian Politics, 53
Indian Press, 149
Indian Princes, 84, 217, 218, 230, 308, 356, 362
Indian Reserve Bank, 140, 319
*Indian Review* (paper), 250
Indian Rulers, 19
Indian Scripts, 151
Indian Shipping Companies, 320
Indian States, 16, 84, 166, 188, 217, 241, 362
Indian States (Protection against Disaffection) Bill, 84
Indian States Inquiry Committee, 279
Indian Struggle for freedom, 29
Indian Trade Union Congress, 282
Indianisation of the Army, 130
Indo-British Agreement, 306
Indo-British Collaboration, 160
Indo-British Textile Agreement, 348
Indo-Irish League, 365
Indo-Japanese Agreement, 306
Insein Jail, 154
Inspector-General of Prisons, 144, 146, 147
Inspector-General of Prisons of Bengal, 152
Intelligence Branch, 148
Intelligence Branch of the Bengal Police, 337
International Committee, 305
International Committee on India, 365
International Federation of Trade Unions of Amsterdam, 35
International Labour Conference, 185
International Labour Office, 255
Iqbal, Sir Mohammed, 33
Ireland, 29, 73, 124, 179, 191, 260, 294, 358, 364, 365
Irish, 230
Irish Convention, 191
Irish Free State, 323, 358
Irish political prisoners, 226
Irish Sinn Fein, 252
Irish Sinn Fein Movement, 64
Irish Sinn Fein Party, 50
Irwin, Lord, 29, 101, 139, 140, 158, 186, 189, 190, 192, 193, 213, 219-222, 226, 233, 235, 238, 239, 251, 382
Islam, 40
Islamic Church, 43
Italy, 124, 126, 255, 256, 327, 364

409

Iyengar, Mr. A. Rangaswami, 54, 93
Iyengar, K. R. (Madras), 90
Iyengar, Mr. Srinivasa, 30, 31, 92, 133, 138, 157, 194, 224
Iyer, Sir Sivaswami, 32
Jackson, Sir Stanley (Governor), 155, 156, 235, 306, 339

Jaffar, (Nawab) Mir., 19, 355
Jallianwalla Bagh, 39-42, 101
Jallianwalla Bagh Massacre, 110
Jamiat-ul-ulema, 271
Jamshedpur, 91
Jana or Tribe, 4
Janapada, 6
Japan, 6
Japanese, 25
Japanese forces, 388
Japanese Government, 390
'Jathas' (groups of men & women), 68
Jayakar, M. R., 128, 131, 133, 213, 217, 221, 279
Jayaswal, K. P., 5
Jessore, 50
Jessore Provincial Conference, 126
Jewish State, 358
Jharia, 171
Jinnah, Mr. M. A., 27, 33, 47, 48, 108, 125, 132, 160, 172, 173, 181, 217, 237, 384
Jinnah's fourteen points, 237
Johannesburg, 44
Joint Committee, 343
Joint Committee's Report, 345
'Joint Free Conference', 162
Joint Parliamentary Committee, 150, 279, 304, 305, 309, 317, 341, 343
Joint Select Committee, 281, 303, 304
Joshi, 279
Joshi, N. M. (Bombay), 34, 184
Joshi, Mr. S. C., 282
Jowitt, Sir William, 217
Justice Party of Madras, 34
Jute Mills in and near Calcutta, strike in, 171

Karachi, 31, 33, 37, 63, 68, 74, 207
Karachi Congress, 224, 225, 236, 237, 239, 242, 244, 247, 257, 298
Karachi Jail, 269
Karnataka, 166
Kashmir, 283
Kashmir Legislative Assembly, 283
Kautilya, Arthashastra of, 9
Kelkar, Mr. N. C., 33, 53, 93, 128, 130, 131, 133, 296
Kelappan, Mr., 278
Kelsal, Lieut-Col., 154
Kenya, 100

Kenya Indians, 100
Kenya Legislature, 100
'Kesari' (Marathi paper), 93
Khaddar, 55
Khadi, 55, 56, 70, 77, 105, 137, 210, 341
Khadi Campaign, 58, 113
Khalifa (Head of the Islamic Church), 28, 43-45, 67
Khalifate, 33, 103, 114, 115
Khaliquzzaman Mr., 32
Khalsaistan, 358
Khan, Aga, 14, 33
'Khan Bahadur' (title), 368
Khan, Hakim Ajmal, 75, 90
Khan, Abdul Gaffar, 31, 204, 220, 262
Khan, Moulana Akram, 95
Khan, Sir Sikandar Hayat, 319, 368
Kharagpur, 157, 170, 282
Khilafat, 40, 78
Khilafat Campaign, 115
Khilafat Committee, 67, 68, 134
Khilafat Conference, 45, 63 68
Khilafat Movement, 28, 33, 44, 45, 134
Khilafat Moslems, 68
Khilafat Organisations, 68, 69
Khilafatist Moslems, 78, 79
Khoda-i-Khidmadgar, 205
Kidwai, Rafi Ahmad, 267
Kifayetulla, Mufti, 271
King Harsha, 6
Kirti (workers), 306
Kirti (workers) Kisan (peasant) Party, 36
Kisan (Peasant), 306
Kisan (Peasant) League, 36, 263
Kisan Sabha, 383
Kitchlew, Dr. S., 30, 31, 96, 190
Kohat, 138
Krishak (Peasant) Samities (Societies), 36
Kshatriya tribes, 151
Kshudrakas, 5

Labour Cabinet, 183, 184, 251
Labour Commission, 184
Labour Conference, 282
Labour Government, 103, 184
Labourites, 159, 253
Labour Party, 118, 134, 158, 183, 186, 211, 219, 280
Labour Secretary of State for India, 117, 118
Lalbazar Central Police Station, 234
Lalbazar Police Station, 142
Lancashire, 59, 250
Lansbury, George, 134
Lahore 30-33, 37, 91, 164, 194, 224, 242

# INDEX    411

Lahore Congress, 76, 161, 175, 177, 194, 197, 199, 214, 224, 225, 229, 249, 341
Lahore Conspiracy Case, 177, 178, 226, 269
Laski, Mr. Harold, 370
Law, Mr. Bonar, 85, 103
Law-Breaking Campaign, 301
Law Courts, 335
Law of Sedition, 202
League against Imperialism, 171, 184
League of Nations, 255, 352, 364, 365
Lee Commission, 99
Left Wing, 26, 30, 31, 39, 46, 47, 130, 161, 162, 171, 174-176, 192-194, 227, 270, 349, 369, 372, 373, 375, 388
Left Wing Congressmen, 36, 191, 270
Left Wing of the Congress, 228
Left Wing Labourites, 270
Left Wing Leaders, 26
Left Wingers, 48, 49, 169, 184, 187, 225, 331, 332
Legislative Assembly, 107, 283, 321
Legislative Council, 12, 16, 185
Legislatures, 193, 198, 218, 345
Legislatures, Central, 249
Legislatures for the Depressed Classes, 245
Legislature, Provincial, 249
Lenin, 124, 126, 399
Liberals, 26, 64, 72
Liberal (Moderate), 108
Liberal Federation, 35, 160
Liberal Leaders, 64
Liberal Party, 32, 35, 109, 153
Liberal Politics, 153
*Liberty* (paper), 186, 205
Lichchavis, 5
Lieutenant-Governor, 12
Lieutenant-Governor of the Punjab, 41
Lillooah, 171, 282
Lingua Franca, 77
Linlithgow, Lord, 303, 370
Lloyd, Lord, 303
Local Legislative Council, 96
Lokamanya Tilak, 26
London, 34, 119, 122, 124, 218, 241, 244, 251, 253, 254, 265, 272, 277, 280, 304, 318, 350, 356, 363, 381
London Conference, 257
Lord Curzon of Kedleston, 336
Lord Mayor of Cork, 179
Lord North's Regulation Act, 11
Lothian Committee's Report, 321
Lower House, 16, 215, 309, 312, 321, 362
Lowman, Mr., 142, 143, 155, 259
Lucknow, 27, 169, 170, 282 290

Lucknow Congress, 27, 32
Lucknow Pact, 299
Lucknow Session of the Congress, 366
Lytton, Lord, Governor of Bengal, 91, 119, 124, 156

Macaulay, 336
Macdonald, Ramsay, 188, 216, 217, 220, 233, 245, 248, 253, 272, 332
McSwiney Terence, 179. 294
Madras, 11, 24, 30-32, 34, 47, 85, 92, 93, 136, 160, 207, 282, 300, 305, 324, 344
Madras Congress, 161, 162, 169, 173-175
Madras Council, 278
Madras Legislative Council, 138, 278, 287
Madras Penitentiary, 181
Madras Presidency, 37, 48, 53, 81, 94, 138, 272, 368
Mahabharata, 3, 4, 7, 9
Maharajahs, 308
Maharaja of Bikaneer, 217
Maharaja of Burdwan, 90
Maharajas in India, 100
Maharaja of Nabha, 100
Maharaja of Nepal, 357
Maharashtra, 24, 53, 91, 296
Maharashtra Chamber of Commerce, 285
Maharashtra Provincial Conference at Poona, 168
Maharashtra Youth Conference, 182, 270
Maharashtrian Swarajists, 128, 129
Maharashtrian Swarajist leaders, 130
Maharsi (a great saint), 21
Mahavira, 327
Mahila Rashtriya Sangha, 182
Mahmud, Dr. Syed, 288
Mahrattas, 325
Mahratta Power, 9
Majority Report, 131
Malabar, 68, 69, 73
Malavas, 5
Malaviya, Pandit Madan Mohan, 32, 33, 46-48, 73, 74, 133, 182, 190, 203, 209, 267, 268, 273, 278, 288, 289, 298, 299, 332, 353
Malayan Campaign, 388
Malkana Rajputs, 102
Manchester Guardian, 203, 393
Mandalay, 143-145, 147, 148, 152
Mandalay Jail, 153, 154
Mandalay Prison, 142
Mandaleswara, 5
Mani Bhawan, 58
Manufacture of salt, 177
Marseilles, 241

Martial Law, 40, 41, 281
Marx, 399
Mathura, 207
Matters, Leonard, 286
Matunga, 282
Maurya Emperors, 5, 6
Maurya Imperialism, 8
Maurya Period, 5
Maya (illusion), 127
Mayor, 104, 105, 202
Mayor of Calcutta, 205, 214, 234, 304
Mayoral Chair, 119
Meerut Communist Conspiracy Case, 98
Meerut Conspiracy Case, 231, 258, 302
Meerut Conspiracy Case Trial, 171
Mehta, Jamnadas, 282, 296
Mehta, Sri Pherozshah, 26, 31
Menon, Krishna, 286
Messiah, 126
Midnapore, 61, 62, 68, 73, 85, 204, 205, 234, 259, 261, 272, 282, 338
Mid-Victorian Parliamentary Democracy, 354
Ministers, 88, 108
Minister of Education, 64, 85
Minister for Local Self-Government, 104
Minister in the Punjab, 132
Minorities Committee, 217, 241-245
Minority Community, 167
Minorities Pact, 244, 245
Minto, Lord, 14, 323, 357
Misra, Pandit Dwarka Prasad, 31
Mitra, Dinabandhu, 50
Mitra, J. N., 282
Mitra, Santosh, 260
Mitra, S. C., 117, 153
Moderate, 24, 26, 27, 49, 52
Moderates (or Liberals), 32, 46
Moderate Congressmen, 42
*Modern Review*, 33
Moghul Emperors, 7
Moghul Empire, 9
Moghul Kings, 7
Mohammedans, 3, 23, 325
Mohammedan Communities, 7
Mohammedan Invaders, 7
Mohammedan Rulers, 3, 8
Mohani, Moulana Hasrat, 45, 76
Mohants, 68, 85
Mohenjodaro, 4
Mohunt, 111, 112
Montagu, E. S., 15, 27, 39, 42, 43, 64, 83-85, 99, 101, 158
Montagu-Chelmsford Reforms, 40
Montagu-Chelmsford Report, 16, 27, 42
Moonje, Dr. B. S., 33, 53, 190, 275

Moplah, 68, 69
Moplah Rebellion, 73
Morarji, Amritlal, 303
Morley, Lord, 14, 357
Morley-Minto Reforms, 14
Morley-Minto Reforms of 1909, 26, 323
Moslems, 27, 45, 63, 67, 101, 102, 104, 105, 112, 124, 135, 164, 167, 172, 199, 237, 238, 276, 278-280, 295, 298, 321-323, 329, 346, 347
Moslem block, 136
Moslem Community, 42, 43, 61, 69, 132, 313
Moslem Electorate, 135
Moslem Group, 32
Moslems, Indian, new awakening among, 54
Moslems of India, 73
Moslem League, 132, 165, 166, 173
Moslem League Conference in Calcutta, 172
Moslem Mosque, 134
Moslem world, 73
Muddiman, Alexander, 108, 131
Muddiman Committee, 108, 131
Mukundlal, S., 258
Mullick, S. N., 72
Multan, 101
Mulvany, Lieut-Col., 152, 153
Munich, 376
Munich Pact, 371, 373
Municipal Schools, 105
Municipality, 106
Muslims, 359
Muslim India, 358
Muslim League, 359, 384
Mussalmans, 245
Mussalmans of India, 40
Mussolini, Il Duce (Signor), 124, 126, 201, 254, 255, 364
Muttra, 257
Mymensingh, 259

Naba Bidhan or New Dispensation, 21
Nadia, 50
Nagpur, 33, 47-49, 51, 56, 57, 138, 369, 383
Nagpur Congress, 48, 49, 58, 125, 341
Nagpur Textile Workers Union, 258
Naidu, Mrs. Sarojini, 32, 33, 38, 127, 132, 182, 190, 213
Naini Prison, 213, 214
Nair, Sir Sankaran, 162
Nair, Dr. T. M., 34
Napoleon's march to Paris, 201
'Nari Karma Mandir', 182
Nariman, K. F., 30, 37, 171, 172 293, 294, 342

## INDEX    413

Nasik Jail, 303
Nation in Making, 40
National Assemblies, 295
National College, 70
National Congress, 172, 363
National Demand, 131, 137
National Education, 81
National Exhibition, 180
National Flag, 97
National Flag Satyagraha Campaign, 98
National Front, 363
National Government, 246, 247, 251, 335, 397
National Institutions, 56
National Missionaries, 24
National Movement, 31
National Planning Committee, 371
National Right, 294
National Socialism, 364
National Volunteer Corps., 76
National Week, 383
National Week Celebration, 267
Natioalism, 102, 124, 352
Nationalists, 15, 26, 32, 115, 127, 136, 165, 169, 203, 235, 285, 347, 367
Nationalist Block, 173
Nationalist Hindus, 237, 347
Nationalist Leaders, 228
Nationalist Members, 211
Nationalist Moslem, 33, 136, 160, 185, 199, 237, 238, 242, 244, 271, 299, 300
Nationalist Moslems in India, 134
Nationalist Movement, 22, 50, 134, 276, 297
Nationalist Muslim leader of Delhi, 160
Nationalist Party, 250, 306
Nationalist Party in Burma, 151
Nationalist Press, 93, 266
Nationalist Strength, 136
Nationalist Wafd Party, 73
Naujawan Bharat Sabha, 37, 138, 178, 192, 227, 257
Near East Policy, 103
Nehru Committee, 165-169, 172, 173
Nehru, Messrs. (father and son), 190
Nehru, Pandit, 341, 367
Nehru, Pandit Jawaharlal, 30-33, 35, 53, 66, 162, 169, 170, 174, 182, 184, 187, 188, 190, 192, 194, 212, 213, 221, 222, 263, 293, 350, 363, 364, 369-371, 374, 376, 384, 389, 390
Nehru, Pandit Motilal, 30, 31, 46, 53, 54, 66, 78, 82, 85, 90, 92-94, 96, 97, 105, 107, 113, 124, 128-131, 133, 137, 139, 149, 157, 162, 165, 174, 176, 186, 187, 190, 191, 201, 212-214, 221, 232, 267, 295
Nehru, Mrs. Motilal, 267, 288
Nehru Reoprt, 166, 172-174
Nepal, 18, 23, 206
New Constitution, 39, 41, 42, 48, 63, 77, 107, 150, 174, 187, 237, 272, 367
New Constitution Act, 309
New Constitution for India, 165, 168, 366
New Reforms, 42
New Turkey, 67
Nil-Darpan, 50
'No-Change', Party, 88, 96
'No-Changers', 93, 95, 128, 176
'No-Changer' Congressmen, 109
No-Tax Campaign, 168, 234
Non-Co-Operation, 51, 53, 71
Non-Co-Operation Movement, 40, 64-66, 132
North-West Frontier, 209
North-West Frontier Province, 138, 199, 204, 206, 220, 264, 324, 359
North-West Provinces, 13
North-Western India, 4, 22
Northern India, 5, 24

O'Dwyer, Sir Michael, 41
Oil and Petrol Works at Budge-Budge, 171
Olcott, Col., 24
Olivier, Lord (Labour Secretary of State for India), 110, 117, 118, 148
Opposition Party, 131
Ordinances, 235
Ordinance (of 1924), 120
Orissa, 11, 280, 308, 324, 368
Ottama, Rev. U., 150
Ottawa Agreement, 225, 286, 301, 306
Ottawa Pact, 282, 348
Oudh, 13
Oxford, 44, 250

Pact, 228, 229, 231-233, 235, 239, 240
Paddison, Sir George, 140
Pagan, 151
Pagecroft, Sir Henry, 303
Pagodas (temples), 151
Pakistan, 358, 359, 384
Pal, B. C., 26, 31, 39, 46, 47, 50
Palestine, 358
'Panch', 350
Panchayat, 8
Pandit, Mrs. V. L., 367
Pandits (old-fashioned), 21
Panipat, 9
Pan-Pacific Trade Union Secretariat, 184

Paranjpye, Dr. (Poona), 108
Paris, 201, 255, 364, 384
Parliament, 59, 273, 274
Parliamentary Board, 296, 299
Parliamentary Commission, 159
Parliamentary Wing of the Congress, 366
Parmanand, Bhai, 33
Partition of Bengal, 25
Pasha, Ghazi Mustafa Kemal, 67, 73, 103, 114
Pasha, syed Zaglul, 73
Pataliputra, 5
Patel Brothers, 53
Patel, Sardar, 36
Patel, Sardar V., 263
Patel, Sardar Vallabhbhai, 32, 53, 168, 169, 189, 190, 213, 227, 229, 233
Patel, Vithalbhai J., 31, 53, 90, 93, 98, 105, 130, 140, 189, 190, 206, 209, 291, 304, 365
Pathans, 206, 359
Pathanistan, 359
Patna, 5, 27, 32, 33, 57, 120, 296, 298, 331
Patna Bar, 53
Patterson, Mr., 146, 147
Paul, K. T., 83
Paura, 8
Peasants' League, 263
Peddy, Mr., 259
Peel, Lord, 63
Peel, Viscount, 85
People's Party, 150
Perambur Railway Workshop, 282
Persia, 5, 73
Peshawar, 206, 207, 234
Pitt's India Act, 11
Playing of music before mosque, 134
Poland, 29, 364
Political Branch of the Bengal Police, 148
Pondicherry, 117
Pondicherry Ashram, 172
Pontius Pilate, 83
Poona, 15, 26, 31, 33, 53, 56, 93, 128, 270, 274, 275, 291, 296, 385
Poona Agreement, 194, 274, 275
Poona Conference, 291, 294
Poona Pact, 245, 274, 313, 322
Portuguese, 9, 18
Pradhan, C. R., 165
Prakasam, Mr., 54
Prarthana Samaj, 21
Prasad, Dr. Rajendra, 32, 53, 361
Presidencies of Bengal, Bombay and Madras, 11
Presidency Jail, 74
President of the Congress, 92, 194
President of the Delhi Congress, 95
President of the Labour Association, 91
President of the Lahore Congress, 188
President of the Relief Committee, 90
Press, 201
Press agitation, 179
Prime Minister, 40, 218, 220
Prime Minister's Communal Award, 238, 244, 321
Princes, 85, 357, 358
Prince of Wales, 69, 73, 84, 164, 218
Principal of the National College, 71
Prisons' Department, 127, 145, 153
Prison Superintendent, 146
Prisoners (classes, A, B and C), 181
Private Bill, 134
Privy Council, 166
Privy Councillor, 101
Professor-President of America, 253
Proposals for Indian Constitutional Reforms, 308
Protection Versus Free Trade, 103
Province or Suba, 8
Provincial Assembly, 321
Provincial Autonomy, 76
Provincial Committees, 211
Provincial Conference, 88, 112, 129, 161
Provincial Congress Committee, 30, 48, 263, 342
Provincial Congress Committee of Bengal, 70, 137
Provincial Council, 321
Provincial Government, 62, 382, 387
Provincial Legislative Assembly, 321
Provincial Legislative Council, 13, 215
Provincial Legislatures, 88, 97, 136, 137, 273, 275, 319, 320, 322
Provincial Lower House, 344
Provincial Public Service Commission, 319
Provincial Students' Association, 182
Provincial Youth Association, 182
Provincial Youth Congress, 257
Public Servants, 106
Public Service Commission, 319
Punjab, 16, 22, 23, 26, 28, 29, 34, 36, 37, 39, 40, 46, 53, 66, 68, 73, 85, 91, 96, 101, 136, 138, 164, 166, 206, 216, 288, 305, 319, 324, 368
Punjab Atrocities, 41, 42
Punjab Congress Committee, 85
Punjab Hindus, 299
Punjab horrors, 39
Punjab Legislative Council, 69
Punjab Students' Conference in

# INDEX    415

Lahore, 182
Puritans, 68
Purna Swaraj, 195, 197

Qureshi, Shuaib, 162, 165
Quit India, 391-393

Rahim, Sir Abdur, 33, 89, 132, 303
Rai, Lala Lajpat, 26, 31, 46, 53, 66, 78, 82, 85, 102, 131, 133, 144, 161, 163, 164, 177, 178
Railwaymen's Federation, 282
Rajagopalachari, C., 32, 53, 90, 92, 300, 390, 393
Rajah, M. C., 274
Rajah-Moonje Pact, 275
Rajasuya, 5
Rajmundry Jail, 269
Rajshahi Jail, 269
Rajasthan, 358
Ramarajya, 327
Ramayana, 3, 327
Ramgarh, 383
Ramkrishna Mission, 22, 23
Ramkrishna Paramahansa, 22
Ranade, Justice, M. G., 24
Ranchi, 296, 304
Rangoon, 143, 154
Rani of Jhansi, 357
Rao, Shiva, 35, 258
Reading, Lord, 62, 73, 80, 83, 99, 122, 124, 139, 192
Reciprocity Bill, 100, 101
Red Shirt Volunteers, 262
Red Trade Union Congress, 35, 36, 258
Reforms, 39
Reforms of 1919, 158, 189
Reforms Enquiry Committee, 131
Regulation, 235
Regulation III of 1818, 116, 117, 130, 141
Regulation 25 of 1827, 233
Report of the Public Debt Enquiry Committee, 247
Reserve Bank Bill, 309
'Reserved' department, 109
'Responsive Co-operation', 128
Responsivist Party, 129, 131-133, 136
Retrenchment Committee, 99
Revolution of 1857, 328
Revolutionary Party, 51, 65, 235
Right Wing, 26, 31, 35, 46, 258, 282
Right Wing of the Labour Movement, 184
Right Wing Leaders, 26, 282
Right Wing Trade-Unionists, 185
Right Wingers, 48, 184, 185, 258, 332
Ripon, Lord, 239

Rishis, 21
Rolland, M. Romain, 255
Rome, 6, 201, 364
Round Table Conference, 17, 34, 74, 75, 107, 131, 158, 173, 189, 190, 191, 194, 200, 211-213, 215, 217-219, 223, 225, 299, 230, 232, 233, 236-239, 241, 242, 244, 247, 248, 250-254, 259, 264, 270, 272, 274, 277, 279-281, 284, 285, 304, 305, 308
Round Table Conference (Second), 236
Rowlatt Act, 39, 40
Rowlatt Bills, 44, 51
Roy, Anil Baran., 117
Roy, B. C., 33, 153, 206, 295
Roy, Kiron Sankar., 158, 205
Roy, M. N., 35, 36, 258, 366, 376, 387
Roy, P. C., 90, 299
Roy, Raja Ram Mohan, 20
Royal Charter, 10
Royal Commission, 17
Royal Commission on Labour, 184
Royal Proclamation, 12
Royal Warrant of November 26th, 1927, 159
Ruikar, 258
Ruling Chiefs, 84
Russell, Earl, 217
Russia, 124, 126, 149, 327, 252, 364
Russians, 25
Russian Revolution of 1905, 29

Sabarmati, 75, 163
Sabarmati Ashrama, 172
Sabha, 4
Sadharan Brahmo Samaj, 21
Safeguards, 231
Saha, Gopinath, 112, 113, 115
Saints, 21
Salisbury, Lord, 343
Salt Law, 199, 200
Salt Tax, 99, 111, 200
Samgati or Samgrama, 4
Samiti, 4
Samudragupta, 6
Samyavada, 352
Sands, Lieut-Col., 155
Sankey, Lord, 216
Sanskrit, 151
Sapru, Tej Bahadur, 32, 64, 85, 108, 139, 160, 165, 190, 213, 217, 221, 279, 281
Saraswati, Swami Dayananda, 22, 23
Saraswati, Swami Sahajananda, 369, 383
'Sardar' (meaning leader), 169
Sarkar, Nilratan, 155

S. S. Pilsna, 257
S. S. Rajputana, 240, 242
Sasmal, Mr. B. N., 62, 85, 86, 137
Sastri, Pandit Hari Nath, 35
Sastri, V. Srinivasa, 32, 42, 100, 140, 190, 217, 221, 250
Satyagraha, 44, 51, 97, 169, 199, 276, 353, 360, 363
Satyagraha campaign, 112
Satyagraha in South Africa, 44
Satyagraha Movement, 139
Satyagrahi, 204, 205, 208, 302
Satyagrahi prisoner, 292
Satyamurti, Mr., 54
Saunders, Mr., 177
Savarkar, Mr., 384
Scotland Yard, 253
Second International, 35
Second Round Table Conferece, 272
Secretariat of the Assembly, 190
Secretary of Bengal Congress Committee, 85
Secretary of State for India, 27, 42, 63, 64, 83, 122, 249
Select Committee, 285
Self-Government, 61
Self-Government within the British Empire, 47
Sen, Keshav Chandra, 21
Sen, Mr. Surjya Kumar, 209, 302
Sen, Tarakeshwar, 260
Sengupta, Mr. J. M., 31, 61, 136, 186, 187, 202, 214, 235, 260, 288, 289, 304, 339
Separate Electorate, 14, 27, 104
Sepoy Mutiny, 12, 23, 356
Servants of God, 205
Servants of India, 100
Servants of India Society, 24
Service Committee, 216-217
Service of India, 24
Setalvad, Sir Chimanlal, 32
Sethna, Sir Pheroze, 32
Setubandha-Rameswara, 2
Shafi, Sir Mohammed, 173
Shah, Bahadur, 357
Shah, King Nadir, 302
Shankaracharya, 3
Shanti, 261
Sheppard, Major, 148
Sherwani, Mr., 32, 238, 263
Shillong, 325
Shiva, 111
Shivaji, 9
Shivaji Festival, 24
Shivaji, 9
Shraddhanand, Swami, 102
Shuddhi (purification), 102
Sikh (s), 23, 34, 68, 100, 101, 167, 172, 245, 313, 322, 323, 325, 353
Sikh League, 165

Sikh Power, 9
Sikh Shrines, 85
Simon Commission, 64, 160, 161, 162, 163, 164, 165, 166, 169, 170, 173, 175, 184, 187, 188, 189, 211, 214, 217, 274
'Simon go back', 164
Simon Seven, 163, 164
Simon, Sir John, 17, 158, 162, 163, 188, 189
Simpson, Lieut-Col., 259
Sindh, 166, 280, 308, 324, 368
Singapore, 388
Singh, Maharaja Ranjit, 9
Singh, Sardar Ajit, 144, 178
Singh, Sardar Bhagat, 177, 178, 192, 226, 227, 228, 229
Singh, Sardar Kishen, 229
Singh, Sardar Mangal, 165
Singh, Sardar Sardul, 32, 373, 388
Sinha, S. P., 14-15, 61
Sinn Fein, 153
Sinn Fein Movement, 73
Sinn Fein Party, 124, 191
Sinn Fein Revolution, 29
Sirajganj, 112
Sirajganj Conference, 113
Sirajudowla, Nawab, 11, 19, 355
Skeen Committee, 130, 139
Slade, Miss Madeleine, 208
Slocombe, Mr. George, 211, 212, 213
Smith, Captain, 145, 148
Smith, Sir Osborne, 319
Smith, Mr. Vincent A., 2
Socialist, 162, 188
Socialist Party, 297, 302, 332, 349
Socialist Republic, 160
Solicitor-General in England, 133
Soviet Russia, 73, 162, 353
South Africa, 25, 27, 29, 44, 45, 51, 65, 80
South African Government, 27, 44, 140
South Africans, 230
South India, 10, 24, 37, 73, 93, 94, 151, 277
Special Congress at Bombay, 42
Special Power Ordinance 1932, 281, 286
Spencer, Herbert, 327
Spoor, Mr. Ben, 49
Stalin, 254
*Statesman* (newspaper), 69, 118, 201
Statute, 167
Statute Book, 286, 301
Statutory Commission, 158, 159
Statutory Railway Board, 319
'Steel frame speech', 110
Stephenson, Sir Hugh, 89
Strathcona, Lord, 158

INDEX 417

Students' Movement, 170, 334, 369
Subdivisional Congress Committee, 30, 48
Subjects Committee of the Congress, 92, 193, 228, 268
Suhrawardy, Saheed, 104
Sultan of Turkey, 28, 43, 44, 45
Suniti, 261
Supreme Court, 246, 317, 318
Supreme Court for India, 166
Supreme Executive of the Congress, 38, 48, 342
Surat Congress, 26
Suri Jail, 269
Swadeshi (i.e. home-made), 105, 323, 328, 336
Swadeshi Movement, 223
Swadeshmitram (Tamil daily), 93
Swaraj, 47, 48, 58, 59, 61, 66, 69, 74, 76, 78, 80, 88, 91, 94, 95, 123, 126, 176, 230, 238, 257, 294, 296, 327, 329
Swarajism, 110, 136
Swarajist Conference, 94
Swarajist Councillors, 105
Swarajist Members, 137
Swarajist policy, 127, 291
Swarajist policy of non-co-operation, 135
Swarajists, 92, 93, 95, 96, 97, 98, 100, 104, 105, 106, 108, 110, 114, 117, 118, 119, 120, 124, 128, 131, 162, 176, 181, 182, 193, 331, 342
Swaraj Party, 92, 93, 94, 95, 97, 102, 104, 107, 108, 111, 113, 114, 116, 124, 125, 127, 128, 129, 130, 131, 132, 133, 136, 137, 297
Swaraj Party of the Central Provinces, 130
Swiss Sanatorium, 365
Switzerland, 154, 155, 255

'Tabligh', 101
Tagore, Devendranath, 21
Tagore, Rabindranath, 21, 64
Tambe, S. B., 130
Tamil Kingdom, 9
Tamil Nadu, 48
Tamil speaking, 48
Tandon, P. D., 31
'Tanzeem', 101
Tarakeshwar, 111, 112, 117
Tarakeshwar Satyagraha, 111, 115, 116
Tarapore, Lieut.-Col., 145, 146
Tarun Sangha, 37
Tata Iron & Steel Company, 91
Tata Iron & Steel Works at Jamshed-170
Tata Strike, 170
Taylor, J. B., 319

Tegart, Charles., 112
Telegu Speaking, 48
Temple Entry Bill, 278, 287
Terrorist Campaign, 306
Terrorist Movement, 281, 335
Textile Strike in Bombay, 170
Textile Workers Union, 258
Theosophical Society, 24
Third International, 35
Thomas, J. H., 217
Thompson, Edward, 383
Thoreau, 51
Thrace, 43
Tibet, 18
Tilak, Lokmanya B. G., 15, 24, 27, 31, 46, 47, 49, 51, 53, 61, 93, 128, 129, 144
Tinplate Company at Jamshedpur, 171
Tippera, 338
Tolstoy, Leo, 50, 51
Tory, 84
Tory Cabinet, 101
Tory Government, 158
Trade Agreement, 345
Trade Union Congress, 36, 171, 184, 185, 258, 305
Trade Union Federation, 35
Trade Union Movement, 258
Tramcars in Calcutta, 335
'Transferred' departments, 108
Treasury Benches, 130
Treaty of Serves, 43
Treaty of Versailles, 364
Tricolour National Flag, 71
Triple Boycott, 60
Tughlak, Mohammed Bin, 7
Tumandar's seat, 325
Turks, 29, 43, 44, 78, 115, 134
Turkish, 43
Turkey, 6, 16, 28, 29, 40, 42, 43, 103, 360
Turkey, Sultan of, 28
Tsar, 25
Twentyfour Parganas, 282
Twenty one Party, 151

U. P. Ordinance, 264
Ulster, 358
Under-Secretary of State for India, 84, 85
Union Boards, 61, 62
Union Congress Committee, 30, 48
Union Jack, 76
United Kingdom, 319, 344
United Provinces, 13, 22, 31-33, 36, 37, 46, 57, 64, 76, 81, 85, 91, 97, 154, 204-207, 216, 220, 234, 239, 250, 262-264, 271, 272, 282, 297, 321, 324, 344, 368
United States 291

United States of India, 76
Unity Conference, 114, 157, 160
'Unity of Culture', 65
University, 20
University Authorities, 64
University of Calcutta, 306
Upanishads, 6
Upper Burma, 142, 147
Upper Chamber, 344
Upper India, 73, 93
Upper House, 16, 309, 312, 321, 362
Utkal, 207

Vaishnava devotee, 123
'Vajapeya', 5
Valera, President de, 365
Vedantism, 20
Vedanta, 6
Vedanta Philosophy, 21
Vedas, 23
Vedic Communities, 4
Vedic Literature, 4
Vedic Periods, 5
Versailles Treaty, 253
'Veto', 108
Viceregal Ordinance, 281
Viceroy, 77, 84, 88, 200, 207
Viceroy's Executive Council, 14, 85, 139
Victoria, Queen, 12
Vienna, 290, 291, 366
Vijayraghavachariar, P., 47
Village Congress Committee, 30 48
Village Self-Government Act, 85
Vivekananda, Swami, 22
Vote, 8

Wadla Salt Depot, 267
Walsh, Stephen, 158
War Cabinet, 388
Wardha, 300, 391, 393
Wedgwood, Col., 49

West, 25
Western Culture, 23
Western India, 24
Whately, Monica., 286
White, Lt.-Col. Denham., 206
Whitehall, 101
White Paper, 17, 343, 346
'White' standard of Life, 140
'Whiter India', 293
Whither Congress, 294
Whitely, Mr., 184
Whitley Commission., 184, 185
Wilkinson, Ellen., 219, 286, 330
Wilkinson, O. J., 106
Willingdon, Lord., 233, 238, 239, 251, 361
Wilson, President., 253
Winterton, Lord, 84, 85, 101
Women's Movement, 334
Wood, Edward, 101
Wood-Winterton Agreement, 101
Workers' and Peasants' Party, 98
Working Committee, 30, 32, 38, 48, 95, 161, 170, 193, 195, 198, 206, 220-222, 224, 229, 232, 236, 263-265, 268, 271, 342
Workers' movement, 334
World revolution of 1848, 29
World War, 357

Yakub, Mohammed, 33
Yervada Prison, 211, 213, 214
Youth Congress, 172, 182, 231
*Young India*, 39, 82, 127, 164, 180, 197, 199, 202, 207, 208
Young Men's Conference, 91
Yuba Samity, 37

Zamorin, 277
Zetland, Lord, 370
Zinovieff, 118
Zurich, 35